ENGLISH EXPERIENCED

Teach  *s by Staging Communication*

by Richard C. Bedford

DOSHISHA WOMEN'S COLLEGE
KYOTO, JAPAN

A Savoyard Book

Wayne State University Press/Detroit/1972

Published simultaneously in Canada
by the Copp Clark Publishing Company
517 Wellington Street, West
Toronto 2B, Canada.

Library of Congress Catalog Card Number 70 156 068

International Standard Book Number 0 8143 1453 8

Contents

Preface

Most texts about teaching English as a second language or teaching English as a foreign language make use of various behavioristically oriented methods, all stemming essentially from the idea of the conditioned reflex. Based on a view of language as oral expression, they provide drill materials of various kinds designed to etch into the student's consciousness what are considered basic English patterns. The goal is automatization of learned responses to the series of oral cues. It is assumed, although the mechanism has remained somewhat mysterious, that students will learn along the way to create statements having patterns similar to those they have learned to associate with triggering cues.

Because language is defined as oral expression, considerable energy and not a little ingenuity has been expended on means to induce automatization of phonological and syntactic patterns. Less attention has been paid to the question of how that huge leap from mere echoing of conditioned response to an associated stimulus to actually selecting and creating suitable responses to unfamiliar or only partly familiar stimuli is to be accomplished. There has been even less concern for identification and provision of patterns of situational context to help students who are thought to have adequate control over the basic phonosyntactic patterns. Very little has been done to teach the social values underlying the communication situation and limiting response possibilities. Accordingly, these methods have proven far more effective with students of European language backgrounds than with students of Oriental language backgrounds.

Since it is by aural-oral means alone that the student is taught—varied only occasionally by audio-visual stimuli requiring oral response—deterioration of fluency is likely to be fairly rapid once his formal language classes are ended. He is provided with no means to bridge the gap between the mechanistic method by which he has been taught and the organic nature of the communication situation he must confront.

This text, however, is built on entirely different assumptions, utilizes an entirely different approach, contains entirely different materials, and has entirely different goals.

First, the definition of language as oral expression has been replaced by the definition of language as an integration of communication behavior patterns only some of which are aural-oral. This text further recognizes that some oral communication signals now untaught must be taught as significant parts of the integrated communication behavior, and that language may be thought of, in a gestalt sense, as involvement of the entire personality configuration rather than merely as involvement of the sound-producing mechanism. That is, there are visible as well as oral communication signals, some of which operate in conjunction with oral signals, some of which communicate autonomously. In fact, language learning involves creation of a new personality manifested in postures, facies, and gestures as well as in pace of speech delivery, phrasing, syntax reflecting attitudes appropriate to the society in which the target language is spoken.

Second, this text is built on the realization that by total mimicry of his teacher, the student learns the complexly integrated communication behavior patterns. He learns systematically what only a few students acquire haphazardly under traditional language teaching methods.

Third, this text gives recognition to the fact that the student does not learn as a disembodied ear and mouth before a desk but while sitting, standing, moving, speaking, interacting in the manner characteristic of ordinary communicational exchanges. In learning to mimic what he has observed, the student feels himself involved in the communication situation: in a sense he *performs* as if the communication behavior were native to him. And as any behavior pattern in the integration reinforces the others—the student learns configurations rather than assemblies—he is more likely to retain what he has learned.

Fourth, the student taught in this manner learns by observing very carefully the entire communication behavior of his teacher and such total mimicry focuses his realization of the interaction of signaling systems. The student not only automatizes the requisite behavior patterns but also develops a learning habit which is not a mere oral-intellectual process. The audio-visual, bodily process is a means of learning a language and, when automatized, is a means to continue to learn after the formal language program is terminated. The communication situation is familiar as the process by which he has learned.

Inherently such an approach shifts language teachers from sedentary desk work to a performing stage on which mimicry of total behavior patterns is possible. Moreover, instead of either the usual lists of disconnected drill sentences or the so-called situational spoken dialogues, learned as if the student were being trained to perform in a radio drama, especially designed *stagings* are used, requiring integration of various communication behavior patterns. These stagings are ordinary, daily life situations—not dramatic or theatrical in the sense of demanding projection of heightened emotion. Although they may be used traditionally, as culmination of language learning, they are designed as learning processes. A staging differs from a play in structural characteristics, in the use made of it, and in the function it serves in the new approach to language learning which I have called *staging communication.*

Accompanying the scenarios for these stagings—each of which appears in three versions to accommodate mixed, all female, or all male classes—is explanatory material which the teacher may use to clarify the nature of the situation which the staging projects. Not only are truncated forms and intonational patterns peculiar to nonwritten English—as distinct from the oralized written English provided by many textbooks—explained with reference to the situational context but also pertinent underlying value assumptions are suggested.

And although the stagings are designed for the teaching of English to non-native English speakers, it is anticipated that the method might be applied to the teaching of other languages as well. It is even likely that such an approach might prove useful to those involved in standard dialect acquisition. Both applications would be grounded on the recognition that language learning for communication is more than the development of control over a few elements of oral expression; communication is the consequence of integration of behavior patterns, one of which is oral. This integration can best be learned by total mimicry through role playing by staging communication.

Finally, then, since this approach is a departure from various language teaching procedures now used, my book is invitational. That is, experimented with widely enough, the approach it contains can be appropriately modified and suitably enhanced.

PART 1

A NEW APPROACH TO LANGUAGE TEACHING

A new approach to language teaching and specifically, although not exclusively, to the teaching of English as a foreign or second language is offered here. Certainly there is no intention of presenting a completely worked out method or system. In fact, cardinal to the approach offered is the conviction that no single workable method for the teaching of all languages to students of various backgrounds is likely to be found. This conviction, product of several years of experimentation abroad as well as a decade of experience in teaching English to foreign students in the United States, is grounded on observation that a language exists as part of a cultural matrix the values of which are not only incommensurable with those of other cultural matrices but which influence the means by which some understanding of those matrices may be acquired.

Thus, although I suggest means for implementation of my approach, I prescribe no program of obligatory procedures which can only stifle the individual ingenuity or intuition that makes teaching an art and the teacher an artist rather than a mere technician substituting inefficiently for a machine. Hoping mainly to induce a desire for speculation, experimentation, I urge teachers willing to accept this approach to develop methods quite pragmatically, in terms of their own experience and needs. Perhaps their experimentation will provide support for my belief that a complete and comprehensive language learning program, based on what I have called *staging communication,* is entirely feasible. But I submit that by adopting the skeptical pragmatism of the scientist, we can

profitably escape from the dogmatism and narrow concern with methodology—ludicrously premature in a field where so little is known—that have stifled us.

The new approach which I am presenting involves situational-contextual learning. And in presenting certain suggestions, tentative and preliminary ideas, I realize that a so-called situational approach, in the form of very brief convernsational exchanges or skits, has long been widely accepted as the best way for a student to get the "feel" of a language. For many years, phrase books—unhappily too often failing to point up structural similarities and parallels—have emphasized the position of an utterance with a stimulus-response pattern of a conversational exchange situation. Many texts have presented "methods" that, by way of short dialogues to be memorized, induced and reinforced the learning of structural patterns. Teachers have often required students to learn and play roles on stage as demonstration of acquired fluency. And all these attempts at sitauational-contextual learning have doubtless been more or less successful, just as virtually any language learning—when implemented by convinced and dedicated, trained and imaginative teachers having sufficient concentration of time and highly motivated students—is likely to prove successful.

In a sense, instead of some radically new or revolutionary panacea, my approach may then seem merely to suggest the need for a more thorough and systematic exploitation of some ideas that have been with us a long time. Yet, the newness of this approach lies in the realization that these ideas have been inadequately exploited and that distorting inadequacy stems from a thorough misunderstanding, a fundamental misapprehension as to the nature of communication, as well as from a failure to recognize significant aspects of the process of language learning.

And although this may seem an arrogantly presumptuous claim, I submit that neither appreciation of nor respect for the accomplishment of those who have worked or yet work in the field can block our questioning speculation. Only the wrongheaded will find derogation in my attempts to point out past deficiencies or errors.

All that we have is built on the past to which we must turn to discover the origin of any possible flaw in the present; we must retrace our way down the track to the point of derailment. But, since the history of language learning is probably almost as old as the discovery of people speaking another language, we cannot here chart the entire course of that history. The evolution of both language teaching and linguistics evidences the common historic fact that decisive turns often set the course of development for many years. Equally commonplace is the fact that there is some distortion in the assumption that such decisions are the unique product of a single mind.

The most significant development in research related to modern language teaching, however, is often seen to date back more than a quarter century when Charles Fries pioneered his now classical survey of thousands of telephone conversations. This was a shattering event, for the very design of this project helped tear us out of the fantasy world of prescriptive grammar and dedicated us irrevocably to the proposition that we can fruitfully consider language in terms of usage: what is actually said and not what should have been said.

It is quite true that the doctrine of usage which emerged from this experiment weaned us from prescriptivism which had tied us to an indefensible grammar that could not describe English. The emphasis on oral expression helped move us away from our earlier concern with the written form and we were, from that point, freed from the confusion of oral and written expression—a development highly beneficial from the standpoint of systematic linguistic analysis. But it was also soon evident that we were saddled henceforth with the notion that language should be only and exclusively oral behavior. Unfortunately, the doctrine of usage also encouraged the misconception that fluency in oral patterns alone—in "language"—was communication. The limitations of the aural-oral encompassed by the linguists' language went largely unrecognized. Paradoxically, the new conception of language was remarkably similar—in terms of limitation, incompletion, and poverty of possible utterance—to the written expression now excluded as a mere notation system.

Had our early researchers been less interested in language and more interested in communication, perhaps they might have wondered whether an experimental design based on the use of telephone conversations was not inherently defective. But even if they had ignored that, they might have been able to draw from those thousands of telephone conversations valuable observations as to how many people will smile, frown, nod, shake their heads, raise or lower their eyebrows, shrug and make other visible gestures while on the phone. Although all of these visible, physical manifestations are dysfunctional in the strictly oral-aural telephone situation, they are, nevertheless, evidence both that there is a felt need for such visible manifestations in communication and, in fact, that the visible-physical complements the oral in communication.

This clear evidence of integrated behavior patterns received little attention from the linguists and only a few apparently would speculate about the possibility that telephone speech, rather than characteristic colloquial expression, might instead be quite heavily charged with audio devices to compensate for the visual cues we find significant in integrated audio-visual behavior patterns of off-phone conversation but which are, of course, denied us by the phone, a strictly audio instrument. Indeed, study of the radio actor's performance, his peculiar form of exclusively oral interpretation, might also have supplied us with valuable information concerning these compensatory mechanisms, for many of us have experienced how badly the ordinary person who has not been trained for radio work is likely to communicate in this entirely oral-aural medium. Valuable work could have been done to determine how many visible behavior patterns are learned by sightless people and how those patterns can be acquired; we might speculate about the source of our feeling of awkwardness in attempting to communicate with the blind. And it might be pointed out that rather than unfamiliarity with phonological and syntactic patterns which could conceivably account for the fact that the telephone situation is widely recognized as the most difficult a foreign student must face, the lack of the integrated audio-visual behavior patterns makes the phone conversation at times an incomplete and unsatisfying experience, even between native speakers and particularly when they are not intimately acquainted.

Various technological developments, particularly in the field of electronics, reinforced the common confusion of language and communication. It cannot be denied that after World War II, when the tape recorder was developed to take over much of the drilling activity of native speaker-informants, the possibility for greater uniformity and fidelity of statement was greatly enhanced as distortion products of human fatigue were eliminated. But certain human communication factors were sacrificed and the subsequent development of the language laboratory not only magnified the illusion that language is exclusively oral but also, through the use of isolated booths, reinforced the very dubious assumption that language learning is largely mechanical oral activity to be accomplished by nonhuman, nonvisual means.

The development and application of audio-visual techniques have caused an even more serious hardship, however, for the binary stimulation they afford produces only oral response in an otherwise passive audience. It could be—and has been—argued that a distinction must be made between the inherent limitations of equipment and the limitations of those using it. Yet, patently, the audio-visual people typically have conceived of their role as that of supplier of stimulating devices to provoke the oral response of the traditional classroom situation. For the most part they do not seem to have realized that they might induce an audio-visual response as well as provide an audio-visual stimulus. And these audio-visual methods tend to produce mere oral response which is defective, since usually no systematic attention is paid to the complete gamut of voice features which communicate meaning. The so-called teaching machines have been recognized, interestingly enough, as much more limited in their capabilities for any kind of teaching than their enthusiastic champions have led us to believe possible, but since such gadgets have been rigged to check only audio recognition rather than to produce audio-visual response, at best they merely support what seems to me the general misconception of communication.

In reacting against the visual, perhaps at least partly as a means of dissociating themselves from the traditional focus on the written language, many linguists contributed to the increase of mutual suspicion and even hostility between them and those dedicated to teaching language mainly through literature. The consequent loss of mutual stimulation between linguistics and literature, the loss to literary criticism in particular, attributable to the virtual split between what might fruitfully have been complementary disciplines, is incalculable. Wooed away from the old translation method of language teaching and convinced by the linguists that language is oral expression, language teachers have, nevertheless, seen the need for investigation of whatever possible links may exist between oral and written expression. Seriously retarded by the oral-aural emphasis, language teachers have only gradually begun to question the validity of the four phase learning sequence of hearing, speaking, reading, writing which had developed out of the emphasis on oral expression. There has been mounting suspicion that the essentially visual phases could have little relation to the oral-aural phases, since language as oral expression is characterized by quite different structures than those visual structures of writing. Some teachers, who would not return to the old translation system of language teaching once prevalent when language was seen as written expression, have begun to wonder if there might not be some efficient way to teach reading and writing apart from hearing and speaking. Unfortunately, intriguing as such speculation is, the process of separating oral from visual in communication continues.

As applied scientists, however, most language teachers could only try to utilize what theoretical linguists provided. And the fact is that the classroom practitioner has been able to make little direct use of that product. Even those working in teaching English as a foreign language or in foreign language teaching, in both of which the oral-aural approach is well entrenched, have experienced a sense of disappointment and frustration at the results of application of the products of the linguists' labors. Since most theoretical structural linguists have been primarily concerned with analysis—and often with analysis of quite "exotic" or unusual languages—their work has been of minimal value to the classroom teacher or practitioner on the firing line who has been concerned, for the most part, with synthesis. We may speculate that the linguists' focus on syntactic analysis, on grammar construction, and on a search for language universals has widened the gap between theoretical and applied linguistics and tended to make an artificial separation between the interrelated processes of analysis and synthesis. Generative-transformational theories, although grounded on a concept of language synthesis rather than analysis, have been only partly implemented for classroom application, and their partial reliance on a complex schematization and notation system has apparently made them seem formidable or even forbidding to most language teachers. The classroom teacher has been made to feel hesitant about developing material of his own on the few practical models supplied him. And the reluctance is not merely a product of timidity; the insistence on the austerity of linguistics as a science seems to have alienated many of those who practice teaching as an art. In short, the absence from the classroom of many practical applications of the ideas which structural and generative-transformational linguists have formulated over the past twenty-five years can no longer be attributed entirely to ignorance or obstinate traditionalism among language teachers. In fact, it seems clear that the schism, separating the language teachers from the theoretical linguists, has been grounded largely on the unformulated recognition of a difference between communication and language. And although Paul Roberts and other teachers, reflecting the work of the theoretical linguists, were welcome contributors of useful teaching material, many teachers have remained sadly aware that language is, in the practical sense of communication, much broader than the concerns of most theoretical linguists.

The definition of language supplied by the linguists not only is too narrow to be useful to us in teaching communication but also might make us wonder what function it serves the linguist. Not only does the linguist exclude from his consideration all behavior which is not oral expression but, in consigning various aspects of communication to a kind of metalinguistic limbo, he has also slighted even certain features of oral expression. Turning our attention to voice qualification, for example, we find that whisper and rasp, excluded from the linguists' systematic consideration, can convey as much significance as the differential loudness of stress which the linguist does consider. It must seem questionable that pitch change should usually be dealt with so grossly in terms of sentence or phonological phrase contour when the intonation contour is really a complex of highly significant shifts in pitch within words or syllables, within phonemes or morphemes. It seems odd that we should have no means to expose foreign students to the meaning shifts available by the fullest exploitation of suprasegmentals and voice qualifiers. Curiously enough, one of the best proofs of the importance of voice qualification, in conveying meaning in terms of communication, may be found in the fact that inexperienced American teachers of foreign students are quite frequently annoyed, and antagonized even, by what is really the foreign student's retention of the voice qualification patterns of his native language that in English communicate a feeling of harshness, of sullenness, or of belligerence.

Even if we accept the very dubious argument that various so-called metalinguistic manifestations cannot convey anything specifically meaningful by themselves, it clearly does not mean those features do not communicate by complementation. Yet many linguists exclude them from consideration, even while insisting on the nonautonomy, the integrated functioning of even those few systems they have categorized as components of language. Although the question of the limits or components of contexts is surely crucial, it is very difficult to see how the linguist can avoid challenging the validity of his own dictum that language is a system of systems when he excludes elements of the system.

But it has long been recognized that the linguist, by definition, is not really interested in communication at all but in language, that the two are not at all the same. Understandably the language teacher has felt dissatisfied, however, that the definition of language has omitted certain oral features from the linguist's consideration so that he might not be distracted while busily engaged in what he considers his main task of cracking the syntactic code. From the standpoint of the teacher this linguistic mechanic who spends all his time tinkering with the engine while neglecting to check the wheels on our vehicle of expression, the condition of the road situation, and the attitude of the talkative driver, is not likely to set us moving down the road of using the language practically, even if he finally learns to tune that engine properly.

Where the "new" linguist's definition of language has been the dominant influence on language teaching, then, the formal learning of language is almost entirely an oral process. The student learns to speak a language and after that he must try to learn all of the signals which permit him to go on to complete communication. This does not imply, of course, that a language student first learns to speak and then in sequence learns to communicate; he must, in fact, learn both at once. My point is that his formal language training provides at best only a systematic control of a sharply limited number of acceptable oral patterns; the rest of communication behavior the student must try to learn informally, perhaps intuitively, and certainly haphazardly. Within oral-aural limits his teacher could not and did not teach him to communicate.

Curiously, although Sapir, Whorf, Hall, and others have voiced the need to link the spoken word to other aspects of behavior, language teachers saw most American linguists ignoring the fact that language usage is part of a total behavior pattern of communication. The fact that situational language learning has received most serious attention at the University of Edinburgh and in Australia seems a significant commentary on the direction of development of American applied linguistics which, paradoxically, is usually thought to have had its origins mainly in anthropology.

Yet, while the main thrust of linguistic research has, in a sense, deprived language teachers of what might be called systematic contrastive studies of essential communication patterns for speakers of various languages, many of us have remained aware that a different way of behaving must be learned in order to speak another language—different from the way the student behaves when speaking his native language. Moreover, we have had reason to suspect that the different behavior patterns we have observed as characteristic of the speakers of various languages were somehow linked to the thought patterns—the values and attitudes, let us say—of the speaker. In fact, it seemed reasonable to suppose that the thought was, in a sense, itself part of the total behavior pattern. And even while we advocated the thoughtless automatization of overlearning as we diligently pattern-practiced, we have remained uneasily aware that we could not entirely abandon the ancient exhortation to "think in the language"—although we had no better idea how students were to attain that noble goal. Worried about how to provide for the development of necessary communication patterns, many of us—converted by total immersion in the area and culture study concept—have discovered that the expected development of a "feel" for the "flavor" of the language remained tantalizingly elusive. Perhaps most disturbing has been our observation that even when a native speaker has been assigned to such area and culture programs, he is likely to be asked mainly to demonstrate various aspects of pronunciation, and attempts to mimic his other communication patterns have been incidental if not ignored. Often his "mannerisms" are considered a source of amusement because they are erroneously thought to be a kind of personal eccentricity. Indeed, in answer to the widespread complaint abroad that foreigners teaching English are often paid more than native teachers, it might be noted parenthetically that the foreign teacher communicates not only by way of oral expression but also by his presence, by his ability to exemplify a foreign way of living, of behaving, of communicating. Recreating even partly the way of life of those whose language he speaks as a native, the foreign teacher will often need a considerably higher salary than is paid to a native teacher.

It must be recognized, however, that speech is not the entirety of communication and that the student learns a language not just to speak it but to communicate in it. Communication is contextual, and language becomes communication only in a context which is nonlinguistic. In an attempt both to clarify this point and to obviate the possibility that the reader may decide that I have involved him in mere word play, too common in linguistics applied or otherwise, I hasten to point out that by communication I mean the significant projection of an attitude which may be verbalized but certainly is characterized by visual and kinesic manifestations—postures, facies, and gestures—and by oral elements—voice qualifiers, pacing of delivery speed, differential pausing, varying degrees of silence, and varying degrees of spatial distance between the speaker and the spoken to. Communication is not affected by linguistic means alone but is, in fact, a product of total behavioral response.

It is time we acted on our realization that unless *all* aspects of communication are taught, communication is likely to be defective. We have certainly witnessed its collapse consequent upon the failure to integrate all its aspects. Even today the sometimes miserably inadequate visual aspects of acting by opera singers jar with the aural aspects of an opera performance, rendering the tenderest lyrics ridiculous. In fact, except for delights in the lavish costuming and settings, and except for what might be said for the superiority of the "live" voice in contrast to the electrified voice, an opera performance might occasionally be better heard than seen. At the other end of the cultural scale, all of us familiar with television overseas are aware that although some foreign singers may astound us with their ability to capture—usually by mimicking of recordings—every nuance of the voice "style" of some American popular singer, we have sometimes been equally impressed with the comically unsuitable visual presence of that skillful oral mimicking. And, on a still more humble level, how often have language teachers been struck by the complete incongruity existing between what a language student says and how he appears as he says it.

Yet, we need not entertain ourselves further with evidence that the devices exploited in communication—which is, after all, the prime concern of the language teacher—are far more extensive than those included in the linguist's narrower concept of language as the knowledge and control of a limited number of verbal patterns. Clearly, most language students whose training was grounded on the narrow concept of language as oral expression have remained, quite literally, mere disembodied voices rather than what we might label *total personalities,* despite the fact that this term is admittedly less clear than the more precise but loaded and perhaps more offensively jargonistic term *communicants*. Once the student is shown, however, that his speech in another language cannot be understood if he uses the sound patterns of his native language and that he cannot merely substitute the words of the other language in the sentence patterns of his native language, he should also be taught that he will not be fully understood if his verbal expressions in a foreign language are accompanied by the behavior patterns of speakers of his native language.

To communicate in a foreign language, entirely new and strange emotions, stemming from new valuations in new and strange situations, have to be learned. The means of conveying those emotions—the way to stand, hold one's hands and tilt one's head, the facial expression needed, and many other aspects of appropriate behavior—have to be taught and learned until they become as automatic as the pertinent verbal response. Moreover, in order to practice and learn the behavior patterns, language students have to behave in typical situations; they must somehow be taught to play various roles in various situations.

Those who have attempted to use plays in teaching languages, even with the obvious confusion of purpose and implementation, have been on the right track, for it is only as an active and total participant—and not merely as a disembodied voice—that the student is really communicating. Although dialogue skits or even full length plays have, to that end, long been the stock-in-trade of language textbook writers and those language teachers dedicated to what has been thought of as situational learning, it must be admitted that usually the student's total behavioral response has been subjected to as little systematic development under this approach as it was when he was earlier required to participate in debates, oratorical contests, and the like, contrived with a similar intention. The usual emphasis is almost exclusively on accuracy in syntax and clarity of pronunciation, while emotional toning, variation in pacing, and other aspects of vocal production are neglected. An exaggerated and artificial declamatory or theatrical projection is often fostered. Context in dialogue memorization is limited to contiguous phrases at best, if not to mere words in a phrase, although context is much broader in actual communication. And, saddest of all, the communication significance of culture-linked movement, as well as postures, facies, and all of those patterns encompassed by what Birdwhistell has labeled kinesics, is usually ignored.

We must also be aware that often the dialogue of plays used in past attempts at situational learning resembles in another way that expression found in debates and oratorical contests, that is, a formal usage far closer to written English than to the everyday spoken word. That colloquial usage has far less syntactic variation than written or pseudo-written formal speech to written English than to the everyday spoken word. We might, of course, trace this difference to the immediate, instantaneous nature of colloquial usage as against the prepared-in-advance nature of the written statement or formal speech, and we might profitably speculate about the fact that colloquial usage tends to rely for communication on behavior patterns other than the words and syntactic structures of the written expression.

In any event, the peculiarly distinct audio-visual behavior patterns of ordinary communication must be learned and can only be learned by student mimicry of teacher modeling. The language student is, by means of total mimicry, learning, in a very real sense, to be an actor. He must be taught to utilize the basic mim-mem concept broadly, as does the actor in the synthesis of a role. But whereas the actor, creative yet concerned with theatrical conventions, usually heightens and intensifies his projection in an artfully exaggerated illusion of reality, the language student, in creating his role, must be taught to duplicate behavior patterns of those offstage living instances of the character he is playing. Unlike the dramatic actor, then, the quality of whose performance is dependent in large measure on the creativity displayed in his imaginative interpretation of his role, the language student learns to perform as he must eventually perform on life's stage as a communicant with those whose means of expression he has mastered.

I want to point out, too, that, even though many foreign students today have been long acquainted with American movies and American television shows, such largely naturalistic theater uses theatrical behavior not at all the same as is found offstage in everyday life. Thus, some students will have to be taught to act less dramatically. Moreover, all linguists agree, the mere passive awareness and knowledge of the finest details of language are not likely to produce a speaker of that language; we might rephrase this by stating that unless a student is actively immersed in and actually exercising the behavior patterns of the society whose language he studies, he is not likely to communicate.

Clearly, however, I do not mean to use the staging—as has been the case with plays—as a mere test of verbal fluency otherwise acquired, but instead will employ it as in itself the means of acquisition of a greater fluency. The stage I have in mind is quite different from that of the playwright, for mine is not set for great and gripping drama. Although our ultimate goal is to implement communication, we must remain aware that the value of role playing, as a language learning device, is far less for an audience than for our participating language student. That is, the foreign student must perform in a way acceptable to those native speakers with whom he would come into ordinary, daily contact—not as an entertainer filling the leisure time of recreation seekers expecting more or less conformity to theatrical conventions. Although the quality of his performance ultimately will be measured by audience recognition, then—by the degree to which he has communicated by integration of behavior patterns—the value for the student lies in the process of learning this integration and not in the entertaining end result of the performed staging. Unlike the ordinary play production situation, in this approach the final performance may be thought of as incidental.

Experience taught me quickly that, in fact, the teacher, attempting to use this situational play approach I have called staging communication, is sharply limited by a very practical consideration: there are very few suitable stagings available. A *staging* differs from a play in structural characteristics, in the use made of it, and in the function it serves in the new approach I have developed for learning communication. Yet, the sense hangs on the meaning of my term *suitable*. Ignoring matters of limited availability of time and money—serious concerns everywhere but particularly, I have found, for the American teacher of English overseas—all period pieces which have elaborate costuming and sets must be avoided. This does not mean that no costumes or properties may be used. On the contrary, in fact, I should also point out that role playing as language learning seems to require that costumes and properties be real rather than imagined or artificially contrived. That is, the setting and costumes should be current and the stage should be as much like the real-life setting as possible. Some illusion is inevitable—since a stage is a kind of temporary enclave or island in the world native to the student— yet the illusion must be limited to the convincing assumption of a role by the student: he will have to assume he is a legitimate inhabitant of the island. But once he has made that assumption, stepped on the stage and become a part of that island, he should find it a real, habitable place, not one he must furnish out of dream and imagination. To make that assumption, the student must feel—by the presence of real and solid objects—that he is firmly if temporar-

18

ily embedded in a real world where the language he is studying is normally spoken.

Yet it should be understood that I have used the term *staging* in the sense of a total behavioral situation rather than in the sense of a theatrical play and, in fact, I have urged that every effort should be made to emphasize the day-to-day reality rather than the heightened dramatic qualities of the situation. Because plays longer than one act involve place and time shifts difficult to stage realistically, or to the degree that foreign student actors are not distracted by this burden placed on their already heavily taxed imaginations, such plays should be avoided. I have found that plays of more than one act may make too many demands on the memory of the students—particularly since this approach requires that students learn not merely dialogue lines but that they learn also the interrelated physical verbal patterns of communication. As an established feature of dramatic convention, the act-break surely has an acceptable and necessary function, but act-breaks in plays of more than a single act can only intensify the artificiality and reduce the reality of the situation for foreign students since no curtain descends or rises in this offstage world.

This approach to language learning can be attempted virtually from the beginning of a student's exposure to a foreign language, but not all plays are suitable for students of all levels of fluency, all degrees of previous exposure to a language: less advanced students should be cast in roles requiring less line memorization so that they can concentrate particularly on perfecting their verbal projection—

pronunciation, intonation, volume, and pacing—as part of the role creation. I have found it even more important that the roles for these students require less synchronization of movement and speech. All language teachers have discovered that students typically—perhaps because they have been misled to focus too narrowly on the oral projection—cannot move and speak at the same time, but will usually either tramp silently across the stage to a fixed position before speaking or will speak their lines motionlessly and then stolidly take up their new positions. When the oral projection consists entirely of an expletive or ejaculant, the effect of such unsynchronized behavior can be particularly disastrous.

My primary aim is to teach the current patterns of communication used by the majority of native speakers of the language. Although realism would seem to countenance at least the recognition of dialects, teachers should discard plays utilizing narrow regional or ethnic dialects and archaic speech, if the student is to be taught the communication patterns of the majority of current native speakers of the language studied. The choice of plays having a current setting will, of course, automatically resolve the issue of temporal dialect interference. Realistically there are varieties of American English—communication patterns—each of which is native for some teachers, though many language teaching problems might be simplified if we had a standard American English. English teachers should find some comfort in the realization that students ultimately will mimic their teacher, who can effectively teach only that language he habitually speaks.

Yet by far the most serious problem encountered in play selection, I have discovered, is the difficulty in finding plays having roles which can be cast from the student group. Since it is unlikely that a play can be found having a cast exactly the size and sex composition of the class being taught, the teacher usually feels he is confronted with some nasty choices. Quite often he will decide that either he must assign two roles to the same student, if his class group is small; or if he has a large group, and not enough roles to go around, he must require two students to play a single role so as to avoid having many students serving as mere inactive observers. But I have found that either the playing of two parts or the sharing of a single part in performance usually seems comical to both the cast and audience—who will, of course, quickly spot the switch. More importantly, the students playing the roles cannot feel as if they are really totally involved in a total situation. That is, the situation which the staging delineates has a kind of unity, the recognition of which is essential if the student is to learn to communicate adequately. The student who merely plays out a part of the situation obviously cannot actively experience the necessary psychological involvement and identification with the complete situation, although that involvement is the basis of his acquisition of appropriate communication patterns.

Since certain psychological difficulties may be anticipated if a student is left without a role and serves merely as a passive audience, each student should, therefore, be assigned a role. I have found that one way to solve the conflicting needs mentioned is to provide for alternation of students in the same total role. Entire alternate casts can enhance the competition for the opportunity to present the staging in performance as well as provide useful opportunities for the instructor to expose students to repeated corrections while comparing the role playing of one student to that of another in the same part. It should be emphasized, however, that performance of the staging is, clearly, secondary in importance to the more basic learning process of its rehearsal.

Another expedient, which may seem particularly tempting to the harried instructor whose class group is too small for the casting of any of the plays available, is that of reducing or otherwise changing parts in order to accommodate the cast to the class membership. This dropping of parts can sometimes be accomplished by some rather simple dialogue changes, particularly since we are not concerned with the play as a dramatic unity. However, additions and subtractions often can create a kind of artificiality or warping of the reality of a play situation, where there really are neither inessential parts to drop nor additional parts needed. Since students will, of course, be oblivious to such distortion in what to them is already a peculiar situation, the teacher must be especially alert not to succumb to the lure of mere expediency which could seriously impair the value of the play approach as a means for teaching valid total communication patterns.

Either the search for suitable plays or the patching and doctoring of plays can be very tiresome and frustrating. Thus, after tinkering wearily with the shifting, dropping, and adding of roles in various plays from standard anthologies, I finally abandoned the ready-made collections of plays and began to write entire vehicles which I call stagings.

Although such writing may, indeed, seem a formidable task to those who erroneously imagine that the dramatic gifts we usually associate with the professional playwright are required, my experience has convinced me it is less a chore than the cut and paste revamping required by the altering of ready-made plays. This is true because, however simplified, the ready-made play is usually constructed with an emphasis mainly on dramatic plot-character relations and not on the realistic requirements of our staging approach. We are not interested in the dramatic theater. The main point we must keep in mind, then, is that basically what is needed is a realistic situation providing for an exchange between characters whose relationship is clearly and simply established and which progresses to a conclusion without the heightening intensity or dramatic artifice necessary for the projection of the extremes of theatrical comedy or tragedy. Newspaper human interest or feature stories, perhaps expanded and embellished somewhat to allow for a number of roles, may be made to serve quite well as plot nuclei, largely because they sustain and even exaggerate the sense of realism of typical motive and action which must be taught. Moreover, the typicality of such situations encourages precisely the necessary stereotypy and cliché in role creation which will furnish the student with realistic models of communication behavior patterns. And originality in role creation is as undesirable as creative originality would be in a pattern practice class. It should by now be clear that staging communication, in a sense, is merely a kind of pattern practice write large

Again it must be pointed out that the entire situation of the staging—the plot and the roles in it—will of necessity be strange to the student, who is learning to communicate by using a foreign language. Cultural values will determine how a situation will be interpreted; the foreigner will evaluate certain situations quite differently from the native. In fact, part of the job of learning to communicate involves learning new and foreign evaluations. Thus, we cannot, nor should we wish to, provide the student with only those stagings which will require the understanding and projection of values similar to or a familiar part of his native culture. Parenthetically, if the student group is characterized by marked ethnic and cultural heterogeneity, as is characteristic of foreign student classes in the United States, it would be impossible to find situations familiar to all members.

It is true, of course, that not all strangeness is considered amusing by all people; many people merely feel disdain and annoyance with the foreign. Yet, I think that ethnocentricity, which seems so universal as to warrant labeling it a human trait, is grounded on a feeling of superiority which may, for most of us, make anything foreign seem vaguely amusing and comically strange. My experience seems to indicate that their own feelings of strangeness in the foreign situation staged may predispose foreign students of English more easily to project that incongruity we frequently associate with humor. That is, although the essence of the comedy in a situation may elude them, in the "natural" reactions to the strangeness of the situation many foreign students will show those behavior patterns which we recognize as comic manifestations. The skillful teacher may then be able to build student confidence by indicating that such natural behavior is entirely appropriate in the humorous situation, while attempting to develop the student's feeling for the humor in the situation. In other words, the student must, as always, be able to project suitable behavior patterns, even as he is developing some understanding of why they are suitable, while he is learning—through active immersion—the social values underlying those patterns.

Yet, we cannot use stagings based exclusively on comic material, if we are to provide valid patterns of communication for students learning to get along in a realistic if foreign world. In teaching patterns appropriate for sad or unhappy situations, however, we must be particularly alert to discourage any tendency toward the emoting and declaiming which is part of the theatrical conventions of many peoples but which in English is likely to seem overblown, sentimental, banal, and melodramatic. We must keep in mind, then, the fact that although the student's entrance onto the stage must be a signal for him to behave in an entirely foreign and different way, it should not be a signal for him to behave theatrically. The entrance onstage should, as much as possible, be a sortie into the everyday world of those who communicate as natives in the language the student is trying to learn. He must learn, that is, that the theatrical conventions of his society are as unacceptable in the foreign situation staged as his native real life patterns of behavior would be in that foreign situation. And the teacher must guard against his own tendency to impose his theatrical conventions on the student.

The basic problem here, however—and a teaching challenge which this approach can meet by total mimicking in communication—is to alert foreign students to the differences of cultural valuation and attitudes which must be acquired in learning the foreign language. That is, the students must be shown what is considered sad and what happy; they must learn how to manifest these evaluations in acceptable communication patterns. And they will learn this largely by mimicry. Many textbook writers ignore the simple fact that foreign students capable of understanding the explanations in the text would not need the course. Similarly foreigners will derive little from lectures on such abstract matters as cultural valuations and attitudes. However, the teacher must seize every opportunity to reinforce his modeling of behavior patterns with short and simple explanatory statements about cultural values directly underlying the situations. Such accompanying explanations will help the student get used to paying attention to the integration of movement and speech. For the student, such explanation is an end rather than merely a means; it is itself a demonstration of the integration of behavior patterns in communication. Careful attention to the kinds of situations included in the stagings may minimize the ever present danger of oversimplification; patently, degrees of complexity and ambiguity must be adjusted to development of student understanding.

No effort should be spared to provide in stagings the situation, roles, and dialogue suitable to the purposes the particular student group may have in learning language. Only the most directly and immediately pertinent roles, in terms of the needs and goals of fluency of the students, should determine the emphasis and focus of a language course—and middle-aged foreign businessmen may legitimately object, therefore, to learning the "utterly useless" role of slangy American teenagers, let us say. Yet, clearly, as critics of the situational approach sometimes point out, we cannot provide all possible situations which the foreign student might encounter upon entering our world. Similarly, it should not be expected, nor is it advocated that stagings can be contrived which will place students only in those roles they might play in real life. Since the student's social and occupational status is likely to be quite different in the foreign setting from what he has known as a member of his native society, he may profit quite directly from the opportunity to play an unfamiliar role. Often, for instance, it can be instructive, even in the matter of casting, for students to recognize that the social valuations of the foreign society provide very different correlations between physical type and personality, that role relationships are socially created rather than inherent, that acquisition of total communication patterns will require acceptable delineation of relative status. Stagings can be fashioned to fit the special composition of the group; it is also possible to devise roles which can be played by students of either sex, so long as the teacher is aware that such changes in casting will usually require considerable adjustment of the total social situation as well as of the dialogue, since important psychodynamics permeate and operate to influence the entire relationship between the sexes in real life. The sole reservation or caution I might offer about casting, is that the assignment of students to play roles of the opposite sex will inevitably prove seriously disruptive for students, in terms of the psychodynamics of relationship within the student group and, therefore, should be avoided.

The establishment of attitudes and means to further language learning is likely to prove of greater benefit, however, than the more direct but narrower confinement to these matters of immediate pertinence. We are less concerned with the *specific content* of dialogue and with motor patterns than we are with acquisition of the *process* of learning total communication patterns. By this approach, we can provide the student with personal, active experience in total mimicry. More important, we will have sensitized the student to the need to continue to learn the integrated communication patterns after he has finished his formal training. Any program of language study should provide for the inevitable continuation which this approach makes possible; most programs fail to provide a means by which the student can continue to learn.

Since much of this discussion of considerations limiting choice of material must otherwise seem vague and abstract, I have included in this text the scenarios for ten of the stagings which I have written and used in teaching English to foreign students. I hasten to add that I am aware that these are not great plays in the sense of gripping box office successes. The printed versions do not differ greatly in form from other plays, although had there been some way to provide notation for all features of communication with which my approach concerns itself, my main task obviously would be to supply that notation. No complete notation exists to deal with the gamut of speech communication patterns nor does any notation exist to represent the physical patterns which are at least supplemental in communication. From one standpoint, since I recognize that such notation could be created, I might consider the absence as underscoring the fact that there has been no general acceptance or understanding of the nature of communication. However, allied to my view of communication is the conviction that even were such notation devised, it would be no more valuable than what we already have for representing oral features; in fact there can be no notation which can capture the dynamics of the integrated communication patterns. My approach greatly enhances the role of the teacher.

The difference between these stagings and ordinary plays, then, lies not as much in their form as in the use made of them. Contrived primarily for the specific purpose of teaching foreign students ordinary patterns of communication in English by way of a new approach, these stagings may also prove useful to teachers uninterested in or hostile to that approach since there is a great shortage of suitable plays for use with foreign students. Graded in difficulty, largely according to degree of speech-movement synchronization required, they are, nevertheless, all relatively simple everyday life situations in which many of the social values of Americans are embedded ready for demonstration, explanation, and total response acquisition. Since they do not require time shifts, they need no narrator or commentator. Yet, despite their simplicity and peculiar ordinariness, a deliberate attempt has been made to avoid the artificiality of much situational material that often resembles thinly disguised pattern practice listings and that, I have found, is likely to alienate most adult students.

I have provided a diagram of a suitable stage set and a description of that set for each play; all stage directions regarding movement of characters, stage balance, entrances, and exits have been keyed to that set, although it is obvious that some adaptation may have to be made depending on the space and properties available to the individual teacher.

In addition to the dialogue of the original scenario written for a mixed cast, two variations have been supplied, one for a cast composed entirely of women and the other for a cast of men. It is hoped that not only will these adaptations prove useful to the vast majority of English teachers in many countries where coeducation is still not common, but that it may offer helpful hints to those teachers who will need to adapt the roles and appropriate dialogue to the composition of their classes. In its original form each play has a cast about equally divided by sex; where the class is neither of one sex nor so divided as to permit the casting prescribed, the sex of roles will need adjusting; substitution from the alternate dialogue should considerably ease the task of adaptation.

Each scenario is supplemented with general suggestions and guides for discussion or foci for teacher effort. I hope that, in offering an approach rather than a method, I have not only freed the teacher for experimentation but have also encouraged the reassertion of individual teaching skill. The information I have furnished in some half dozen categories may encourage the process but should, in any event, prove of more direct concern to the teacher than to most students who would find it very difficult reading. Since it is hoped that in all cases the teacher will supplement and enlarge on what has been furnished and not merely parrot from the text, I have tried to focus teacher attention on the details of total behavior patterns which must be modeled for student mimicking.

The first category in the supplementary information provided for each play is labeled Glossary. It is hoped that this will not only do the usual job of supplying students with definitions of unfamiliar terms occurring in the play but that it will also encourage the teacher to urge his students to utilize these definitions in paraphrase during play rehearsals. Moreover, as teachers may not choose to do all plays in the text, each glossary is separate rather than related to all others; terms occurring in several plays are defined in the glossary for each play in which they appear. Since a term can be defined only within its situational context, all definitions have been thought of less as items to be memorized verbatim than as pegs on which the student may hang a general feeling for the meaning within a context. In a certain sense the glossary may even be an unnecessary burden, since the student is far more likely to learn by guessing and through immersion in a situation than he is by the intellectualizing process of definition. From this standpoint, all expressions may be thought of as idiomatic, and student awareness of context should be encouraged. Although definitions have been offered for exclama-

tions, expletives, and ejaculants, such expressions are particularly difficult to define explicitly since they mainly reflect emotional tone and attitude. The phonemic notation given for each of these expressions provides very general, approximate information, since—as has been noted earlier—these expressions are characterized by the fact that there is no adequate notation for them, despite the frequency of their occurrence colloquially. Most texts evade the problem by disposing of such manifestations as metalinguistic aspects of expression: I instead urge teachers to insist that students, in their mimicry, pay strict attention to *all* oral features as essential to the roles being developed. This is only one of many instances in which the teacher will have to furnish oral models for complex oral phenomena.

If language can be thought of as a structure of structures, quite clearly the label Structure, which I have given to the second category of supplementary information provided for each play, is very vague indeed. Most of the structures considered, and particularly those which characterize colloquial usage, are syntactic. But some attention has also been paid to common features of the phonological structure of English, such as complex patterns of pitch and stress. Lexical structures, particularly those stemming from contraction and elision so common colloquially, are also described under this heading. Because many of the structures of oral statement defy written expression, the teacher will have to be alert in supplying oral models for them. But, as in the case of glossary items, the learning of these structures can be encouraged by frequent paraphrase exercises.

Visual behavior patterns must be correlated with role and situation—and to some extent this has been accomplished in the stage notes supplementing dialogue in each scenario. Any notation I have found for those postures, gestures, facies, ways of moving, etc., has seemed clumsily inadequate. My experimental attempts to elaborate an adaptation of ballet notation seemed promising but have thus far not proven completely successful. The awkwardness of explanation is magnified by the foreign students' limited vocabulary. The teacher must, therefore, provide the models for such patterns as part of the dynamics of role creation. Control of such structures will result from insistence on precision of student mimicry in rehearsal, but many expressions will be acquired as a consequence less of the rehearsal of dialogue than from the repetition in informal conversational exchange taking place between student and teacher—or even between students—during rehearsals of the staging.

In the category labeled Cultural Values, I have attempted to focus teacher attention on those aspects of plot and character relations which I feel may strike foreigners as especially strange. It will be necessary for students to acquire some understanding of and feeling for the peculiar value system which we as natives take for granted, but it should be expected that students will develop the ability to project the behavior patterns before they acquire the feeling and understanding. In fact, the teacher will probably find that through the exercise of such patterns the acquisition will be furthered. Most students will profit little from lectures on these abstract matters and few students would be able to extract much meaning from what I have written. These notes should alert the teacher to the need for special care in the modeling of their visual and oral patterns. It should be recognized that all behavior patterns will reflect such values, that the way something is said is as important as what is said, and that very often what is implied and not said is even more significant.

The delineation of role, by status and sex, may pose serious problems, since the value system of the student's native society will interfere just as the phonological and syntactic structures of his native language will interfere with his attempts to produce their English counterparts. Teachers will probably find that the prevalence of irony and sarcasm will seem particularly puzzling to most foreign students who will tend to interpret all statements quite literally. In the initial stages of exposure, therefore, it may be useful to resort to more exaggerated expression than is normal until students are familiar with this common mechanism of ironic usage.

It has been noted earlier that the need for simplicity of presentation requires considerable generalization regarding American values. My use of hedging words, such as *many, some, usually,* etc., should alert a teacher to the need for restraint. The fact that some

teachers may not agree with the formulas offered here—which they may find too subjective or even eccentric—does not release them from the obligation to be ever sensitive to contrasts in values and to search for ways to make those differences clear to foreign students.

The three categories of supplementary information considered thus far deal with the staging itself, in terms of specific dialogue and action, as well as with the underlying values responsible for such visual and oral manifestations. The fourth category, which I have called General Comment, has to do largely with notes about the organizational structure of the staging generally and with problems of pertinence. Each staging offers certain mechanical problems of exits and entrances, of tempo variation which need student consideration. I have emphasized that although our focus is on projecting believable characterizations rather than on theatricality, the staging situation must be seen as a unified whole, having a beginning and an end; indeed, the recognition of this structure will influence the shaping of the characterization. It is hoped that some of the comment offered under this category of supplementary information may suggest the need for the invention of those gestures and mannerisms often labeled *stage business.* Acquisition of such motor behavior patterns is at least as essential to the impression of fluency as is a facility with such conversational fillers as the introductory Oh or Well.

Finally, since the adaptations require a considerable number of changes in roles, a category of information called Notes on Adaptations has been provided for each play. In addition to a supplementary glossary, these notes—in unified, summary form—contain the information relative to the adaptations provided under separate headings of Structure, Cultural Values, and General Comment in the analysis of the original play. Although the adaptations have mainly been occasioned by my conviction that the playing of parts of the opposite sex should not be encouraged, a contrastive study of the adaptations with reference to the original play may prove quite profitable to many students. They may not only develop a clearer idea of characteristic behavior patterns differentiating the sexes, but they may better understand how differing interests, values, and status of roles may influence the patterns of behavior to be displayed by the member of one sex in communication exchange with a member of the opposite sex, instead of with a representative of his own sex, in what is apparently the same situation. Students should also gain some recognition that the similarity in situation itself may be only a seeming one; thus, the adaptations indicate changes in situation which can be expected when characters of one sex are substituted for those of the other sex.

In any case teachers should find in these notes a source of considerable extra practice material, for the adaptations in many cases offer variant expressions rather than absolutely necessary changes. Obviously, the adaptations are not exhaustive, even in the sense of providing for all possible sex ratios in the student group. Additional suitable voice qualification in the broader sense, as well as changes in pitch and stress, will have to be provided by the teacher as model, as was the case with the original plays. The adaptations do serve, however, as suggestions how the plays can be changed fairly easily for use with various groups.

Effective language learning is, at least in part, the consequence of effective language teaching which, in turn, is largely the product of the relationship of the teacher's understanding of his goal and his ability to reach that goal. Although I am here presenting an approach to language teaching, it has been neither my purpose nor my desire to insist that acceptance of this approach entails the employment of specific methods or techniques of teaching. Each teacher should, in fact, be encouraged to experiment as he sees fit in attempting to implement—or challenge—this approach; such experimentation is a necessary reflection of the individuality and creativity of each person who is truly a teacher.

But, surely a central question that cannot be shirked is that of time or necessary exposure. Obviously, availability of study time or intensity of application not only will dictate the basic organization of the language learning program but will, in large measure, account for results.

Most of my experimentation has been carried on with students in a ten week intensive program comprising six hours exposure a day five days a week. And, although the intensive program has much to recommend it, it cannot be ignored that school administrators generally have not recognized—and are not likely to—the superiority of the intensive program, even from the standpoint of economic efficiency, precisely because intensive language study would require radical reorganization of the entire school curriculum. It is probable that most language learning will be practiced according to the traditional low efficiency scheme of fewer than half a dozen hours exposure per week extended over several years.

However, I must also point out that students with whom I experimented were not exclusively subjected to my approach throughout the intensive program for which they had registered but were, in fact, exposed to it only an hour or so per day. And this raises two questions: first, whether supplementation of this approach—by means of fairly standard classes in syntactic structure, phonology, etc.—is necessary or whether such an approach would in itself suffice; and, secondarily, whether such an approach could be used—exclusively or not—with students who have had various degrees of previous exposure to English.

Quite frankly, I am not sure I can supply answers for these questions satisfactory to everyone. My own experience has convinced me that an entire and complete language learning program could be based on the approach I have labeled staging communication, and I think that such a program could be set up to accommodate beginners as well as advanced students. I certainly do not deny the need for organization based on relative student ability and the consequent need for stratification of levels within a teaching program. Nor do I deny the beginner's need for work in syntactic structures, phonology, etc. But I think that all of these matters could more efficiently be handled within the context of the integration furnished by the approach I have suggested.

The assumption that such an approach must be utilized only

with advanced students, who have otherwise acquired basic abilities, is grounded on the dubious notion that such an approach is somehow more difficult for the beginner than more traditional training. I am inclined to feel that, indeed, the beginner who is not exposed to the integrated experience provided by my approach is unnecessarily handicapped for later exposure. My experience also suggests that some advanced students otherwise taught may be at some disadvantage upon exposure to my approach, precisely because their previous exposure has not provided them with the means to communicate in English; their progress in acquiring such ability to communicate has been obstructed by the ordinary approach to language, which does not present communication as an integration of behavior patterns. Extended exposure to conventional language training reinforces the misconception that communication is oral expression. Students long accustomed to such a misconception usually attempt to learn by assembly rather than by the integration of patterns provided by my approach.

Yet, it should not be supposed that mine is a blanket condemnation of all that has gone before in language learning; surely such an attitude has already been responsible for much unnecessary hostility between linguists and teachers. Obviously, over the years many principles of language teaching have proven generally valid. Indeed, the mim-mem idea—perhaps foremost among those principles—has served, greatly expanded and more fully exploited, as vital underpinning for the implementation of my approach.

I suspect, however, that those who find this approach new or radical would oblige me to suggest specific procedures by which it can be profitably exploited—even as I caution against any assumption that such procedures constitute a method. Perhaps without serious encroachment, therefore, I may offer a few suggestions, based on my personal experience with this approach.

First, then, since recognition has been extended fairly recently to the discovery that students, and beginners particularly, must be trained to listen efficiently, the teacher should begin by reading the staging aloud. Moreover, this first exposure cannot be delegated to a tape recorder. And, in view of the tremendous popularity of the tape recorder and its extensive use in the language lab, many readers may be startled to find me seemingly rejecting its use for this initial exposure. I hasten to explain, therefore, that I certainly do not mean that throughout the entire period of exposure to a staging students cannot profitably make use of a tape recorder for the improvement of pronunciation, intonation, and for facilitating the mimicking of their teacher's various recorded voice patterns. I would even point out that, paradoxically, deceptive simplicity of operation may have encouraged inadequate exploitation of the tape recorder as a teaching device. Few have realized that properly supplemented this machine could be more than a way to eliminate the effects of the fatigue curve. That is, even in the conventional, fairly rigid classroom situation, tape recorders could be utilized fully, for instance, if a rather simple switching device were so constructed that a teacher could activate in turn a tape recorder sitting before each student as he called on the student. The teacher's statement, the student's response, and the teacher's correction of the student could be recorded on the student's tape recorder; at the end of the session the student would have a tape of his own work for that class session, which he might review at his leisure. Extending the idea further, we can imagine a teacher controlling the playing, on a master tape deck, of a taped exercise which would itself activate in turn the recorders of a prearranged random series of students. The recorded statement, the individual student's response, and the teacher's interjected correction of the student, as well as the student's repetition of the correction, would then be recorded on the student's recorder before the teacher switched the master tape deck to produce the next prerecorded statement of the lesson. Pretaping, which makes further demands on the teacher's out-of-class time, would not always be necessary, for I have found that with practice most teachers are able to switch on the tape recording at any point during rehearsals to capture, for immediate playback and consideration, their own modeling as well as the mimicked student response. But by this arrangement can be retained the advantages of reduction of teacher fatigue and lack of distortion provided by the typical language lab program; we can remove students from the isolation of earphones and lab booths; we can still provide for immediate and limitless correction or elaboration by the teacher; and, most importantly, we can provide each student with a tape of his own performance during the class session. By more thorough exploitation of the tape recorder we can thus enjoy many of the best features of classroom and lab.

My main objection to dependence on the tape recorder in the introductory phase is that from the outset the concern of those utilizing this approach should be that communication be experienced realistically as a personal audio-visual relationship between people rather than as an exclusively aural-oral experience with a machine. As I have stated earlier, aural-oral expression alone must, in most instances, be considered incomplete communication. Although the tape recorder has its uses, no amount of ingenuity in exploitation of this machine can change the fundamental fact that as an echo of only the oral expression it is a supplement rather than a substitute for staging communication.

The teacher should from the outset encourage close observation and total mimicry rather than mere oral mimicry. In expanding use of the mim-mem principle and substituting observation for mere listening, the teacher will not only read but will project, by appropriate oral emotional toning and visible behavior patterns, the necessary distinctions in roles. The teacher will, in short, act out the staging, and student observation will, thus, focus on all other aspects of awareness as well as on careful listening. As the degree of student comprehension will vary with previous exposure to English, it should be expected that the beginning student will probably understand little or nothing, in the sense of being able to define or explain meanings of words or phrases. But he should, nevertheless, be required to mimic the patterns of behavior, and stagings should be carefully contrived so as to represent a progression by difficulty, established on the basis of complexity of integration of audio and visual behavior patterns, rather than merely in terms of phonological, lexical, or syntactic difficulty.

The comprehension of students who have had some previous exposure to English can be checked by simple questioning as to plot, character, and plot character relationships. In responding to questions, students should be urged, however, to mimic totally rather than to provide mere oral response. That is, even if some students are only able to demonstrate their comprehension by responding with an echoing of the pertinent section of the staging, rather than with answers in the form of sentences they contrive themselves, they are indicating comprehension and they should be required to mimic the complete, integrated patterns as closely as they can. With the exercise of some imagination, the teacher can—by supplying additional terms, by simple repetition, by single element substitution, by replacement, by expansion, by reduction, by conversion, and by transformation—put students of only slight previous exposure through a kind of pattern practice which will develop more than syntactic fluency, even when those students may know little of the meaning of what they are saying.

Moreover, I should point out that in making corrections to be repeated by the student immediately and totally, the teacher should provide the integrated behavior patterns so that the student will associate the aural and the visual; the teacher should reread and restage the pertinent parts of the staging. And following his questioning of students, the teacher can restage the entire staging, pointing out such linguistic features of communication as intonation, pausing, and pacing, while demonstrating their relationship. The teacher can, by focusing on specific sections of the plot and role projection, indicate which are most essential to the development of certain ideas and attitudes being communicated. The student will gradually see that certain features of behavior distinguish the role and he may even get some sense of the role as both source and consequence of the plot line, which, it should be remembered, is situational.

But, often exaggeration will provide the best means to focus student attention, provided the teacher recognizes that exaggeration may mean underplaying as well as overplaying. Both of these departures from the normal produce the incongruity which we find as a basis of humor. Since it may, of course, be necessary for the teacher to resist the student's tendency to fall into highly stylized and theatrical acting, the teacher's exaggeration in modeling may take the form of underplaying. With more advanced students, exaggerated behavior may provide an entree into examination of the seemingly perverse patterns of irony, particularly the special form called sarcasm, so common in colloquial usage. By limiting the intensity of student projection, the teacher will be providing a necessary distinction between enough and too much.

The foreign student will probably be better able to understand the sources of the comic or the sad by learning, within the situational context of the staging, the behavior patterns manifesting the emotions and underlying valuations. In learning which behavior patterns are appropriate, the student may be provided with a fitting introduction to the important realization that the same objective situation is interpreted variously according to the background of cultural values of those involved or observing—even to the extent that what elicits an active response by members of one society may draw no response from members of another. One effective means to discussing the relationship between behavior patterns and attitudes, without lapsing into abstraction, can be a discussion or demonstration of dialect usage, focusing on that to be found in the play and reflecting such determiners of social status as sex and relative age. That is, although caution has been offered earlier against use of staging involving dialects which are either spatially or temporally narrow and remote, the question of suitability of dialect in terms of characterization may lead to a consideration of what have been called social dialects. The teacher should try to alert the foreign student—perhaps even by a degree of exaggeration—that, despite what may appear as a kind of leveling, certain social distinctions based on relative age, sex, social position, etc., have been preserved and are reflected in the communication behavior patterns. The foreign student will have to learn, for instance, that the peculiar American casual style has definite limits; that is, he must realize that although most American professors—to his surprise—may speak quite readily to janitors and policemen, they also use certain other speech features when they address deans, judges, etc. And, since these distinctions are not entirely oral but are reflected in the entire gamut of communication patterning, the foreign student, eager to assimi-late but unaware of social values, may easily transcend the faint but significant boundaries of deference; his confusion of honorific forms of behavior can produce disastrous communication results.

In any event, while the beginning student is practicing behavior patterns which manifest certain attitudes, the more advanced student should be assisted in his understanding of the attitudes manifest. Obviously, at times some recourse can—and must—be had to the students' native language if any meaning is to be conveyed, for the limits of the exclusively "direct method" approach have by now been well exposed. Yet the teacher would be well advised to accept such recourse cautiously—as a kind of last resort—for the interpretations of the same objective situation by representatives of two cultures are as incommensurable as the phonemic systems of their respective languages. Often student understanding of attitudes may be facilitated, however, by simple descriptive discussions contrasting the foreign values with those familiar to the student.

The main problem in conveying to the student some sense of an underlying value system will lie in the teacher's tendency to wander too far from the situation in the staging being considered. The limitations of student comprehension, as well as the desire to maximize active student communication, require a sharp limitation of mere philosophizing by the teacher. Since one important contribution of linguistic research to practical language teaching has been the recognition that learning about a language is not likely to produce speakers of the language, we must try to arrange, as far as possible, for the student to learn about the language through communicating in it. Similarly, the teacher cannot afford to forget the significant difference between knowing the values and attitudes of a society and the ability to reflect them in suitable behavior patterns. The ability to reflect such patterns effectively is, of course, a product of active practice—preferably in situational context.

Certainly in the course of such active practice there will be interference from native patterns, since they reflect differing native values. But in learning the points of contrast, the teacher can better focus his effort on modeling English patterns for his students to mimic. In any event, the student will be actively immersed in the observation and recreation of integrated characterization and will thereby be acquiring the necessary habit of staging communication. The sole caution I would offer here is that the teacher always be careful, whenever contrasting native and foreign attitudes, not to allow contrast to become evaluation; although what is foreign can seem amusing, neither native nor foreign need be seen as inferior.

Thus far, students have been given no written copy of the staging; they have relied entirely on observation built through numerous repetitions in rehearsal. However, writing need not be neglected, for students can be required to write according to level of ability although the effort may be confined to a kind of collaborative class composition. Outside of class the more fluent may be able to set down parts of the dialogue from memory and to offer some accompanying description of appearance of visible behavior patterns of a character, a summary of part of the plot, or even an explanation of emotions and attitudes in terms of plot-character relations. In order to insure that the focus of attention in such homework remain on the oral presentation—despite the fact students are writing—a kind of written colloquial usage should be encouraged. That is, the gap between spoken and written expression should not be permitted to inhibit or complicate the student's task of expression at this point; contractions, sentence fragments, and other features of informal usage should be accepted. Such outside-of-class work should, in fact, encourage retention offstage of the features of staging.

In all writing students should be encouraged to note as much of the evidence of integration of behavior patterns as they can: they should be urged to write as much detail as possible of *how* something is said (in terms of postures, facies, voice qualification) as well as *what* is said (in terms of the words and sentences of the dialogue). Student writing should be read in class, with student writers staging—whenever feasible—as they read their papers, so that they may themselves be the first to recognize the deficiencies in their written presentation. In order to hint at differences (limitations of written form), attention may be called to the fact that they have not been able to set down all of the patterns and their integration demonstrable in staging communication. Corrections by other students should take the form of restaging the situation described, with the teacher pointing out—by demonstration—the omissions and misinterpretations students have made. That is, correction should be accomplished by student mimicking the teacher rather than by lengthy discussions or explanations.

Throughout the early stages of rehearsal, the teacher may find it both interesting and instructive to act out in pantomime the visual patterns accompanying the oral patterns, as the student reads the dialogue. By soliciting suggestions and inducing the student to correct his patterns, the teacher can ascertain the degree of student acquisition of the integrated patterns. Then, in later rehearsals, he may have students—pantomiming various roles—stage all of the visual patterns which should accompany the teacher's tape-recorded oral patterns. In this way, students may learn not only to observe the two kinds of patterns very carefully but also to develop the ability to integrate them. Moreover, this exercise requires alertness and provides a check on aural comprehension. It also encourages students to "memorize their lines" in the more realistic and meaningful sense of committing to memory—or, rather, to the automatization of overlearning—the audio-visible behavior patterns of communication.

As a kind of summary of goals thus far achieved, then, the teacher can select at random sections of dialogue from the scenario and have students stage them, mimicking from memory the teacher's modeling. This is a form of test of what students have already learned to mimic—and, of course, students should only be tested on what they have been taught. No originality has been required nor has self-expression been encouraged. It is essential at this stage that students overlearn the stereotyped pattern—the cliché of communication; by first learning to communicate he will not call unusual attention to his foreignness; later, he can distinguish himself as an individual, can develop his characteristic style.

At this point, however, it may be fruitful to consider substitution of alternates in the scenario, and many of these alternates can be drawn from either the glossary items or can be suggested as paraphrases by the teacher. In fact, since the student's stock of synonymous expressions will be pretty much limited to those supplied by the teacher, this opportunity for expansion of vocabulary and substitution of syntactic structures should be welcomed. Patently, if the staging is specially designed to meet students' needs, the students should not be permitted to change or make substitutions merely to eliminate sounds or sound sequences they find difficult to pronounce. Students by now should also be aware that the retention of certain lines as written is essential for a specific effect. This may be particularly true with *double-entendre* statements, with puns, or with certain kinds of allusions, but it is also true of much idiomatic statement and particularly of that mildly sarcastic, ironic humor common in English speech.

Both to encourage dependence on eye and ear and to renew student interest, situational analogues as well as consequent dialogue paraphrases can be introduced to expand the significance of the verbal-physical integration beyond the specific situation of the staging. Such situational paraphrasing can provide the material for more elaborate pattern practising as well as furnish the means to acquire a feeling for larger contexts. That is, in attempting substitution by paraphrasing, the foreigner must reveal his understanding of the situation in context, since all substitution is context sensitive. In correction, the teacher can discuss the situation staged, as part of the life pattern of native speakers of the language and as it contrasts with the familiar patterns of the student's native background. By this process students may observe the function of each characterization in relation to others, the necessity of each behavior pattern in the characterization, and the effect of omission in substitution of plot features.

The emphasis should always be on the behavior—both aural and visual—by which mood is generated. Knowing the characters and the basic plot, as well as plot-character relations—and having acquired, by active staging, some feeling for the integration of behavior patterns—the students can be referred to specific scenes in the scenario, copies of which may now be distributed. From their observation of the teacher as model and through their immersion in mimicry, the students should be able to recognize something of the general mood of the staging and possibly of the shifts of mood as plot features. And although continuing to work on communication as integrated behavior patterns by modeling of total active mimicry, the teacher may now turn his main attention to the development and improvement of integration in character relations, in terms of the staging situation. Pacing, continuity, exits and entrances, phrasing and timing generally can be improved. Since most students will probably tend to speak more slowly on stage than is normal for native speakers off stage, staging communication may somewhat enhance opportunities for correction. But certainly most foreign students should not be encouraged to speak faster if distortion, as is likely, increases apace. Students taught to phrase in segments of three or four words are far more likely to be understood, since stressing and elision are more easily controlled, than those students permitted to rattle away in larger segments more characteristic of the native speaker. Not only will such short segment phrasing encourage more care in the pronunciation of segmental phonemes but also intonation contours closer to normal can be retained. Moreover, those dictionary addicted students who tend to speak phrases made up of separate unelided words—with a characteristic staccato sound I have labeled "typewriter English"—can more easily be induced to elide acceptably when such short segment phrasing is used.

However, the process of sensitizing students to the limitations of written expression alone—begun with student experience in writing about the characterization—can also be furthered by contrasting the written notation of the scenario with the staged communication of the staging they have observed and have participated in. Having seen and heard the staging while immersed in it, the student will have imagined or visualized the situation and thus be able to supply what the written statement must of necessity omit. That is, he will have become aware of the dynamics of communication and this experience is likely to encourage the student to exercise such imaginative visualization in *all* his reading.

By this time, most vocabulary items will have been clarified through staging and discussion of their situational contexts. Students should, therefore, be able to read aloud with less fumbling and hesitation, more meaningfully—both as a group and individually—as they follow the teacher's modeling. Reference to written forms may now further the correction of pronunciation, although the teacher must be careful not to encourage dependence on the segmentation of the sound stream which is, of course, the characteristic convention of writing's division into words. That is, pronunciation must be dealt with within the context of the line or the short segment rather than in terms of single words, if all the necessary slurring is to occur properly. However, the teacher must also make the student aware that pronunciation is contextual in still another sense—in terms of the characterization using the dialogue—for the various features of voice qualification necessary to the role are mutually influential, integrated. In a certain sense, the process of learning to read in the language, after having gained some control of listening and speaking seems very similar to learning to play the violin from notes after having learned to pick out tunes by ear. And here I might suggest that the famous Suzuki method of violin teaching, which has produced such dazzling results in Japan, deserves the attention of language teachers, since it gives primacy to ear training rather than to the usual eye training in note reading.

Pattern practice may be expanded to deal with such transformational features as are involved in the use of the negative, the trailer or tag question, the shift from quote to report, and may also deal with the use of modal auxiliaries, etc. All of this will be based on the staging although such exercises really cannot be used as part of a staging. But they will occur on stage rather than within the rigid rows and ranks of the classroom, and in responding students can be encouraged more easily to acquire behavior patterns typical of ordinary conversation among native English speakers. The patterned seating of the ordinary classroom represents a completely artificial language situation, scarcely ever to be found in real life. Thus, even while performing in pattern practice fashion, the student is provided, by the staged communication approach, with the possibility of lifelike fluidity in spatial and physical relationships. Since the pattern practice items are drawn from the scenario as part of an integration of behavior patterns, pattern practice is not merely an exercise in syntactic competence. Moreover, instead of drawing the pattern practice items out of a scenario as isolated units, the teacher can take out several dialogue lines in sequence, giving students practice in active conversational exchange. Discussion of the stage properties and the spatial reference of the stage set, in terms of the stage directions given in the scenario, can also furnish opportunities for significant pattern practice exercise. Moreover, the student can be required to observe and mimic the spatial relations of characters as communicants of emotional attitudes; he can be given practice in making the essential shifts in posture and relative spatial position in conjunction with suitable oral expression.

As the staging is read through repeatedly, the teacher can establish the idea, by careful focusing of effort, that the scenario is a sequence of dialogue exchanges, usually between two characters. Staging one role, the teacher can have students read and act out the dialogue of another character's response to that role in the exchange. Assigning roles at random and alternating roles freely, the teacher can develop student ability to observe and mimic totally, as well as in integrated fashion, the behavior patterns peculiar to the characterization of each role. It is important at this point that the student not become identified with any single role; he should, instead, have opportunity to augment his powers of observation and mimicry, so that he may learn to associate the physical and verbal aspects of a role. In addition to basic segmental phoneme pronunciation, students should be required to pay careful attention to unstressing, elision, pause patterns, pacing, and stress or pitch shifts, as well as to the dynamic relations existing between all of these features, for these along with other forms of voice qualification not only provide meaning but also distinguish the roles.

As students reread and perform the staging and are assigned roles at random and alternately, they will be familiarizing themselves with the situation intellectually; through the active performance of total mimicry, they will be developing a physical sense of themselves in the situation. The teacher should choose a staging with an eye to its suitability in terms of division by sexes within the student group, but some adjustments in part splitting and changes in sex of roles are inevitable. As I have said above, sex role differences are probably reflected in the languages of all societies and so there is no value in having a student play a role of the opposite sex; in fact, such a practice is positively harmful, since the time and effort necessary for the learning of total roles are wasted on the learning of unsuitable behavior patterns.

Some languages more than others seem to be characterized by more explicit reflection of sex distinction, but it is important for a student to be aware that behavior patterns distinguishing the sexes reflect differing social values. As a student can best learn acceptable communication behavior patterns from a member of his or her own sex, ideally teacher and students should be of the same sex. But as this will be impossible to arrange and as it would, in any event, be impossible to provide a teacher of each sex for a mixed group, it is clear that any teacher must—by careful observation and total mimicry—learn the patterns of the opposite sex as well as those of his own sex. In fact, one of the advantages of the approach presented in this book is that the student is encouraged to develop that close observation of all native speakers of the language he is learning. For students trained in close observation, movies and television shows as well as whatever opportunities a student may have for face-to-face meetings with native speakers can supplement the teacher's efforts to supply patterns distinguishing the sexes.

Although the teacher will have foreseen and allowed for such accommodations, adjustment at this point can provide a means to reviewing and reexamining the relations of various structural elements of the situations depicted, as the effect of various changes in roles, dialogue, plot, etc., is explored. The staging can then be performed again and a specific role assigned to each student. From this point on, each student will concentrate on maximizing communication of his role by perfecting his mimicry of the integration of behavior patterns involved.

Obviously, total mimicry can be effective as a language learning approach only if attention is paid to careful memorization in addition to close observation. All students must be able to reproduce patterns as well as recognize and understand them; only the opportunity to perform the required patterns will develop their ability to reproduce them. Once parts have been assigned, the student should be required to begin to practice and memorize his role as a whole, and not to separate oral and visual manifestations, since all patterns in a language system reinforce each other. However, care in selecting a staging having a fairly equal division of lines, and a distribution avoiding the long, unbroken speeches not common in real life situations, will help the student in his task of line memorization. Since the main interest is in acquisition of appropriate behavior patterns rather than in exactness of line memorization, some substitution of suitable lines can be permitted.

Once parts are assigned, the staging should be divided into scenes according to the grouping of roles involved. Again it may be found that rehearsal of scenes at random and out of sequence will not only focus observation on the patterns, and not merely on the plot, but will also allow students to acquire the ability to jump immediately into the behavior patterns required by a situation. Gradually, as patterns of roles are acquired more fully, scenes can be rehearsed in sequence, always stressing integration of response and unity of the situation. Students should become so familiar with their roles in a staging as to experience the illusion of total involvement in a lifelike situation. Along with some idea of the unity of a role, through its composite behavior patterns, rereading of the staging will provide opportunity to experience it as a unified situation consisting of a beginning, a development, and a conclusion. This attention to formal elements of structure will be valuable in teaching students ultimately to read literature in the foreign language; but it is of more immediate concern that the student begin to feel that real life is a composite of a series of scenes, for each of which he must understand the situational context, so that he can select and project an appropriate integration of behavior patterns. In other words, the goal is not merely to learn a role in a staging having initial and terminal points, signaled by a rising and falling curtain, but to learn to perform in the continuous and interlocking situations of real life. The terminal points in one staging situation must be felt as the boundaries of a situation and at the same time as the opposite terminals of other situations. Following from this, it may prove stimulating to encourage student speculation about what they think might have happened before and after the situation staged. That speculation should be communicated as a performance of integrated oral and visible behavior patterns; it should be yet another opportunity for staging communication.

Until they have learned to concentrate completely on mimicking the behavior patterns of the role, beginning students will fail to recognize the need to sustain the separation of themselves, as role players, from their audience. Incompletely immersed in the role, each will still be standing apart observing the scene along with the audience and will self-consciously be outside the staging. They can, therefore, be expected to join occasionally in the reaction of the audience and at times may even disrupt the performance of fellow players. Yet, since the sustaining of the illusion of total involvement is vital—not only for the audience which may witness the performance but, more importantly, for the development of the student's own learning—stepping out of character on stage should be discouraged.

The rehearsal must not degenerate into an unstructured extracurricular activity, and for many foreign students, raised on the notion that only the bitter pill is effective, that any learning must be painful, such degeneration is unlikely. On the other hand, staging communication may dispel the rather gloomy, solemn atmosphere more familiar to most students that has made language learning a very grim kind of puzzle-solving or a desperate code-breaking activity. Too many teachers, that is, may forget that student response to a playful attitude is as good a measure of recognition and production as is student response to some of the very solemn academic nonsense we frequently contrive in our unwisdom. Both teachers and students will be surprised to discover that in the relaxed, casual atmosphere fostered by staging communication they are more likely to feel exhausted only by the intensity and amount of work possible. They will experience less of the nervous exhaustion resultant from the very natural insecurity which arises when the communication structures forming a major part of the ego framework are readjusted to a new language. Yet the advantage of staging, in terms of total involvement of the student learning to communicate, will be lost if the greater range and fluidity in student response afforded by this approach become identified with idle relaxation.

In any event, and in a sense far broader and more authentic certainly than that advocated by those linguists who sent us off duplicating merely what we were told was the child's process of aural-oral acquisition of language, students by means staging communication will learn as a child really does—by total observation and total mimicry—that integration of suitable oral and visual patterns which is truly effective communication.

Every language teacher has at one time or another realized that it should be possible, by careful contrivance, to design a body of material by which various subsystems, or perhaps all subsystems, could be taught simultaneously. The promise of maximized efficiency makes such a possibility seductive, indeed. Yet those who have attempted to develop so-called integrated programs have quickly discovered for various complex reasons—stemming essentially from the mutual influence of subsystems having their own differentials of difficulty—that this is an extremely complicated undertaking. Thus, in the average language program these subsystems are likely to be dealt with separately or the emphasis in any particular class is on only one subsystem at a time. Fully implemented, my approach will go a long way toward providing that ideal integration in teaching of subsystems although, at first sight, the need for the greatly broadened and integrated observation on the part of the student, learning by total mimicry, may appear to complicate the student's task enormously. In fact, I have found no reason to accept the commonly held opinion that the student—and particularly the beginner—is so severely burdened with pronunciation or syntax that he cannot profitably be required to pay attention to all other aspects of communication. Indeed, some students actually seem to learn syntactic patterns more readily in the context of communication—that is, as part of an integrated unity of various behavior patterns. Similarly, hearing and speaking words in context reduces the need for rote memorization of vocabulary. The

context—much larger, of course, than a mere sentence or paragraph—consists of the manifestations of attitudes and values, and one pattern triggers another. As audio-visual people have long contended, in learning one sense tends to reinforce and augment another. Staging communication—providing the physical and visual features of a situation—can reinforce the oral, furnishing mnemonic devices to evoke response.

Accepting the idea that communication is a system of systems—although our unity is much broader than that which most linguists accept—we find that the attempt to teach syntactic structures, let us say, without reference to other, visible behavior patterns, is as questionable as the linguists have told us it is to teach morphology without regard for phonology or syntax without reference to suprasegmentals. In fact, we might go further and suggest that if language is a system of systems, then the attempt to teach only part of the total behavior pattern, by the usual method of presenting syntactic patterns in the vacuum of exclusively oral oriented pattern practice sessions, may actually retard or even block that learning. Further investigation might indicate that those limitations of the typical pattern practice may be traced to the fact that such practice does not encourage the observation of total communication patterns providing supplementary clues to reinforce retention of the syntactic patterns.

Instead of a mechanical assemblage of separate capacities acquired in step-by-step fashion, the ability to communicate is the creation of a configuration of integrated patterns acquired simultaneously. Of course, it would be folly to expect perfect acquisition from the earliest exposure, for the beginning student will neither control nor integrate those patterns well. But, surely it is no less folly to expect, as most of us now do, that drill to perfection in one aspect of the language after another separately will produce a perfect integration of those refined but separate aspects. In short, the student can perfect his ability to communicate only by attempting truly to communicate; and communication, as I have stated repeatedly, is possible only by an integration of behavior patterns such as I have described.

Shifting our attention momentarily, in the opposite direction, to the advanced student, we find that the basic problem in language learning, which has been long recognized by all language teachers, is the fitting of the behavior pattern suitably to the situation. Even when modern principles of applied linguistics are followed, the advanced student must eventually somehow get beyond the mere cued response to voice his ideas and attitudes freely. We really do not know how a student learns to respond in a way he has never learned to a stimulus which has not earlier been provided as a cue. But having developed his powers of close observation by the required exercise of them as he learns by staging communication, the student will simply have more clues as to what is expected in the situation. His experience in staging communication may enable him better to interpret even the unfamiliar situation.

Moreover, the integration of behavior patterns accomplished in staging communication is not a private but a public performance, as it is in real life. And although such exposure might seem to threaten the average self-conscious student reluctant to subject himself to the possible ridicule his attempt to communicate in another language might engender, actually it seems that the self-consciousness of a student may be reduced considerably, because he is completely involved in the integration of total response necessary for the characterization. That is, by concentrating on total mimicry rather than on the oral projection alone—as in the usual language class—the student seems to experience a kind of diffusion of focus which may free him from the concentrated strain of effort in one area of communication alone and its consequent flubs. While on one hand, perhaps because of its inherent artificiality, staging communication may help to foster an atmosphere of psychological experimentation very useful in the acquisition of a totally foreign response pattern, on the other hand, it may make the student—as mimic rather than as creator of a role—feel less responsible for the inadequacy of his projection as he learns the role. It seems that the role, in a sense, protects the student's personality from failure, for on stage the student tends to feel it is the role or character he is playing which is defective and not he himself. Once the inhibition has been dispelled through staging communication, many students are able to stand, move, and speak without that numbing self-consciousness common in the usual language class. A student who might otherwise remain silent often seems to experience a kind of release when he is able to evoke a response while communicating in another language, not only in rehearsal but also in actual performance before an audience. At the same time, he may experience a greater sense of success because he can come closer to simulating the total pattern.

But, in any event, staging communication will help to break down the atmosphere of sedentary study in scholarly isolation which, paradoxically, the most sophisticated use of the language lab has encouraged. The student learns in an active situational context including other people whose roles he must understand fully while integrating his responses, as in realistic communication. Nor need we ignore the function of the audience, for good teachers have always known that there is usually a learning incentive in public performance which not only spurs a kind of competition but also helps the student to become aware of the performance of his fellow students, to become sensitized to the need to strive for control over those communication devices which will enable him to project his own role better.

Moreover, I have not found that the average student, exposed to my approach, finds the burden of correction intolerable. In fact, correction is likely to be more gracefully received, because apparently, the role the student is learning may protectively mask his ego from the threats which correction usually represent. The student is thus likely to be more ready to accept the need for repeated "rehearsals" of a phrase that he is trying to project authentically, since he knows that such repetition is a convention of all play production.

I have noted, furthermore, that a student's classmates are better able to volunteer both comment and correction of his particular performance, since the total response required on stage usually affords them a better understanding of the situation and its behavior requirements than is made available in the usual classroom setting. And even when these interpretations of classmates are quite wrong, there is likely to be active involvement. In addition, it is quite surprising how many of the behavior patterns learned in communication of various roles find their way into the conversation of the students—the final test of effective language learning.

Focusing more sharply on specific elements of communication, we find that many students in performance, both as active participant and as passive observer, may also become aware of the need for appropriate pacing; they will become aware that the language is not spoken at a constant speed, that fluency is not measured by speed of utterance but by comprehensibility. In fact, greater attention to the matter of timing generally may result, for the student will find that he must be alert to pick up his cues both visual and oral.

Moreover, students can become acquainted with a far broader spectrum of communication sounds—other than words—than the usual textbook-based-approach to language provides. And while confronting the curious paradox that linguists must insist—in their written texts on language—that language is aural-oral, we must also be aware that certain communication effects cannot be expressed in writing because no practical way has been found adequately to phonemicize them, and, therefore, they cannot be found in textbooks. In merely mentioning these features we often find it necessary, in the absence of any better, to resort to something like the gross representations to be found in the dialogue balloons of comic strips. Thus, only by staging communication is the student provided a context within which the expression of amenities or softening devices or of those idiomatic communication openers and fillers that lubricate conversation in every language is meaningful. By staging communication such odd yet important expletives, for example, as the English interrogative "huh?" the surprising "ahah," the negative "uh-uh," the musing "h-mmm"—all of which are so common colloquially and of such significant parts of communication that they have defied spelling or written expression—are provided with suitable visual coordinates in context.

Since the context transcends the immediate situation and the individuals involved, it should be clear that there are historical, sociological, and psychological aspects of the context which must be understood. Yet another advantage of staging communication, therefore, lies in the fact that it provides a natural entree for the explanatory demonstration in context—and by contrast, perhaps, with those of the student's own background—of the values and attitudes lying behind the communication patterns of the people whose language the student is studying. Social dialects and sex role delineation by dialogue can readily be demonstrated and acquired as reflections of these appropriate values and attitudes. And, with regard to the latter, one of the curiosities of literature in English is that so little attention is paid even by major authors to delineation of the sex of characters by dialogue. There is a general unawareness of sex differences in speech patterns, but since such delineation is also a product of visual behavior patterns integrated with complexly related aural patterns, written material cannot easily provide such evidence of sex delineation. Yet, perhaps this merely suggests the obvious yet ignored fact that the spoken language cannot be learned by reading and writing.

While the student is led, on the one hand, to depend less on the written word and more on his eyes and ears in his experiencing of language as communication, on the other hand, staging communication encourages him to examine the written scenario carefully for all clues as to how a role should be created. We can, thus, teach close reading which will focus student attention on devices of written expression.

It should be recognized—and particularly by those who could

look upon this approach as fostering mere supplementation—that if imaginatively employed, staging communication can facilitate fluency in all four of what are generally accepted as the main aspects of language learning: hearing, speaking, reading, and writing. That is, these four aspects—clearly divisible into the two broad categories of recognition and production—collectively imply the need for just such an integration of the aural and the visual. This does not mean that those as yet scarcely understood distinctions of oral from written forms of expression are here somehow minimized or reconciled. Certainly this approach does not suggest that students can or should be taught to read or write as they speak; neither is there any implication that spoken expression should approximate written forms. But it is clear that both close listening and close reading depend on that habit of close observation which this approach fosters. And it should be apparent that any validity to the long held notion that better student writing is somehow induced by exposure to written models can be demonstrated only if students are trained in such careful observation. Surely, if we avoid the often confused blurring of development of literacy and development of individual style, it is clear that acquisition of basic ability to convey ideas and experience understandably cannot be expected unless the student has first learned to mimic his models carefully.

In staging communication, these four aspects of language learning may be seen more realistically as greatly extended; once it is accepted that communication is more than the linguist's language, the student ear can be tuned to other than the comparatively few aural signals which presently concern most linguists, while the student eye can be focused on other than the written forms.

In talking about both the staging content and the written expression of it, we will practice speaking in the language—again extending the use of communication devices beyond their use in the staging itself, as students learn to express their feelings and thoughts about the staging in the language they labor to learn. And, clearly, the dialogue of the staging is more likely to encourage a dialogue among the students than are the artificial language forms on which most novels, short stories, and essays depend, particularly since the stagings we employ are realistic communication situations rather than theatrically heightened drama. Idioms which in the usual text are merely listed essentially without situation, are plentiful not only in the stagings provided—for without them the expression is unreal—but, also in this text, based on staging communication, in which idioms are highly situation sensitive and immerse the student in the situation appropriate to the idiom's usage.

When, by practice-rehearsal, the distance diminishes between written expression and oral expression, between staging as written script and staging as performed communication, between the staging and real life, the artificiality of the language learning process is reduced. Totally involved in role recreation, the student can be encouraged, for example, to expand the stage notes, so as to set down in writing the communication patterns necessary for the recreation of the role in the situation. All of this, growing out of active discussion of and participation in the play, can, of course, exercise the student's grasp of essentials of language structure.

We can focus the student's attention on the complex relation of sight and sound in non-written communication by making him aware of the limits of written forms of expression to effect communication. Surely it should be obvious that the distinction between oral and written expression can be recognized far more easily by openly discussing and demonstrating those differences than by the usual focusing on oral expression while bootlegging the reading, as if reading were in some mysterious and inexplicable way merely the written version of what is spoken. On the other hand, a better awareness of those limits can be used to encourage more careful attention to situational interpretation in reading and a greater concentration on ways of attaining clarity and precision in the student's own writing.

The process of language learning by staging communication will then be a kind of continuous rehearsal, in which is invested naturally the necessary repetition which can be so dull and hypnotic in the average, merely verbal pattern practice. As he rehearses, the student will actively participate but, as importantly, his observation of the performance of his fellow students will furnish him with repeated instances of correction, of total response in context until he may develop a critical sensitivity to integration of movement and speech, to the synchronization of physical and aural presence necessary for communication. As both audience and actor, the student will experience the dynamics of a situation he cannot possibly catch by the essentially static flashcards, felt board recreations, transparent overlays, or by dialogues and discussions providing only the verbal aspect of communication. And it is this dynamic interrelatedness of communication, available only through the student's participation in the play, which he most needs to experience; for by his developing sense of confidence in playing a total role in staged communication, he will be encouraged to assume total roles in other English communication situations. In the process of staging communication the student will have had the opportunity to practice in context such ordinary but necessary conversation as "Come over here," "How does that look?" "Put that over there," "Is it O.K. now?" etc. In fact, the greater spatial dispersal and fluidity of student visual relationships will have fostered an exchange which is unavailable in the ordinary static, passive classroom situation.

Gradually the student can, perhaps, synthesize a unified personality–different from his native personality but quite complete and integrated to a remarkable degree. It is as if, by stepping on stage, the student exchanges his personality for another and this metamorphic experience is precisely that of anyone who in real life shifts from communication in one language to communication in another. Thus, in a very real sense true language learning may be likened to the development of what might–with some admitted exaggeration,–be called a kind of controlled schizophrenia. And the student who has experienced this metamorphosis will be able to go beyond even that experience which has eluded most of us who have never been taught systematically how to attain the ability to "think in the language"; he will, in addition, be able to feel, to communicate, to live in the language.

This approach, thus, has a very important advantage. By breaking down the artificiality of language learning and by involving the total behavioral response, there is not only a carry over into the attempt at communication outside the play of patterns learned in role creation of a staging but also a sensitization of the student to the need to observe, even while he is outside of class, all communication patterns of those who speak the language he is learning.

In focusing on the value of the *process* of staging communication rather than on the final and finished performance of the staging, I have indicated it is preferable that the student be exposed to the idea of total mimicry, as embodied in the staging, as early as possible in his language learning experience. But it is well to remember that all formal training programs have two terminal points and that whereas most are concerned about how and with whom to begin, most do very little about the even more critical problem of what will remain when the program is over. This does not mean that these programs have no goals, that the goals are not reached, or that no provision is made for determining whether goals have been reached. There is, in fact, a great deal of concern for such matters. But, patently, at the end of the program many students are left to enroll in a new program which will develop and refine what has been acquired or–and this I have found far more likely–they regress measurably and very shortly after leaving the program. Actually, language learning is not readily confined within the limits of a program but is a process requiring continuous exercise over a lifetime.

It can be argued that those who genuinely wish to learn to communicate will make every effort to arrange for such exercise. Yet the problem is not quite that simple. Those who have spent any time teaching overseas will certainly be aware that despite the ingenuity displayed in students' desperate efforts to retain fluency by informal group study, once their formal studies are ended, passive listening to guest speakers, or the equally passive watching of movies, too often supplants active involvement in the language. The student who learns in the usual way will have acquired limited and essentially isolated behavior patterns which are not readily retained. He will not have been physically and visually–or even orally– engaged in active communication. That is, even those who have been exposed to dialogue learning, as an attempt at situational context, are not likely to have experienced any of the distraction of movement and speech of the real world of integrated behavior patterns, whereas the student exposed to my approach has been totally involved in real life contexts.

Moreover, the graduate of the usual program has acquired no systematic habits of integrated observation by which he can reinforce or acquire aspects of that integration. And this provision for development of the habit of careful observation of integrated behavior patterns is, then, the significant difference between the approach outlined in this book and all other approaches of which I am aware. Whatever weaknesses the New Critics may have had, it seems clear to most of us teaching literature that they did help foster close reading. It should be equally clear that we can extend this idea of focused attention on details to the fostering of close observation of the integrated behavior patterns by which communication is accomplished. Indeed, by this approach the student has learned more than the integration of behavior patterns; he has learned how to learn in such a way that he can continue to develop genuine communication ability.

Thus, for the student exposed to my approach, language learning is no longer a narrow intellectual activity but becomes a means of confronting reality. We find that, paradoxical as it may seem, the character building of role playing in stagings is directly related to character building in that different sense we have long been told is perhaps the main profit of language learning.

Guide to Pronunciation

There is no conventional notation for the features which we are attempting to illustrate. The following may therefore be considered an approximation of them.

Phonemes used in the glossary and commentary following each staging are:

Vowels: i ɨ u
      e ə o
      æ a ɔ

   Note: a tilde (～) marks a nasalized vowel

Stops: p   t   k   b   d   g

Affricates: č   ǰ

Fricatives: f   v   θ   ð

Sibilants: s   š   z   ž

Nasals: m   n   ŋ

Lateral: l

Semivowels: r   w   y   h

Stresses: ´   ˆ   ˋ   ˘

Pitches: 1   2   3   4

Junctures: + | || #

PART 2
STAGINGS

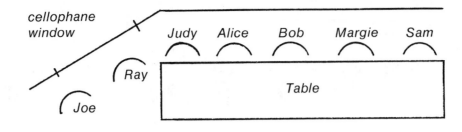

SETTING

The dining room of a middle class home. The cast is sitting around the dining table (as shown in sketch above). A window, made of a sheet of cellophane, is on the backdrop stage right rear. As the curtain rises, a club meeting is in progress and the chairman is trying to conclude the discussion.

Mixed cast (all in midteens)

Bob (chairman)
Margie
Sam (at whose home the discussion takes place)
Judy
Joe
Ray
Alice (secretary)

Bob.   O.K. then ... we've finally got two possibilities ...
Margie   *(annoyed and interrupting).* Yeah, and I don't like either of them. *(looks disgusted and speaks sarcastically)* A picnic or a visit to the planetarium! *(Pause as everyone looks at her)* How about a dance?
Sam   *(sighing and trying to be patient).*

Girls' cast (all in midteens)

Betty (chairman)
Margie
Sandy (at whose home the discussion takes place)
Judy
Jane
Ruth
Alice

Betty.   O.K. then ... we've finally got two possibilities ...
Margie   *(annoyed and interrupting).* Yeah, and I don't like either of them. *(Looks disgusted and speaks sarcastically)* A picnic or a visit to the planetarium! *(Pause as everyone looks at her)* How about a dance?
Sandy   *(sighing and trying to be pa-*

Boy's Cast (all in midteens)

Bob (chairman)
Mac
Sam (at whose home the discussion takes place)
John
Joe
Ray
Al

Bob.   O.K. then ... we've finally got two possibilities ...
Mac   *(annoyed and interrupting).* Yeah, and I don't like either one of them. *(Looks disgusted and speaks sarcastically)* A picnic or a visit to the planetarium! *(Pause as everyone looks at him)* How about a dance?
Sam   *(sighing and trying to be patient).*

44

mixed

Look, Margie, we've been all through that. Why can't we get down to choosing which it's going to be . . . a picnic or the planetarium . . . and start arranging the details.

Judy   *(enthusiastically).* That's a good idea! What day was it again, Bob?

Bob.   Next Saturday.

Joe.   Yeah—but don't you think it will be a little cool for a picnic?

Ray.   No . . . just right. We can have a weenie roast with a campfire. Then we can sing songs after we eat. And . . .

Alice   *(writing furiously).* Wait a minute . . . I can't keep up with all of you.

Bob.   Sorry, Alice—but you don't need to take down all this.

Alice, seemingly oblivious, continues writing furiously.

Joe   *(kidding).* No, and particularly that part where Ray was trying to work things so we'd have to listen to his guitar playing *(in a mocking sarcastic tone)* "sing songs after we eat . . . ."

Margie.   But we still haven't decided whether it's to be a picnic or the planetarium trip . . . if we can't have a dance, that is.

Sam   *(giving Margie a chilling look).* Anybody here ever been to the planetarium?

Judy   *(wearily).* Yes, I went once . . . and it was very dull. It's so dark that you fall asleep right away. And the lecturers aren't always so

girls

tient). Look, Margie, we've been all through that. Why can't we get down to choosing which it's going to be . . . a picnic or the planetarium . . . and start arranging the details.

Judy   *(enthusiastically).* That's a good idea! What day was it again, Betty?

Betty.   Next Saturday.

Jane.   Yeah—but don't you think it will be a little cool for a picnic?

Ruth.   No . . . just right. We can have a weenie roast with a campfire. Then we can sing songs after we eat. And . . .

Alice   *(writing furiously).* Wait a minute . . . I can't keep up with all of you.

Betty.   Sorry, Alice—but you don't need to take down all this.

Alice seemingly oblivious, continues writing furiously.

Jane   *(kidding).* No, and particularly that part where Ruth was trying to work things so we'd have to listen to her guitar playing *(in a mocking, sarcastic tone)* "sing songs after we eat . . . ."

Margie.   But we still haven't decided whether it's to be a picnic or the planetarium trip . . . if we can't have a dance, that is.

Sandy   *(giving Margie a chilling look).* Anybody here ever been to the planetarium?

Judy   *(wearily).* Yes, I went once . . . and it was very dull. It's so

boys

Look, Mac, we've been all through that. Why can't we get down to choosing which it's going to be . . . a picnic or the planetarium . . . and start arranging the details.

John   *(enthusiastically).* That's a good idea! What day was it again, Bob?

Bob.   Next Saturday.

Joe.   Yeah—but don't you think it will be a little cool for a picnic?

Ray.   No . . . just right. We can have a weenie roast with a campfire. Then we can sing songs after we eat. And . . .

Al   *(writing furiously).* Wait a minute . . . I can't keep up with all of you.

Bob.   Sorry, Al—but you don't need to take down all this.

Al, seemingly oblivious, continues writing furiously.

Joe   *(kidding).* No, and particularly that part where Ray was trying to work things so we'd have to listen to his guitar playing *(in a mocking, sarcastic tone)* "sing songs after we eat . . . ."

Mac.   But we still haven't decided whether it's to be a picnic or the planetarium trip . . . if we can't have a dance, that is.

Sam   *(giving Mac a chilling look).* Anybody here ever been to the planetarium?

John   *(wearily).* Yes, I went once . . . and it was very dull. It's so dark that you fall asleep right away. And the lecturers aren't always so

mixed

stimulating either.

Alice   *(throwing down her pencil).* I give up . . . I can't get it all down.

Margie   *(ignoring Alice and answering Judy).* It's educational.

Ray   *(jokingly).* Is that good? *(Everybody laughs)*

Bob   *(teasingly).* Did you go alone, Judy?

Ray   *(also teasing).* Yeah . . . maybe that's why you found it dull.

Judy   *(slyly).* You mean it was dull because I was alone or because I wasn't?

Alice.   It probably depends on the guy you were with. *(Smiling slyly at Judy)*

Bob   *(wearily trying to be businesslike).* O.K., O.K. . . . but we've got to cut this out and decide.

Joe.   Say, do any of you know what days the planetarium is open?

Sam.   Ahah! A man with an idea! *(Gets up)* I'll phone them right away. *(Exits stage left)*

Margie.   How long does the show take at the planetarium?

Ray.   I think it's only about an hour, but there are some exhibits outside of the auditorium.

Judy   *(mildly interested).* Yes, and they're pretty interesting—might even be better than the lecture, in fact.

Alice.   I think they have lectures every couple of hours . . . at 2, 4, and 6 P.M.

Bob.   What about the price? How much does it cost?

Joe.   They get a dollar for the lecture.

girls

dark that you fall asleep right away. And the lecturers aren't always so stimulating either.

Alice   *(throwing down her pencil).* I give up . . . I can't get it all down.

Margie   *(ignoring Alice and answering Judy).* It's educational.

Ruth   *(jokingly).* Is that good? *(Everybody laughs)*

Betty   *(teasingly).* Did you go alone, Judy?

Ruth   *(also teasing).* Yeah . . . maybe that's why you found it dull.

Judy   *(slyly).* You mean it was dull because I was alone or because I wasn't?

Alice.   It probably depends on the guy you were with. *(Smiling slyly at Judy)*

Betty   *(wearily, trying to be businesslike).* O.K., O.K. . . . but we've got to cut this out and decide.

Jane.   Say, do any of you know what days the planetarium is open?

Sandy.   Ahah! A woman with an idea! *(Gets up)* I'll phone them right away. *(Exits stage left)*

Margie.   How long does the show take at the planetarium?

Ruth.   I think it's only about an hour, but there are some exhibits outside of the auditorium.

Judy   *(mildly interested).* Yes, and they're pretty interesting—might even be better than the lecture, in fact.

Alice.   I think they have lectures every couple of hours . . . at 2, 4, and 6 P.M.

Betty.   What about the price? How

boys

stimulating either.

Al   *(throwing down his pencil).* I give up . . . I can't get it all down.

Mac   *(ignoring Al and answering John).* It's educational.

Ray   *(jokingly).* Is that good? *(Everybody laughs)*

Bob   *(teasingly).* Did you go alone, John?

Ray   *(also teasing).* Yeah, . . maybe that's why you found it dull.

John   *(slyly).* You mean it was dull because I was alone or because I wasn't?

Al.   It probably depends on the girl you were with. *(Smiling slyly at John)*

Bob   *(wearily trying to be businesslike).* O.K., O.K. . . . but we've got to cut this out and decide.

Joe.   Say, do any of you know what days the planetarium is open?

Sam.   Ahah! A man with an idea! *(Gets up)* I'll phone them right away. *(Exits stage left)*

Mac.   How long does the show take at the planetarium?

Ray.   I think it's only about an hour, but there are some exhibits outside of the auditorium.

John   *(mildly interested).* Yes, and they're pretty interesting—might even be better than the lecture, in fact.

Al.   I think they have lectures every couple of hours . . . at 2, 4, and 6 P.M.

Bob.   What about the price? How much does it cost?

Joe.   They get a dollar for the lecture.

mixed

There's no charge to get into the planetarium building.

Ray   *(sighing relieved).* That's the best news I've heard!

Sam   *(reentering from stage left).* Well— that settles it! We can forget the planetarium idea. It's closed for two weeks while they do some painting and repairs. Probably getting ready for the Christmas vacation crowd.

Judy   *(sarcastically).* That's nice! Well, I guess it's going to be a picnic then.

Margie   *(quickly, smiling archly at everyone).* Unless we have a dance.

Everybody groans disgustedly and stares at her until she wilts.

Joe.   And it's the old story . . . where are we going to have the picnic?

Alice   *(nodding).* Uh–huh . . . in fact it's older than that . . . who's going to bring what?

Judy   *(agreeing with Alice's implied protest).* Yeah, usually it's the girls who are stuck with bringing the food, and I object.

Sam   *(with mock solemnity).* It's only fair that the girls bring the food . . . since they eat most of it.

Margie   *(faking laughter).* Last time we had a picnic I brought six sandwiches and Sam ate them all.

Ray.   Well, after all, it's a kind of compliment. *(Pauses, smiling at Margie)* Your sandwiches *are* delicious.

Joe   *(ignoring Ray).* O.K., but how about going to Belle Isle Park. Then

girls

much does it cost?

Jane.   They get a dollar for the lecture. There's no charge to get into the planetarium building.

Ruth   *(sighing relieved).* That's the best news I've heard!

Sandy   *(reentering from stage left).* Well–that settles it! We can forget the planetarium idea. It's closed for two weeks while they do some painting and repairs. Probably getting ready for the Christmas vacation crowd.

Judy   *(sarcastically).* That's nice! Well, I guess it's going to be a picnic then.

Margie   *(quickly, smiling archly at everyone).* Unless we have a dance.

Everybody groans disgustedly and stares at her until she wilts.

Jane.   And it's the old story . . . where are we going to have the picnic?

Alice   *(nodding).* Uh–huh . . . in fact it's older than that . . . who's going to bring what?

Judy   *(sighing).* Wouldn't it be nice if we could get the boys to supply the food.

Sandy   *(sarcastically).* You're dreaming! (Pause) . . . Although they eat most of it.

Margie   *(sadly).* Yeah–last time we had a picnic I brought *six sandwiches . . . (emphasizing loudly)* SIX OF THEM . . . and Sam ate them all.

Ruth.   Yeah, and he said it was a kind of compliment . . . because your sandwiches were so good . . . the pig!

boys

There's no charge to get into the planetarium building.

Ray   *(sighing relieved).* That's the best news I've heard!

Sam   *(reentering from stage left).* Well— that settles it! We can forget the planetarium idea. It's closed for two weeks while they do some painting and repairs. Probably getting ready for the Christmas vacation crowd.

John   *(sarcastically).* That's nice! Well, I guess it's going to be a picnic then.

Mac   *(quickly, smiling archly at everyone).* Unless we have a dance.

Everybody groans disgustedly and stares at him until he wilts.

Joe.   And it's the old story . . . where are we going to have the picnic?

Al   *(nodding).* Uh–huh . . . in fact it's older than that . . . who's going to bring what?

John.   Well, I'm in favor of the girls bringing the food, as usual–since we're supplying the transportation, as usual.

Sam   *(with mock solemnity).* It's only fair that the girls bring the food . . . since they eat most of it.

Mac   *(faking laughter).* Come off it, Sam . . . last time Margie brought six sandwiches and you ate them all.

Ray.   Well, after all, it's kind of a compliment . . . she does make good sandwiches.

Joe   *(ignoring Ray).* O.K., but how about going to Belle Isle Park. Then we'd have barbecue pits and it's not

mixed

we'd have barbecue pits and it's not too far away.

Alice   *(enthusiastically).* That's a good idea–usually we spend too much time just getting to the place where we're having the picnic.

Bob.   Belle Isle sounds good to me. *(Calling for a vote)* All those in favor . . . *(Chorus of "yes")*

Sam.   So it's Belle Isle Park then.

Alice   *(starting to write again).* Wait a minute; I'll make a note of that.

Ray.   Yeah, Belle Isle's a good spot and I'll bring my guitar.

Joe.   Uh-oh . . . there he goes again with that guitar business!

Margie   *(enthusiastically).* And maybe we can dance there too!

Judy.   O.K., so let's decide what to bring and who's bringing what.

Bob   *(suddenly looking out the window).* Hey, look *(pointing toward the window),* isn't that snow?

Someone offstage behind the window drops tiny pieces of white paper from above so that the audience will see snow falling. Ray and Joe rush to either side of the window, gaze out, and return to their chairs, nodding glumly.

Ray.   Uh-huh–and really coming down too.

Joe   *(attempting to be cheerful).* Well, it's two days away yet. Might stop snowing by then.

Sam.   Should I phone the weather bureau?

girls

Jane   *(ignoring Ruth).* O.K., but how about going to Belle Isle Park. Then we'd have barbecue pits and it's not too far away.

Alice   *(enthusiastically).* That's a good idea–usually we spend too much time just getting to the place where we're having the picnic.

Betty.   Belle Isle sounds good to me. (Calling for a vote) All those in favor . . . (Chorus of "yes")

Sandy.   So it's Belle Isle Park then.

Alice   *(starting to write again).* Wait a minute; I'll make a note of that.

Ruth.   Yeah; Belle Isle's a good spot and I'll bring my guitar.

Jane.   Uh-oh . . . there she goes again with that guitar business!

Margie   *(enthusiastically).* And maybe we can dance there too!

Judy.   O.K., so let's decide what to bring and who's bringing what.

Betty   *(suddenly looking out the window).* Hey, look *(pointing toward the window),* isn't that snow?

Someone offstage behind the window drops tiny pieces of white paper from above the window so that the audience will see snow falling. Ruth and Jane rush to either side of the window, gaze out, and return to their chairs, nodding glumly.

Ruth.   Uh-huh and really coming down too.

Jane.   *(attempting to be cheerful).* Well, it's two days away yet. Might stop snowing by then.

boys

too far away.

Al   *(enthusiastically).* That's a good idea–usually we spend too much time just getting to the place where we're having the picnic.

Bob.   Belle Isle sounds good to me. *(Calling for a vote)* All those in favor . . . *(Chorus of "yes")*

Sam.   So it's Belle Isle Park then.

Al   *(starting to write again).* Wait a minute; I'll make a note of that.

Ray.   Yeah, Belle Isle's a good spot and I'll bring my guitar.

Joe.   Uh-oh . . . there he goes again with that guitar business!

Mac   *(enthusiastically).* And maybe we can dance there too!

John.   O.K., so let's decide what to bring and who's bringing what.

Bob   *(suddenly looking out the window).* Hey, look *(pointing toward the window),* isn't that snow?

Someone offstage behind the window drops tiny pieces of white paper from above the window so that the audience will see snow falling. Ray and Joe rush to either side of the window, gaze out, and return to their chairs, nodding glumly.

Ray.   Uh-huh and really coming down too.

Joe   *(attempting to be cheerful).* Well, it's two days away yet. Might stop snowing by then.

Sam.   Should I phone the weather bureau?

Bob.   Yeah, you'd better call them,

mixed

Bob. Yeah, you'd better call them, Sam.

Sam exits stage left.

Alice. Well, while we're waiting, let's settle the food question anyway.

Margie. I'm in favor of the boys bringing the food for a change.

Judy. And we can bring the cake and cokes—but *(severely) no* onion sandwiches, Bob.

Bob *(smiling but protesting)*. But I'm very fond of onion sandwiches.

Joe *(pointing at Bob as if ordering him)*. Bring one for yourself then . . . and don't sit too close to me.

Sam returns briskly, entering from stage left.

Sam *(resignedly)*. Well, of course they don't promise anything but *(shrugging)* they told me we could probably expect snow for four or five days.

Ray *(sarcastically)*. Fine, fine. Delightful for a picnic!

Everybody looks sad and disappointed.

Margie *(brightly)*. Well, since we can't go to the planetarium and the picnic is out *(pause while everybody turns to look at her)*, how about a dance?

Bob *(exaggerated disgust)*. Oh, shut up!

CURTAIN

Glossary

ahah! /^{1}a + ^{3}ha$^\prime$ /—a sound of surprised discovery and approval

barbecue pits—concrete boxes in which a

girls

Sandy. Should I phone the weather bureau?

Betty. Yeah, you'd better call them, Sandy.

Sandy exits stage left.

Alice. Well, while we're waiting, let's settle the food question anyway.

Margie. I still favor Judy's idea that we get the boys to bring the food—for a change.

Judy. And we could bring the cake and cokes *(pause while reflecting)*, except Bob will bring those terrible onion sandwiches.

Betty *(turning away disgusted at the thought)*. Phew! and last time he sat right next to me. *(Makes a wry face)*

Jane *(sighing resignedly)*. Oh well, I guess they don't know how to make decent sandwiches anyway so we're stuck with the job, as usual.

Sandy returns briskly, entering from stage left.

Sandy *(resignedly)*. Well, of course they don't promise anything but *(shrugging)* they told me we could probably expect snow for four or five days.

Ruth *(sarcastically)*. Fine, fine. Delightful for a picnic!

Everybody looks sad and disappointed.

Margie *(brightly)*. Well, since we can't go to the planetarium and the picnic is out *(pause while everybody turns to look at her)*, how about a dance?

Betty *(exaggerated disgust)*. Oh, shut up!

CURTAIN

boys

Sam.

Sam exits stage left.

Al. Well, while we're waiting, let's decide whose car we're going to use.

Mac. Sam's got the biggest car.

John. Yeah, but it's a real gas hog, and Sam's father is touchy about filling that gas tank before we bring it back.

Bob. Since one car won't hold all of us anyway, let's use mine and Al's . . . they're the easiest on gas.

Joe *(smiling broadly)*. Suits me *(chuckling)* and I'm sure Mac and John won't mind having chauffeurs!

Sam returns briskly, entering from stage left.

Sam *(resignedly)*. Well, of course they don't promise anything, but *(shrugging)* they told me we could probably expect snow for four or five days.

Ray *(sarcastically)*. Fine, fine. Delightful for a picnic!

Everybody looks sad and disappointed.

Mac *(brightly)*. Well, since we can't go to the planetarium and the picnic is out *(pause while everybody turns to look at him)*, how about a dance?

Bob *(exaggerated disgust)*. Oh, shut up!

CURTAIN

Glossary

a real gas hog—a big, heavy car which uses a lot of gasoline

come off it—stop talking nonsense, don't try to fool us

mixed

cooking fire can be built

cut this out—stop doing this, wasting time

don't promise anything—can't be completely sure, don't guarantee anything

get down to—start

give up—admit defeat, inability to do a job

keep up—continue (to write down everything that is said)

old story—a problem that has developed many times before

really coming down—snowing heavily (also used for heavy rain)

say—an introductory word expressing a desire to be listened to

spot—place

stuck with—be obligated to do something (usually unpleasant)

take down—make notes

there he goes again with that guitar business—he is mentioning his guitar playing again

to work things—to arrange, to scheme

uh-huh / ə + hə/—yes

uh-oh /³ə + ²ow/—a sound indicating both a mock warning and mild disapproval or suspicion of impending disaster

we can forget the planetarium—it is no longer practical to consider the plan of going to the planetarium

weenie roast—a kind of picnic at which the main food is a sausage, called a frankfurter or hot dog, which is roasted over a campfire

we've been all through that—we have discussed it thoroughly already

wilt—to lose confidence and poise because of embarrassment

yeah /yeh/—yes

girls

Glossary

decent—good

phew / fiyuw /—an expression of disgust with a bad smell

pig—a derogatory word commonly used for a person who is selfish or greedy

you're dreaming—you are fooling yourself, it is impossible

boys

suits me—I agree

they're the easiest on gas—they do not use much gasoline

touchy about filling the tank—becomes very angry when they do not replace gasoline which they have used

won't mind having chauffeurs—will be happy to ride as passengers while the other boys drive the cars

Structure

1. When Judy says, "What day was it again, Bob?" she indicates that she has forgotten which day they are planning for, and she wants Bob to tell her again; she is not requesting that the day occur again, although some students may puzzle confusedly over this apparent interpretation of her statement.
2. Note that Judy uses *it* to refer to the day of the week while Joe uses *it* to refer to the weather. The use of *it* as a subject is, of course, very common in English.
3. Sam says, "Anybody here ever been to the planetarium?" and later "Getting ready for the Christmas vacation crowd probably," and then Joe, still later, comments, "Might stop snowing by then." All of these are examples of abbreviated structure commonly found in ordinary spoken expression. Sam's question means, "Has anybody here ever been to the planetarium?" and he is suggesting that the workers at the planetarium are probably preparing to receive a large crowd of visitors at Christmas time. Because he has dropped part of the verb, Sam probably would project the first statement with a rising intonation contour to show that he is asking a question. In his second statement, Sam again drops part of the verb and this time he also drops the subject of the sentence. Joe also drops the subject in his statement, for what he means is that it might stop snowing by then. Americans very often drop subjects and auxiliary verbs in conversation, although such omissions are not acceptable in written English. Students should be alerted to the occurrence of such truncated structures in colloquial English and, of course, should be required to mimic the model provided by their teacher.
4. *Well* has many meanings, as a half-dozen instances in the dialogue of this play indicate. Frequently it is used, with a rising pitch, as a kind of informal sentence introducer. Students should acquire the ability to use automatically such conversational transitions, not only to give an authentic tone to their speech but to provide themselves with time for the thought necessary to consider and choose the more difficult structures needed to sustain the conversation.

Cultural Values

1. This is a typical informal meeting in which formal parliamentary procedure, such as we find in Roberts' Rules, is not followed. Americans usually favor this type of meeting as "democratic," and some are even suspicious of more formal meetings; that is, some may suspect that those well acquainted with the technical rules tend to control more formal meetings in order to deny other people a chance to present their views. Those students who are acquainted with a standard parliamentary procedure will note that although Bob does ask for a kind of formal vote, nobody has made a formal motion before that vote.
2. There is a prevalence of sarcasm in the dialogue. This tone or attitude is very common, particularly among young people who typically hide their true feelings while mildly hinting that they are critical. Often this attitude is a form of irony, as in Judy's statement, "That's nice!" in which she means exactly the opposite: she really disapproves of the situation. Ray similarly says, "Fine . . . fine . . . delightful for a picnic!" when he really means that the weather is miserable and it is impossible to have a picnic. Usually pitch is somewhat higher and more exaggerated in sarcastic statements. Sometimes an attitude of a kind of mock solemnity is used with sarcastic–ironic intent, as in the case of Sam's comment, "It's only fair that the girls bring the food . . . since they eat most of it." He knows that what he has said is not true and he merely hopes to tease the girls. Students should be advised that in America it is usually considered comical for a girl or woman to eat a great deal, particularly since thin women are thought to be more attractive.
3. When Margie says "It's educational," she is really implying, somewhat sarcastically, that it may be very practical and informative but it is not interesting or exciting. The foreign student may be surprised to discover that American students are often dissatisfied with the presentation of mere technical facts, such as in many movies used in schools, and they demand more imaginative and entertaining material.
4. Notice that the teasing about the date at the planetarium, suggests that each partner was too busy impressing the other to

listen attentively to the lecture. This kind of teasing, implying some romantic interest, is very common among Americans. Boys use such teasing in flirting with girls and girls must learn to be clever enough to counterattack. Note that in answering the boys, Judy suggests that it might be more interesting to attend such a lecture alone than to attend with a boy—thereby implying that at least some boys are not very interesting.

5. The student should learn the social values underlying Judy's insistence that Bob not bring onion sandwiches. That is, although they eat onions in various foods, some Americans find the smell of onions unpleasant. They usually avoid eating onions, therefore, if they are going to be in close contact with people at a social gathering. Joe thus tells Bob that if Bob brings an onion sandwich, he should sit far away from Joe because Joe doesn't like the smell of onions.

6. Notice that Bob is the chairman and Alice is the secretary at the meeting. Although there is considerable equality between boys and girls or men and women, it is still quite common for a boy or a man to be in charge as chairman or president of various organizations, while a girl or a woman is asked to serve as vice president or secretary. Part of the reason for this may be that it is widely believed that girls or women write more neatly and clearly than boys or men do; a secretary should, of course, take readily legible notes about what happened at a meeting.

General Comment

1. There is very little movement in this staging. Ray and Joe get up briefly to confirm that it is snowing, but Sam, in whose house the meeting is being held, is the only character who has several exits and entrances. Thus, the parts are relatively easy to play because there is little synchronization of movement and dialogue necessary. Moreover, since this is a meeting, and not a mere accidental gathering of people, the attention of all those characters not speaking can be shifted to the character who is speaking.

Even though there is so little movement, the characters must not appear too stiff, for it is a rather casual meeting and young people are not likely to sit at attention but instead will tend to sprawl rather awkwardly, yet in a completely relaxed way. Moreover, as young people (teenagers), all characters should speak in quite exaggerated, animated fashion. In modeling for student mimicry the teacher should try to distinguish each character by appropriate facies and intonation patterns; the expression of girls should be quite distinct from that of boys.

2. Since this staging is constructed as a fairly informal exchange of views between all the various characters rather than an alternation of conversational exchange between two individuals, it is not easy to divide it into scenes. Yet the staging can be considered and rehearsed in five parts: the first three separated by Sam's exits and entrances, the fourth when Bob suddenly discovers it is snowing, and the last when Sam returns from making his confirming phone call to the weather bureau.

3. Approximately the same number of lines are assigned to each character—although all characters do not appear in every scene—so that no student will feel either slighted or overburdened in the role assigned him.

4. Notice that various exclamations—ahah /^{1}a+^{3}há/, uh-huh /ə̃+hə̃/, and uh-oh /^{3}ə̃+^{2}ow/—are very commonly used in speaking and communicate a great deal of meaning. Since practical notation actually provides no spelling for these peculiar sounds made in the throat and nose, the student will have to learn them by ear, mimicking the model presented by his teacher, and try to remember the sounds so that they can be recognized, understood, and used in conversation. Approximate phonemic qualities of such expressions have been presented in this text; however, it should be recognized that, as mere approximations, these serve largely to emphasize the limits of notation available; certainly the notation is secondary to the modeled sound.

5. The set for this staging is deliberately simple. If the students seem to be too rigid or uniform, some of their chairs may be moved forward or backward and adjusted to face at slightly

different angles. If large lounge chairs are available, some members of the cast could be seated, away from the table, in those.

Notes on Adaptation

1. Young people, and teenagers particularly, usually behave quite freely and equally toward each other, and have little regard for status so it seems that the seven roles in this staging could be played by either men or women. Bob, Joe, Sam, and Ray could be called Betty, Jane, Sandy, and Ruth respectively, if only women are available to play the parts. Alice, Margie, and Judy could become Al, Mac, and John respectively, if we use an all male cast. Essential to the plot in the original staging is who is to bring the food and the consequent byplay between boys and girls which would be impossible with a cast of one sex. Appropriate changes in dialogue have, therefore, been offered in the adaptations.

2. Many students will be surprised that young people mix so freely in America and have so much freedom to plan and engage in various social activities together. It will be difficult for some to realize that for the most part teenagers take responsibility for their own entertainment without interference from their parents or from other adults. Although dating may seem particularly strange to those students from strongly status conscious societies which practice some form of arranged marriage, they will learn that it is an essential part of maturation process in America. The foreign student should be advised that parents, who feel that individual dating may be dangerous, are likely to encourage such group activities as that described in this staging.

3. Despite the fact that discussion as to who will bring the food has required these two adaptations, actually girls usually bring the food. Thus, the girls are expressing a kind of futile sense of rebellion, since all activities related to food are generally taken care of by women in our society, an exception would be the large scale cooking found in restaurants; such commercial cooking is usually done by men, since the large quantities of food are usually thought to be too heavy for women to handle.

4. It is expected, however, that the boys will provide the transportation. Boys are expected either to pay the fare for girls when escorting them on public transportation or else supply the automobile and do the driving. Many boys, even those of high school age, either have access to their family's car or own their own cars. In this staging the boys are interested in using smaller, more economical cars since they will all share the expense of the gasoline. Such sharing is particularly common among young people who don't have large amounts of money. For instance, students frequently form "car pools", which means either that each rider, picked up and brought to school each day, pays the student who owns the car or that several students who own cars may take turns picking up all the others, thereby reducing the transportation expense for everyone. This cooperative arrangement also reduces the acute parking problem in urban areas. Incidentally, students should be advised that in American society a boy is expected to go to the girl's home to meet her and also to escort her back to her home after the entertainment. As her escort, the boy is considered responsible for protecting the girl. Despite the degree of equality enjoyed by women in American society, this tradition is still widely practiced. It will be completely unfamiliar to many students from other cultures who may even find it quite peculiar in view of the apparent freedom of American women.

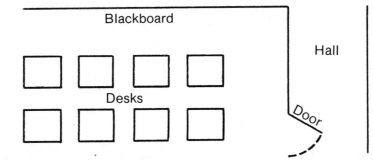

SETTING

A classroom in a high school, furnished with several desks. The backdrop is a blackboard. A door is at stage left front. The set is arranged so that the hall just outside the door can be seen far stage left.

Mixed cast	*Girls' cast*	*Boys' cast*
Martha	Martha	Martin
Phil	Phyllis	Phil
Stan	Esther	Stan
Ruth	Ruth	Ross
Lois	Lois	Lou
Bob	Bobby	Bob
Al	Alice	Al
Chauffeur (Peter)	Secretary (Miss Carter)	Chauffeur (Peter)

Martha (standing alone midstage rear and talking to herself aloud in a thoughtful manner). Now let me see— there'll be Ruth, Lois, Phil, and Bob, Stan . . . that's about all we can expect, I guess, at this reunion.

Phil (entering stage left). Martha Moran! How are you? (Holding hat in hand, he walks quickly to Martha)

Martha (standing alone midstage rear and talking aloud to herself in a thoughtful manner). Now let me see— there'll be Ruth, Lois, Phyllis, and Bobby, Esther . . . that's about all we can expect, I guess, at this reunion.

Phyllis (entering stage left). Martha Moran! Darling, how are you? (Holding purse in hand, she walks quickly to

Martin (standing alone midstage rear and talking to himself in a thoughtful manner). Now let me see—there'll be Ross, Lewis, Phil, and Bob, Stan . . . that's about all we can expect, I guess, at this reunion.

Phil (entering stage left). Martin Moran! How are you? (Holding hat in hand, he walks quickly to Martin) Golly, you

mixed

Same round face and bangs! Golly, you haven't changed at all!

Martha.　Phil! The class math whiz! *(Holding out her hand, which Phil takes and shakes)* It's been so long, hasn't it? *(Mildly sarcastic)* Yet... same face... a little longer now though, isn't it, Phil? *(Chuckling)* What happened to all that hair?

Phil　*(laughing).* Went like that math reputation, I guess. I've been in advertising, writing jingles for soap almost since I finished high school. But, it was swell of you to contact me. Ten years since we graduated!

Martha　*(nodding).* Yes, exactly. And, although I really didn't know whether I still had the title *(attitude of mock dignity),* I *was* class secretary, you remember, and well, I thought it would be a good idea if we all got together again.

They walk toward the desks and Phil sits down on one of them midstage.

Phil　*(enthusiastically).* A great idea! Will everybody be here? Old Bob Gray, and Stan Barlow, and Ruth Olson and Lois, *(frowning)* what was her last name?

Martha.　Well, it was Martin, but she's been Mrs. Billings for a long time now. *(Chuckling)* Has three kids, one has almost finished grade school.

Phil　*(surprised).* Wow! Time really flies! *(Then, thoughtfully)* But there was another kid I can't quite remember his

girls

Martha) The same pretty eyes and cute bangs! *(Exclaiming happily)* Why, you haven't changed at all!

Martha.　Phyllis! The class math whiz! *(Reaching out and grabbing Phyllis's wrists)* It's been so long, hasn't it? *(Scrutinizing Phyllis carefully, head tilted slightly to one side, says teasingly)* Not quite so dumpy now as the kid was I knew. And *(smiling)* what's become of that pug nose?

Phyllis　*(laughing).* Vanished like that math reputation, I'm afraid. I've been working in advertising writing jingles for soap almost since I finished high school. But it was awfully sweet of you to contact me. My, it doesn't seem possible, it's ten years since we graduated, does it?

Martha　*(Shaking her head).* It sure doesn't. And, although I really didn't know whether I still had the title *(attitude of mock dignity),* I *was* class secretary, you remember, and well, I thought it would be a good idea if we all got together again.

They walk toward the desks and Phyllis sits down on one of them midstage.

Phyllis　*(enthusiastically).* A lovely idea! And I suppose everybody will be here, won't they—Bobby Gray and Esther Barlow and Ruthie Olson, and Lois *(pauses, trying to remember)*, I seem to have forgotten her last name.

Martha.　Well, it was Martin; but she's been Mrs. Billings for a long time now.

boys

haven't changed at all!

Martin.　Phil! ... the class math whiz! *(Holding out his hand, which Phil takes and shakes vigorously)* Gee, it's been a long time. *(Scrutinizing Phil, and then mildly sarcastic)* But its the same face... a little longer now. *(Chuckles)* What happened to all that curly hair, fella?

Phil　*(laughing).* Went like that math reputation, I guess. I've been in advertising, writing jingles for soap almost since I finished high school. But it was swell of you to contact me. Ten years since we graduated!

Martin　*(nodding).* Yes, exactly. And, although I really didn't know whether I still had the title *(attitude of mock dignity),* I *was* class secretary, you remember, and well, I thought it would be a good idea if we all got together again.

They walk toward the desks and Phil sits down on one of them midstage.

Phil　(enthusiastically). *A great idea! Is everybody coming, Old Bob Gray, and Stan Barlow, and Ross Olson, and Lou* (frowning, as if trying to remember) *what was that guy's last name?*

Martin.　*I guess you mean Lou Billings* (chuckling) *our annual field day champion. Has three kids now, one almost ready for high school, I guess.*

Phil　(surprised). *Wow! Time really flies!* (Then, thoughtfully) *But there was another kid I can't quite remember his*

mixed

name, although I'll never forget him! You know, the kid who was always playing tricks, never did the homework. We all figured he'd be in jail five years after he left school!! Don't you remember him!

Martha   *(nodding)*. I think you mean Al McGuiness. He's dropped out of sight. Nobody has seen him since before the war. Sent him a card, but there isn't much chance I reached him.

Phil.   There never was with him. *(Musing)* Wonder what's happened to him.

Stan enters stage left, stopping just inside the door.

Stan.   Wonder what happened to who, you old numbers man?

Phil   *(jumping up and whirling around toward the door, happily surprised).* Stan, you son of a gun! How are you, boy? *(Rushes over and pounds Stan on the back)*

Stan   *(enthusiastically)*. Great! Boy, it's good to see you again, both of you. How have you been, Martha M. Moran, our class poet and secretary?

Martha   *(extending her hand, showing the wedding ring. Stan looks at the ring and then shakes the hand).* The name's Green now, Stan. And my two haven't left me any time for poetry, believe me. But how has our favorite geographer been doing? Working for an airline or mapping the Sahara for an oil company?

Stan   *(a little sadly)*. Me? That's a laugh!

girls

(Chuckling) Has three kids, one has almost finished grade school.

Phyllis   *(surprised)*. My—time goes so fast, doesn't it! *(Then, thoughtfully)* But there was another kid *(trying to remember)*. I'll never forget her, I suppose. I can't remember her name, full of tricks, never did any homework. Don't you remember her?

Martha   *(nodding)*. I think you mean Alice McGuiness. She's dropped out of sight. Nobody has seen her since before the war. Sent her a card, but there isn't much chance I reached her.

Phyllis.   There never was with her. *(Musing)* Wonder what's happened to her.

Esther enters stage left, stopping just inside the door.

Esther.   Wonder what happened to who, you old numbers woman?

Phyllis   *(jumping up and whirling around toward the door, happily surprised)*. Esther, it is you, darling, isn't it! *(Rushes over and embraces Esther)* How are you?

Esther   *(holding Phyllis at arm's length and gazing at her, smiling warmly).* My, but it's good to see you again *(turning toward Martha)*, both of you *(releasing Phyllis)*. How have you been, Martha M. Moran, our class poet and secretary?

Martha   *(extending her hand, showing the wedding ring. Esther looks at the ring and then shakes the hand).* The name's Green now, Esther. And my

boys

name, although I'll never forget him! You know, the kid who was always playing tricks, never did the homework. We all figured he'd be in jail five years after he left school! Don't you remember him?

Martin   *(nodding)*. I think you mean Al McGuiness. He's dropped out of sight. Nobody has seen him since before the war. Sent him a card, but there isn't much chance I reached him.

Phil.   There never was with him. *(Musing)* Wonder what's happened to him.

Stan enters stage left, stopping just inside the door.

Stan.   Wonder what happened to who, you old numbers man?

Phil   *(jumping up and whirling around toward the door, happily surprised).* Stan, you son of a gun! How are you, boy? *(Rushes over and pounds Stan on the back)*

Stan.   Great! Boy, it's good to see you guys again! How have you been Martin M. Moran, our class poet and secretary?

Martin   *(extending his hand, which Stan shakes)*. Stan, old boy, two kids to feed and clothe and a fat mortgage payment don't leave me much time for poetry, believe me! *(Chuckles)* But how about our favorite geographer? Working for an airline or mapping the Sahara for an oil company?

Stan   *(a little sadly)*. Me? That's a laugh! Why, I haven't even left the neighbor-

mixed

Why, I haven't even left the neighborhood. In fact, until last week I ran an elevator just around the corner. Ten years on the job. Now I've been promoted to head janitor.

Ruth enters quietly stage left, pauses, looking around smiling.

Phil   *(spying her and shouting enthusiastically).* Well, will you look at that. If it isn't Ruthie Olson, our gift to Broadway! *(Rushes over to greet her)* Come on in and tell us who's understudying for you at the theahtah today, my deah!

Martha   *(warmly).* Hi! Say *(exaggeratedly)*, don't you look simply gorgeous though!

Ruth   *(walks over to them and speaking with suppressed emotion).* It's just like a dream. You're all here . . . I never expected it . . . I thought you'd all forgotten me by now.

Stan   *(laughingly).* Who could forget that Joan of Arc. *(Assumes a pose as if against a stake with hands tied behind his back and gazing soulfully at the ceiling. Then, enthusiastically, breaking the pose)* How are you, Ruthie. *(Pumps her hand vigorously)*

Ruth.   You *have* a long memory. But the "arc" part is right anyway. I'm a welder at Ford's.

Martha.   Oh. *(Disappointed, then after a pause, as all fidget nervously, changes the subject to mask her disappointment)* Say, does anybody know if Mrs.

girls

two haven't left me any time for poetry, believe me. But how has our favorite geographer been doing? Working for an airline or mapping the Sahara for an oil company ?

Esther   *(a little sadly).* Me? That's a laugh! Why I haven't even left the neighborhood. I've been a salesgirl at Walcott's, just around the corner until just last week *(with mock pride).* Now I've been promoted to assistant department supervisor.

Ruth enters quietly stage left, pauses, looking around smiling.

Phyllis   *(spying her and shouting enthusiastically).* Well, will you look at that. If it isn't Ruthie Olson, our gift to Broadway! *(Rushes over to greet her)* Come on in and tell us who's been understudying for you at the theahtah today, my deah!

Martha   *(warmly).* Hi! Say *(exaggeratedly)*, don't you look simply gorgeous though!

Ruth   *(walks over to them and speaking with suppressed emotion).* It's just like a dream. You're all here . . . I never expected it . . . I thought you'd all forgotten me by now.

Esther   *(laughingly).* Who could forget that Joan of Arc. *(Assumes a pose as if against a stake with hands tied behind her back and gazing soulfully at the ceiling. Then, enthusiastically, breaking the pose)* How are you, Ruthie? *(Pumps her hand vigorously)*

boys

hood. In fact, until last week I ran an elevator just around the corner. Ten years on the job. Now I've been promoted to head janitor.

Ross enters quietly stage left, pauses, looking around smiling.

Phil   *(spying him and shouting enthusiastically).* Well, will you look at that. If it isn't Ross Olson, our gift to Broadway! *(Rushes over to greet him)* Come on in and tell us who's standing in for you at the theahtah today, old boy!

Martin   *(warmly).* Hi! Say, you haven't changed a bit, Ross!

Ross   *(walks over to them).* Gee, I can't get over it. All of you here together again! I never expected we'd see each other again. In fact, I figured you'd probably all forgotten me.

Stan   *(laughing).* Who could forget that Hamlet *(assumes a pose, holding his hat as if it is a skull in his outstretched hand, and looking very gloomy)*, "to be or not to be." *(Dropping the pose, they all laugh, and shake hands with Ross)* How are you, Ross, old boy? *(Pumps his hand vigorously)*

Ross.   You guys *have* got long memories. But the "ham" part of that Hamlet is right anyway. I've been working at the packing plant for the past ten years. *(They all laugh nervously)*

Martin.   Oh. *(Disappointed, then after a pause, as all fidget nervously, changes*

Lois Martin Billings will be able to get here?

Phil   *(shaking his head).* Wouldn't know her if I saw her, I bet. Three kids, she's probably big as a house by now.

Lois enters stage left as he speaks and quietly walks up behind him.

Lois   *(prodding him in the back with her finger).* Oh, is that so! *(Mock indignation)* Just pretend you don't know me then, Phil, because after that nasty crack, I don't know you! *(Phil jumps in surprise and is mildly embarrassed)*

Ruth   *(laughing).* He'll apologize, or I'll kill him on the spot, Mrs. What-was-the-name? *(Then, looking Lois up and down, says admiringly)* Lo, you haven't changed a bit.

Phil   *(hat held humbly in both hands before his chest and smiling).* My humble apologies, Lovely Lois.

Lois   *(to Ruth).* Billings is the name, and you *have* changed. *(Touching Ruth's hair lightly)*

Ruth   *(nodding).* Yes, it's as black as yours now to cover up the gray here and there. *(They both laugh nervously)*

Bob   *(who has tiptoed in, stage left, and seated himself quietly at the last desk seat near the door, as if startled).* Oh, did somebody mention Gray?

Everybody, suddenly noticing him, shouts.

Martha   *(rushes over to him as he stands up).* You did get my card then! Mar-

Ruth.   You *have* got a long memory. But the "arc" part is right anyway. I'm a welder at Ford's.

Martha.   Oh. *(Disappointed, then after a pause, as all fidget nervously, changes the subject to mask her disappointment)* Say, does anybody know if Mrs. Lois Martin Billings will be able to get here?

Phyllis   *(shaking her head).* I don't think I'd know her if I saw her, would you? Three kids. Must be rather *(artificial cough for emphasis)* ahem! matronly by now, don't you think?

Lois enters stage left as she speaks and quietly walks up behind her.

Lois   *(prodding her in the back with her finger).* Matronly! *(Mock indignation)* Well, you can just forget you ever knew me, then, Phyllis. After a crack like that, I don't even recognize you! *(Phyllis jumps in surprise and is mildly embarrassed)*

Ruth   *(laughing).* She'll apologize, or I'll scratch her eyes out, Mrs. What-was-the-name? *(Then, looking Lois up and down, says admiringly)* Lo, you really haven't changed a bit.

Phyllis   *(catching up her skirt and curtsying stiffly).* My humble apologies, Lois, ma'am.

Lois   *(to Ruth).* Billings is the name, and you *have* changed. *(Touching Ruth's hair lightly)*

Ruth   *(nodding).* Yes, it's as black as yours now to cover up the gray here

the subject to mask his disappointment)* Say—anybody know if Lou Billings is coming?

Phil   *(shaking his head).* Wouldn't know him if I saw him, I bet. Three kids, the guy must be an old worn-out shell by now!

Lou enters stage left as he speaks and quietly walks up behind him.

Lou   *(prodding him in the back with his finger).* Worn-out shell, huh! *(Mock threat)* Well, I can still tie you in knots. *(Smiling)* and if I can't, I can still outrun you. *(Phil jumps in surprise and is mildly embarrassed)*

Ross   *(laughing).* He'll apologize, or I'll kill him on the spot. *(Then, looking Lou up and down)* Lou, you haven't changed a bit. *(Smiling)* You still look like nothing! *(Slaps Lou on the shoulder)*

Phil   *(hat held humbly in both hands before his chest and smiling).* My humble apologies, *sir.*

Lou   *(to Ross).* But, you have changed, Mr. Olson, or else *(smiling)* your hair was always that thin and I never noticed.

Ross   *(with mock indignation as he strokes his hair back).* Ridiculous! It's the bad light in here *(smiling),* the way the light hits the gray, that is!

Bob   *(who has tiptoed in, stage left, and seated himself quietly at the last desk seat near the door, as if startled).* Oh, did somebody mention Gray?

mixed

velous and so good to see you again! *(Kisses him lightly on the cheek)*

Stan   *(jokingly to Bob, as Martha and Bob walk over to the others stage right, arm in arm).* Well, you old fiddler, I didn't get kissed when I came in! What is this power you've always had with the ladies?

Ruth   *(going up to Bob).* What would a party be without music? How have you been, Robert? *(Pumps his hand vigorously)*

Phil   *(enthusiastically).* Bob, you old romantic! Let me shake your hand after all these years! *(Reaches for Bob's hand, shakes it vigorously)* How about giving us a tune? Got the fiddle with you? *(Looks past Bob toward the doorway, searching for the violin)*

Lois   *(exaggerating).* There he is, the man of my dreams. Bob, did you know I'd be here? *(Links her arm through his so that Bob stands between two women)*

Bob   To tell you the truth, Lois, I didn't even know *I'd* be here! The boss was kind of reluctant to let his ace shoe salesman have the afternoon off.

Martha   *(mildly shocked).* Shoe salesman! *(Disappointed, pause, then, turning to Mrs. Billings in an affort to hide the disappointment)* Come, come, Mrs. Billings, that romance died ten years ago!

Lois   Well, I guess we're all here anyway. No . . . wait a minute. There was

girls

and there. *(They both laugh nervously)*

Bobby   *(who has tiptoed in, stage left, and seated herself quietly at the last desk seat near the door, as if startled).* Oh, did somebody mention Gray?

Everybody, suddenly noticing her, shouts.

Martha   *(rushes over to her as she stands up and says excitedly).* Oh, you did get my card then, after all! My, it's marvelous to see you again, Bobby. *(Embraces Bobby happily)*

Esther   *(jokingly as Martha and Bobby walk over to the others stage right, arm in arm).* Well, our old dancing school accompaniest has arrived! I can just hear that minuet now, and see all of us clumsy kids trying to be graceful young ladies. *(Laughs)*

Ruth   *(going up to Bobby).* What would a party be without music? How have you been, Bobby? *(Pumps her hand vigorously)*

Phyllis   *(kissing Bobby on the cheek).* Bobby, dear! If only we had a piano, you could play all those old tunes . . . and I think I'd cry. *(Makes a crying face)*

Lois   *(jokingly).* Well, I know I would if we had to dance to them! . . from the sheer pain of the exercise! *(To Bobby)* You're looking marvelous, Roberta. *(Links her arm through Bobby's and the three women–Martha, Bobby, and Lois–stand linked together)*

Bobby   *(flustered at the enthusiastic re-*

boys

Everybody, suddenly noticing him, shouts.

Martin   *(rushes over to him as he stands up).* You got my card then, you old faker! Great! Boy, it's good to see you again! *(Reaches up and musses Bob's hair)*

Stan   *(jokingly to Bob).* Well, you old fiddler, at least you've still got enough hair to muss up. *(Laughs)* But I guess that's part of the musician's disguise, huh?

Ross   *(going up to Bob).* What would a party be without music? How have you been, Robert? *(Pumps his hand vigorously)*

Phil   *(enthusiastically).* Bob, you old romantic! Let me shake your hand after all these years! *(Reaches for Bob's hand, shakes it vigorously)* How about giving us a tune? Got the fiddle with you? *(Looks past Bob toward the doorway, searching for the violin)*

Lou   *(excitedly).* There he is, our own Jascha Heifetz. Hey, you guys, now the talent has arrived. *(As a kind of mock serious announcement)* He is here!

Bob.   To tell you the truth, Lou, I didn't even know I'd be here! The boss was kind of reluctant to let his ace shoe salesman have the afternoon off.

Martin   *(mildly shocked).* Shoe salesman! *(Disappointed, pause, then, weakly, as if covering his embarrassment)* Well, you're soothing their soles anyway! *(Chuckles)*

mixed

one more . . .

Phil   Yeah Al McGuinness. Voted unanimously Most Likely to Fail! *(Jokingly)* Wonder which jail he's in.

Bob   *(with mock sternness)*. Don't be unkind, Phil. It could have happened to any one of us. Although I'll have to admit he was the most likely candidate. *(They all laugh)*

Ruth   Oh, he wasn't so bad. He was just a natural born clown who . . .

Lois   *(interrupting)*. Who has doubtless become a first class bum!

Bob   *(shaking his head)*. I have never met anybody since who has impressed me less. A completely lazy, hopelessly stupid kid. *(Chuckles, shaking his head from side to side)*

Lois   *(pleadingly)*. Oh, come on now—he wasn't so stupid. He just had no ambition . . . except to fool around and play tricks all day . . .

Sound of voices interrupting offstage left.

Chauffeur   *(voice offstage)*. Are you sure this is the place, sir?

Voices grow louder as Al and Chauffeur appear in the hall, stage left rear.

Al   *(positively)*. I certainly am, Peter . . . *(Slightly annoyed)* Now just look around for the right room.

Chauffeur.   Yes, sir.

Al comes downstage left, enters the room through the door stage left. He is dressed with a banker's conservative dignity and is followed into the room by a man dressed in chauffeur's uniform.

girls

ception). It's so good to see you all again. I hardly know what to say. *(Smiling)* It's almost as if we were all still kids in school here again, isn't it? I can almost forget all the typing I had to leave back at the office.

Martha   *(mildly shocked)*. Typing! *(Disappointed, pauses, then, to Lois, as if covering her embarrassment)* Yes . . . yes . . . it's just as if we were all kids here together again in this old schoolroom.

Lois.   Well, I guess we're all here anyway. No . . . wait a minute. There was one more.

Phyllis.   Let's see. *(Reflecting)* Why, of course, Alice McGuiness is missing! How could I have forgotten that crazy kid. *(Thoughtfully)* I wonder what's become of her.

Bobby   *(sarcastically)*. Alice McGuiness? Is there anybody who has the slightest doubt as to what happened to her? *(They all laugh)*

Ruth.   Oh, she wasn't so bad. She was just a natural born clown who . . .

Lois   *(interrupting)*. Who has doubtless become a first class tramp!

Bobby   *(nodding)*. She was a real character all right. She just didn't have a chance from the beginning.

Lois   *(pleadingly)*. Oh, come on now—she really wasn't so stupid, was she? I think it was just that she really had no goal in life . . . except to fool around and play tricks on the teacher all

boys

Lou.   Well, I guess we're all here anyway. No . . . wait a minute. There was one more . . .

Phil.   Yeah, Al McGuinness. Voted unanimously Most Likely to Fail! *(Jokingly)* Wonder which jail he's in.

Bob   *(with mock sternness)*. Don't be unkind, Phil. It could have happened to any of us. Although I'll have to admit he was the most likely candidate. *(They all laugh)*

Ross.   Oh, he wasn't so bad. He was just a natural born clown who . . .

Lou   *(interrupting)*. Who has doubtless become a first class bum!

Bob   *(shaking his head)*. I have never met anybody since who has impressed me less. A completely lazy, hopelessly stupid kid. *(Chuckles, shaking his head from side to side)*

Lou   *(pleadingly)*. Oh, come on now—he wasn't so stupid. He just had no ambition . . . except to fool around and play tricks all day . . .

Sound of voices interrupting offstage left.

Chauffeur   *(voice offstage)*. Are you sure this is the place, sir?

Voices grow louder as Al and Chauffeur appear in the hall, stage left rear.

Al   *(positively)*. I certainly am, Peter . . . *(Slightly annoyed)* Now just look around for the right room.

Chauffeur.   Yes sir.

Al comes downstage left, enters the room through the door stage left. He is dressed with a banker's conservative dignity and is

mixed

Al *(happily surprised upon catching sight of the group, which has been staring at the doorway, attracted by the noise).* Ah, here they are! *(Turning to the chauffeur)* There . . . you see, Peter—I told you we'd find them, if you just did as I told you.

Chauffeur. Yes, sir.

Al *(advancing briskly on the group stage right and with joviality).* Well, well, well . . . and how are you all? All of my *dear old classmates! (Each of these last three words must be said slowly and stressed strongly)*

All are obviously stunned as he shakes hands with each in turn; all continue to look shocked.

Al *(shaking Bob's hand and speaking jovially).* Bob, good to see you. Lois *(shaking her hand)*, you're still beautiful. Phil *(shaking his hand)*, delightful to meet you again like this. Ruth *(shaking her hand)*, wonderful, wonderful. Stan *(shaking his hand)*, how are you, old fellow . . . and Martha. *(Holds her hand and gazes at her)*

Martha *(her hand still held by Al).* Then . . . you did get my card?

Al *(still holding on to her hand).* Just this morning, as a matter of fact. My secretary brought it to me as soon as it arrived. Uh . . . *(chuckling)* . . . apparently she noticed all of the forwarding addresses. *(Holding Martha's hand tightly with both his hands and speaking slowly with mock feeling)*

girls

day . . .

Sound of voices interrupting offstage left.

Secretary *(voice offstage).* Are you sure this is the place, ma'am?

Voices grow louder as Alice and Secretary appear in the hall, stage left rear.

Alice *(positively).* Certainly I am, Miss Carter. *(Slightly annoyed)* Now please help me find the right room.

Secretary. Yes, ma'am.

Alice comes downstage left, enters the room through the door stage left. She is very stylishly dressed and is followed by a plainly dressed woman wearing eyeglasses.

Alice *(shrilly in happy surprise, upon catching sight of the group who have been staring at the doorway, attracted by the noise).* Ah, here they are! *(Glance toward Secretary)* I told my secretary we'd find you, if she just did as I asked.

Secretary. Yes, ma'am.

Alice *(advancing briskly on the group stage right and with joviality).* Well, well, well . . . and how are you all. All of my *dear old classmates! (Each of these last three words must be said slowly and stressed strongly)*

All are obviously stunned as she shakes hands with each in turn; all continue to look shocked.

Alice *(shaking Bobby's hand).* Bobby, so good to see you. Lois *(shaking her hand)*, oh, isn't this nice! Phyllis *(shaking her hand)*, such a delightful surprise! Ruth *(shaking her hand)*,

boys

followed into the room by a man dressed in a chauffeur's uniform.

Al *(happily surprised upon catching sight of the group, which has been staring at the doorway, attracted by the noise).* Ah, here they are! *(Turning to the chauffeur)* There . . . you see, Peter—I told you we'd find them, if you just did as I told you.

Chauffeur. Yes, sir.

Al *(advancing briskly on the group stage right and with joviality).* Well, well, well . . . and how are you all. All of my dear old classmates! *(Each of these last three words must be said slowly and stressed strongly)*

All are obviously stunned as he shakes hands with each in turn; all continue to look shocked.

Al *(shaking Bob's hand).* Robert, good to see you! Louis *(shaking his hand)*, still the dashing young man! Phillip *(shaking his hand)*, you are looking well! Ross *(shaking his hand)*, great, great!! Stanley *(shaking his hand)*, how are you, old fellow . . . and Martin. *(Holds on to his hand and slaps him several times on the shoulder)*

Martin *(his hand still held by Al).* Then . . . you did get my card?

Al *(holding on to his hand).* Just this morning, as a matter of fact. My secretary brought it to me as soon as it arrived. Uh . . . *(chuckling)* . . . apparently she noticed all of the for-

mixed

Thank you, Martha. I wouldn't have missed this for anything. *(To everybody, looking around at them all)* And I just wish I could stay . . .

Phil   *(as if half recovered from shock).* You're pretty . . . busy then . . . eh, Al?

Lois   *(as if stunned).* You . . . you . . . have something else . . . to do?

Stan   *(who has been eyeing Al's clothing).* Can't stick around for a while then, eh Al?

Ruth   *(recovering).* Well, it's . . . it's certainly good to see you looking so well and . . . prosperous!

Al   *(beaming at them paternally).* Thank you, thank you all. *(Apologetically)* But I've got a conference at the bank . . . then I have promised my sales director I'd discuss some problem with him after that. Just dropped in. I really wish I could stay, but . . . *(smiling)* you know how it is.

Bob   *(still shocked but smiling weakly).* Sure, Al . . . sure . . . you go right ahead. *(Smiling weakly)* Glad to have had the chance to see you again.

Martha   *(nodding).* Yes, it certainly has been a nice surprise.

Al.   Yes . . . well . . . *(Raising one hand in a kind of goodbye wave)* Goodbye to you all. *(Exits through the door stage left, followed by his chauffeur who closes the door as all gaze after him dumbfounded)*

Inside the room the members of the group

girls

wonderful, wonderful! Esther *(shaking her hand),* how are you, my dear? . . . And Martha. *(Holds her hand and gazes at her smiling)*

Martha   *(her hand still held by Alice).* Then . . . you did get my card?

Alice   *(holding on to her hand).* Oh yes, it came just this morning. My secretary *(motioning toward the girl who follows her, with her pencil poised above the notebook)* Miss Carter here, brought it to me as soon as it arrived. *(Turning to Martha)* Thank you, Martha dear. I'm so glad you remembered me. *(To everybody)* And I do wish so much I could stay with you all. *(Looking around at them all and smiling)*

Phyllis   *(as if half recovered from shock).* You're pretty . . . busy then . . . eh, Alice?

Lois   *(as if stunned).* You . . . you . . . have something else . . . to do?

Esther   *(who has been eyeing Alice's clothing).* Can't stick around for a while then, eh Alice?

Ruth   *(recovering).* Well, it's . . . it's certainly good to see you looking so well and . . . prosperous!

Alice   *(beaming at them graciously).* Thank you, thank you all. *(Apologetically)* But I do have a perfectly dreadful conference at the bank that I must attend . . . and then I have promised to go over advertising for our new line of cosmetics with my sales director, after

boys

warding addresses. *(Holding Martin's hand tightly with both his hands and speaking slowly with mock feeling)* Thank you, Martin. I wouldn't have missed this for anything. *(To everybody, looking around at them all)* And I just wish I could stay . . .

Phil   *(as if half recovered from shock).* You're pretty . . . busy then . . . eh, Al?

Lou   *(as if stunned).* You . . . you . . . have something else . . . to do?

Stan   *(who has been eyeing Al's clothing).* Can't stick around for a while then, eh Al?

Ross   *(recovering).* Well, it's . . . it's certainly good to see you looking so well and . . . prosperous!

Al   *(beaming at them paternally).* Thank you, thank you all. *(Apologetically)* But I've got a conference at the bank . . . then I have promised my sales director I'd discuss some problem with him after that. Just dropped in. I really wish I could stay, but . . . *(smiling)* you know how it is.

Bob   *(still shocked but smiling weakly).* Sure, Al . . . sure . . . you go right ahead. *(Smiling weakly)* Glad to have had the chance to see you again.

Martin   *(nodding).* Yes, it certainly has been a nice surprise.

Al.   Yes . . . well . . . *(Raising one hand in a kind of goodbye wave)* Goodbye to you all.

Exits through the door stage left, followed

mixed

stare at the door for a few seconds and then slowly look around at each other unbelievingly.

Outside the door Al quickly slips off his topcoat and hands it to the chauffeur along with the fedora and cane, while the chauffeur places the chauffeur's cap on Al's head and Al slips into the chauffeur's coat.

Chauffeur   (hurrying Al nervously and hissing in a stage whisper). Old man Wayne will skin you alive if he ever hears about you taking his coat, cane, and hat—and what about the car. We gotta get it back in the garage before he sees it's missing.

Al   (laughing softly all the while he dresses). Yeah, yeah . . . there was a lot of risk to it and, Gus, I want you to know I really appreciate your helping me out by playing chauffeur. (Nudging the other man with his elbow and smiling) Kind of a change from painting too, wasn't it? Boy, did you see the looks on their faces!! (Mimics their look of surprise and chuckles)

Turning upstage they both laugh heartily as they exit into the wings.

CURTAIN

Glossary

ace—best

a little longer now—Phil's face seemed longer because he had become bald

girls

that. So you see (pauses and shrugs), I could just stop by for a minute. Really (smiling) I wish so much I could stay, but (as if pleading for their sympathy) you do understand, don't you?

Bobby   (still shocked but smiling weakly). Sure, Alice . . . sure . . . you go right ahead. (Smiling weakly) Glad to have had the chance to see you again.

Martha   (nodding). Yes, it certainly has been a nice surprise.

Alice.   Yes . . . well . . . (Raising one hand in a kind of goodbye wave) Goodbye to you all.

Exits through the door stage left, followed by her secretary who closes the door as all gaze after her dumbfounded.

Inside the room the members of the group stare at the door for a few seconds and then slowly look around at each other unbelievingly.

Secretary   (hurrying Alice nervously and hissing in a stage whisper as she takes off the glasses and puts them into the pocketbook Alice has handed to her). Alice, come on—we've got to get back behind the counter at Frank's joint . . . and if his wife ever hears we borrowed her coat and stuff from the back room, Frank'll fire us both. Easy on that coat . . . but let's go.

Alice   (laughing softly as she gently removes the coat). Yeah, yeah . . . we've got to get back and wait on the customers. (Nudging the secretary with

boys

by his chauffeur who closes the door as all gaze after him dumbfounded.

Inside the room the members of the group stare at the door for a few seconds and then slowly look around at each other unbelievingly.

Outside the door Al quickly slips off his topcoat and hands it to the chauffeur along with the fedora and cane, while the chauffeur places the chauffeur's cap on Al's head and Al slips into the chauffeur's coat.

Chauffeur   (hurrying Al nervously and hissing in a stage whisper). Old man Wayne will skin you alive if he ever hears about you taking his coat, cane, and hat—and what about the car. We gotta get it back in the garage before he sees it's missing.

Al   (laughing softly all the while he dresses). Yeah, yeah . . . there was a lot of risk to it and, Peter, I want you to know I really appreciate your helping me out by playing chauffeur. (Nudging the other man with his elbow and smiling) Kind of a change from painting too, wasn't it? Boy, did you see the looks on their faces!! (Mimics their look of surprise and chuckles)

Turning upstage they both laugh heartily as they exit into the wings.

CURTAIN

Glossary

can't get over it—can't quite believe it; can't

mixed

arc—kind of pun: Joan of *Arc* and the electric *arc* used for welding

banker's dignity—very well dressed, wealthy looking, and impressive; bankers are thought to be dignified

big as a house—very fat; it is sometimes believed that older women who have had several children become very fat

come on now—you are exaggerating or trying to fool me

dropped out of sight—has disappeared; nobody has seen him in a long time

eh/²ey³/—an expression indicating a question and pronounced with a rising intonation

fiddler—a violin player

first class bum—the most worthless person imaginable: *first class* means the extreme example

golly /galiy/—an exclamation of enthusiasm, pleasure

gorgeous—very beautiful

gotta—a common colloquial contraction of *got to*, meaning *must*

gray—a kind of pun: Ruth has said her hair is gray and Gray is Bob's family name

great!—very good, very well

hi! /hay/—a colloquial form of *hello;* it is very widely used in America among friends

I bet—I think, I imagine

I'll kill him on the spot—Ruth is pretending to threaten to punish Phil for his tactlessness

it could have happened to any of us—any of us might have become as worthless as Al probably has become

girls

her elbow and smiling broadly)* But did you see the look on their faces, Dottie? *(Mimics their look of surprise and shock)*

Turning upstage they both laugh heartily as they exit into the wings.

CURTAIN

Glossary

behind the counter—working in a shop, probably works as a waitress at the counter where customers sit to eat

curtsying—a kind of respectful bow formerly used only by girls and women. One foot is placed behind the other and the knees are bent while the skirt is held out at the sides with each hand

dumbfounded—so surprised that they cannot speak

dumpy—short and slightly fat

easy on that coat—be careful that you don't damage the coat

fired—to be discharged from a job

from the sheer pain of the exercise—they have gotten older and can no longer bend their bodies so easily and comfortably

go over advertising—look at the plan for advertising

joint—slang for a very low quality shop or restaurant

ma'am—a short form of madam; it is often used as a term of respect to women who are older or who are considered social superiors

boys

quite realize it

fat mortgage—a large mortgage; he still owes a great deal of money that he borrowed to buy a house

field day champion—good athlete, field day is an annual athletic contest

ham—slang term for an untalented actor

Jascha Heifetz—a famous concert violinist; they are sarcastically referring to Bob's violin playing

looks like nothing—are not handsome (friendly sarcasm)

musician's disguise—musicians are commonly thought of as having long hair

muss—to disarrange

my humble apologies—a mock apology, used sarcastically

packing plant—meat processing factory

talent—the person who has skill or ability; Lou is imitating the exaggerated way that talented people are often introduced to an audience

tie you in knots—best you in a fight

worn-out shell—exhausted from overwork

mixed

jingles—simple verses or rhymed slogans

just dropped in—came temporarily and informally

Lo—a kind of nickname for Lois; such nicknames are usually used only by close friends

marvelous—exaggerated expression used mostly by women and meaning good

math whiz—an exceptionally good mathematics student

Mrs. What-was-the-name—Ruth hasn't caught Lois's married name

nasty crack—unpleasant remark

now let me see—an expression used when talking to oneself, while puzzled about something

numbers man—Stan is recalling that Phil was an excellent student in arithmetic: he is also sarcastically hinting that Phil may have become a gambler, since one form of gambling is called the *numbers racket*

old man Wayne—an uncomplimentary reference to their elderly employer

reach—contact, also, as in Stan's reply, to become acquainted with or understand

skin you alive—punish you severely

son of a gun—mostly an affectionate term of address used between men

stick around—stay, remain

swell—very kind, wonderful; this word is widely used as a term of approval or agreement

that's a laugh—it's so entirely wrong that it is ridiculous (usually used sarcastically)

theahtah—pronunciation imitating the broad *a* which is sometimes thought to be a

girls

minuet—a kind of slow, formal, old-fashioned dance music used very commonly for children's dancing lessons

new line of cosmetics—new type of cosmetics or cosmetics made by another company

tramp—homeless, wandering beggar; a word used to describe an immoral woman

what's become of those cute, short legs—her legs are not short now, she has grown up

mixed (continued)

feature of the pronunciation of cultured people. Similarly, *dear* is pronounced *deah*

understudying—substituting for the actor who usually plays the role

wow /⁴wæuw/—an exclamation of excitement, surprise

you haven't changed a bit—you look the same as you used to, you don't look older

Structure

1. Note that the following are examples of the shortened sentence structure used in the informal spoken language and that the subject of the sentence has been omitted:
   a. Phil: Went like that math reputation.
   b. Martha: Sent him a card, but there isn't much chance.
   c. Phil: Wonder what happened to him.
   d. Phil: Wouldn't know her if I saw her, I bet . . .
2. Note also the use of the statement form with rising intonation to indicate a question, as Lois asks Al: "You have something else to do?" This construction is a very common feature of the spoken language although students should be cautioned that often such a construction unintentionally conveys a kind of sarcastic tone and it must, therefore, be employed cautiously.
3. Emphasis on one word can often convey a great deal of meaning. When Ruth tells Stan: "You *have* a long memory," she is implying that she has forgotten she had played the part of Joan of Arc when she was a student; she may also feel mildly surprised because she has forgotten, or she may be indicating a kind of annoyance at Stan's reminder that she is getting older. Later, when Lois tells Ruth: "Billings is the name, and you *have* changed," she is frankly admitting that Ruth has aged and, in fact, looks much older. Also, as Al greets his old classmates later, he stresses "my *dear old classmates*," to get a kind of exaggeration which seems ironic: none of them ever really liked him and he knows it.
4. Expressions such as Martha's use of "believe me" in her statement; "And my four haven't left me anytime for poetry, believe me," are used for emphasis. Other such expressions which can be found in colloquial usage, are: "I'm telling you," "I swear that . . . ." We even find expressions such as "by God" used for this purpose of emphasis.
5. Note that the word "Boy" /bɔiy/ as used by Stan is an exclamation of pleasure or delight and is neither a term of direct address nor reference to the age of anybody. This usage is probably much more common in man's speech than in woman's. Although it may sound the same and there is possibly some ironic reference to age, the use Phil makes of *boy* in greeting Stan is quite different. Phil is using the term, that is, as a common form of address between men who are close friends.

Cultural Values

1. Notice that Martha can joke with Phil about his baldness because they are old friends. Such comments about a person's physical appearance are considered tactless or even insulting if made by a person who is not a close friend.
2. Martha says, "The name's Green now, Stan," and later Lois says, "Billings is the name." Each woman is referring to her own married name but by using the definite article *the* instead of the more personal *my*, each pretends to be quite objective. Such objectivity seems to be a kind of ironic reservation or mock dignity. We are given another aspect of this use of names to convey a certain reserved tone when we find Ruth saying, "How have you been, Robert?" and later Bob says, "Don't be unkind, Philip." In both cases the speaker is pretending to be formal and paternalistic, and so uses the full name rather than the nickname. This exaggerated formality is considered comical because it contrasts sharply with the ordinary casualness of relationships.
3. Although these people have not been in contact with each other for many years, they very quickly become quite familiar again as they recall the very casual relationship they had with each other as childhood classmates. Such excited enthusiasm and familiarity in relationships are quite common among Americans, who often think that somebody who behaves in a very stiff and dignified way, not displaying his emotion, is being undemocratic and unfriendly.
4. The usual greeting, particularly between people who have not seen each other in a long time, is a handshake. However, the man must wait to see if the woman will offer her hand; it is considered impolite for the man to grab the woman's hand when

she hasn't offered to shake hands with him. Phil greets Stan very enthusiastically. Men commonly greet each other by striking each other lightly on the back at almost shoulder level. This is also a gesture used for congratulating somebody. This gesture is not used by women. Although we do not find an example in this staging, it is common for women to kiss each other lightly on the cheek when they meet. In this staging we find Martha kissing Bob in this way, which indicates she is quite excited. This kiss is only a kind of greeting and does not indicate any romantic interest between them. However, Stan immediately makes a joke about the power Bob "always had with the ladies," because it is easy, of course, to misinterpret this kind of kissing. Such joking, called *kidding*, is very common among close friends; to hint jokingly to a friend that you suspect he is involved in a secret romance, is thought to be quite funny. We find Lois also pretending such a romantic interest in Bob when she says, "There he is, the man of my dreams," as she tries to give the impression she has had romantic dreams about him. To remind Lois that she is married—and therefore should not have such ideas—Martha emphasizes the *Mrs.* as she says, "Come, come, *Mrs.* Billings, that romance died ten years ago!"

5. It should also be noted that expressions like "you old devil" are a means of showing affection between men. Since men are expected to control their emotions, the affection is masked ironically by what may seem a kind of mild insult but which actually is not.

General Comment

. The pace in this staging is very lively at the beginning because all of the characters are quite excited to be seeing each other again after many years of separation. Then, as Al enters, the pace slows down. All of the characters are shocked to see him looking so rich and behaving in such a dignified way; they are slightly embarrassed because they never imagined he would be a success and they do not know what to say to him.

2. The basic emotion of the characters in this staging is a peculiar mixture of joy at seeing each other—and reliving, in their memories, their happier childhood days—and a kind of sad disappointment upon discovering that all of the promise and talent each displayed have been wasted. Students must be made aware that attitudes are frequently ambivalent, just as they are in their native societies.

3. The ironic impact of the staging depends on the shock felt by the group at the realization that Al, who has shown the least promise and who in childhood appeared to have no worthwhile future ahead of him, has apparently been the only one of the group who has succeeded. Unless it is clearly established that Al was thought to be an inevitable failure, the impact of his splendid entrance will be lost. Students coming from societies in which social fluidity is greatly restricted may find this situation peculiar and will need to be made aware that in America rags-to-riches has been the pattern of many people. To establish the basis for the group's shocked surprise, the pacing of comments about Al should be fairly slow to impress the audience with his lack of success-potential. In addition, it will be necessary for Al to pace his presentation slowly enough so that the audience recognition of who he is or what he has become—in contrast to what has been said about him by his classmates—can be achieved.

Notes on Adaptation

1. Intensifiers and modifiers, such as *so*, *awfully*, and *lovely*, are very commonly used by women and are rather rare in men's speech. Examples of typical feminine combinations are shown in "perfectly dreadful" and lexical items such as *sweet*, particularly in the expression "awfully sweet."

2. Note also the use of the diminutive endings on Ruth*ie* and Bobb*y* which are typically feminine devices and may be seen as additional examples of softening effects used by women to avoid seeming too direct or aggressive.

3. A kind of mild sarcasm is also generated by exaggerated deferential behavior, such as Phyllis's curtsying to Lois and her use of the honorific *ma'am*. There is often an element of humor in such deference in America, perhaps because of the importance placed on personal equality. Thus Alice's use of "my dear girl," in addressing her secretary, must inevitably sound somewhat quaint and mildly amusing.

4. The term *fella*—a sound spelling of the word *fellow*—and "old faker" or "old boy" are other affectionate terms of address widely used between close men friends. Although it might be thought odd that the word *old* should express affection in a society which places such a high valuation on youth, it seems likely that the word conveys the idea that two people have known each other, have remained friends for many years, and have—in that sense—grown old together.

5. Ten years have passed since the characters in this staging have last seen each other. They separated as youths and now are meeting again much later. They are, therefore, quite conscious of the passage of time, of their changed appearance as they have aged. Students should be made aware that most Americans are often particularly concerned with physical appearance and especially with maintaining a youthful appearance. Many foreign students may, indeed, find quite peculiar the typical American consciousness of white teeth and condition of hair. In this staging the characters are taking a rather amused attitude toward the loss of their hair. In pointing out the other fellow's loss of hair, each person is recognizing and admitting to his own age. We note the slyly sarcastic reference that Ross has become bald, as Lou says, "or else your hair was always that thin and I never noticed." And Ross replies with the comically weak excuse, "it's the bad light in here," indicating that he doesn't want to admit he is aging, although, ironically, he admits they are not able to see well and blames it on the poor light. There is, again, a kind of friendly atmosphere created by their sharing their common experience of the effects of time's passage. Note that they still behave boyishly in mussing each other's hair.

6. Students should recognize the pun in Ross's comic disclosure that although he has not remained the *ham*, or unskilled amateur actor, who once played the role of *Ham*let, by working in the packing plant he has at least remained in close touch with hams. And the first syllable of Hamlet's name may be seen both as an ironic reference to the fact that all actors (hams) are said to desire to play the role of Hamlet and that Hamlet was himself a ham actor, when he acted in the famous play within a play sequence in order to goad the King.

Martin's rather clever attempt to cover his shock at hearing that the talented Bob has become a mere shoe salesman also contains a pun, for, indeed, the musician soothes the soul by making his audience feel calm and rested, while the shoe salesman soothes the sole, or the bottom of the foot, by giving the customer a comfortable shoe.

A pun is, of course, based on the existence of homonyms and probably all students can think of examples of such homonyms in their own native languages. Inviting them to relate some of those in English is often a good way to encourage the use of English.

Pole

O ———————————————————

Backdrop

SETTING

A city street corner. Buildings are painted on the backdrop. On a pole painted far stage right is a street sign labeled Woodward Avenue. A sidewalk reporter carrying a microphone is standing about midstage as the curtain rises.

Mixed cast	*Girls' cast*	*Boys' cast*
Interviewer	Interviewer	Interviewer
Old Man (deaf)	Old Woman (deaf)	Old Man (deaf)
Woman	Woman	Man
College Student	Coed	College Student
Wife (Mabel)	Mother	Father
Husband (Herbert)	Daughter (Debbie)	Son (Herbie)

Interviewer *(very glibly and gaily talking into the microphone. The clichés of his speech should be exaggerated as should the falsity of his optimistic attitude).* It's a beautiful day out here on the corner of Woodward and Grand River, ladies and gentlemen. The streets are crowded with busy shoppers, as usual . . . lots of traffic . . . Oh, and here comes a distinguished looking

Interviewer *(very glibly and gaily talking into the microphone. The clichés of her speech should be exaggerated as should the falsity of her optimistic attitude).* It's a beautiful day out here on the corner of Woodward and Grand River, ladies and gentlemen. The streets are crowded with busy shoppers, as usual . . . lots of traffic . . . Oh, and here comes a distinguished looking

Interviewer *(very glibly and gaily talking into the microphone. The clichés of his speech should be exaggerated as should the falsity of his optimistic attitude).* It's a beautiful day out here on the corner of Woodward and Grand River, ladies and gentlemen. The streets are crowded with busy shoppers, as usual . . . lots of traffic . . . Oh, and here comes a distinquished look-

69

mixed

elderly gentleman. I think I'll ask for his opinion on our topic for today *(grabbing the arm of an old fellow who has entered from stage right and is slowly and haltingly walking across the stage, leaning wearily on his cane. They meet at midstage)*

Old Man   *(surprised and annoyed)*. Eh, eh? . . . no, I never give to beggars. *(Shrugs off the Interviewer's hand from his arm)* Why . . . you're old enough to be working! *(This should be said with indignation and mild anger)*

Interviewer   *(slightly embarrassed but smiling as if to humor the old fellow)*. Sir . . . sir, I'm not a beggar. I'm a sidewalk reporter and I'd like to ask you a question.

Old Man   *(complaining crankily)*. That's the trouble with you young fellows . . . always standing around on street corners instead of working. I suppose you drink too, eh?

Interviewer   *(speaking confidentially into the microphone)*. Apparently, folks, this elderly gentleman is slightly deaf. *(Shouting to the old man, who has begun to walk away)* Sir, . . . say, sir . . . What do you think is the best way to learn a foreign language. *(Very loudly)* A FOREIGN LANGUAGE?

Old Man   *(drawing back as if shocked and indignant)*. Eh! . . . what's that? . . . A b e e r a n d sandwich? . . .*(Indignantly and barely controlling his temper as he raises his*

girls

elderly lady. I think I'll ask for her opinion on our topic for today *(grabbing the arm of an old woman who has entered from stage right and is slowly and haltingly walking across the stage, leaning wearily on her cane. They meet at midstage)*

Old Woman   *(surprised and annoyed)*. Eh, eh? . . . no, I never give to beggars. *(Shrugs off the Interviewer's hand from her arm)* Why . . . you're old enough to be working! *(This should be said with indignation and mild anger)*

Interviewer   *(slightly embarrassed but smiling as if to humor the old woman)*. Madam . . . madam, I'm not a beggar. I'm a sidewalk reporter and I'd like to ask you a question.

Old Woman   *(complaining crankily)*. That's the trouble with you young kids . . . spend your whole time loafing. *(Sourly)* Just waiting for somebody to marry you, aren't you?

Interviewer   *(speaking confidentially into the microphone)*. Apparently, folks, this elderly lady is slightly deaf. *(Shouting to the old lady, who has begun to walk away)* Madam . . . say, madam . . . What do you think is the best way to learn a foreign language. *(Very loudly)* A FOREIGN LANGUAGE?

Old Woman   *(drawing back as if shocked and indignant)*. Eh! . . . what's that? . . . A beer and sandwich? . . .*(Indignantly and barely con-*

boys

ing elderly gentleman. I think I'll ask for his opinion on our topic for today *(grabbing the arm of an old fellow who has entered from stage right and is slowly and haltingly walking across the stage, leaning wearily on his cane. They meet at midstage)*

Old Man   *(surprised and annoyed)*. Eh, eh? . . . no, I never give to beggars. *(Shrugs off Interviewer's hand from his arm)* Why . . . you're old enough to be working! *(This should be said with indignation and mild anger)*

Interviewer   *(slightly embarrassed but smiling as if to humor the old fellow)*. Sir . . . sir, I'm not a beggar. I'm a sidewalk reporter and I'd like to ask you a question.

Old Man   *(complaining crankily)*. That's the trouble with you young fellas . . . always standing around on street corners instead of working. I suppose you drink too, eh?

Interviewer   *(speaking confidentially into the microphone)*. Apparently, folks, this elderly gentleman is slightly deaf. *(Shouting to the old man, who has begun to walk away)* Sir, . . . say, sir . . . What do you think is the best way to learn a foreign language. *(Very loudly)*, A FOREIGN LANGUAGE?

Old Man   *(drawing back as if shocked and indignant)*. Eh! . . . what's that? . . . A beer and sandwich? . . . *(Indignantly and barely controlling his temper as he raises his cane threaten-*

| | mixed | girls | boys |

mixed

cane threateningly at Interviewer)...not with my money, you loafer.

Interviewer   (cupping his hands around his mouth and shouting into the old man's ear). No...no...sir...I'm a sidewalk reporter, sir.

Old Man   (smiling as if reassured). Well, don't apologize...at least it's honest work. (Starts to walk away)

Interviewer   (placing his hand on the old man's arm to detain him, and shouting). But, sir...sir, what do you think is the best way to learn a foreign language?

Old Man   (indignantly pushing the Interviewer's hand away). I'm not interested in learning a foreign language, young man...I don't like foreigners. And, furthermore, I'm 75 years old and I have no time for nonsense. Good day, sir. (Walks on across the stage and exits stage left, leaving Interviewer standing dazed and baffled at midstage)

Interviewer   (using a fake laugh). Well, takes all kinds...(Looks around) But, here comes a pretty young lady. (Touching her arm lightly as a young woman enters from stage left) Good afternoon, Miss...how are you this lovely day? (Smiling)

Woman   (jumping back and raising her purse as if to strike Interviewer, and speaking in an annoyed, loud voice). Now, you stop bothering me or I'll call

girls

trolling her temper as she raises her cane threateningly at Interviewer)... not with my money, you loafer.

Interviewer   (cupping her hands around her mouth and shouting into the old woman's ear). No...no...madam ...I'm a sidewalk reporter, ma'am.

Old Woman   (smiling as if reassured). Well, don't apologize...at least it's honest work. (Starts to walk away)

Interviewer   (placing her hand on the old woman's arm to detain her, and shouting). But madam...ma'am, what do you think is the best way to learn a foreign language?

Old Woman   (indignantly pushing Interviewer's hand away). I'm not interested in learning a foreign language, young woman...I don't like foreigners. And, furthermore, I'm 75 years old and I have no time for nonsense. Good day, miss. (Walks on across the stage and exits stage left, leaving Interviewer standing dazed and baffled at midstage)

Interviewer   (fake laugh). Well, takes all kinds...(Looks around) But here comes a sweet young thing. Touching her arm lightly as a woman enters from stage left and speaking with exaggerated friendliness) Good afternoon, Miss...and how are you this gorgeous day?

Woman   (pulling her arm away and speaking indignantly). I beg your pardon! Now, look, I don't want to buy

boys

ingly at the Interviewer)...not with my money, you loafer.

Interviewer   (cupping his hands around his mouth and shouting into the old man's ear). No...no...sir...I'm a sidewalk reporter, sir.

Old Man   (smiling as if reassured). Well, don't apologize...at least it's honest work. (Starts to walk away)

Interviewer   (placing his hand on the old man's arm to detain him, and shouting) But, sir...sir, what do you think is the best way to learn a foreign language?

Old Man   (indignantly pushing Interviewer's hand away). I'm not interested in learning a foreign language, young man...I don't like foreigners. And, furthermore, I'm 75 years old and I have no time for nonsense. Good day, sir. (Walks on across the stage and exits stage left, leaving the Interviewer standing dazed and baffled at midstage)

Interviewer   (fake laugh). Well, takes all kinds...(Looks around) But here comes a fellow who looks as if he might have some interesting views. (Addressing Man who has entered from stage left) Sir, I wonder if you could help us out on this splendid spring day.

Man   (motions him away with a wave of his arm and shouts in an annoyed way). No, get away from me. I don't want to sign any election petitions.

mixed

a cop. I know your kind. Mashers! A girl isn't safe in broad daylight nowadays.

Interviewer   *(stunned and embarrassed).* No, no, Miss. I'm a sidewalk interviewer and I would like you to tell our radio audience what you think would be the best way to learn a foreign language. *(Smiles artificially)*

Woman   *(smiling and very enthusiastic).* Oh . . . oh, radio . . . you mean I'm really on the radio? Well, wait just a minute. *(Turns her back, quickly touches up her hair, looking into her purse mirror, and examines her lipstick)*

Interviewer   *(impatiently).* It's not TV, you know . . . I said radio, Miss . . . Miss, they can't see you . . .

Woman   *(turning toward the Interviewer, speaks very mechanically and monotonously, like a tape recorder).* Now I think that the best way to learn a foreign language would be to follow the sequence of hearing, speaking, reading, and writing. First, however, you've got to learn the phonemes of the language . . . there are forty-five or so of those in English. And then you've got to learn the basic sentence patterns, and particularly the ones that are different from those in your own, native language. And then . . .

Interviewer   *(overwhelmed, steps back).* Well, thank you very much, Miss. I'm sure we all appreciate your help.

girls

anything and I'm not interested in political surveys, so just go away and stop bothering me.

Interviewer   *(stunned and embarrassed).* No, no, Miss. I'm a sidewalk interviewer and I would like you to tell our radio audience what you think would be the best way to learn a foreign language. *(Smiles artificially)*

Woman   *(smiling and very enthusiastic).* Oh . . . oh, radio . . . you mean I'm really on the radio? Well, wait just a minute. *(Turns her back, quickly touches up her hair, looking into her purse mirror, and examines her lipstick)*

Interviewer   *(impatiently).* It's not TV, you know . . . I said radio, Miss, they can't see you . . .

Woman   *(turning toward Interviewer, speaks very mechanically and monotonously, like a tape recorder).* Now, I think that the best way to learn a foreign language would be to follow the sequence of hearing, speaking, reading, and writing. First, however, you've got to learn the phonemes of the language . . . there are forty-five or so of those in English. And then you've got to learn the basic sentence patterns, and particularly the ones that are different from those in your own, native language. And then . . .

Interviewer   *(overwhelmed, steps back).* Well, thank you very much, Miss. I'm sure we all appreciate your help.

boys

(Grumbling as he keeps walking) It's getting so you can't walk down the street without being mobbed by a bunch of political parasites, bothering you for your signature on petitions. It's a lot of nonsense.

Interviewer   *(stunned, holds up his hand in a peaceful gesture, and smiles).* Now wait a minute, sir . . . let's calm down. I'm afraid you didn't understand me. I'm not collecting signatures on a petition. *(Very slowly and patiently)* I'm a sidewalk interviewer and I would like you to tell our radio audience what you think would be the best way to learn a foreign language.

Man   *(looking surprised and somewhat embarrassed).* Huh? . . . radio audience? Well, uh . . . you mean I'm really on the radio? Well, gee *(Quickly adjusts his coat and fixes his necktie, smiling),* why didn't you say so . . .

Interviewer   *(still rather shaken but impatiently).* Look, mister . . . sir *(man pulls out his handkerchief and dusts his shoes)* . . . look, it's not TV. *(Man takes off his hat and adjusting the brim replaces it carefully on his head)* I said RADIO, sir . . . sir, they can't see you . . .

Man   *(turning toward interviewer speaks very ponderously and mechanically).* Now—*(clears his throat)* ahem—I think that the best way to learn a foreign language would be to follow the sequence of hearing, speaking, reading,

mixed

(Turns toward stage left, trying desperately to get away from the over talkative woman)

Woman *(following Interviewer and refusing to stop speaking)* . . . You also have to learn the patterns of behavior used by people who speak the language as natives and this . . .

Interviewer *(pulling the microphone away from her).* Yes . . . Yes . . . well, thank you . . . thank you. *(Moving quickly toward stage left)* Goodbye!

Woman *(shrugging and shaking her head in a puzzled way).* Well, he asked me . . . and . . . *(Turns and walks away toward stage right and exits)*

Interviewer *(speaking nervously into the microphone as he stops at stage left and looks back toward the woman exiting stage right).* Well, folks, we've had two . . . er . . . interesting responses and . . . er . . . here comes a serious looking young man. Say, young fellow (smiles), I wonder if I could ask you a question? *(Young man approaches from stage right and stops at midstage)*

College Student *(chewing gum energetically).* O.K. . . . what's on your mind?

Interviewer *(smiling and with fake friendliness).* Yes . . . well . . . er . . . what do you think is the best way to learn a foreign language?

College Student. You couldn't have picked a worse time to ask me about that! As a matter of fact, I flunked a

girls

(Turns toward stage left, trying desperately to get away from the over talkative woman)

Woman *(following Interviewer and refusing to stop speaking)* . . . You also have to learn the patterns of behavior used by people who speak the language as natives and this . . .

Interviewer *(pulling the microphone away from her).* Yes . . . Yes . . . well, thank you . . . thank you. *(Moving quickly toward stage left)* Goodbye!

Woman *(shrugging and shaking her head in a puzzled way).* Well, she asked me . . . and . . . *(Turns and walks away toward stage right and exits)*

Interviewer *(speaking nervously into the microphone as she stops at stage left and looks back toward the woman exiting stage right).* Well, folks, we've had two . . . er . . . interesting responses and . . . er . . . here comes a serious looking young lady. Say, young lady *(smiles)*, I wonder if I could ask you a question? *(Young woman approaches from stage right and stops at midstage)*

Coed *(chewing gum and giggling).* Uh-huh, well—what do you want to know?

Interviewer *(smiling and with fake friendliness).* Yes . . . well . . . er . . . what do you think is the best way to learn a foreign language?

Coed *(laughing).* Oh my—well, that is a problem, isn't it—and especially since I

boys

and writing. *(Clears his throat again)* Ahem—But, first, you've got to learn the phonemes of the language . . . there are forty-five or so of those in English, I believe. And then you've got to learn the basic sentence patterns and particularly those different from the ones in your own language. And then . . .

Interviewer *(overwhelmed, steps back).* Well, thank you very much, sir. I'm sure we all appreciate your help. *(Turns toward stage left, trying desperately to get away from the over talkative man)*

Man *(following Interviewer and refusing to stop speaking)* . . . You also have to learn the patterns of behavior used by people who speak the language as natives and this . . .

Interviewer *(pulling the microphone away from him).* Yes . . . Yes . . . well, thank you . . . thank you. *(Moving quickly toward stage left)* Goodbye!

Man *(shrugging and shaking his head in a puzzled way).* Well, he asked me . . . and . . . *(Turns and walks away toward stage right and exits)*

Interviewer *(speaking nervously into the microphone as he stops at stage left and looks back toward the man exiting stage right)* Well, folks, we've had two . . . er . . . interesting responses and . . . er . . . here comes a serious looking young man. Say, young fellow *(smiles)*, I wonder if I

mixed

French exam just this morning.

Interviewer   *(enthusiastically)*. Ah, you're a student then, I take it! Well, your views should be very interesting. Now, what method would you suggest?

College Student   *(with mock seriousness)*. I wish I knew. One guy told me I should try using phonograph records. Another guy told me I should forget about everything else until I understand the grammar. Sometimes I think the best way might be to get a girl friend.

Interviewer   *(puzzled)*. A girl friend? . . .*(Then, smiling)* . . . Oh, you mean just forget about learning a language and go dancing . . . or something. *(Laughing mildly and nervously)*

College Student   *(earnestly)*. No . . . I mean get a girl who understands the language . . . one with an apartment. Then *(smiling)* I figure after we've had a couple of drinks to loosen us up, y'know *(nudges Interviewer in the ribs)* . . . I can . . .

Interviewer   *(wincing)*. Yes, well that sounds like an unusual approach . . . and I'm sure our audience would like to hear more . . .*(shooing the student away)* sometime. *(Holding his hand over the microphone and stage whispering)* Beat it, kid . . . you've had it! *(aloud, glibly into the microphone)* But time moves on, folks . . . *(chuckles hollowly)* heh, heh, heh.

girls

flunked a French exam just this morning. *(Giggles)*

Interviewer   *(sympathetically)*. Oh, isn't that too bad . . . but since you're a college student I'll just bet you have some interesting views on our question. I wonder if you could tell us something about methods you think might work?

Coed   *(reflecting)*. Hm-m-m. Well, everybody has a different idea, it seems. One of the kids at the dorm told me I should use phonograph records. Another kid said I should forget everything else until I had the grammar down cold. But, I don't know—sometimes I think it might be best to just go to the movies.

Interviewer   *(puzzled)*. The movies? *(Then, smiling)* Oh, I see, you mean to learn a language by seeing movies in that language . . .

Coed   *(with a bland innocence)*. No, I just mean going to any movies . . . forgetting about learning a language and just go to the movies. *(Giggles)* What do I need to know a foreign language for, anyway?

Interviewer   *(sputtering)*. Well . . . but *(pompously)* don't the possibilities for better cultural understanding, for exchange of ideas interest you at all, as a student? After all *(puzzled)* . . . well, why are you attending college?

Coed   *(candidly)*. Me? Are you kidding? I'm just going to school to find a

boys

could ask you a question? *(Young man approaches from stage right and stops at midstage)*

College Student   *(chewing gum energetically)*. O.K. . . . what's on your mind?

Interviewer   *(smiling and with fake friendliness)*. Yes . . . well . . . er . . . what do you think is the best way to learn a foreign language?

College Student.   You couldn't have picked a worse time to ask me about that! As a matter of fact, I flunked a French exam just this morning.

Interviewer   *(enthusiastically)*. Ah, you're a student then, I take it! Well, your views should be very interesting. Now, what method would you suggest?

College Student   *(with mock seriousness)*. I wish I knew. One guy told me I should try using phonograph records. Another guy told me I should forget about everything else until I understand the grammar. Sometimes I think the best way might be to get a girl friend . . .

Interviewer   *(puzzled)*. A girl friend? . . .*(Then, smiling)* . . . Oh, you mean just forget about learning a language and go dancing . . . or something. *(Laughing mildly and nervously)*

College Student   *(earnestly)*. No . . . I mean get a girl who understands the language . . . one with an apartment. Then *(smiling)* I figure after we've had a couple of drinks to loosen us up,

mixed

College Student   *(looking disappointed and grumbling).* O.K. . . . O.K. . . . You asked me and I'm trying to give you my opinion . . . *(Shrugs his shoulders and shakes his head as he exits stage left)*

Interviewer   *(looking back over his shoulder nervously, as if to make sure the student has really gone, as he continues talking mechanically into the microphone).* Well, we'll have time for about one more opinion, folks.

Interviewer looks toward stage left as he walks toward stage right. Bumps into the husband and wife who have entered from stage right and have reached midstage.

Interviewer   *(quickly turning toward the couple and apologizing in a very exaggerated way).* Oh, I'm *very* sorry . . .

Husband holds one shin and groaning slightly limps comically but painfully in a little circle.

Wife   *(annoyed, addresses Interviewer in a harsh voice).* Why don't you look where you're going . . . before you hurt somebody or something?

Interviewer   *(still very apologetically).* Very careless of me. *(And then smiling broadly)* Er . . . I'm a sidewalk interviewer and the question today is what do you think is the best way to learn a foreign language.

Husband   *(still rubbing his shin, stops limping and looks very serious).* Say . . . I never thought about that. That's a very interesting problem.

girls

husband.

Interviewer   *(wincing).* Yes, well that sounds like an unusual approach . . . and I'm sure our audience would like to hear more . . . *(shooing the coed away)* sometime. *(Holding her hand over the microphone and stage whispering)* Beat it, kid . . . you've had it! *(Aloud, glibly into the microphone)* But time moves on, folks . . . *(chuckles hollowly)* heh, heh, heh.

Coed   *(puzzled).* But you did ask me for my opinion—although I told you I flunked the French exam . . . and . . . therefore, it all seems so silly and such a waste of time . . . *(Shrugs her shoulders and, shaking her head disapprovingly, exits stage left)*

Interviewer   *(looking back over her shoulder nervously, as if to make sure the coed has really gone, as she continues talking mechanically into the microphone).* Well, we'll have time for about one more opinion, folks.

Interviewer looks toward stage left as she walks toward stage right. Bumps into the mother and daughter who have entered from stage right and have reached midstage.

Interviewer   *(quickly turning toward the mother and daughter and apologizing in a very exaggerated way).* Oh, I'm terribly sorry, really I am.

Daughter holds one shin and groaning slightly limps comically but painfully in a little circle.

Mother   *(annoyed, addresses Interviewer*

boys

y'know *(nudges Interviewer in the ribs)* . . . I can . . .

Interviewer   *(wincing).* Yes, well that sounds like an unusual approach . . . and I'm sure our audience would like to hear more . . . *(shooing the student away)* sometime. *(Holding his hand over the microphone and stage whispering)* Beat it, kid . . . you've had it! *(Aloud, glibly into the microphone)* But time moves on, folks . . . *(chuckles hollowly)* heh, heh, heh.

College Student   *(looking disappointed and grumbling).* O.K. . . . O.K. . . . You asked me and I'm trying to give you my opinion . . . *(Shrugs his shoulders and shakes his head as he exits stage left)*

Interviewer   *(looking back over his shoulder after him nervously, as if to make sure the student has really gone, as he continues talking mechanically into the microphone).* Well, we'll have time for about one more opinion, folks.

Interviewer looks toward stage left as he walks toward stage right. Bumps into the father and son who have entered from stage right and have reached midstage.

Interviewer   *(quickly turning toward the father and son and apologizing in a very exaggerated way).* Oh, I'm *very* sorry . . .

Son holds one shin and groaning slightly limps comically but painfully in a little circle.

mixed

(Stops rubbing his leg and straightens up)

Wife   *(looking at her husband threateningly)*. Oh . . . well, just get any funny ideas out of your head *right now!*

Interviewer   *(smiling mechanically and placatingly at her)*. Well, I'm sure, Madam, your husband was merely expressing his interest in our little problem for today and had no intention of . . .

Wife   *(turning on Interviewer and interrupting angrily)*. Oh, yeah . . . well if he thinks he's going to skip out on me and take off to some foreign country, he's crazy!

Husband   *(turning toward his wife soothingly)*. Mabel . . . I had no such thought. The man only asked and I was trying to be . . . helpful. *(Turning in a friendly way to Interviewer)* I hear your program pretty often and you certainly get some nutty people. But I figured you practiced with them beforehand.

Interviewer.   No, sir, our programs are all unrehearsed. Just people passing by . . . people like yourself. Now, about our question for today . . .

Wife   *(threateningly to Interviewer)*. I told you to cut out putting ideas into Herbert's head.

Husband   *(whining)*. But, Mabel . . .

Wife   *(turning to husband)*. Shut up, you! *(Turning to Interviewer)* And as

girls

in a harsh voice). Why don't you look where you're going . . . before you hurt somebody or something?

Interviewer   *(embarrassed and still very apologetic)*. That was awfully clumsy of me, wasn't it? *(Mechanically to daughter)*. And I do hope I haven't hurt you badly . . . have I? *(Smiling broadly and mechanically)* Er . . . I'm a sidewalk interviewer and I wonder if you'd mind telling us what you think is the best way to learn a foreign language.

Daughter   *(still rubbing her shin, stops limping around and looks very serious)*. Oh, well—er—I've often thought about that *(glances toward her mother)*—because it's so interesting to meet foreigners, I think.

Mother   *(looking sternly at her daughter, speaks with harsh sarcasm)*. Uh-huh. Well, just don't get any funny ideas, Debbie . . .

Interviewer   *(smiling mechanically and placatingly at her)*. Oh, I'm sure she meant nothing by it, madam; you know how girls are—and your daughter was . . .

Mother   *(turning on Interviewer and interrupting angrily)*. Oh, is that so . . . well, if you think I'm going to let her go off alone to some foreign country at her age, you're crazy!

Daughter   *(turning to her mother soothingly)*. Momma . . . I wasn't even thinking of anything like that. Gee,

boys

Father   *(annoyed addresses Interviewer in a harsh voice)*. Why don't you look where you're going . . . before you hurt somebody or something?

Interviewer   *(still very apologetically)*. Very careless of me. *(And then smiling broadly)* Er . . . I'm a sidewalk interviewer and the question today is what do you think is the best way to learn a foreign language.

Son   *(still rubbing his shin, stops limping and looks very serious)*. Say . . . I never thought about that. That's a very interesting problem. *(Stops rubbing his leg and straightens up)*

Father   *(looking at his son threateningly)*. Oh yeah. Well, just get any funny ideas out of your head right now!

Interviewer   *(smiling mechanically and placatingly at the father, as he interrupts)*. Oh, come now, sir. Don't be too hard on the boy. *(Chuckling hollowly)* After all, he was merely expressing a natural curiosity about our little problem for today. I don't think he had any intention of . . .

Father   *(turning toward Interviewer and interrupting angrily)*. How do you know? . . . And who asked for your opinion, anyway? I guess I know my own kid.

Interviewer   *(placatingly)*. Yes, of course you do, sir, but . . .

Father   *(interrupting)*. And if you think

mixed

for you ... what are you trying to do, destroy our marriage? Isn't it enough I have to cut all the pictures of those foreign girls in bikinis out of the newspaper before I let him read it?

Interviewer   *(stunned and rather frightened by her strong reaction).* Foreign girls? ... bikinis? But, Madam, all I want to know is what you think is the best way to learn a foreign language.

Wife   *(waving her umbrella at Interviewer threateningly).* I know what you want ... and I know what you're going to get too *(shaking the umbrella at Interviewer pointedly)* ... you h o m e w r e c k e r! *(Grabbing her husband's arm and dragging him away)* Come along, Herbert!

Wife drags the husband away and they exit stage left.

Interviewer   *(adjusting his collar nervously and speaking into the microphone).* Well *(laughs nervously)* heh, heh, heh—some days are more difficult than others ... but ... that is all the time we have today, friends. Listen in tomorrow when we'll ask another ... *(wincing)* ... timely question of the man in the street. *(Glances quickly toward stage left as if to be sure that the pair has gone)* This is your Sidewalk Interviewer ... saying *(fake gaiety)* goodbye for today!

CURTAIN

girls

the lady just asked a simple little question *(whining exasperatedly)* and I was just trying to help her out ... Gee *(turning in a friendly way toward Interviewer)* I hear your program pretty often and you certainly get some nutty people. But I guess you usually rehearse with them beforehand, don't you?

Interviewer.   Oh, no, dear—none of it is rehearsed at all—we just take people passing by—like you and your mother. *(Smiling mechanically)* But won't you please say something about the question for today?

Mother   *(angrily to Interviewer).* Now just a minute, Miss. I've already told you I don't want Debbie to get any strange ideas about things that we can't afford. It seems to me you ought to realize that it is tough enough to raise kids nowadays without ...

Daughter   *(interrupting whiningly).* But Momma, she ...

Mother   *(turning to her daughter).* Just be quiet! *(Turning angrily to Interviewer)* People like you are the cause of all the juvenile delinquency. Parents have a hard enough time with kids as it is, without you people encouraging them in every crazy idea. Who do you think has to pay for all of the nonsense you put into their heads?

Interviewer   *(stunned and rather frightened by the mother's outburst).* But, madam, all I wanted ...

boys

I'm going to let you talk him into taking an expensive trip that I'll be stuck with the bills for, you're crazy!

Son   *(turning to his father, puzzled).* But, Pop ... he didn't even mention a trip. *(Turning in a friendly way to Interviewer)* I hear your program pretty often and you certainly get some nutty people. But I figured you practiced with them beforehand.

Interviewer.   No, sir, our programs are all unrehearsed. Just people passing by—people like you yourself. Now, about our question for today ...

Father   *(angrily to Interviewer and emphasizing each word with a stab of his index finger)* Look, I've told you before to cut out putting ideas into Herbie's head. It's tough enough to raise kids nowadays, without ...

Son   *(interrupting).* Aw, gee, Pop ... what are you getting so excited about?

Father   *(turning to his son).* Just be quiet! *(Turning angrily to Interviewer)* People like you are the cause of all the juvenile delinquency. Parents have a hard enough time with kids as it is, without you people encouraging them in every crazy idea. Who do you think has to pay for all of the nonsense you put into their heads?

Interviewer   *(stunned at the father's outburst).* But, sir, all I wanted ...

Father.   I don't care what you want ... but I know what you're going to get *(shaking his fist at Inter-*

mixed

Glossary

beat it, kid—slang meaning *go away*

bikini—a very brief, two piece bathing suit for women

clichés—words or statements used too often so that they have no real meaning anymore

cut out—stop

distinguished looking—dressed modestly in dark and very dignified clothing

eh?/²e³y/—a questioning expression, meaning *Isn't that true?*

flunked—student slang meaning *failed*

funny ideas—peculiar and suspicious ideas

glibly—very quickly and thoughtlessly

guy—slang word for *man*

Herbie—nickname for Herbert

he's crazy—he is wrong, he is mistaken

homewrecker—a person who destroys a marriage by interfering in the relationship of husband and wife

I take it—I imagine, I guess, I think, I suppose

loafer—a lazy, idle person

loosen us up y'know—help us to speak freely; the student is implying that a few drinks of whiskey will help him to seduce the girl

mashers—slang meaning a man who annoys or accosts girls or women who are walking along the street

nutty—peculiar, unusual, crazy

Oh /³o⁴u/—a sound of suspicion

O.K., O.K. /²oké³y + ²oké³y/—grudging acceptance of the fact he has been

girls

Mother   *(waving her umbrella at Interviewer threateningly).* I know what you want . . . and I know what you're going to get too *(shaking the umbrella at Interviewer pointedly)* . . . you . . . you . . . tramp! *(Grabbing her daughter's arm and dragging her away).* Come along, Debbie. *(Angrily)* I've heard enough from that . . . that creature!

Mother drags Daughter away and they exit stage left.

Interviewer   *(touching up her hair nervously and speaking into the microphone).* Well *(laughing nervously)* heh, heh, heh—some days are more difficult than others, aren't they? But, I guess that is all the time we have today, friends. Listen in tomorrow, won't you, and we'll ask another *(wincing)* timely question of the man in the street. *(Glancing quickly and nervously toward stage left, as if to be sure that the pair has gone)* This is your Sidewalk Interviewer saying *(fake gaiety)* goodbye for today.

CURTAIN

Glossary

after all—finally

are you kidding?—your statements are ridiculous and certainly are not to be taken seriously, I imagine

at her age—the girl is too young to travel

boys

viewer) if you don't stop trying to corrupt our kids. Now let's go, Herbie. *(Pushes his son ahead of him and turning back to Interviewer)* . . . and don't you forget it, mister!

Father drags the son away and they exit stage left.

Interviewer   *(adjusting his collar nervously and speaking into the microphone).* Well *(laughs nervously)* heh, heh, heh—some days are more difficult than others . . . but . . . that is all the time we have today, friends. Listen in tomorrow when we'll ask another . . . *(wincing)* . . . timely question of the man in the street. *(Glances quickly toward stage left as if to be sure that the pair has gone)* This is your Sidewalk Interviewer . . . saying *(fake gaiety)* goodbye for today!

CURTAIN

Glossary

ahem /ə+héhm/—clearing the throat in preparing to speak

be too hard on—act severely toward, be too demanding or stern

corrupt—influence badly

don't you forget it—a kind of warning: if Interviewer tries to influence the boy further, the father will attack him.

election petitions—lists of signatures collected from persons who believe that some candidate or issue should be pre-

mixed	girls	boys
rejected	abroad alone	sented for the decision of voters on election day.
phonemes—the significant sounds which distinguish a language	gee—an expression indicating emotion and intensifying the statement which follows	political parasites—minor politicians who live off of major politicians
shin—lower part of the leg, between the knee and the ankle	gorgeous—beautiful (used mainly by women)	Pop—affectionate, colloquial address for one's father
shooing the young man away—using a motion of the hand, such as is used in chasing birds away	had the grammar down cold—knew the grammar very well	shaking his fist—a kind of threatening gesture: the father is threatening to strike Interviewer
shut up—be quiet, stop talking	hard enough time—have serious difficulty	stuck with the bills for—be responsible to pay for
skip out on me—desert me, run away	h-m-m hūm/—expression indicating reflection and speculation	
take off—leave	I *beg* your pardon—sarcastic expression of indignation and annoyance	
what's on your mind—what do you want	kids—children or young people	
wincing—sudden nervous reaction, usually an abrupt pulling back of the head and a sudden painful expression on the face	loafing—idle, not working	
you've had it—you are not going to be given any further attention or consideration	now, look—pay attention; usually reflects rising annoyance or exasperation	
	sweet young thing—a pretty, young girl	
	uh-huh/ə̃ + hə̃/—pression of skeptical agreement or doubt	

Structure

1. We find several examples of truncated sentence forms in the dialogue of this staging. The missing parts are in parentheses.

   (a) lots of traffic *(There is)*

   (b) always standing around *(Young fellows are)*

   (c) Just people passing by *(I talk with)*

   We note that (a) is an example of a sentence without a verb; (b) is a sentence without a subject and with part of the verb missing; and (c) is an example of a sentence from which both the subject and its verb have been omitted. All are common types of abbreviation found widely in spoken English.

2. The ordinary structure of the tag or trailer question—statement ±, question ∓?—is sometimes abbreviated by the use of "eh?" /³ey / meaning *don't you* in this case but actually merely a sign of the question. This "eh?" is frequently used as a kind of request for agreement, with a meaning similar to *isn't that true?*

3. In the expression "say, sir" the word "say" is only a kind of signal used informally to attract somebody's attention. Less formal usage in America might be "Hey" and more formal might be, "Excuse me/Pardon me, but . . .". Some British dialects use "I say," but this is not used by Americans. The "sir" is a term of respect when the Interviewer uses it, although when the Old Man uses it, its main function is to request deference. Notice that the Old Man's "Good day, sir" expresses a kind of frosty formality; the Old Man is dismissing the Young Man.

4. The expression "Takes all kinds" is part of a common proverb, "It takes all kinds of people to make a world," meaning that we must realize that a vast population must inevitably consist of some oddly behaving people whom we must, nevertheless, accept. Americans often use only part of a well known proverb, since the listener can easily supply the missing part.

5. "I wish I knew," is an expression of puzzlement or even of mild disappointment or despair. The student is disappointedly admitting that although he would like to learn French, he has been unsuccessful and doesn't know how to improve.

6. The expression "Well, just get any funny ideas out of your head *right now*" is a kind of warning or threat, as is shown by the stressing of the last two words. Those two words, meaning *immediately*, are equally stressed; their pitch contour is /²ra³it + ²næuw/.

7. Students should be shown that "er" / ər / is commonly used to indicate a pause for thought when the speaker is not sure or needs time to consider his words more carefully.

Cultural Values

1. The Interviewer is a very common type who speaks routinely, using language automatically without thinking. Most of what he says is mere cliché and nonsense which is used only to fill the time. But, since many people want their friends to hear them on a radio or TV program, such Interviewers are quite popular.

2. The old man becomes annoyed because he has assumed that the Interviewer is really a beggar. Begging is rather rare in America now and it is generally thought that a person who begs is not really in need but is merely too lazy to look for a job. The old man expresses the common feeling that people who don't work, and particularly young people, are merely lazy and, therefore, deserve no sympathy, consideration, or help. It is widely assumed that such people are drunkards and we note that the deaf old man readily misinterprets "a foreign language" as "a beer and sandwich."

    Later, when the old man finally understands that the Interviewer is really an interviewer, he says "Don't apologize . . . at least it's honest work," implying that he thinks such a job is really not important and, in fact, is not much better than being a beggar and is really a form of idling.

3. Young men quite commonly are very much interested in girls and it is even common for men to whistle or try to talk with girls who happen to be passing in the street. Although young girls may consider this kind of attention rather flattering, many girls consider it insulting and in this staging the young girl is quite annoyed because she assumes that the Interviewer is merely a man trying to flirt with her. Angered by such behavior a girl may strike such a fellow or even report him to a policeman, who may either chase the fellow away or give the fellow a ticket for being a public nuisance. Some cities have so-called anti-masher laws which specify fines or other punishment for men who bother women in public places. Notice also how quickly the girl in the play changes her attitude, however, when she learns that she may have a chance to appear on a radio program. Many people are very anxious to appear on radio or T.V.

4. The student is implying that he could learn a foreign language quicker if he had a romance with a girl who spoke the language. He is not really interested in learning a foreign language, but would merely like to meet a girl with whom he could have an affair. Although some foreigners may think it odd, American boys are frequently greatly interested in such romantic matters and spend a great deal of time pursuing girls. In fact, the coeducational system makes relationships between boys and girls quite easy and very common. Dating is encouraged as an educational device so that young people will become acquainted with many different personality types before they make a decision about a marriage partner. But foreign students also should note that sexual relationships are usually not openly discussed, particularly over the radio, and when the Interviewer realizes that the student may be about to suggest a sexual relationship, the Interviewer chases the student away.

5. The wife in this play dominates her husband, who from the American standpoint, seems very henpecked. The foreign student from a male dominated society may find the situation grotesquely unbelievable. He may have to learn that usually this is considered a comical situation in America, not so much because of a belief in male dominance, as he may suppose, but

because the relationship between husband and wife is usually considered an equal partnership—which the foreign student may also find difficult to understand—although the husband may dominate in some lower class marriages.

The student must be shown that Mabel's dialogue in speaking to her husband is much like that of a man in its direct, unsoftened bluntness; in fact, the essence of their marriage is that as the dominant member she is really playing the part of a man.

Moreover, it should be noted that although it is a kind of standard joke for an American wife to pretend to suspect that her husband is romantically interested in other women, in this play Mabel is quite serious and really is angered by the interest in women which she imagines Herbert has.

Students will have to realize that Americans quite commonly think of men and women as being engaged in a continuous contest against each other and a wife may, therefore, assume that her husband's male friends will inevitably sympathize with him against her. Similarly, the husband expects that other women will sympathize with his wife rather than with him. It should be noted that Mabel accuses the Interviewer of encouraging Herbert's rebellion against her domination.

6. Some students will be interested to know that Americans generally imagine that foreign women—and particularly the French—are most attractive sexually. In this play, Mabel is determined that Herbert will not have the opportunity to become interested in the provocative pictures of foreign girls in brief bathing suits. She even accuses the Interviewer of encouraging her husband to become interested in other women, and, thereby, of threatening her marriage. Many students will be shocked not only at her threatening attitude toward a man, but also at her mentioning of the possibility of the collapse of her marriage, since such attitudes would be impossible in some societies and particularly in those in which arranged marriages are common.

General Comment

1. Each interview is like a separate scene, not connected to the other interviews except that we see the increasing frustration of the Interviewer who is repeatedly surprised and disappointed by the reactions of the various characters. Division for rehearsal is fairly simple, therefore, and students have an opportunity to see the varying responses to a casual introduction such as that attempted by the Interviewer. Moreover, care will be necessary in arranging entrances and exits as well as in plotting each conversational exchange.

2. Since there is very little synchronization of physical movement and dialogue, those students having little experience with English should be able to play the parts fairly successfully. Each character walks to midstage to meet the Interviewer and then the exchange begins. When the exchange ends, the character exits and is replaced by another character. However, students should be required to pay particular attention to postures, facies, pitch, stress, and pacing as they project the different emotions of the characters. Careful pronunciation will be particularly necessary, since the audience must get the meaning of the exchange virtually from the dialogue alone. The pace of dialogue of each character starts out fairly briskly and then slows up, as the exchange develops, only to speed up again toward the end of each exchange. It should be noted, also, that the pace of speaking of the student is much quicker than that of the old man; in fact, each role is characterized by a distinct pace.

3. All characters are mildly annoyed, at least at first, when the Sidewalk Interviewer stops them. The annoyance of the deaf, old man and of Mabel continues and increases; the annoyance of the young girl vanishes quickly, changing first to enthusiastic cooperation and then to puzzlement and, finally, back to mild annoyance again. The student is more indifferent, perhaps, than annoyed, but when his attempt at cooperation is rejected, he is also puzzled and mildly annoyed. Annoyance should be shown by above average loudness and by somewhat exaggerated pitch

changes.

4. The Interviewer must give the impression of being very cocky and self-confident, by talking exaggeratedly and with a kind of mechanical glibness, so that his disappointment, as he talks with each character, will seem comical in contrast.

5. Although this staging is made up of a series of comical exchanges, students should not feel that these characters are trying to be funny. That is, the characters are behaving quite naturally and would be surprised to learn that their behavior was at all unusual. When, in the course of rehearsals, students are allowed to improvise dialogue, they should not be encouraged to use the theatrical tricks of the comedian or clown. It should always be remembered that the plays are not designed to appeal to the audience, as a theatrical production would be, but are intended, instead, to teach participating students how to project all aspects of roles such as they will have to play in real life when speaking the foreign language. Students should be shown that the comedy lies in the fact that although the Interviewer remains optimistic and tries to give the impression that the program is a success, actually it is a failure, since every interview turns out disappointingly. Thus, the humor is grounded in the incongruity of the contrast between the happy impression the Interviewer attempts to convey and the sad reality.

Notes on Adaptation

1. There are only two women's roles in this staging but to adapt it for a cast made up entirely of either women or men is equally difficult, since the young woman is reacting against what she initially believes is the unwelcome romantic intention of the Interviewer, while Mabel's role is that of the dominant wife dealing with her henpecked husband. Some rather radical shifts, therefore, have been necessary in the adaptation for women. In the male version, not only has the role of the young woman been changed to that of a young man, but the role of the dominant wife has been changed to that of a father. However, another of the men's roles must also be greatly modified, for the role of the henpecked husband would be meaningless without the conversational exchange with his wife. Thus, the role has been changed to that of a teenage son, which will permit an exchange between parent and child such as was provided in the adaptation for women.

2. The conflict between the mother and daughter is quite evident but the foreign student should be made to realize that the mother becomes angry because she assumes that the Interviewer is trying to influence the daughter. The relationship between parents and teenage (13-20 years old) children is often very difficult in America, because the children are encouraged to be independent and yet this independence leads them to resent the authority of their parents and they may rebel against it.

3. The Old Woman also reflects some of the generation conflict in accusing the Interviewer of loafing while awaiting marriage. The Old Woman's statement "Just waiting for somebody to marry you, aren't you?" is a kind of rhetorical question, combining both an opinion and a kind of insult. We note, however, that the coed admits quite frankly that she is going to college mainly to find a husband, and such an admission is commonly accepted here. Although many foreign students may feel that coeducation is wasteful, therefore, they should recognize that college attendance for such a reason indicates that most college educated men would not be interested in marrying a girl who had not attended college; from this it is quite possible to see that marriage in America is largely a companionship of partners rather than the male dominated formal arrangement for continuing the family line that it is in many other societies.

4. There are many examples of the devices of woman's language apparent in this adaptation for women. Note that certain words such as *sweet* in "sweet young thing" or *lovely* in "lovely day" have much more limited usage by men. And in addition to the very common and characteristic woman's use of intensifiers, we have "*so* silly," "*such* a waste of time" used by the coed who otherwise sounds quite blunt and masculine in her directness.

Note also that the Interviewer attempts to get greater emotional intensity or emphasis—more typical of woman's speech-by reinforcing the "terribly sorry" with "really I am." She attempts to get a similar reinforcement in her "I *do* hope I haven't hurt you badly." The "I wonder if . . ." construction, used by the Interviewer in requesting the coed's opinion, is also typical feminine usage conveying the sense of a rather indirect question.

5. The use of *dear* in the Interviewer's, "Oh, no, dear," reflecting a kind of affection, is quite commonly used by older women in addressing young people and particularly young women. This may be seen as evidence of a rather veiled attempt to assert the authority of age or a request for deference.

6. It might be pointed out that the dialogue for the old man need not be greatly changed when the part is shifted to that of an old woman, since a kind of interchangeability—or, rather, the blurring of social distinction between the sexes—is characteristic of aging.

   Similarly, the dialogue of the Interviewer would probably not be much different whether the role were played by a man or a woman, since the lines consist largely of rather mechanical and impersonal clichés, typical of the speech of radio announcers.

7. Note that the mother and father are equally annoyed and resentful about attempts by strangers to interfere with their children. And although this may be understandable to foreign students, the fact that these parents are quite concerned about expense may not be very understandable to those foreigners who come from societies in which the teenager is not considered as important a part of the society as he is here. The foreigner may have difficulty understanding that many parents may attempt to use their money to exert authority over their children. Moreover, the foreigner will be quite surprised to find that strangers have a great deal of influence over children because industries, such as popular music and clothing, depend very heavily on the spending of teenagers and use vast amounts of advertising to stimulate their demands. Thus, in order to keep control and possibly to gain the respect of children, many parents are led to feel they must meet these demands. Not only is generational conflict intensified—particularly when the demands cannot be met—but the parents may view all outside influence as a genuine threat which they will resist as angrily as the two parents do in our play adaptation. In other words, the rather harsh reaction by the parents often may reflect the fear of parents who realize that their authority is being challenged. The psychodynamics underlying this relationship are too complex, of course, to present at once to foreign students, but teachers should take every opportunity to make students aware of certain manifestations and ramifications of generational conflict in the behavior patterns of members of our society. That awareness will be best gained not through lectures but through the mimicking of behavior patterns—first those modeled by the teacher and then those of the natives whom the foreigner learns to observe.

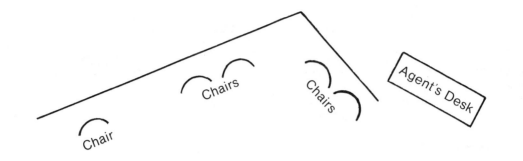

SETTING

The passenger lounge of an airline terminal. A row of chairs extends in a half rectangle running from stage right downstage to upstage and across almost to stage left upstage where a high desk faces diagonally toward stage right downstage. Behind the desk sit Airline Agent and Assistant. A microphone is on the desk before Agent. There is a narrow passage, serving as a kind of gateway between the end of the row of chairs and Agent's desk so that those entering the lounge area have to pass before Agent's desk. A person in uniform sits in the last chair in the row, far stage right, slumped, reading a newspaper. Other characters sit on chairs in the row running across the stage from stage right to stage left.

Mixed cast	*Girls' cast*	*Boys' cast*
Airline Agent	Airline Agent	Airline Agent
Woman #1	Woman #1	Assistant
Woman #2	Woman #2	Old Man
Assistant	Assistant	Old Man's Son (Al)
Businessman	Businesswoman	Businessman
Student	Coed	Student (Stan)
Student's Mother	Coed's Mother	Student's Father
Man in Uniform	Woman in Uniform	Man in Uniform

Agent   *(in loud commanding tone into microphone).* Attention, please. May I

Agent   *(in loud commanding tone into microphone).* Attention, please. May I

Agent   *(in loud commanding tone into the microphone).* Attention, please.

mixed

have your attention. *(Pause)* Flight 641 to New York due at 4:16 will be delayed until 4:46. Thank you.

Woman #1 *(nervously to her companion)*. Oh, they talk so fast! Did he say Flight 446 would be delayed until 6:41?

Woman #2 *(shrugging)*. I couldn't hear it either. *(Shaking her head disqustedly)* It's always the same problem. Air terminals, train stations, bus depots . . . lots of anouncements, but you can never hear any of them clearly enough so you can understand them.

Woman #1 *(anxiously)*. I guess we'd better ask that girl.

They walk over to the Assistant, stage left

Assistant *(looking up and speaking in a very sweet voice)*. Why, hello. May I help you? *(This should be spoken very mechanically)*

Woman #1. Miss, did he just announce that Flight 446 would be delayed until 6:41, or Flight 416 would be delayed until 6:14?

Man rushes across from stage right upstage, pushing in front of the passengers.

Businessman *(out of breath)*. 'Scuse me, ladies. *(Puffing breathlessly)* Say, look, I got to get that 641 outa here for New York. I sure hope I haven't missed it.

Agent *(looking up from his paperwork at the three people in front of the desk, reaches for the microphone and*

girls

have your attention. *(Pause)* Flight 641 to New York due at 4:16 will be delayed until 4:46. Thank you.

Woman #1 *(nervously to her companion)*. Oh, they talk so fast! Did she say Flight 446 would be delayed until 6:41?

Woman #2 *(shrugging)*. I couldn't hear it either. *(Shaking her head disqustedly)* It's always the same problem. Air terminals, train stations, bus depots . . . lots of announcements, but you can never hear any of them clearly enough so you can understand them.

Woman #1 *(anxiously)*. I guess we'd better ask that girl.

They walk over to Assistant, stage left.

Assistant *(looking up and speaking in a very sweet voice)*. Why, hello. May I help you? *(This should be spoken very mechanically)*

Woman #1 Miss, did she just announce that Flight 446 would be delayed until 6:41, or Flight 416 would be delayed until 6:14?

Woman rushes across from stage right upstage pushing in front of the passengers.

Businesswoman *(out of breath)*. 'Scuse me. Sorry—but I've just got to get through *(puffing breathlessly)* Say, I simply must catch that 641 out of here for New York. I haven't missed it, have I?

Agent *(looking up from her paperwork at the three people in front of the desk, reaches for the microphone and*

boys

May I have your attention. *(Pause)* Flight 641 to New York due at 4:16 will be delayed until 4:46. Thank you.

Old Man *(annoyed)*. What's that? Did he say Flight 446 would be delayed until 6:41? The fellow talks too fast—can't hear him.

Old Man's Son *(in a fairly loud voice)*. I didn't catch it either, Pa. *(Frowning)* You never can hear them in a place like this. *(Noticing the old man's puzzlement, raises his voice and shakes his head from side to side)* No. I didn't get it.

Old Man *(loudly)*. Well, let's ask that young fellow over there. *(Points toward Assistant)*

They walk over to Assistant, stage left.

Assistant *(looking up and speaking in a bored, slightly annoyed voice)*. Yes, sir. Need some help? *(Smiles mechanically)*

Old Man. Young man, did that fellow just say Flight 446 won't be here until 6:41, or that Flight 416 won't arrive 'til 6:14, or what *did* he say?

Man rushes across from stage right upstage pushing in front of the passengers.

Businessman *(out of breath)*. 'Scuse me, fellas. *(Puffing breathlessly)* Say, look, I got to get that 641 outa here for New York. I sure hope I haven't missed it.

Agent *(looking up from his paperwork at the three people in front of the desk, reaches for the microphone and*

mixed

says in a loud, deliberate voice). Attention, please. May I have your attention. Flight 6-4-1 to New York will be delayed until 4-4-6, Thank you.

Businessman *(excited).* What! Now, look, I've *got* to be in New York at 6. Haven't you got *anything* going out before 4:46?

Assistant *(shaking her head negatively and smiling mechanically).* Sorry.

Businessman *(fuming in annoyance).* Well, where're the pay phones then, damn it? I'll have to call the office long distance.

Woman #2 *(sympathetically).* It's always the same story, isn't it? It seems to me you just can't count on them.

Assistant *(frostily to Businessman).* The public telephone booths are on the lower level, sir.

Businessman *(exits hurriedly stage right grumbling disgustedly).* Damned airlines—always hold you up. Shoulda taken a train!

Assistant *(to Woman #1).* Which flight are you on, madam?

Woman #1 *(opening a huge pocketbook and digging inside).* Well—I'm not sure ... but I have the ticket somewhere here. (Pulls out all sorts of junk, handing her umbrella, a magazine, and a package to Woman #2) It's right here somewhere. (Pulls out eyeglass case, removes glasses, hands case to Woman #2 and putting*

girls

says in a loud, deliberate voice). Attention, please. May I have your attention. Flight 6-4-1 to New York will be delayed until 4-4-6. Thank you.

Businesswoman *(whining).* Oh, no! But, I've just got to be in New York at 6. Isn't there anything leaving before 4:46?

Assistant *(shaking her hand negatively).* Not a thing. *(Then, as an afterthought)* Sorry!

Businesswoman *(wailing in frustration and annoyance).* Oh-h-h! Why, that's terrible! I rushed so to get here too. *(Shrugs)* But ... I'll just have to call long distance—do you happen to know where the pay phones are, miss?

Woman #2 *(sympathetically).* It's always the same story, isn't it? It seems to me you just can't count on them.

Assistant *(frostily to Businesswoman).* The public telephone booths are on the lower level, madam.

Businesswoman *(exits stage right, complaining).* Oh, that makes me just furious. It's always the same story— just when you need them!

Assistant *(to Woman #1).* Which flight are you on, madam?

Woman #1 *(opening a huge pocketbook and digging inside).* Well—I'm not sure ... but I have the ticket somewhere here. (Pulls out all sorts of junk, handing her umbrella, a magazine, and a package to Woman #2) It's*

boys

says in a loud, deliberate voice). Attention, please. May I have your attention. Flight 6-4-1 to New York will be delayed until 4-4-6. Thank you.

Businessman *(excited).* What! Now, look, I've *got* to be in New York at 6. Haven't you got *anything* going out before 4:46?

Assistant *(shaking his head negatively and smiling mechanically).* Sorry.

Businessman *(fuming in annoyance).* Well, where're the pay phones then, damn it? I'll have to call the office long distance.

Old Man's Son *(shaking his head sympathetically).* It's always the way—when you need them, they fail you. *(Louder, to his father)* Can't count on them!

Assistant *(frostily to Businessman).* The public telephone booths are on the lower level, sir.

Businessman *(exits hurriedly stage right grumbling disgustedly).* Damned airlines—always hold you up. Shoulda taken a train!

Assistant *(to Old Man, in dull, flat voice).* What's your flight number, sir?

Old Man *(taking a larger envelope full of papers from his inside breast pocket and opening it).* I've got it right here. Never can remember. (Pulls out various papers, lays them on the counter, and his son picks them up. Frowns, squints at the papers. Reaches into breast pocket, takes out eyeglasses,*

mixed

on glasses resumes the search, taking items out and handing them to Woman #2 who soon has both hands full)

Woman #2   *(desperately trying to hold all the stuff)*. Martha, let's sit down so you can look for the ticket. *(They move toward the chairs midstage. Desperately struggling with the stuff, Woman #2 finally drops the umbrella)*

Student   *(leaning over to pick up the umbrella)*. Here you are, lady.

Student presenting umbrella to Woman #2 who, in reaching for it with a nervous "Thank you," drops the magazine. Student stoops to pick up the magazine, returns it to Woman #2 who again says "Thank you."

Mother   *(nervously to Man in Uniform)*. Pardon me, but are the planes usually late? The weather was fine today and I don't see why they're late.

Man in Uniform   *(looking up from his newspaper, bored and disinterested)*. H-m-m? Late? Oh—*(looking at wristwatch)* I guess so, lady. May've had to set down someplace, I s'pose. *(Resumes reading)*

Mother   *(frightened)*. Set down! *(Whining in exasperation)* Oh dear! You mean the plane may have . . . crashed? But the weather has been so nice. *(Shaking her head dazedly)* Why, I just can't understand it. I just knew I should've had Stanley take the train.

Man in Uniform   *(peering intently at his newspaper, as if trying to shut her off)*. Maybe, lady . . . but the railroads

girls

right here somewhere. *(Pulls out eyeglass case, removes glasses, hands case to Woman #2 and putting on glasses resumes the search, taking items out and handing them to Woman #2 who soon has both hands full)*

Woman #2   *(desperately trying to hold all the stuff)*. Martha, let's sit down so you can look for the ticket. *(They move toward the chairs midstage. Desperately struggling with the stuff, Woman #2 finally drops the umbrella)*

Coed   *(leaning over to pick up the umbrella)*. Here, lady, you dropped this.

Student presenting umbrella to Woman #2 who, in reaching for it with a nervous "Thank you," drops the magazine. Student stoops to pick up the magazine, returns it to Woman #2 who again says "Thank you."

Mother   *(nervously to Woman in Uniform)*. Pardon me, but are the planes usually late? The weather was fine today and I don't see why they're late.

Woman in Uniform   *(looking up from her newspaper, bored and disinterested)*. Late? Oh—*(looking at wristwatch)* I guess so. Maybe they had to set down someplace. I really don't know. *(Resumes reading)*

Mother   *(frightened)*. Set down! *(Whining in exasperation)* Oh dear! You mean the plane may have . . . crashed? But the weather has been so nice. *(Shaking her head dazedly)* Why, I just can't understand it. I just knew I

boys

puts them on, tilts head back, and looks at papers from envelope. His son puts down a suitcase and also examines the papers he is holding)* It's here—somewhere . . .

Old Man's Son   *(turning slightly, knocks over suitcase and in reaching for it drops a couple of the papers. As he picks them up, he says)* Pa, let's go sit down so we can look for the ticket in all this stuff. *(As they move toward chairs midstage, he again drops the papers)*

Student   *(leaning over to pick up the papers)*. Here you are, sir. *(Reaching for them and murmuring "Thanks," the Old Man's Son drops several other papers)*

Student again presents paper to Old Man's Son who, slightly embarrassed at his clumsiness, says "Thank you."

Father   *(nervously to the Man in Uniform)*. Pardon me, but are the planes usually late? The weather was fine today and I don't see why they're late.

Man in Uniform   *(looking up from his newspaper, bored and disinterested)*. H-m-m? Late? Oh—*(looking at wristwatch)* I guess so, mister. May've had to set down someplace, I s'pose. *(Resumes reading)*

Father   *(looking startled)*. Set down! You mean the thing might have . . . crashed . . . *(frowning)* even in this weather? Doesn't seem possible. Hm-m-m—maybe the train would've

mixed

have their problems too, y'know.

Mother   *(to her son who has returned to sit down after retrieving the dropped articles)*. Oh, I told both you and your father you shouldn't fly. It's too dangerous.

Student   *(with bravado)*. Aw, don't worry, Mom. All the fellas come back to school by plane. Besides Pop wouldn't let me drive the car . . . so there was nothing else I could do.

Mother   *(irritated)*. You could have taken the train, as I suggested . . . but you two wouldn't listen to that. Now just see what's happened.

Student   *(disgustedly)*. The train! Nobody can afford to waste time on trains nowadays, Mom . . . only hogs and cows and things like that. Gee, that's ancient history. Besides . . . nothing's happened. Stop worrying!

Mother   *(pointing)*. That man just told me the plane might've crashed somewhere . . . and he looks like a pilot himself.

Student   *(peering at Man in Uniform)*. Him? He doesn't look like a pilot to me. *(Scornfully)* What does he know about it?

Mother.   Well, it doesn't make any difference. Planes are not safe.

Woman #1 finds the ticket and, holding it up triumphantly, rushes to the Assistant, followed by Woman #2.

Woman #1   Here it is . . . my ticket . . . for Flight 614!

girls

should've had Mildred take the train.

Woman in Uniform.   Uh-huh. *(Shrugs)* But I guess trains aren't always on time either, are they?

Mother   *(to her daughter who has returned to sit down after retrieving the dropped articles)*. Oh, I told both you and your father you shouldn't fly. It's too dangerous.

Coed   *(frowning and with a whine of annoyance)*. Oh, Mother! Why, all the girls come back to school by plane. Besides, Dad didn't want me to drive back with Margie . . . *(with annoyance)* for some reason I certainly never will comprehend . . . So what else could I do?

Mother   *(irritated)*. You could have taken the train, as I suggested . . . but you two wouldn't listen to that. Now just see what's happened.

Coed   *(frowning and gazing at the ceiling in disgust and then sarcastically)*. Oh, yes, the train would be *lovely*. *(Pause)* I don't think they even run coaches anymore . . . It's all freight. But *(consolingly)* . . . why are you making such a fuss when nothing's happened?

Mother   *(pointing to Woman in Uniform)*. That woman just told me the plane might've crashed somewhere . . . and she looks like an airline hostess.

Coed   *(staring at Woman in Uniform who sits reading a newspaper)*. Her?

boys

been better.

Man in Uniform   *(peering intently at his newspaper, as if trying to shut him off)*. Maybe, mister . . . but the railroads have their problems too, y'know.

Father   *(to his son who has returned to his seat after retrieving the dropped articles)*. Maybe you should've taken the train, Stan. The plane's late and may've come down somewhere.

Student   *(with bravado)*. Aw, don't worry, Pop. All the fellas come back to school by plane. Besides Mom wouldn't let me drive the car . . . so there was nothing else I could do.

Father.   Well, there's the train. It's slow and would take a lot longer—and *(frowning and looking concerned)* now, I don't know—

Student.   Aw, Pop . . . trains are old stuff. They're too slow . . . they use them nowadays only for hogs and cows . . . and things like that. The plane could've just run into some strong wind. *(Reassuringly)* There's nothing to worry about.

Father   *(nodding toward Man in Uniform)*. That guy over there just told me the ship might've crashed somewhere. And he looks like he might be a pilot.

Student   *(peering at Man in Uniform)*. Maybe—but he doesn't look like a pilot to me. *(Reassuringly)* And he probably doesn't know anything about

mixed

Woman #2 Yeah, and I'll bet that one will be late too.

Agent *(acidly)*. No, madam, that flight was *not* late. In fact, it left at exactly 1:46 *on* schedule *(Slowly, to emphasize each word)* . . . two and a half hours ago.

Woman #1 *(stunned, then shouting)*. What! Why wasn't it announced? *(Looking shocked, she turns to Woman #2 and they whisper to each other animatedly)*

Businessman *(returning and pushing through, past the ladies)*. 'Scuse me, ladies. Beg your pardon. *(To Assistant)* Say, I couldn't find any phone booths . . . and can you break a five. I need some change to make that call.

Woman #1 *(confused)*. Call? What call? I was never called. Now *(beginning to cry)* my plane's gone. *(Starting to cry louder)* I've missed it! *(Everybody stares at her)*

Businessman *(consoling her)*. Don't take it so hard, lady. You can probably get the next one. They got lots of them all day. *(To Assistant)* About that change . . .

Assistant *(mechanically, with an icy smile)*. The telephone booths are on the lower level, sir. You will find change machines to the left of the booths. We are not permitted to make change here, sir.

Businessman *(unbelievingly)*. What! Aw, come on now, come off it . . .

girls

She doesn't look like anything of the kind to me. *(Scornfully)* And what could she know about it anyway?

Mother. Well, it doesn't make any difference. Planes are not safe.

Woman #1 finds the ticket and, holding it up triumphantly, rushes to Assistant, followed by Woman #2.

Woman #1. Here it is . . . my ticket . . . for Flight 614!

Woman #2. Yeah, and I'll bet that one will be late too.

Agent *(acidly)*. No, madam, that flight was *not* late. In fact, it left at exactly 1:46 *on* schedule *(Slowly, to emphasize each word)* . . . two and a half hours ago.

Woman #1 *(stunned, then shouting)*. What! Why wasn't it announced? *(Looking shocked, she turns to Woman #2 and they whisper to each other animatedly.)*

Businesswoman *(returning and pushing through the crowd)*. Excuse me again. I'm so sorry. *(To Assistant testily)* Miss, I didn't find a single phone booth down there . . . and *(digging into her pocketbook)* anyway I'll need change to make my call.

Woman #1 *(confused)*. Call? What call? I was never called. Now *(beginning to cry)* my plane's gone. *(Starting to cry louder)* I've missed it! *(Everybody stares at her)*

Businesswoman *(consolingly)*. Oh, I'm so sorry I've upset you so. But you'll

boys

it anyway.

Father. Yeah, but your mother doesn't like planes and if she was here she'd— *Old Man finds the ticket and, holding it with both hands, triumphantly rushes to Assistant, followed by his son.*

Old Man. Here it is, young man. Here's my ticket . . . for Flight 614!

Old Man's Son *(somewhat wearily setting down the suitcase)*. Yeah, but I suppose that one will be late too.

Agent *(scornfully)*. Nope . . . that one wasn't late. In fact, it left here on schedule at exactly 1:46 . . . two and a half hours ago.

Old Man *(excitedly, turning to his son)*. What's that! Did this fellow say the plane left already? *(Turning to Agent)* Well, why wasn't it announced, young man?

Businessman *(returning and pushing through, past the men)*. 'Scuse me, sir. Beg your pardon. *(To Assistant)* Say, I couldn't find any phone booths . . . and can you break a five. I need some change to make that call.

Old Man *(unbelievingly)*. Call, call? There was no call. *(Shouting angrily)* Now, you say the plane's gone . . . without me? *(Everybody stares at him.)*

Businessman *(trying to quiet the Old Man)*. Why get so excited, mister. You can catch a later one. *(To Assistant)* Say, look, about that change . . .

Assistant *(mechanically, with an icy*

mixed	*girls*	*boys*

mixed

Assistant *(mechanically smiling)*. Sorry!

Businessman *(walks off stage right, grumbling and mumbling)*. Damned airlines!

Woman #2 *(trying to console Woman #1, who continues weeping and shaking her head sadly)*. Don't worry, Martha—you'll get on a later plane. *(To Assistant)* When's the next flight to New York, miss?

Agent *(glancing up at her, looks scornful and, picking up the microphone, announces)*. Attention please. May I have your attention. Flight 641 to New York has been delayed and is now scheduled to arrive at 4:46. Thank you.

Woman #2. Good! You can make that one easily, Martha. *(To Assistant)* You can change her ticket, can't you?

Assistant *(to Woman #2)*. Sorry. *(Shaking her head but with a big smile)* But she will have to go to the Adjustment Office. We are not permitted to make reservation adjustments here, madam.

Woman #2 *(obviously annoyed)*. All right, all right. But, look *(glancing at her wristwatch)*, it's 4:40 now. Where's the Adjustment Office? Quick!

Assistant Sorry. *(Big smile)* The Adjustment Office is located on the lower level, to the right of the escalator, madam.

Mother *(jumping up)*. And I think that is exactly where we're going too. Air-

girls

be able to get the next one, won't you? They must have lots of flights, don't you think so? *(Coolly to Assistant)* But, Miss, I *would* like to have that change . . .

Assistant *(mechanically, with an icy smile)*. The telephone booths are on the lower level, madam. You will find change machines to the left of the booths. We are not permitted to make change here, madam.

Businesswoman *(unbelievingly)*. What! Oh, now look—after all—

Assistant *(mechanically smiling)*. Sorry!

Businesswoman *(flounces off stage right, complaining)*. What a nerve!

Woman #2 *(trying to console Woman #1, who continues weeping and shaking her head sadly)*. Don't worry, Martha—you'll get on a later plane. *(To Assistant)* When's the next flight to New York, miss?

Agent *(glancing up at her, looks scornful and, picking up the microphone, announces)*. Attention please. May I have your attention. Flight 641 to New York has been delayed and is now scheduled to arrive at 4:46. Thank you.

Woman #2 Good! You can make that one easily, Martha. *(To Assistant)* You can change her ticket, can't you?

Assistant *(to Woman #2)*. Sorry. *(Shaking her head but with a big smile)* She will have to go to the Adjustment Office. We are not permitted to make

boys

smile). The telephone booths are on the lower level, sir. You will find change machines to the left of the booths. We are not permitted to make change here, sir.

Businessman *(unbelievingly)*. What! Aw, come on now, come off it . . .

Assistant *(shrugging his shoulders)*. That's what the regulations say. Sorry.

Businessman *(walks off stage right, grumbling and mumbling)*. Damned airlines!

Old Man's Son *(consolingly)*. Don't worry, Pa—everything will work out O.K. *(To Assistant)* When's the next flight to New York?

Agent *(glancing up at him, looks scornful and, picking up the microphone, announces)*. Attention please. May I have your attention. Flight 641 to New York has been delayed and is now scheduled to arrive at 4:46. Thank you.

Old Man's Son *(straining hard to hear the announcement, smiles)*. There, you see, Pa! *(Speaks louder as the Old Man looks puzzled)* There's another flight in a few minutes, Pa. *(To Assistant)* You can change his ticket, can't you?

Assistant *(to Old Man's Son)*. Sorry. *(Shaking his head but with a big smile)* He will have to go to the Adjustment Office. We are not permitted to make reservation adjustments here, sir.

Old Man's Son *(obviously annoyed)*. All right, all right. But, look *(glancing*

mixed

planes are too dangerous and I'd be worried sick if you took a plane. We can get a refund on that ticket, and you can catch the six o'clock train.

Student *(disgustedly whining).* Aw, gee, Mom. There's nothing to worry about. Why are you getting excited. A plane shows up a few minutes late and *(. . . voice dying out in a grumble).*

Woman #2 *(to Assistant, exasperatedly).* But we'll never make it all the way down there and back in five minutes. Can't you phone them and do something to her ticket so she can catch that plane?

Assistant *(shaking her head negatively).* Sorry! *(Big smile)* We're not permitted to . . .

Woman #2 *(interrupting, annoyed).* But, for heaven's sake, there isn't time for all that now!

Woman #1 *(wearied).* Don't argue with her, Mildred. I've decided not to go, after all. I just don't feel like making the trip now . . . after all of this . . . this confusion.

Mother *(emphatically to son).* And you're not going either. I've made up my mind and that settles it!

Businessman *(pushing his way to the desk).* 'Scuse me, ladies. *(To the Agent and Assistant)* Just thought you two might like to know that I got the deal settled by long distance phone so I don't have to fool around with you people anymore.

girls

reservation adjustments here, madam.

Woman #2 *(obviously annoyed).* All right, all right. But, look *(glancing at her wristwatch),* it's 4:40 now. Where's the Adjustment Office? Quick!

Assistant. Sorry. *(big smile).* The Adjustment Office is located on the lower level, to the right of the escalator, madam.

Mother *(jumping up).* And I think that is exactly where we're going too. Airplanes are too dangerous and I'd be worried sick if you took a plane. We can get a refund on that ticket . . . and you can catch the six o'clock train.

Coed *(disgustedly whining).* Oh, Mother! Must you get so excited? After all, the plane is only a few minutes late and . . . *(Voice dying out in a grumble)*

Woman #2 *(to Assistant, exasperatedly).* But we'll never make it all the way down there and back in five minutes. Can't you phone them and do something to her ticket so she can catch that plane?

Assistant *(shaking her head negatively).* Sorry! *(Big smile)* We're not permitted to . . .

Woman #2 *(interrupting, annoyed).* But, for heaven's sake, there isn't time for all that now!

Woman #1 *(wearied).* Don't argue with her, Mildred. I've decided not to go, after all. I just don't feel like making

boys

at his wristwatch), it's 4:40 now. Where's the Adjustment Office? Quick!

Assistant. Sorry. *(Big smile)* The Adjustment Office is located on the lower level, to the right of the escalator, sir.

Father *(lurching awkwardly to his feet).* Well, I think we'd better go down there too and cash in your ticket. This plane business is too risky. You can make the six o'clock train— and your mother will be happier with that arrangement, I'm sure.

Student *(disgustedly whining).* Aw gee, Pop. Why get so excited, just because the plane is a few minutes late. Mom doesn't even know it . . . *(Voice dying out in a grumble as he stoops to pick up his bag, etc.)*

Old Man's Son *(to Assistant, exasperatedly).* Look, we can't get down there and back in five minutes. Why can't you phone them or mark his ticket here somehow so he can make that plane?

Assistant *(shrugging his shoulders).* Sorry! The regulations say we're not permitted . . .

Old Man's Son *(interrupting impatiently and shouting in annoyance).* Yeah, yeah . . . I know, but look, there isn't time for all that now!

Old Man *(wearily grabbing his son's arm).* Aw, don't argue with him, Al. I don't think I want to go now anyway.

mixed

Woman #2   *(consolingly to Woman #1).* Well, if you don't feel like it, Martha . . . maybe you should wait a couple of days. After all, there's no rush. Let's go down to that Adjustment Office and get your refund.

Mother   *(to son).* Yes, and we'll go there too. Come along, Stanley. We'll get your refund and I'll phone your father to get you a seat on the evening train.

Student   Aw gee, Mom . . .

Woman #1 and Woman #2 start walking toward the door stage right, followed by Mother and sulking son.

Businessman   *(turning to follow them, stops just beyond the Agent's desk, turns, looks at Assistant and mimicking her false smile).* Sorry!

All exit stage right.

Agent   *(into microphone).* Attention, please. May I have your attention. Flight 641 to New York is now arriving and will load at Gate 3. Thank you.

Assistant   *(glancing around the waiting room and then sadly to Agent).* Well, it seems that we have nobody leaving on that flight now.

Agent   *(drily).* They all changed their minds?

Assistant   *(apologetically).* I guess so. *(Then, illogically)* Sorry! *(Mechanically smiles)*

Agent   *(looking disgustedly at her).* What happened to that guy in the uniform who was reading the paper?

girls

the trip now . . . after all of this . . . this confusion.

Mother   *(emphatically to daughter).* And you're not going either. I've made up my mind and that settles it!

Businesswoman   *(pushing her way through).* I'm so sorry. *(Icily, to Agent and Assistant as she reaches their desk)* I don't suppose you have the slightest interest, but since I've taken care of my business by phone, I won't have to waste any more time on your delightful service.

Woman #2   *(consolingly to Woman #1).* Well, if you don't feel like it, Martha . . . maybe you should wait a couple of days. After all, there's no rush. Let's go down to that Adjustment Office and get your refund.

Mother   *(to daughter).* Yes, and we'll go there too. Come along, Mildred. We'll get your refund and I'll phone your father to get you a seat on the evening train.

Coed   Oh, Mo-ther . . .

Woman #1 and Woman #2 start walking toward the door stage right, followed by Mother and daughter grumbling.

Businesswoman   *(turning to follow them).* Me too. *(Turns back toward Agent's desk, waves goodbye mockingly, and with imitation of Assistant's mechanical smile)* Sorry!

All exit stage right.

Agent   *(into microphone).* Attention, please. May I have your attention.

boys

(Sighing) I'm too tired . . . with all this confusion . . . to take the plane.

Father   *(to son).* You'd better not take the plane either. It's just too much of a headache.

Businessman   *(pushing his way to the desk).* 'Scuse me, gents. *(To Agent and Assistant).* Just thought you two might like to know that I got the deal settled by long distance phone so I don't have to fool around with you people anymore.

Old Man's Son   *(agreeing).* Sure, Pa. There's no rush and maybe in a couple of days you'll feel more like going. *(Leads his father toward the chairs)* You can sit down here while I go down to that Adjustment Office to get your refund. *(Old Man shakes his head negatively and steers his son toward the gate.)*

Father.   O.K., Stan—let's get going. I'll get your refund and call up to get you a seat on the evening train. You'd better phone your mother to kind of reassure her.

Old Man and his son start walking toward the door stage right, followed by Father and his son.

Student   *(sulking and grumbling.)* O.K., Pop—although I sure did want to ride that jet.

Businessman   *(turning to follow them, stops just beyond Agent's desk, turns, looks at Assistant and mimicking his false smile).* Sorry!

mixed

Assistant (*glancing around the room again*). Oh . . . he's still there. (*Gets up and hurries over to Man in Uniform who continues to read the paper and eat peanuts*) Sir (*mechanically smiles*), Flight 641 to New York is now loading.

Man in Uniform (*shrugging*). Yeah. (*Continues to read, then after a pause*) So what?

Assistant (*puzzled*). But . . . what flight do you have a ticket for, sir?

Man in Uniform (*looking up*). Ticket? Me? I'm not waiting for any flight. Look, sister, I drive an airport bus (*looking at wristwatch*) and my shift doesn't begin 'til 5. (*Pointedly*) I'm trying to catch up on the ball scores and absorb a little more of this air-conditioning . . . so if you don't mind . . . (*Turns back to his newspaper*)

Assistant, thoroughly deflated, walks slowly back to the desk and shakes her head negatively at Agent.

Agent (*in a loud voice over the microphone*). Attention please. May I have your attention. Flight 641 . . .

CURTAIN

Glossary

all right, all right—expression of annoyance at statement of the obvious

anything—a plane of any kind

girls

Flight 641 to New York is now arriving and will load at Gate 3. Thank you.

Assistant (*glancing around the waiting room and then sadly to Agent*). Well, it seems that we have nobody leaving on that flight now.

Agent (*drily*). They all changed their minds?

Assistant (*apologetically*). I guess so. (*Then, illogically*) Sorry! (*Mechanically smiles*)

Agent. But what happened to that girl in the uniform . . . the one who was reading the paper?

Assistant (*glancing quickly around the waiting room*). Oh . . . she's still here. (*Gets up and hurries over to Woman in Uniform who sits with pencil poised over a folded newspaper.*) Miss (*mechanically*), Flight 641 to New York is now loading.

Woman in Uniform (*shrugging and without looking up*). Really! (*Pauses while she writes on the newspaper*) I couldn't care less.

Assistant (*puzzled*) But . . . what flight do you have a ticket for, miss?

Woman in Uniform (*looking up*). Ticket? Me? But I'm not waiting for any flight. I'm on duty at the Traveler's Aid desk at 5 (*looks at wristwatch and then, pointedly*), and I would like to finish this crossword puzzle . . . so if you don't mind. (*Turns back to her newspaper and*

boys

All exit stage right.

Agent (*into microphone*). Attention, please. May I have your attention. Flight 641 to New York is now arriving and will load at Gate 3. Thank you.

Assistant (*glancing around the waiting room and then sadly to Agent*). Well, it seems that we have nobody leaving on that flight now.

Agent (*drily*). They all changed their minds?

Assistant (*shrugging his shoulders*). Looks like it. (*Nodding toward the departing group*) They're all heading for the Adjustment Office.

Agent. What about that guy in the uniform . . . (*Nodding toward Man in Uniform*) reading the paper over there?

Assistant (*glancing at Man in Uniform, shrugs, gets up and goes over to him. He continues to read his newspaper and eat peanuts*). Flight 641 to New York is now loading, sir.

Man in Uniform (*shrugging*). Yeah. (*Continues to read, then after a pause*) So what?

Assistant (*puzzled*). But . . . er . . . haven't you got a ticket for that flight, sir?

Man in Uniform (*looking up*). Ticket? Me? I'm not waiting for any flight. Look, fella, I drive an airport bus (*looking at wristwatch*) and my shift doesn't begin 'til 5. (*Pointedly*) I'm

mixed

aw / ɔɔ /—expression of disappointment or frustration

aw come on—stop trying to fool me

ball scores—scores of the major baseball games

beg your pardon—courtesy form of *excuse me*

booths—telephone booths

bravado—pretended bravery typical of boys

break a five—exchange $5 for smaller money

can make that one—will be on time to get on it

catch up on—to acquire knowledge or experience after some postponement of it

change—money of smaller denominations

come off it—a slang expression meaning *don't pretend*

count on—rely on, depend on

damn it—used by Businessman, expresses his annoyance

damned—an expression of annoyance or disgust (profanity); used by Businessman, expresses his annoyance

escalator—a moving stairway found in large buildings

fool around with—be involved with, have dealings with

for heaven's sake—an expression of annoyance

frostily—inconsiderately

gee—expression of excitement or sometimes enthusiasm, very commonly used by children

here you are—an expression calling attention when giving or presenting something

hold you up—delay you

girls

reads mumbling) H-m-m, a five-letter expression of regret—*(reflecting)* must be S-O-R-R-Y.

Assistant, thoroughly deflated, walks slowly back to the desk and shakes her head negatively at Agent.

Agent   *(in a loud voice over the microphone).* Attention please. May I have your attention. Flight 641 . . .

CURTAIN

Glossary

doesn't look like anything of the kind—does not look like it at all

don't you think—an abbreviated form of *don't you think so?*, meaning *isn't it true?*

h-m-m-m /hūm/—an expression of reflection, speculation, or thought

I couldn't care less—I don't care about it at all; I'm not interested

making such a fuss—behaving so excitedly

really!—an ironic or mock expression of disinterest, usually spoken with pitch rise

Travelers' Aid—a voluntary organization to help travelers. Members can be found in most large train stations, bus depots, or airline terminals. They will help travelers buy travel tickets, find hotel or restaurant accommodations, arrange for a taxi, give directions, make telephone calls, and furnish all sorts of other services. Members who speak foreign languages meet arriving travelers who do not speak English.

boys

trying to catch up on the ball scores and absorb a little more of this air-conditioning . . . so if you don't mind . . . *(turns back to his newspaper)*

Assistant, thoroughly deflated, walks slowly back to the desk and shakes his head negatively at Agent.

Agent   *(in a loud voice over the microphone).* Attention please. May I have your attention. Flight 641 . . .

CURTAIN

Glossary

always the way—always true, so, the same

cash in your ticket—get refund for the ticket

catch it—hear it

everything will work out—finally everything will be good

get it—understand it, hear it

how come?—why?

I sure did want—I wanted very much

jet—airplane drive by a jet engine

look—sentence introducer to give a kind of emphasis to what follows

make that plane—catch that plane, be on time for the plane

Mom/mam/—colloquial term of address or reference to your mother

nope / nowp /—colloquial form of *no*

old stuff—old-fashioned, out-of-date

Pa—familiar, colloquial term of address or reference to your father

risky—dangerous

mixed

junk—various kinds of small articles, any worthless thing

lower level—first floor (often a kind of lobby or entrance in a large building)

make it—be there, or sometimes it means *catch* as when Woman #2 says, "You can make that one easily."

may've / mey+əv/—a colloquial contraction of *may have*

Mom/mam/—a common, intimate way to address one's mother

now look—an expression indicating mild annoyance or resistance

oh—expression of surprise

oh dear—a mild exclamation of concern

pay phones—telephones operated by deposit of coins

Pop—a common, intimate way to address one's father

refund—return of money

say, look—expression to arouse or focus attention; it may convey some slight annoyance

'scuse me—a common colloquial abbreviation of *excuse me*

set down—landed or crashed

shift—a period of work, usually eight hours

shoulda/šuda/—a colloquial contraction of *should have*

sister—a slang term used in addressing a girl, particularly when annoyed with her

so what?—an expression of disinterest, lack of concern

s'pose—suppose

take it so hard—become so disturbed

that's ancient history—that is outdated, old-

girls

uh-huh / ə̃ + hə̃/—an expression of agreement meaning *yes*

what a nerve!—expression of resentment by someone who feels imposed upon

mixed

fashioned, no longer popular; this is the typically exaggerated usage of the adolescent or teenager

there's no rush—we are not in a hurry

thoroughly deflated—disappointed

worried sick—very worried

boys

too much of a headache—too much trouble and worry

Structure

1. The structures to be found in the dialogue of this staging represent fairly standard syntactic patterns of colloquial usage. Yet since the setting of the staging is a public place we can expect much mixing of idiom as well as many language features representing several different social levels.

    In any event, there is a considerable amount of elision going beyond even that reflected in the ordinary use of contractions. Thus, we find the Businessman using the quite common shortening of the courteous *excuse me* to " 'scuse me," while the Man in Uniform shortens *suppose* in "I s'pose" and *you* in "y'know." In all instances, the unstressed vowel follows its normal tendency in English to approximate the schwa/ə/ and with less care, perhaps in hasty speech, even the sound of the schwa may vanish. Such extreme sound suppression in rapid elision may not only produce the collapsed forms of the Man in Uniform, but may even result in omission of the auxiliary verbs, as in the Businessman's "I got to get that 641," instead of the fuller *I've got to get that 641*. We also note that although the mother uses the standard contraction in "I should've had Stanley take the train" and the Man in Uniform does so in suggesting "May'uv had to set down someplace," the Businessman further reduces the construction as he states, "Shoulda taken the train." In this last instance, the extensive elision plus the truncation brought about by the omission of the subject may make this statement very puzzling to a foreigner who has not been trained to recognize that /sŭd hæv/ may become /sŭd əv/ or even /sŭdə/, particularly with rather casual and somewhat careless native speakers.

2. Note that very often the single noun or verb, usually pronounced with a rising intonation, may be used colloquially to convey a kind of question. That is, the speaker picks out a single word from a statement he has just heard and repeats it as a kind of greatly truncated rhetorical question which is either then embedded in a more fully formed question, as when Woman #1 says, "Call? What call?" or when the Student says, "Him? He doesn't look like a pilot to me."

3. We find another example of the question formed by the statement voiced with a rising intonation contour in the Agent's, "They all changed their minds?" Most textbooks would, of course, show the context in the form *Did they all change their minds?* although the statement as given in the dialogue of this staging is very common colloquially. In fact, the statement is sometimes used, as a question, without the rising intonation contour, as if it were presented as a possibility to be either refuted or assented to. And sometimes an unstressed *then*, added at the end of the statement, serves to signal the question. But in whatever form, the statement elicits a negative positive option for reply.

    In any event, it is not at all clear that the statement is a truncated form rather than a full form stylistic variant and the foreigner may have to depend on the so-called metalinguistic context—in this case, perhaps, a quizzical facial expression or posture of the speaker—to determine whether a question has been posed. It might also be noted that this form of question is often used in a sequential context as a means to corroborate an earlier statement. But here again, we find support for the basic argument of this text: communication is a product of integrated behavior patterns of which language is only a part.

4. In the case of the Businessman's, "About that change—," we have a question implied in the form of a kind of reminder. That is, the statement—which might as commonly occur as *What about that change?* with the introductory interrogative *what* signaling the question—is a greatly truncated form of something like *What are you going to do about that change?* or *What about giving me that change that I asked for?* or *Please give me that change I asked for*. The teacher must try to make clear that this form is used when an earlier request has been ignored.

5. Note that the use of *just* in the Mother's "Now just see what's happened" may be thought of as a mild intensifier to increase the emphasis of the imperative *see* and seems to be somewhat

more common, as a means of emphasis, in women's speech than in men's.

6. The teacher might point out the sharp contrast between the mechanical, formal speech of the airline employees and the informal speech of the passengers. Student attention should be called to the fact that when speaking together, rather than to the customers, the airline employees also speak quite informally. That is, students should be alerted that there are levels of usage dependent upon the social situation as well as the social relation of conversants, and that context must be considered in these broader terms. Playing a role in staged communication, a student will have to mimic various patterns which project the integration of that social situation and social relationship, thereby becoming sensitized to the need for close observation.

Cultural Values

1. Reflected very strongly in this staging is the high valuation placed on time and the sense of urgency generated by that valuation. The businessman becomes quite excited upon learning he has missed the plane and the two women are also seriously concerned although we notice that the man apparently could have concluded his business by telephone from the outset and Woman #2 finally points out that "after all, there's no rush." This may seem contradictory or paradoxical and the teacher will have to impress his students with the fact that concern with time may serve to explain a great deal of otherwise seemingly unmotivated behavior. The expression, "Time is money" is not only widely accepted as wisdom but is indicative of what might be termed a national attitude. We see, in this play, how ill-at-ease people are who unexpectedly must wait, as if they feel somehow guilty about wasting the time. As a kind of container of experience time must be filled. Few people can feel completely satisfied merely to sit and wait for time to pass. We note that Woman #1 apparently has time to waste for "there's no rush." The businessman is able to gloat that he did not have to waste time taking the trip. In real life many people in such a situation will devise unnecessary activities and tasks to fill the time so as not to feel they are wasting it.

2. Although it should not be assumed that foreign students are discourteous, it is clear that they will appear so unless they learn both the situations requiring expressions of courtesy, and the precise forms that expression must take; both situations and the forms of expression are likely to differ from those of their native cultures, since the social values are quite different.

    As for the oral expressions, we notice that in this play *'scuse me* (excuse me) and *thank you* are used and it is well for the student to realize that such expressions are likely to be more commonly used in public with strangers than between intimate friends or relatives.

    But truly "actions speak louder than words" and we also note that the student immediately stoops to pick up the fallen umbrella and magazine for Woman #2. Boys are usually taught to pick up things accidentally dropped by women although it is not likely that a woman will pick up something dropped by a man unless he is very old, obviously sick, or perhaps extremely fat. We also notice that the man in a hurry excuses himself for pushing ahead of the people in line. Usually in a public place, at street bus stops, etc., people form a line for service. Someone trying to push ahead of people standing on such a line is usually thought impolite and often people will become angry at such behavior. Students will need a great deal of practice in linking the situation, the words, and the action.

3. Part of the high national valuation of time, noted above, underlies the boy's comment about trains. Actually most of the railroads in the United States have reduced or abandoned passenger service and trains are used largely for shipment of freight, since most people want to get to their destination as quickly as possible. Trolleys or streetcars have been replaced by buses almost everywhere throughout the country. Although long distance bus traveling is still quite common it is patronized largely for economy reasons or by a few people who are

interested in sightseeing. Personally owned automobiles are very commonly used for long trips, on relatively short trips, and in daily commuting, even where subways and buses are available, since most people prefer privacy and the convenience of arriving and departing whenever they choose rather than keeping to a schedule. And again perhaps we see the American concern with time in attempts to control it rather than to be subjected to it. As we can see from this staging, however, most long distance traveling is done by plane; since it is faster less time is wasted in traveling.

General Comment

1. It is somewhat difficult to establish the scenes in this staging, since the actions and lines of various characters are closely interwovern. However, an analysis of character relations discloses that there is a kind of alternation of dialogue exchanges between Woman #1 and Woman #2. Finally, all characters—except the Man in Uniform, briefly introduced in an exchange with the Mother—come together and the situation closes with the revelation, at the end, of the identity of the person in uniform.

   These exchanges can be rehearsed as separate scenes, but care must be taken to insure that the atmosphere of interruption and disjointedness is sustained. Many interruptions, both oral and physical, distract a foreign student of another language, and he must be taught to sustain his attention even when surrounded by such distraction.

   Proper pacing will be particularly important. Since all the passengers are apparently in a hurry, yet nervous because the plane is late, the pace of their dialogue is fairly brisk throughout the staging. On the other hand, as the situation is quite routine for the airline employees—and for the person in uniform, who is not interested in catching a plane—their dialogue is projected at a much slower pace.

   This staging requires more coordination of movement and speech than the earlier stagings have. Students must be taught to synchronize the two behavior patterns rather than to alternate them. They must be prepared for the fact that there is a lot of merely nervous movement and dysfunctional activity in such a situation, rather than the calm resignation some of them may be used to. This does not mean that the student must actually become nervous or lose the precious equanimity he has learned in his own culture. But he certainly must recognize that his failure to behave the same as others around him may weaken communication and, in any case, he must be prepared to confront excitable people in such a situation. He must even recognize that failure to register excitement in a situation considered excitable may make him seem unusual; he will have to learn what is thought important in the society and by what patterns that evaluation is made manifest. He will have to mimic all patterns to communicate.

3. The atmosphere of bustle and excitement also tends to make announcements incomprehensible in large, highly functional buildings, such as airline terminals, in which the acoustics are likely to be poor. Moreover, there is much distraction and people are preoccupied with their excited anticipation of what is for many of them the fairly unusual or even novel experience of long distance traveling. And they may also be unfamiliar with expressions used by people working as airline or other transportation employees. These employees, on the other hand, are inclined to be rather careless in pronunciation, since they may assume the expressions are easily understood merely because it is routine for them. However, it should be recognized that members of large, bureaucratic organizations may tend to behave rather mechanically. They often are quite callously impersonal and frequently project a kind of insincere courtesy, almost as if they felt annoyed by customers as a kind of necessary evil. We note some of this in the behavior of the Agent and Assistant in this staging. We also note that the customers, such as the Businessman and Woman #2, may tend to resent being treated in this way and sometimes openly voice their annoyance and discontent. This resentment adds to the atmosphere of tension.

The students must be made to feel this tension and, to implement this goal, tape recordings of loud announcements of various kinds can be played during rehearsals and students can, for instance, be required to carry various bags and bundles which will need their attention. They can also be required to mimic various nervous mannerisms although they should be required to enunciate with acceptable clarity and should suitably synchronize their movements and their speech. In trying to generate the necessary atmosphere, the teacher who is staging communication is not so much concerned that the student audience will feel the authenticity of the situation as he is that the student actors can feel immersed in a real-life situation.

Notes on Adaptation

1. In adapting this staging we must recognize that once again we are dealing with fairly formal, public behavior. Although there is, of course, some familiarity and intimacy in the dialogue exchanges between parent and child, between two close friends, and between two employees who work with each other daily, all of these people are aware that since they are in public they must be somewhat more subdued in behavior than they would be if interacting privately. Moreover, there should be a noticeable shift in dialogue and attitude to differentiate the exchange between strangers and between people related or familiar with each other.

2. In commenting on earlier stagings I have pointed out that men favor the more aggressive direct statement forms while women, in speaking, are likely to use question structures, such as the Woman in Uniform, "I guess railroads aren't always on time either, are they?" or the Businesswoman's consoling, "They must have lots of flights, don't you think?" This example also contains a truncated form of what usually is "Don't you think so" which, in turn, is really an elliptical form of "Don't you think they have more flights?"

    We also note that women make extensive use of *just* as intensifier, as in the Businesswoman, "That makes me just furious." *Such* and *so* are other words often used, particularly in combinations, as modifiers by women. We find *just* as feminine intensifier in the Businesswoman's "I've just got to be in New York" and *simply* serves a similar function in the Businesswoman's "I simply must catch that 641."

    Really in the Woman in Uniform's "I really don't know" is yet another intensifier favored to a greater extent by women than by men, although this last example often seems to be used as much to express a kind of annoyance as for emphasis. Certainly words such as *lovely* and *delightful*, are more likely to be used by women, particularly when used ironically, as when the girl student says to her mother, "Yes, the train would be lovely," and the Businesswoman says, ". . . I won't have to waste any more time on your delightful service." Students should be advised that in both quoted instances the usage is ironic, but these words and others, such as *marvelous* and *gorgeous*, are generally part of women's rather than of men's usage.

3. While dealing with lexical matters, the teacher should call attention to the fact that a kind of icy, sarcastic snappishness, rather than a thunderous denunciation, characterizes much feminine usage, as in the Businesswoman's sarcastic "I don't suppose you have the *slightest* interest, but . . . ." We also catch a note of sarcastic disdain in the coed's somewhat stilted rejection, "She doesn't look like anything of the kind to me," which would more commonly appear as *She doesn't look like it to me.* Here the annoyed girl seems to be attempting to mask her emotion by using somewhat formal language. This usage is a typical tactic of the teenage girl, since a more assertive, direct attitude might be interpreted as immature ignorance of socially approved behavior patterns of her sex.

4. Adapting a part for the opposite sex often involves more changes in intonation than in lexicon or syntax, although it would be impractical—even if possible—to attempt notation of all the delicate nuances involved in this intonation. The teacher will have to be alert, nevertheless, to these changes in usage if

suitable mimicry is to be required. Often reinforcing intonational patterns are sex linked exclamations, such as the Businesswoman's "Oh, no!" expressing a refusal to believe or accept what has been stated, or her "Oh, now look," expressing a kind of opposition and warning of resistance, and her drawn-out wailing "Oh-h-h" of frustration and annoyance.

Moreover, we find that girls and women may make use of a kind of peevish whining tone to express annoyance, frustration, or opposition, while men are likely either to remain silent or openly and directly to make their annoyance or frustration apparent, sometimes by use of profanity. Occasionally the feminine whining tone makes for a kind of drawing out of enunciation until juncture and stress are considerably distorted, as in the coed's "Mo-ther" /³mə-²ðər.

5. Finally, men tend to make far less use of gestures while speaking than women do; gesture is a quite acceptable aspect of the feminine behavior pattern, as is clear from the Businesswoman's derisive, sarcastic goodbye wave to the Assistant, for instance.

6. Earlier reference has been made to a kind of bureaucratic objectivity and impersonality which explains many of the peculiarities of dialogue exchange in which personnel of large organizations are involved. The adaptation of this staging for an all male cast shows this bureaucratic impersonality reflected in the reference by the Agent's Assistant to the need for strict observance of regulations: "That's what the regulations say . . . sorry." Although many foreign students are quite accustomed to such an attitude, others may assume it reflects some personal animosity or may feel it is their limited ability to communicate which prevents them from circumventing the bureaucrat's appeal to regulations. It is particularly important, therefore, that the student learn to recognize such patterns of behavior as well as those which he can use in combating them. Students should be particularly advised that bribery or references to one's family are not likely to prove effective and may even lead to further stiffening of the bureaucrat's attitude.

7. Teachers should sensitize students to the relative differences of courtesy in softened speech to members of the opposite sex as contrasted with the direct and sometimes blunt sounding statement used in speaking to a member of one's own sex. This rather stark and unsoftened directness, the sharply reduced use of courtesy forms are particularly obvious in dialogue exchanges between men in this staging.

8. It should be noted that the use of "young man" or "young lady" by old people, particularly in addressing young people, can often imply an awareness of age difference and the fact that more respectful or deferential treatment is desired.

9. Attention is again called to the tendency—particularly of men—to use truncated forms colloquially. In this staging we have examples of the common omission of subject in such lines as "Can't hear him," "Can't count on them," and "Doesn't seem possible." Note also that omission of the article, as in "Weather looks pretty good," is another common type of colloquial abbreviation.

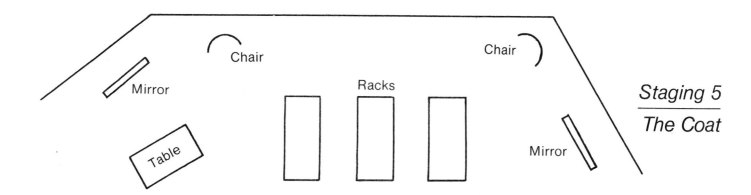

SETTING

Randall's, a typical exclusive department store. Several low racks containing coats are lined up stage center from upstage to down-stage. There is a chair or two and, if possible, a couple of full length mirrors on the walls left and right. As the curtain rises, a sale is being concluded. Another customer is trying on various coats from a rack, stage left. Another customer is standing behind another rack apparently examining one of the coats.

Mixed cast	Girls' cast	Boys' cast

Mixed cast

Salesgirl (Miss Roberts)
Woman Customer A
Dept. Manager (Mr. Jordan)
Man Customer B
Woman Customer C
Store Manager (Mr. Hansen)
Store Detective (Dan Karsh)

Girls' cast

Salesgirl (Miss Roberts)
Woman Customer A
Dept. Manager (Mrs. Jordan)
Woman Customer B
Woman Customer C
Store Manager (Mrs. Hansen)
Store Detective (Doris Karsh)

Boys' cast

Salesman (Mr. Roberts)
Man Customer A
Dept. Manager (Mr. Jordan)
Man Customer B
Man Customer C
Store Manager (Mr. Hansen)
Store Detective (Dan Karsh)

Salesgirl.   Will that be all then, ma'am? _(Pencil poised over her order book)_
Woman Customer A.   Yes, I think so. Charge it . . . I have my plate here in my bag. _(Rummaging through her pocketbook)_ Well, that's funny . . .

Salesgirl.   Will that be all then, ma'am? _(Pencil poised over her order book)_
Woman Customer A.   Yes, I think so. Charge it . . . I have my plate here in my bag. _(Rummaging through her pocketbook)_ Well, that's funny . . .

Salesman.   Will that be all then sir? _(Pencil poised over his order book)_
Man Customer A.   Yes, I think so. Charge it. I have the charge plate here somewhere. _(Pulls out his wallet and looks through it, frowning)_ . . . Right

101

mixed	*girls*	*boys*

mixed

Perhaps I left it in my coat pocket. Oh . . . *(looking around)* where is my coat? Where did I leave it? *(Walks from place to place looking for her coat)*

Salesgirl   *(writing in her order book).* It must be right here someplace . . . Just a minute, madam, I'll look around. *(Closes the book and walks around the clothes rack, glances at the two chairs. Puzzled when she doesn't find the coat)* I'm sorry but I don't seem to see it anyplace. *(Frowning)*

Woman Customer A.   I can't understand what could have happened to it. I put it down just a moment ago. *(Hurries around the rack, following the same route the salesgirl had taken. Returns to center stage, wringing her hands)* Oh I hope it hasn't been stolen.

Salesgirl   *(leafing through all the coats on the rack).* It may have gotten hung up here by mistake; don't worry, we'll find it, I'm sure. *(After going through all the coats on the racks, the salesgirl looks perplexed and slightly frightened)*

Woman Customer A   *(beginning to sob with increasing loudness).* Oh, what am I going to do. My coat has been taken . . . I'm sure of it.

Dept. Manager   *(walking by upstage is attracted by the sobbing sound and walks quickly stage right where the customer is standing with the salesgirl).* Why, what seems to be the

girls

Perhaps I left it in my coat pocket. Oh . . . *(looking around)* Where did I leave it? *(Walks from place to place looking for her coat)*

Salesgirl   *(writing in her order book).* It must be right here someplace . . . Just a minute, madam, I'll look around. *(Closes the book and walks around the clothes rack, glances at the two chairs. Puzzled, when she doesn't find the coat)* I'm sorry but I don't seem to see it anyplace. *(Frowning)*

Woman Customer A.   I can't understand what could have happened to it. I put it down just a moment ago. *(Hurries around the rack, following the same route the salesgirl had taken. Returns to center stage, wringing her hands)* Oh, I hope it hasn't been stolen.

Salesgirl   *(leafing through all the coats on the rack).* It may have gotten hung up here by mistake; don't worry, we'll find it, I'm sure. *(After going through all the coats on the racks, the salesgirl looks perplexed and slightly frightened)*

Woman Customer A   *(beginning to sob with increasing loudness).* Oh, what am I going to do. My coat has been taken . . . I'm sure of it.

Dept. Manager   *(walking by upstage is attracted by the sobbing sounds and walks quickly stage right where the customer is standing with the salesgirl).* Why, what seems to be the trouble here? What's happened?

boys

here . . . someplace. H-m-m . . . That's funny. It must be in my overcoat pocket. Where is my overcoat? *(Looking around)*

Salesman   *(writing in his order book).* Be with you in a minute, sir. *(Closing book, walks around the clothes rack, glances at the two chairs. Puzzled when he can't find the coat)* Sorry, sir, but I don't see it.

Man Customer A.   H-m-m! *(Frowning)* Wonder what happened to it. I just put it down here a few minutes ago. *(Hurries around the rack, following the same route Salesman had taken)* It's a fairly new coat too . . . so I hope nobody stole it.

Salesman.   Could have been hung up by mistake. I'll check the racks quickly. *(Smiles at Customer and begins checking through the clothing on the racks)* It's got to be here somewhere. *(After going through all the coats, Salesman frowns perplexedly and seems somewhat frustrated)*

Man Customer A   *(scowling and muttering).* It looks to me like somebody walked off with it, damn it! *(Pauses as he looks around)* Yeah, I'm pretty sure somebody's picked it up. *(Speaking loudly)* Damn it . . . A brand new coat too, almost. You can't take your eyes off anything for a minute.

Dept. Manager   *(walking by upstage is attracted by the loud voices and walks briskly to stage right where Customer

mixed

trouble here? *(To the salesgirl)* What's happened, Miss Roberts?

Salesgirl *(aside to Manager, so as not to alarm the customer further).* This customer's coat seems to have been picked up.

Dept. Manager *(shocked).* Nonsense, Miss Roberts. That's impossible! We've never had such a situation at Randall's. Have you looked around? It must be somewhere. *(Goes around the rack, tracing the same course the salesgirl and customer had taken. Returns perplexed. By now the customer is crying loudly)*

Woman Customer A *(sobbing).* My gorgeous coat's gone. Oh, I certainly never expected that this would happen at Randall's ... such a good quality store ... Why, I've always shopped here. Who would have thought there could be thieves here? I only took it off ten minutes ago. Just imagine, thieves in a store like this. *(Wails loudly, shaking her head in disbelief)*

Dept. Manager *(flustered and trying to quiet the customer).* Now, now, madam. This is certainly regrettable, but I'm sure you realize that Randall's will do everything possible to make the matter right. *(Customer continues to sob inconsolably. Dept. Manager desperately makes another quick search; as he passes the man customer who has been standing at the other rack he says)* Did you happen to see

girls

Salesgirl *(aside to Manager, so as not to alarm the customer further).* This customer's coat seems to have been picked up.

Dept. Manager. Oh, that can't be, can it, Miss Roberts? Why it seems impossible. Not at Randall's certainly. *(To the salesgirl)* Have you looked around? *(Briskly retraces the route taken earlier by the customer and the salesgirl, but returns perplexed)* I simply cannot understand it. *(By now the customer is crying loudly)*

Woman Customer A *(sobbing).* My gorgeous coat's gone. Oh, I certainly never expected that this would happen at Randall's ... such a good quality store ... Why, I've always shopped here. Who would have thought there could be thieves here? I only took it off ten minutes ago. Just imagine, thieves in a store like this. *(Wails loudly, shaking her head in disbelief)*

Dept. Manager *(soothingly).* Now, now, dear. Everything's going to be all right. You know Randall's will do everything possible to make matters right, don't you? *(Customer continues to sob inconsolably and Manager desperately makes another quick search. As she passes another woman customer who has been standing at the other rack)* Pardon me, but I wonder if you happened to see the lady's coat, madam?

Woman Customer B *(thoughtfully,*

boys

is standing with Salesman) Something wrong here? *(To Salesman)* What happened, Mr. Roberts?

Salesman *(aside to Manager so not to arouse Customer further).* This guy's coat may've been picked up.

Dept. Manager *(shocked and scolding).* Nonsense, Mr. Roberts. That kind of thing doesn't happen at Randall's. It's probably around somewhere. Let's go through the racks in case it got hung up by mistake. *(Quickly leafs through the clothing on all the racks and returns, frowning in puzzlement. By now Customer is obviously annoyed and angered)*

Man Customer A *(shouting in annoyance).* That coat was almost new too. Stolen—in a place like this. I've come in here for years and I never figured there were crooks here. I took my eyes off it only a couple of minutes and ph-t-t ... it was gone. I never expected that in a place like this, believe me.

Dept. Manager *(frustrated yet trying to calm Customer).* O.K., but let's not get excited, sir. I know how you feel about it and, although it might not seem very consoling, I guarantee Randall's will make it right with you. *(Customer continues to grumble and manager desperately makes another quick search. As he passes Man Customer B who has been standing at the other rack)* Say, you didn't happen to see his *(nodding toward Customer A)*

mixed

the lady's coat sir?

Man Customer B *(thoughtfully).* No-o-o . . . unless it could be this one. *(Picks up a coat that has been lying across the rack in front of him)*

Dept. Manager *(relieved).* That must be it! *(Grabs the coat and rushes over to Customer A with it. Smiling, he holds it out)* This is your coat, isn't it, madam?

Woman Customer A *(still sobbing, looks up).* Why . . . why . . . it is! *(Stops sobbing and, smiling happily, reaches for the coat)* Where did you find it? *(Looks at the coat in amazement)* Oh . . . I'm so happy to see it again!

Dept. Manager *(helping her into the coat).* Well, it was just misplaced. It had to be here somewhere. *(Having helped the customer into the coat)* There you are!

Woman Customer A *(happily).* Oh, thank you . . . thank you so much. I was so sure that such a thing couldn't happen at Randall's.

Dept. Manager *(beaming).* Certainly not. Well, goodbye, madam. *(Shakes the hand she extends and Customer A exits, stage left. Customer B, still standing near the rack, quickly and quietly exits, stage right)*

Customer C appearing from stage right, wandering coatless and looking at the coats on the racks. Stops at the rack where Customer B had been standing. Frowns,

girls

shaking her head negatively). Why, no, I wasn't paying much attention . . . unless it could be this one. *(Picks up a coat that has been lying across the rack in front of her)*

Dept. Manager. Oh, that must be it, I think. *(Grabs the coat and rushes over to Customer A with it. Smiling, she holds it up)* Now, here it is right here, madam, isn't it?

Woman Customer A *(still sobbing, looks up).* Why . . . why . . . it is! *(Stops sobbing and, smiling happily, reaches for the coat)* Where did you find it? *(Looks at the coat in amazement)* Oh . . . I'm so happy to see it again!

Dept. Manager *(helping the customer into the coat).* Why, of course you are. It had to be somewhere, didn't it? *(Having helped the customer into the coat)* There, now, everything is just fine again, hm-m-m?

Woman Customer A *(happily).* Oh, thank you . . . thank you so much. I was so sure that such a thing couldn't happen at Randall's.

Dept. Manager *(smiling).* Well, it certainly couldn't. *(Holding Customer A's elbow lightly)* I'm sure we won't have such unpleasantness when you come again. *(Smiling broadly)* Goodbye. *(Customer A exits, stage left. Customer B, still standing near the rack, quickly and quietly exits, stage right)*

Customer C appearing from stage right,

boys

coat, did you?

Man Customer B *(thoughtfully).* No-o-o . . . .unless it could be this one. *(Picks up a coat that had been lying across the rack in front of him)*

Dept. Manager *(relieved).* Phew! That must be it. *(Grabs the coat and rushes over to Customer A with it, holds it out)* I think I've got it.

Man Customer A *(turned the other way and still muttering, turns around and beaming, exclaims).* Yeah, it sure is! *(Big smile)* I thought I'd never see it again. Where was it? *(Sticks his arm into the sleeve and starts to put the coat on)*

Dept. Manager *(helping Customer into the coat).* I figured it had to turn up. We've never lost a coat; it just got misplaced *(Having helped Customer into the coat)* There you are; all set. And no hard feelings, I hope.

Man Customer A *(beaming).* Thanks a lot. I couldn't believe anything would be stolen in a place like this.

Dept. Manager. Not very likely, eh! Well, goodbye. *(Raises his right hand to his temple in a kind of half salute. Customer A exits stage left. Customer B exits quickly and quietly stage right)*

Customer C appearing from stage right, wandering coatless and looking at coats on the racks. Stops at the rack where Customer B had been standing. Frowns, looking puzzled, but walks quickly around the rack. Then, after looking across at the other rack

mixed

looking puzzled, but walks quickly around the rack. Then, after looking across at the other rack and glancing at the chairs, walks toward Manager who has been chatting quietly with Salesgirl, stage right downstage.

Woman Customer C *(pleasant although puzzled).* Pardon me, but I wonder if you've seen my coat? I left it over there while I was looking around. And now I don't see it anywhere.

Both Salesgirl and Dept. Manager, obviously stunned, turn toward her.

Salesgirl. Your coat? . . . It's . . . er . . . missing, you say?

Woman Customer C *(continuing to smile).* Yes, isn't that funny. I just put it down over there and now it seems to be gone. *(Puzzled)*

Dept. Manager *(astounded).* Your . . . your coat is missing. *(Louder and pitch rising)* Yours too!

Woman Customer C *(nodding).* Yes, it certainly seems to be. I just can't understand it. Why, it's ridiculous! *(As if suddenly aware of what the manager had said)* What do you mean, "yours too"?

Dept. Manager *(smiling mechanically and trying to control himself).* Well, we just had a little excitement in locating a coat which another customer thought was missing.

Woman Customer C *(coolly).* But I *know* I left my coat right here. So, apparently somebody hung it up—or something. *(Quickly looking through*

girls

wandering coatless and looking at the coats on the racks. Stops at the rack where Customer B had been standing. Frowns, looking puzzled, but walks quickly around the rack. Then, after looking across at the other rack and glancing at the chairs, walks toward Manager who has been chatting quietly with Salesgirl, stage right downstage.

Woman Customer C *(pleasant although puzzled).* Pardon me, but I wonder if you've seen my coat? I left it over there while I was looking around. And now I don't see it anywhere.

Both Salesgirl and Dept. Manager, obviously stunned, turn toward her.

Salesgirl. Your coat? . . . It's . . . er . . . missing, you say?

Woman Customer C *(continuing to smile).* Yes, isn't that funny. I just put it down over there and now it seems to be gone. *(Puzzled)*

Dept. Manager *(astounded).* Your . . . your coat is missing. *(Louder and pitch rising)* Yours too!

Woman Customer C *(nodding).* Yes, it certainly seems to be. I just can't understand it. Why, it's ridiculous! *(As if suddenly aware of what the Manager had said)* What do you mean, "yours too"?

Dept. Manager *(smiling mechanically and trying to control herself).* Well, we just had a little . . . er . . . difficulty locating a coat—which seemed to be missing. *(Laughs artificially trying to make light of the incident)*

boys

and glancing at the chairs, walks toward Dept. Manager who has been chatting quietly with Salesman, stage right downstage.

Man Customer C *(smiling).* Say, did you happen to see my coat? I left it over there while I was looking around, but I can't find it.

Both Salesman and Dept. Manager, obviously stunned, turn toward him.

Salesman. Your coat? . . . It's . . . er . . . missing, you say?

Dept. Manager *(smiling mechanically and trying to control himself).* Well, we just had a little excitement in locating a coat which another customer thought was missing.

Man Customer C *(a little annoyed).* Look, I left my coat right here. Maybe somebody hung it up. *(Quickly looking through the coats on the rack and scowling grumbles)* It's not here though. *(Frowns)*

Dept. Manager *(quietly yet with scarcely suppressed exasperation to Salesman).* Why are some days like this! Two of them within an hour!

Man Customer C *(completing his fruitless search and raising his voice in complaint).* Look, this is no joke, and I'm tired of fooling around. Let me speak to the Store Manager.

Dept. Manager. Certainly, sir . . . but I'm sure everything will be all right . . . if *(smiling mechanically but obviously suppressing his own exasper-*

mixed

the coats on the rack) No—it isn't there either.

Dept. Manager *(quietly yet with scarcely suppressed exasperation to Salesgirl).* Why are some days like this! Two of them within an hour!

Woman Customer C *(completing her fruitless search and speaking crisply in growing annoyance).* This is no longer funny and I've had just about enough. I'd like to speak to the Store Manager.

Dept. Manager Certainly madam . . . but I'm sure everything will be all right . . . if *(smiling mechanically but obviously suppressing his own exasperation)* we just remain . . . calm. *(To salesgirl)* Miss Roberts, please ask Mr. Hansen to come down for a moment. *(Salesgirl exits stage right)*

Woman Customer C *(seriously).* You say the same thing happened earlier today? Well, what was the outcome then?

Dept. Manager *(laughing in a hollow way).* Oh . . . the coat was found, of course. It had been somehow mislaid. Let's look through the coats on this other rack . . . just on the chance . . . *(They both go to the opposite rack and look through the coats)*

Store Manager *(appearing stage right, followed by the salesgirl).* What seems to be the trouble, Mr. Jordan?

Dept. Manager. Well, Mr. Hansen, this customer apparently left her coat here someplace . . . and now we can't find

girls

Woman Customer C *(coolly).* But I *know* I left my coat right here. So, apparently somebody hung it up—or something. *(Quickly looking through the coats on the rack)* No—it isn't there either.

Dept. Manager *(quietly yet with scarcely suppressed exasperation to Salesgirl).* Oh my, now we seem to have another one missing. It *is* a bad day isn't it?

Woman Customer C *(completing her fruitless search and speaking crisply in growing annoyance).* This is no longer funny and I've had just about enough. I'd like to speak to the Store Manager.

Dept. Manager Certainly, madam . . . but I'm sure everything will be all right. We'd just better be calm and not get . . . excited.

Woman Customer C *(seriously).* You say the same thing happened earlier today? Well, what was the outcome then?

Dept. Manager *(smiling mechanically).* Yes, but we found the coat, of course . . . Right where it was left. *(Reassuringly)* Don't worry. Let's look through the coats on the other rack. Just on the chance. *(They both go to the opposite rack and look through the coats)*

Store Manager *(appearing stage right, followed by the salesgirl).* What seems to be the trouble, Mrs. Jordan?

Dept. Manager. Well, Mrs. Hansen, this

boys

ation) we just remain . . . calm. *(To Salesman)* Mr. Roberts, please ask Mr. Hansen to come down for a moment. *(Salesman exits stage right)*

Man Customer C *(seriously).* Say, what happened to the other coat—the one you say was lost a while ago?

Dept. Manager *(casually, trying to sound unperturbed).* We found it. It was just mislaid somehow. I'll take another look through the coats on this other rack. There's a chance . . . *(He goes to the rack, followed by Customer C, and they paw through the coats)*

Store Manager *(appearing stage right, followed by Salesman).* What seems to be the trouble, Mr. Jordan?

Dept. Manager. Well, Mr. Hansen, this customer apparently left his coat here someplace . . . and now we can't find it.

Store Manager *(frowning).* Hm-m-m . . . that's odd . . . and Mr. Roberts tells me the same sort of problem developed earlier today. I suppose you've looked through all the coats on the racks? *(Looking at both Salesman and Dept. Manager)*

Dept. Manager *(nodding).* Not a sign of his coat.

Salesman. Yes, sir, we've looked everywhere. It's not like the other time . . . when Mr. Jordan found that blue coat for the man.

Store Manager *(to Jordan).* That one

mixed

it.

Store Manager *(frowning).* Hm-m-m ... that's odd ... and Miss Roberts tells me the same sort of problem developed earlier today. I suppose you've looked through all the coats on the racks? *(Looking at both the salesgirl and the department manager)*

Dept. Manager *(nodding).* Not a sign of her coat.

Salesgirl. Yes, sir, we've looked everywhere. It's not like the other time ... when Mr. Jordan found that blue coat for the lady.

Store Manager *(to Jordan).* That one was a blue coat that you gave to the other customer, eh, Jordan? And what color was *your* coat, madam? *(Turning to Customer C)*

Woman Customer C. Mine was blue too. A light blue, knobby wool coat, double breasted, with raglan sleeves.

Salesgirl *(surprised).* Why that's exactly like the coat that belonged to the other customer! *(Gloomily, with the vaguely uneasy realization that a serious error has been made)* ... the one ... that Mr. Jordan found ... and ... gave ... to that lady earlier.

Store Manager. Now wait a minute ... there's something very peculiar here. Jordan, how did you happen to locate that other coat?

Dept. Manager. Well, I was looking all through the racks ... and a

girls

customer apparently left her coat here someplace ... and now we can't find it.

Store Manager. This *is* odd, isn't it? And Miss Roberts tells me we had a similar problem a little earlier today. I suppose you've looked through all the coats on these racks, haven't you? *(Looking at both Salesgirl and Dept. Manager)*

Dept. Manager *(nodding).* Yes, we have, but there's not a sign of her coat, I'm afraid.

Salesgirl. Yes, Mrs. Hansen, we've looked everywhere. It's not like the other time ... when Mrs. Jordan found that blue coat for the lady.

Store Manager *(to Mrs. Jordan).* Then, you gave the other customer a blue coat, Mrs. Jordan? *(Turning to Customer C)* And what color was *your* coat, madam?

Woman Customer C. Mine was blue too. A light blue, knobby wool coat, double breasted, with raglan sleeves.

Salesgirl *(surprised).* Why that's exactly like the coat that belonged to the other customer! *(Gloomily, with the vaguely uneasy realization that a serious error has been made)* ... the one ... that Mrs. Jordan found ... and ... gave ... to that lady earlier.

Store Manager. Oh my, that does seem peculiar, doesn't it. *(Frowning)* I wonder how you happened to locate that other coat? *(To Mrs. Jordan)*

boys

was a blue coat that you gave to the other customer, eh, Jordan? And what color was *your* coat, sir? *(Turning to Customer C)*

Man Customer C. Mine was blue too. Kind of navy blue, fly front, sort of sporty.

Salesman *(frowning).* Say ... that's exactly like the coat that belonged to the other customer. *(Gloomily, as if beginning to realize disaster)* ... the one that ... Mr. Jordan found ... and gave to that fellow earlier.

Store Manager. Now wait a minute ... there's something very peculiar here. Jordan, how did you happen to locate that other coat?

Dept. Manager. Well, I was looking all through the racks ... and a customer—a man who was looking at some coats—spotted it.

Salesman. Yeah—the man handed the coat to Mr. Jordan and he took it to the customer *(shaking his head for emphasis)* ... and he was really glad to get that coat back!

Store Manager. Yes ... of course. *(Pause)* By the way, did he buy the coat he wanted, Mr. Roberts?

Salesman *(disappointed).* Well, no sir, he didn't ... he was so happy to get his coat back, he just left.

Store Detective *(enters from stage left, walking quickly).* Sorry for the delay, Mr. Hansen. Your secretary's call didn't reach me until I got to Sporting

mixed

customer—a man who was looking at some coats—spotted it.

Salesgirl *(brightening)*. That's right. The man handed the coat to Mr. Jordan and he took it to the customer. *(Smiling and enthusiastic)* Boy, was she happy to get her coat back!

Store Manager. Yes . . . of course. *(Pause)* By the way, did she buy the coat she wanted, Miss Roberts?

Salesgirl *(disappointed)*. Well, no sir, she didn't . . . she was so happy to get her coat back, she just left.

Store Detective *(enters from stage left, walking quickly)*. Sorry for the delay, Mr. Hansen. Your secretary's call didn't reach me until I got to Sporting Goods.

Dept. Manager *(to Customer C)*. This is Mr. Karsh, our store detective.

Store Manager *(to Store Detective)*. Dan, this customer seems to have lost her coat and this is the second time this morning that we've had this problem in this department. Oddly enough, blue coats have been involved both times.

Salesgirl *(chattily to Store Detective, as if to be helpful)*. Mr. Jordan found the first lady's coat—a knobby wool with raglan sleeves—and gave it back to the customer.

Store Detective *(to Dept. Manager)*. How did you know it was her coat?

Dept. Manager. Well, I brought the coat over to her . . . after a man—another

girls

Dept. Manager. Oh, I was looking through our racks when another customer—who was looking at some coats—happened to locate it . . . and gave it to me.

Salesgirl *(brightening)*. That's right. The woman handed the coat to Mrs. Jordan and she took it to the customer. *(Smiling and enthusiastic)* Boy, was she happy to get her coat back!

Store Manager. Yes . . . of course. *(Pause)* By the way, did she buy the coat she wanted, Miss Roberts?

Salesgirl *(disappointed)*. Well, no Mrs. Hansen, she didn't . . . she was so happy to get her coat back, she just left.

Store Detective *(enters from stage left)*. I'm awfully sorry I've been delayed, Mrs. Hansen. Your secretary's call didn't reach me until I got to Sporting Goods.

Dept. Manager *(to Customer C)*. This is Mrs. Karsh, our store detective.

Store Manager *(to Store Detective)*. Doris, I wonder if you'd help us out here. We seem to be losing coats today. That is, we've lost two this morning and, oddly enough, both of them were blue coats.

Salesgirl *(chattily to Store Detective, as if to be helpful)*. Mrs. Jordan found the first lady's coat—a knobby wool with raglan sleeves—and gave it back to the customer.

Store Detective *(to Dept. Manager)*.

boys

Goods.

Dept. Manager *(to Customer C)*. This is Mr. Karsh, our store detective.

Store Manager *(to Store Detective)*. Dan, this customer seems to have lost his coat and this is the second time this morning that we've had this problem in this department. Oddly enough, blue coats have been involved both times.

Salesman. Dan, Mr. Jordan found the first guy's coat—a navy blue with raglan sleeves . . . and gave it back to him, and then . . .

Store Detective *(interrupting, to Dept. Manager)*. And how did you know it was his coat?

Dept Manager. Well, I brought the coat over to him . . . after a man—another customer—handed it to me, and he immediately said it was his.

Store Detective *(very coolly to Dept. Manager)*. But you didn't know what his coat had looked like . . . I mean until the customer said the coat was his?

Dept. Manager *(puzzled, but rather embarrassed)*. No . . . no, I didn't.

Store Manager. Jordan says that another customer . . . a man . . . happened to spot it and gave it to him, Dan.

Man Customer C *(to Dept. Manager)*. Wait a minute . . . if you didn't know what the man's coat looked like, I don't see how you could be sure it was

mixed

customer—handed it to me, and she immediately said it was hers.

Store Detective *(very coolly to Dept. Manager).* But you didn't know what her coat had looked like . . . I mean until the customer said the coat was hers?

Dept. Manager *(puzzled, but rather embarrassed).* No . . . no, I didn't.

Store Manager. Jordan says that another customer . . . a man . . . happened to spot it and gave it to him, Dan.

Woman Customer C *(to Dept. Manager).* Wait a minute . . . if you didn't know what the woman's coat looked like, I don't see how you could be sure it was really her coat that you gave her.

Store Manager *(quickly, as if suddenly aware of what has happened).* Yes, Jordan . . . it could have been *any-body's.* (Glancing quickly at Customer C, who stands scowling with hands on hips)

Woman Customer C *(very annoyed). Yes, it could.* In fact, I think *he* (nodding toward Dept. Manager) gave her *my* coat!

Store Detective *(nodding slowly and speaking very drily).* I suspect that is exactly what happened. *(To Jordan)* You say a man customer *happened* to spot the coat which you gave to the woman. Well, recently we've had word that a couple has been working a

girls

How did you know it was her coat?

Dept. Manager. Oh—well, when I brought it over to her, she immediately said it was hers . . . so I thought—

Store Detective *(smiling at Dept. Manager).* But I suppose that until then you didn't really know what the coat looked like, did you . . . I mean . . . hers?

Dept. Manager *(puzzled, and rather embarrassed).* No . . . no, I guess I didn't . . . but . . .

Store Manager. It seems that another customer spotted it and gave it to Mrs. Jordan, Doris.

Woman Customer C *(to Dept. Manager).* Wait a minute . . . if you didn't know what the woman's coat looked like, I don't see how you could be sure it was really her coat that you gave her.

Store Manager *(quickly, as if suddenly aware of what has happened).* Yes, Mrs. Jordan . . . it seems to me that if your didn't know what the customer's coat looked like she might easily say *any* coat was hers. *(Glancing quickly at Customer C)* Don't you think so?

Woman Customer C *(very annoyed). Yes, I do,* and, in fact, I think *she* (nodding toward Dept. Manager) gave her *my* coat!

Store Detective *(frowning and shaking her head from side to side).* I'm afraid that may be exactly what happened. *(To Mrs. Jordan)* It all seems to fit a

boys

really his coat that you gave him.

Store Manager *(quickly, as if suddenly aware of what has happened).* Yes, Jordan . . . it could have been *any-body's.* (Glancing quickly at Customer C, who stands scowling with hands on hips)

Man Customer C *(very annoyed and looking at Dept. Manager almost threateningly).* Yeah, and in fact, I think you gave that other guy *my* coat!

Store Detective *(nodding slowly and speaking very drily).* I suspect that is exactly what happened. *(To Jordan)* You say a man customer *happened* to spot the coat which you gave to the man. Well, recently we've had word that a pair has been working a racket . . .

Dept. Manager *(shocked as he begins to be aware of his error).* You mean . . . that those two fellows were actually crooks who were working together, is that it?

Store Detective *(nodding in confirmation).* Yeah, I'm afraid so. One of them watches for a customer to lay down his coat. Then the other one— who has been posing as a customer, while trying on various coats says that his coat is missing. The store employees usually start searching for his coat.

Salesman *(interrupting excitedly).* I get it! And the other guy hands a coat to

mixed

racket ...

Dept. Manager   *(shocked as he begins to be aware of his error).* You mean ... that *man* and the woman *customer* ... were actually thieves who were working together.

Store Detective   *(nodding in confirmation).* Yes, I'm afraid so. The man watches for a customer to lay down her coat. Then, the woman, who works with him while posing as a customer, declares that her coat is missing. The store employees search for the coat ...

Salesgirl   *(interrupting).* And ... and *(as if afraid to believe it)* and the man hands the other customer's coat to somebody ... to one of the employees ... like Mr. Jordan. *(As if shocked, she suddenly holds her hand over her mouth, her eyes open wide)*

Woman Customer C   *(interrupting and now very annoyed)* .... Who hasn't *bothered* to find out what the missing coat looks like.

Store Manager   *(now glaring at Jordan).* And Jordan *(acidly)* gives the coat to the thief who quickly leaves with her accomplice! *(Turning to Customer C)* Now, madam, I think I see what has happened and I am, of course, very sorry that this has occurred. Randall's will, of course, reimburse you for your loss. Just go along with Miss Roberts and tell her the value of your lost coat so that we can make out a report, and

girls

pattern we've had word of recently.

Dept. Manager   *(shocked, holding her hand up against her cheek).* Oh, my! It seems that those two ... customers ... were actually ... thieves ... working together then.

Store Detective   *(nodding sadly).* Yes ... one of them watches ... Then the other woman, who works this racket with her, declares that her coat is missing. *(Sighing)* Then it seems that the store employees search for the coat.

Salesgirl   *(interrupting).* And ... and *(as if afraid to believe it)* and the woman hands the other customer's coat to somebody ... to one of the employees ... like Mrs. Jordan. *(As if shocked, she suddenly holds her hand over her mouth, her eyes wide open)*

Woman Customer C   *(interrupting and now very annoyed)* ... Who hasn't *bothered* to find out what the missing coat looks like.

Store Manager.   And it appears that Mrs. Jordan *(acidly)* gives the coat to the thief, who quickly leaves with her accomplice! *(Turning to Customer C)* It does seem clear that there has been a terrible *mistake (Glancing at Mrs. Jordan)* although Randall's will, of course, reimburse you for the loss of your coat. I am so sorry this has occurred. Won't you please go along with Miss Roberts and tell her the value of your lost coat so that we can

boys

one of the employees—like Mr. Jordan ...*(His voice fades down almost to a whisper as if he is suddenly shocked at his awareness of what he is saying)*

Store Manager   *(now glaring at Jordan).* And Jordan *(acidly) gives* the coat to the thief who quickly leaves with his accomplice! *(Turning to Customer C)* Now, sir, I think I see what has happened and I am, of course, very sorry that this has occurred. Randall's will, of course, reimburse you for your loss. Just go along with Mr. Roberts and tell him the value of your lost coat so that we can make out a report, and we'll get a check ready for you.

Man Customer C, glancing witheringly at Dept. Manager, follows Salesman; they exit stage left.

Store Manager   *(turning grimly to Dept. Manager who stands glumly downcast).* As for *you*, Mr. Jordan, kindly come along with me to my office. You'd better come along too, Mr. Karsh. *(With biting sarcasm)* I think we're going to have a *very interesting* discussion.

Store Manager exits stage right, followed by Dept. Manager and Store Detective.

CURTAIN

Glossary

acidly—in an annoyed or angry way

mixed	*girls*	*boys*

mixed

we'll get a check ready for you.

Woman Customer C, glancing witheringly at Dept. Manager, follows Salesgirl; they exit stage left.

Store Manager　*(turning grimly to the department manager who stands glumly downcast).* As for *you*, Mr. Jordan, kindly come along with me to my office. You'd better come along too, Mr. Karsh. *(With biting sarcasm)* I think we're going to have a *very interesting discussion.*

Store Manager exits stage right, followed by Department Manager and Store Detective.

CURTAIN

Glossary

accomplice—a thief's helper or partner

as for you—an expression indicating a shifting of attention to consideration of a problem raised by another person

beaming—smiling or grinning

boy—expression of emphasis, enthusiasm; it is not an address or a reference to age

by the way—incidentally; an expression used to signal a phrase of less importance

charge it—add the cost to her charge account

coolly—with exaggerated stiffness expressing annoyance

double-breasted—front overlaps with two parallel rows of buttons

eh /²ey³/—a questioning expression meaning *is that true*?

er /ər/—a sound used to indicate a pause

girls

make out a report. We'll have a check ready for you right away.

Woman Customer C, glancing witheringly at Dept. Manager, follows Salesgirl; they exit stage left.

Store Manager　*(turning with an icy smile to Mrs. Jordan, who stands glumly, downcast).* Oh, and Mrs. Jordan, I think we'd better go along to my office and have a little talk about all of this, don't you? I suppose you'd better come along too, Mrs. Karsh.

Store Manager exits stage right, followed by Dept. Manager and Store Detective.

CURTAIN

Glossary

hm-m-m? /²hū̃m³/—an interrogative exclamation meaning *isn't it*? Not that the pitch contour distinguishes this from the puzzled or speculative /²hū̃ ¹m/

I'm afraid—I'm sorry to say; this is not an expression of fear or fright

Make light of the incident—to pretend it is not serious

Oh my—a mild exclamation of concern, (used mainly by women)

boys

all set—ready, complete, restored

consolation—attempt to make someone feel happier; to relieve of worry

crooks—thieves

damn it—expression of annoyance or displeasure or disgust (profanity)

figured—thought

flyfront—a clothing design in which the buttons holding the coat closed are not visible

fooling around—waiting unnecessarily, wasting time, accomplishing nothing

h-m-m /²h-m¹/—an expression of puzzlement or reflection

I get it—I understand

look—sentence opener indicating some mild annoyance, disagreement, resistance

navy blue—dark blue, as an American sailor's winter uniform

O.K. /ow + key/—an expression of agreement; yes

phew /fyuw/—an expression of relief, similar to a sigh

ph-t-t /ft/—an imitation of the swishing sound of something being snatched up and disappearing quickly (made by prolonging the pronunciation of /f/ followed by /t/)

sporty—not formal, casual

this is no joke—this is serious, important

turn up—appear, be found

yeah /yeh/—yes

mixed

while thinking of what to say next

fruitless—without positive results

get a check ready—write a check (for the amount lost)

good quality store—an expensive, exclusive store with a reputation for quality

gorgeous—beautiful

isn't that funny—isn't that strange, peculiar, unusual; *funny* does not mean comical or humorous here

I've had just about enough—I am annoyed, angry, and unwilling to listen to any more nonsense; some effective action must be taken

knobby wool—a weave having occasional lumps in the texture

ma'am—an abbreviated form of *madam*, commonly used by salesgirls in addressing older women customers

make the matter right—solve the problem, probably by either finding the missing coat, giving the customer a new coat as a replacement, or paying the customer for the coat

mislaid—placed and then forgotten

no longer funny—has become a very serious matter

now, now—an expression used to soothe or calm someone

now wait a minute—impatient expression of interruption

oddly enough—although it may seem peculiar or strange

of course—expression of impatience in this case

perplexed—puzzled

mixed

picked up—carried away, stolen

plate—a metal or plastic disk used as identification by a person who has a charge account

raglan sleeve—a sleeve starting at the neck instead of at the edge of the shoulder

reimburse—give some money to replace something lost

spot it—see it, find it

store detective—person hired by a department store to circulate with the customers and catch anyone who tries to steal anything from the store

that's funny—that is strange, peculiar

there's something very peculiar here—the account of the incident seems suspicious

there you are—a kind of courtesy expression when giving or returning something; sometimes *here you are* is used with the same meaning

well—a common sentence opener which may signal that an opinion will follow; this expression also serves as a kind of softening device

why—expresses a kind of emphasis or, sometimes, surprise; one of a series of sentence openers with no definite meaning; *why* does not signal a question here.

why are some days like this—a kind of rhetorical expression of exasperation or frustration; it is not addressed to anybody specifically

witheringly—angrily

working a racket—involved in an illegal scheme to steal

wringing her hands—a nervous gesture of

mixed

squeezing one hand with the other

yeah /yeə/—yes

STRUCTURE

1. In this staging there are a few truncated and elliptical expressions typical of colloquial usage on which foreign student attention should be focused for purposes of developing recognition ability if not for increasing production facility:

   a. Often triggering of communication can be accomplished by the use of a mere noun phrase, such as the Salesgirl's "Your coat?" meaning *Did you say something about your coat?* which contains the complete subject and verb. We may also note that often *you say* is substituted for *did you say*, as in "It's—er . . . missing . . . you say?" meaning *Did you say your coat is missing?* Quite commonly, and particularly when the speaker is under emotional stress, the subject-verb interrogative clause is moved from the opening position as most textbooks state, "You say the same thing happened earlier today?" to the end of the statement. Since the intonation contour rises at the end of the statement to indicate a question, it will probably not receive more than secondary level of pitch, when *you say* is used at the beginning of a sentence.

   b. Similarly, the introductory or anticipatory *There is* is often dropped in colloquial usage without loss of meaning, as in the Dept. Manager's "Not a sign of her coat." Frequently such usage implies a kind of exclamation, or a comment unconsciously verbalized.

   c. Immediate emotional reaction as comment may be conveyed by single words, as in the Dept. Manager's shocked, "Nonsense, Miss Roberts," meaning *It is nonsense to even suggest such a possibility. Ridiculous* or *absurd* could be substituted for *nonsense* to convey the same idea of immediate dismissal of a suggestion. As such an attitude may easily seem blunt and peremptory, the teacher should focus student attention on situational aspects of such usage.

   d. Note that in the Dept. Manager's emotional "Two of them within an hour!" we have an interesting ambiguity of meaning. That is, he seems to be expressing dismay at the fact that two coats have been declared missing within an hour, but he may also be expressing his annoyance and frustration at having to deal with two excited disgruntled women customers within one hour. Moreover, such ambiguity is not merely a literary witticism consciously contrived but may, in fact, reflect covert hostility of which the speaker is only partly aware himself.

   e. Often, of course, and particularly in men's speech, the subject and verb may be omitted, as in the Detective's "Sorry for the delay," meaning *I'm sorry for the delay.* In a sense the same clipping which accounts for the destressing of segmental phonemes and entire syllables may operate to account for this word omission, although here the fact that subject and verb are implicitly understood in a continuous conversation is, perhaps, more influential than mere speed of utterance.

   f. The Store Manager's agreement with the salesgirl shows his impatience, as he says "Yes . . . of course," by the reinforcing *of course*, which is unstressed, without pitch change and spoken very rapidly. Although this device is widely used in the written English with which foreign students are usually better acquainted, they should be apprised of the fact that *of course* must be carefully and sparingly used in speaking, if the foreign student is to avoid conveying an attitude of cocky derision.

2. In colloquial English one form of question is communicated by a rising intonation contour applied to the statement pattern. But often the question signal eh /²ey³/ is used to reinforce the question conveyance, and, incidentally, to create a kind of truncated tag or trailer question, as in "That one was a blue coat that you gave the other customer, eh Jordan?" Similarly, *I suppose,* often without rising intonation contour and coming either at the beginning or at the end of the sentence, may signal a question, as in the Store Manager's "I suppose you've looked through all the coats on these racks?"

3. Note the use of the definite article *the*, rather than the pronoun, to give an effect of objectivity, as in the Store Detective's "Sorry for *the* delay," and in the Department Manager's "Isn't this *the* coat, madam?" The foreign student will have become acquainted with a series of such signals of the speaker's desire to project a kind of anonymity or objectivity, since such signals are cues to situational attitudes and social values which the student must understand and acquire to communicate in English.

4. The present perfect compound verb form is often used in the passive voice to express the anonymity of the actor, as in the thief's "My coat has been taken" or the Salesgirl's "This customer's coat seems to have been picked up." The teacher may attempt to show that the perfect tense always reflects a kind of vagueness as to actor or time of action unless a clarifying time phrase or contingency clause is added. Unfortunately, since most texts do not indicate that this usage is highly situation sensitive and cannot be dealt with as a syntactic problem, foreign students usually have a great deal of difficulty with present perfect usage particularly, and will need a great deal of situational practice.

   Note further that in the dialogue lines quoted, a careful attempt is made to speak euphemistically and avoid use of the word *stolen*. Part of the job of language learning, of course, is the acquisition of synonyms, but foreign students should learn to recognize that synonymity is situationally determined and all paraphrasing should be attempted with that in mind.

5. Many foreign students will be baffled by the Dept. Manager's very common expression, "There you are," which sometimes becomes *Here you are* or even *Here (or There) we are,* since the meaning seems to refer neither to spatial position nor to the person addressed. Probably it is best to explain this idiom as a kind of verbal gesture of reassurance and courtesy on the part of someone presenting something, and indicating that he believes a transaction has been completed. The teacher's frequent use of such expressions during classroom activities will help students acquire a feeling for their meaning. As in the case of many conversational fillers—such as the introductory *Why, Well, Oh,*

Now—the student's use of them along with an appropriate attitude of presentation, should be encouraged to give an authentic ring to his English.

6. Again, the salesgirl's query, "Will that be all, then, ma'am?" may seem confusing to foreign students, since the future tense reinforced by *then* is used to inquire about a present situation. The teacher should point out that actually the future and present tense forms are frequently mutually substitutable and, moreover, that *then* has no temporal reference but serves as a kind of redundant softening device, reinforcing the rising pitch contour which, if omitted, may make the query sound abrupt, harsh, and surly. It might be noted that the query will almost certainly seem abrupt, harsh, and surly if the present tense is used while the pitch rise, the *then*, and the *ma'am* are all omitted. Since most English texts do not give enough attention to such softening devices—and, indeed, many linguists seem unaware of their existence—a particular effort should be made to acquaint students with their function and usage.

7. Often we find a commentary exclamation couched in the form of an address without an addressee, as in Customer A's "Just imagine, thieves in a store like this." Usually such an expression is almost an unconscious verbalization of the user's shocked incredulity. Just as in the case of rhetorical questions, these are not designed to evoke any reply, although they do signal the speaker's state of mind or his attitude toward the situation, and are, therefore, valuable aspects of communication.

8. Although sound duration is usually given little attention by linguists, who may relegate it to that enormous ragbag summarily labeled "metalinguistics," it should be made clear to the foreign student that this feature may be as phonemic as intonation. When the thief's accomplice says "No-o-o," he is communicating an attitude of reflective indecisiveness, conveying far less finality than the word *no* usually does. The listener may, in fact, expect some following expression of reservation and even of resistance to decisive action. Frequently such stretching in the use of *yes* or *no* is employed to indicate a kind of reluctance,

doubt, or lack of conviction which may seem less harsh and, therefore, may be thought of as a softening device. Some foreigners may find this kind of expression annoyingly uncertain, but they should learn that very often it is all that can be expected in a situation requiring consensus.

Another example of the meaningful stretching out of the vowel sound occurs when Bob/Bobbie says, "⁴Óh, ⁴nó!" In this instance, the vowel sound in each of these two words is drawn out to produce a whining, exasperated blend of disappointment and disbelief. The emotional quality of the reaction is indicated by the fourth level pitch, the primary stress, and the exclamation mark.

9. There is the usual lexical evidence of women's language in this staging, for in addition to the use of *so* and *such* as intensifiers, we find the woman thief bemoaning the loss of her "gorgeous" coat. It might be pointed out that since the dialogue in the role should reflect the thief's calculated deception, pitch and stress can be somewhat exaggerated and "gorgeous," in particular, is likely to be strongly stressed. Since the thief hopes that the store officials will want to quiet his comments and complaints to avoid bad publicity, the words should be drawn out whiningly.

Cultural Values

Some typical social values in American society are revealed in three relationships presented in this staging:

1. The attitude of the customer toward salespeople is likely to reflect the widespread social class fluidity. That is, there is no sharply distinguished class which supplies salespeople, and it is not safe to assume the social class of a person by the fact he/she works as a salesperson. Many college students work part-time to contribute to their tuition and other expenses. Many housewives work both to occupy themselves after their children are grown up and to earn money, although it should be noted that large numbers of women work to supplement the family income even when they have children still of school age. The work of many people, such as students and housewives, is made possible because the system of part-time employment is very prevalent and, in fact, many businesses depend to a large extent on part-time employees.

Thus, the attitude of customers toward salespeople is generally fairly casual and equal. The salesperson does not feel inferior nor does the customer feel superior. In fact, however, the customer is aware that the continuation of the store depends on the patronage of customers, since competition is keen and dissatisfied customers may decide to buy at another store. The customer does not hesitate, therefore, to complain of discourtesy, poor quality merchandise or bad service generally. Frequently in larger stores there is a complaint department where dissatisfied customers may-go, and where some action will be taken if the complaint is justified.

2. The attitude of the salesperson toward the customer can be summed up in the very common slogan, "The customer is always right." This means that since the business depends ultimately on the customer, every effort must be made to please the customer. Thus, service to the customer is based on the realistic fact that jobs depend on customers rather than on the idea that the salesperson must demonstrate social class deference toward the customer. The store officials, in any event, are very anxious to avoid the bad publicity which might stem from a customer's dissatisfaction, and we see in this staging the readiness of the manager to "make the matter right," to reimburse a customer whose coat has been stolen. Partly to protect the customer, therefore, large stores frequently employ men and women to serve as detectives who circulate throughout the store to catch criminals.

Another aspect of the store's relations with its customers is revealed, for the store must be protected against people who may pretend to be customers but are actually thieves called shoplifters, ready to steal merchandise from the store. In a large city people live fairly anonymously, as contrasted with life in a small town where everybody knows everybody else. There is likely to be a great mixture and variety of ethical/moral standards in a city and the store officials must take precautions to prevent theft of merchandise by people who are not motivated by immediate personal need but who steal instead of working. Indeed, some of them engage in systematic crime as a kind of employment. Other people who are not professional thieves sometimes cannot resist temptation; this is particularly true of young people who are victims of advertising propaganda and feel they must have some item. Impulsively they may try to steal it. Despite the existence of store detectives and the fact precautions are taken, however, it is quite possible that anything left unwatched, even for a moment, will be quickly stolen. This is particularly true of light, expensive objects such as cameras, and foreign students should be particularly careful to watch their property in public places.

As everywhere the main purpose of a business is to make a profit for its owners and one means of doing this, while at the same time providing a kind of convenience for customers, is the various forms of credit available everywhere in the United States. Charge accounts are very common not only in department stores but in smaller shops, in gasoline stations, and almost every other kind of business. By these various credit devices the customer may obtain various articles or services without paying cash; periodically, he is sent a bill for the total amount he owes and he can pay that bill in monthly installments. Businessmen and salespeople encourage customers to have charge accounts because the interest charged on these accounts, sometimes called "service fees" or "carrying charges" is additional profit. Moreover, even when no interest is charged directly to the customer who has a charge account, the price of the merchandise in the store can be raised to cover the cost of making charge account facilities available. This means, of course, that additional profit is obtained from every customer rather than only from those who have charge accounts.

But, of course, there are ways in which a charge account can be convenient for the customer also. For instance, the customer does not have to carry money which might be stolen from him. Credit cards, which many Americans use in place of money when making purchases, are not as easily used by thieves who may steal them from the owners. Moreover, the person who has charge accounts or other credit devices may find it more convenient to budget his expenses by receiving monthly statements showing how much he has purchased and, therefore, owes and becomes more aware that he is spending too much each month. And here it can be pointed out that since by this device a husband can get a clear picture of his wife's buying habits, the use of charge accounts can lead to periodic family arguments; occasionally the husband may feel his wife is finding it too easy to put purchases on her charge account and he may decide to close his wife's charge account as a means of forcing her to reduce her shopping, to economize.

3. In order to understand why employees are likely to behave equally toward each other, it is necessary to realize that most employees feel that they are selling their services to the owner of a business and that the owner, in turn, cannot make a profit unless people are willing to work for him. Employees also recognize that the owner will continue to employ them only as long as the business is profitable. Workers usually feel no particular personal loyalty to an employer, therefore, and the employer knows they will leave their jobs to take other jobs if they are dissatisfied or if they believe they can find better conditions elsewhere. The relation between employer and employee is likely to be quite equal, objective, and based on mutual need. Thus, all employees are likely to have very similar attitudes toward the business, and unusual attempts by one worker to put excessive pressure or use authority over another worker are not likely to be very effective. Each worker is thought to be responsible for the job he was hired to do and he expects to be scolded or even discharged from his job if he does not do his job well. This is what happens in this staging, for we can guess that

at the end of the staging when the Dept. Manager goes to the Store Manager's office, he will be severely scolded, because his stupidity has cost the store a loss; he may even be fired.

Yet, despite this relative equality among employees, we can see in this staging evidence of recognition of different social levels among workers. Note that the employees address each other quite formally before customers although they might not do so when alone. Also notice that the Store Manager can address the Store Detective by his first name, Dan, because the Manager is the Detective's immediate boss within the store. The Detective could not call the Store Manager by his first name while they are working together, although it might be possible when they are outside the store.

Notice that at the end of the staging the Store Manager addresses the Dept. Manager in a severely formal way to express a kind of objectivity and yet to make clear that the Store Manager is of higher occupational rank. The Store Manager does not wish to be on the same level as the Dept. Manager because it is his duty to punish the Dept. Manager. Despite this formal objectivity, the Store Manager's annoyance is quite apparent from the sarcastic understatement, reinforced by pitch-stress contour exaggeration, in his final speech.

General Comment

1. This staging can be divided into four scenes:
   a. Until Dept. Manager gives the coat to Customer A and says goodbye showing how the thieves operate, although it is not yet revealed that Customers A and B are actually thieves. This scene helps us understand the explanation which comes later in the staging.
   b. From our introduction to Customer C until the arrival of the Store Manager—we learn of the disappearance of another coat.
   c. From the arrival of the Store Manager until the arrival of the Store Detective—we learn the details regarding the missing coats and see Customer B's reaction to the loss.
   d. From the arrival of the Store Detective until the end of the staging—we realize that the coat in Scene a and in Scene b is the same coat, that Customers A and B in Scene a were thieves, and that the Dept. Manager has behaved foolishly.

   This scene division can be useful in planning rehearsals.

2. Students must be taught that there is a change of pacing differentiating these four scenes. Scene a) opens very briskly, slows while people are searching for the coat, and then closes briskly after the Dept. Manager takes the coat from the man customer. Scene b) is presented at a slightly slower pace as the characters react to what seems to be a rather puzzling repetition of the same situation. In Scene c) the slow paced presentation continues as the characters try to puzzle out the facts and what has happened. And, finally, the pace is speeded up considerably in Scene d) after each of the characters realizes what has happened and particularly after the Store Manager recognizes that the Dept. Manager has made a serious mistake.

   These differences in pacing of scenes reflect differences in emotional attitudes toward the situation and are not merely descriptions of formal dramatic structure. The differences in pacing are projected by differences in speed at which dialogue is spoken and by difference in speed of physical movement of the characters, since those are the communication patterns by which the underlying emotional attitudes are conveyed.

3. There are in particular four emotional attitudes which students playing the various roles must be taught to convey:
   a. The objective and correct—even somewhat snobbish—attitude of all employees and customers of a rather exclusive department store. Note that although contractions are used as part of standard colloquial patterns, no slangy expressions are used and the atmosphere is one of quiet courtesy.
   b. The rather exaggerated sense of loss expressed by Customer A, which upon reflection we will recognize was false, and the typical behavior of a thief. Students must learn suitable behavior patterns for the conveyance of the emotion of such loss, but it is also necessary for students to learn how much

is too much, so that they may be alerted and suspicious of such exaggerated behavior. The problem is one of recognition rather than one of production, but they can better learn to recognize the excessive by learning to project such behavior patterns themselves. It is important that they thereby learn not to project what may be interpreted as insincerity.

c. The genuine annoyance and anger of Customer B at the loss of her coat must be believable. Here, again, it is important for the student to recognize the difference between minor irritation and major annoyance or anger. The foreigner often tends to interpret behavior in a way incommensurate with the causal facts. This disproportion is a consequence of (1) his limited understanding of the accepted behavior patterns and (2) his different emotional evaluation of the situation stimulating the response. The student must learn, by mimicking, the suitable reaction patterns for the emotion he feels; but he must also understand how the situation is evaluated within the unfamiliar cultural setting of the people whose language he learns. That is, he must understand the social relations between communicants in the situation. Gradually, through the psychodynamics of interplay between his reaction and the reaction to him, he will himself acquire the new values.

Notice also that Customer B's behavior reflects a gradual realization of what has happened or, from another standpoint, a mounting sense of loss and anger. Although the focus of Customer B's reaction may seem to be on the Dept. Manager, who has given away her coat, actually the Dept. Manager is only a kind of target for Customer B's sense of disappointment. In real life, foreigners frequently seem to overreact and the typical American response is to tell them—sometimes rather impatiently—not to get "excited," although such a response is likely to seem callous and insensitive to the foreigner, resulting in the breaking down of communication.

d. Since both are employees, the Store Manager cannot simply denounce the Dept. Manager; instead, he must give the customer the feeling that the store is responsible—although he may feel the customer's carelessness in leaving the coat unwatched was the real cause of the trouble. The Store Manager's annoyance and anger must also be seen as gradually mounting, although more slowly in this case. It must also be understood that he cannot reveal his anger completely but must continue to be courteous and solicitous toward the customer. That is, while seeming objective he must also seem to sympathize with the customer. This again points up the interrelation of social relationships and emotional attitudes, and the need to vary behavior patterns accordingly.

4. Not only must every attempt be made to recreate the reality of a real life situation—by utilizing a real coat, racks of clothing, etc. which will involve the student actors in the situation—but students must be taught behavior patterns to express genuine concern. That is, their movements as they search for the coat must not be peremptory or pale imitations; they walk around between the racks searching. The acquisition of behavior patterns which communicate suitably is, of course, in direct proportion to the degree of immersion in the situation, in the authenticity and totality of mimicry required.

Notes on Adaptation

1. This staging like the others in this text has approximately half of the roles for one sex and half for the other. The fact that behavior patterns of salespeople may seem fairly standardized and largely geared to women customers, since they do most of the shopping, may lead the teacher to feel he can use the staging with few changes in the dialogue other than in gender of nouns and pronouns. It is true, of course, that the customers could believably be women and the teacher should explain that in many large stores department managers and even store managers

may be women. It is also common to hire women as store detectives, since they are, of course, less conspicuous, particularly while circulating in areas of the store where women's clothing is sold. In many instances the dialogue would be the same lexically and syntactically for both sexes, although intonation contours would vary much more extensively. For example, the Dept. Manager's

> ^{2}"Why what seems to be the ^{3}trou^{2}ble here? . . . ^{2}What's ^{3}hap^{2}pened?"

is likely to be rendered, by a woman as

> ^{1}"Why ^{3}what ^{2}seems to be the ^{4}trou^{2}ble ^{3}he^{2}re? . . . ^{1}What's ^{4}hap^{2}pened?"

Several other examples of the typically extreme pitch variation reflecting the emotional coloring characteristically projected by women's speech are:

a. The Dept. Manager: ^{1}"Oh ^{2}that ^{4}can'^{2}t ^{2}be, ^{2}can ^{3}it, ^{3}Miss ^{3}Rob^{2}erts? ^{1}Why ^{2}it seems im^{4}poss^{2}ible. ^{2}Not at ^{3}Ran^{2}dall's ^{3}cer^{2}tainly. ^{2}I ^{3}sim^{2}ply ^{2}can^{3}not under^{4}stand ^{2}it."

b. Customer A: "^{2}Why . . . ^{2}why, . . . ^{2}it ^{4}is! ^{2}Where did you ^{4}find ^{2}it? ^{4}Oh . . . I'm ^{4}so ^{2}happy to^{3} see ^{2}it again↓"

c. Dept. Manager: "^{2}Why, ^{1}of ^{3}course ^{1}you are. ^{2}It ^{3}had ^{2}to be here ^{3}some^{2}where, ^{2}didn't it↓ ^{2}There ^{1}now ^{3}every^{2}thing is just ^{3}fine ^{2}again, ^{2}hm-^{3}m-m.↑"

d. Customer A: "^{2}Oh, ^{2}thank ^{1}you . . . ^{3}thank ^{2}you ^{4}so ^{2}much↓"

e. Dept. Manager: "^{1}Well, ^{2}we ^{2}just ^{3}had a ^{2}little . . . er . . . ^{3}diff^{2}iculty locating a ^{3}coat . . . ^{2}which ^{3}seemed ^{2}to be ^{3}miss^{2}ing↓"

f. Dept. Manager: ^{3}Oh ^{2}my, ^{2}now we seem to have ^{2}an^{4}oth^{2}er one missing. ^{2}It ^{3}is ^{1}a bad day, ^{3}isn't ^{2}it↓"

The melodious quality of the pitch alternation in the speech of the Dept. Manager seems to have a kind of soothing, consoling, reassuring effect. The pacing is likely to be slower in women's speech, perhaps in keeping with the greater fluctuation within the intonation pattern. Yet, even when the sex of the role is not changed, the original dialogue of that role must be modified lexically and syntactically, since the way either sex speaks may depend as much on the sex of the person spoken to as upon the sex of the speaker; the way men talk to men or women talk to women is usually quite different from the way men and women talk to each other. This important fact should be apparent in the adaptations supplied.

2. In the adaptation for women we also find the following linguistic devices illustrating that in most instances the dialogue of women has a relatively tentative, unassertive, and indecisive tone, as if what is stated is only the opinion of the speaker and not actually factual:

a. The conversion of direct statements to trailer/tag questions, as in the Dept. Manager's "You know Randall's will do everything possible . . . don't you?" or in her, "It is a bad day, isn't it?" and in the Store Manager's "That is odd, isn't it?"

b. The use of certain rhetorical question forms, such as in the Store Manager's "Won't you please go along with Miss Roberts." Note that the negative seems to convey additional softening by indirection, although we often find the positive *will you* or *would you* similarly used.

c. Another means of softening can be found in the prefatory *I wonder* of the Store Manager's "I wonder how you happened to locate that other coat," expressing a question indirectly, or the Dept. Manager's "I wonder if you happened to see the lady's coat, madam." In the latter usage the courteous indirection is reinforced by the preceding stock "Pardon me" and the use of the tentative *if* after *wonder*.

d. The apparent sharing of loss or blame, by use of such forms as *let's* or *we*, seems to soften the blow and we find the Dept. Manager saying, "Let's look through the coats." We might note also how the usage is compounded with other softening devices in the Store Manager's request to the Store Detective, "*I wonder* if you'd help *us* out here. *We* seem to be losing coats . . . *we've* lost two . . ." The underlined terms all represent softening by the rhetorical question and the indefinite verb. The following lines of the Store Manager are another example, "it *seems to me* that *if* you didn't know what the customer's coat looked like she might identify any coat as hers, don't you think so?"

e.   The indefinite adverbs and verbs, such as *perhaps, apparently, seem,* and *appear* are used to produce a typically tentative, non-assertive tone, which is similarly obtained by the use of such verbs as *think, suppose, imagine, guess.* And we also find extensive use made of the contingent *if* as well as of the mildly advisory *N better V* construction, as in the Store Manager's "And I suppose you'd better come along too, Mrs. Karsh." Incidentally, we note that even the male Store Manager's courteous, "You'd better come along too, Mr. Karsh" has been further softened by the addition of *I suppose* in the woman's version. The trailer question form is compounded with the *suppose* construction in the Store Detective's "But I suppose that until then you didn't really know what the coat looked like, did you?"

Of course, such restrained usage is neither confined to women nor can it be found in the language of all women. Although it reflects general modes of courteous deferential usage, it is well to recognize that through extensive usage of these forms, women quite typically reveal their acceptance of the less aggressive, retiring role assigned them by our social values.

f.   In addition to the lexical and syntactic devices noted, women tend to employ rather mild exclamations, such as *Oh my* or *Oh dear*, as in the Dept. Manager's "Oh my, now we seem to have another one missing" rather than the blunter,

more violent sounding, and often profane usages of men. It should be pointed out that the male Dept. Manager is exasperated and driven to despair whereas the female Dept. Manager rather matter-of-factly accepts the confusion. Even the rather ominous man's "We're going to have a very interesting discussion" is rendered somehow milder by the diminutive in the woman's "have a little talk." And as if to project a sharing of those feminine values which are not a man's concern, we find women tending to extend sympathetic understanding, by addition of such expressions of agreement as "of course you are," while terms of affection such as *dear* are quite commonly used between women, no matter what their relationship, as in the Dept. Manager's "Now, now, dear," although this usage is much less common between women and men and is impossible between men.

3.   As shopping for most men is handled by their mothers or wives, they are usually less familiar with the surroundings in a department store and, therefore, may tend to be somewhat ill-at-ease, off-hand, impatient and particularly anxious to establish a reassuring familiar relationship with salespeople. Men tend to be more familiar and less distant with members of their own sex than women are, and may reveal this in their ready usage of colloquialisms and slang.

4.   Colloquial usage tends to favor a considerable degree of truncation of structure and this is particularly true in men's speech. Men often omit the sentence subject, as in the Customer's "Wonder what happened to it" and the Salesman's "Could have been hung up by mistake." But we also find that the auxiliary verb is omitted quite commonly, as in the Salesman's "Be with you in a minute, sir." The foreign student not only must be alerted to such truncation if his recognition of English is to be adequate—and particularly since few texts handle this feature of colloquial usage—but he must also be made aware that the occurrence of such usage may indicate a kind of relaxation and acceptance and that the other party feels able to speak informally. The fact that this usage thus serves as a clue to the

attitude or tone of the conversation may be very useful to the foreigner attempting to ascertain the degree of intimacy required in the situation. He should also be warned that such usage may be part of a strategy of exploitation or manipulation when used by salesmen or other propagandists.

5. Similarly, we often find commentary in the form of a sharply truncated expression, as in the Customer's "You can't take your eyes off anything for a minute." For many foreign students this expression may appear a nonsequitur or wholly unrelated to the rest of the dialogue and here, again, it will be necessary for the teacher to impress on the student a sense of the informality of the situation, the mutual understanding between the people involved in the situation. The meaning of such truncated commentary is clear only because all parties can interpret what is unstated. In this instance, the customer means, *If you don't watch your coat, etc., it will be taken.*

6. Under stress many men resort to the use of profanity, as in the case of the Customer's use of "Damn it" upon discovery that his coat is missing. Such usage is considered an acceptable male outlet for feelings of annoyance, hostility, and frustration, although most women will either avoid the use of profanity or may at least avoid utterance of it aloud and in public.

7. When speaking together close men friends or associates are likely to use the colloquial *guy*, meaning *fellow* or *man*, in referring to another man, although ordinarily in less casual usage this term may be thought to have a rather slangy tone; *fellow* or *gentleman* will then be substituted. The colloquial usage is not restricted to men and, in fact, is widely used by women of all ages, but since women are expected to be somewhat more reserved than men, they are likely to be somewhat more formal in all usage until the tone of the situation is very clearly established. Again, we may observe the high social valuation placed on lack of assertiveness and forwardness in women.

8. The Salesman and the Customer in this staging speak quite casually together, with very little indication of deference extended or demanded. Foreign students may be quite surprised at the readiness of Americans generally to assume an attitude of equality toward salespeople. This attitude is a reflection of the large measure of social fluidity in America, or the fact that the correlation between types of job and social class level is neither rigid nor permanent. Foreigners are often surprised to learn that many college students engage in various kinds of manual labor and that the job history of many highly respected and renowned public figures contains evidence of such employment. Moreover, the national mythology reinforces notions of equality which, for most Americans, are vaguely related to the principles of democracy. Thus, most people feel it necessary to avoid giving the impression they think themselves superior to others. In fact, the curious felt necessity of the very wealthy in this country to behave humbly, and even more common than most common men, may be a source of wonder to many foreigners who are far more familiar with the wealthy man's assertion of superiority, his insistence on deference and favoritism, and even his overbearing arrogance.

9. In expressing his annoyance and displeasure at the loss of his coat, the customer emphasizes that it is new rather than it is beautiful, as the woman customer did when she bemoaned the fact that her "gorgeous coat" was missing. Although there are, of course, many exceptions to such a generalization, foreign students should be acquainted with the fact that men in our society are expected to be more concerned with practical matters, such as price or value in terms of newness, rather than with aesthetic matters which are generally considered quite subjective, emotional, impractical—and feminine—concerns.

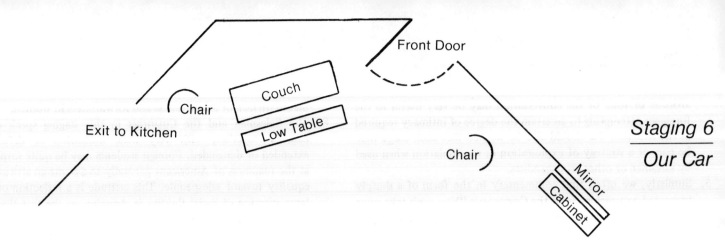

SETTING

The living room of a middle class home. Friday evening about 6. Father or Aunt Doris, who has just arrived home from work, enters from stage left and stops by the couch, left of stage center, where a grandparent is seated and reading a newspaper.

Mixed cast

Father (George)
Grandmother
Mother
Bob (son)
Nancy (daughter)
Mr. Slocum

Father   *(tiredly)*. Good evening, Mother.
Grandmother   *(looking over the top of the newspaper she is reading)*. Good evening, George. *(Glancing at her wristwatch)* A little late, aren't you?
Father.   Yup, a little. Had to stop off at the garage to get that damned car fixed again. *(Shaking his head in disgust)* Second time this week.
Grandmother.   Cars are nothing but

122

Girls' cast

Aunt Doris
Grandmother
Mother
Bobbie (younger daughter)
Nancy (older daughter)
Mrs. Slocum

Aunt Doris   *(tiredly)*. Good evening, Mother.
Grandmother   *(looking over the top of the newspaper she is reading)*. Good evening, Doris. *(Glancing at her wristwatch)* A little late, aren't you?
Aunt Doris   *(sighing)*. Oh, yes, a little, I guess. I had to stop off at the garage to get that car fixed again—that's the second time this week.

Boys' cast

Father (George)
Grandfather
Uncle Ed
Bob (younger son)
John (older son)
Mr. Slocum

Father   *(tiredly)*. Hello, Pop.
Grandfather   *(looking over the top of the newspaper)*. Evening, George. *(Glancing at his wristwatch)* A little late, h-m-m?
Father.   Yup, a little. Had to stop off at the garage to get that damned car fixed again. *(Shaking his head in disgust)* Second time this week.
Grandfather.   Cars are nothing but

mixed

trouble. You could take a cab, George, for what it costs you to keep that thing going. *(Looking pointedly at George's bulging profile)* You could even walk occasionally and be better off for it. *(Emphatically)* Cars are a constant headache and the cause of trouble.

Mother   *(entering from kitchen stage right, with apron on and holding a large towel and dish, addresses Father).* Oh, I thought I heard you come in, George. Something kept you working overtime?

Father   *(sitting down on a chair stage right, with part of the newspaper snatched up from the couch where Grandmother sits reading).* No—just that car of ours acting up again. Mac says it will be ready by seven or so.

Mother.   Well, I hope so, because I have a club meeting tonight, you know.

Father.   You do, huh. I'd forgotten about that. In fact, the boss left early this afternoon and I promised I'd stop by his house with some reports on my way home. Then that clunker of ours died and I had to be pushed to the garage. So, I didn't get to the boss's place and figured I'd run out when I got the car back after supper.

Mother   *(peeved).* George, how could you forget my meeting? It's only once a month, after all. And I will need the car because I told Helen Johnson I'd pick her up.

girls

Grandmother.   Cars are nothing but trouble. You could take a cab, Doris, for what it costs you to keep that thing going. *(Looking pointedly at Doris's profile)* You could even walk occasionally and be better off for it. *(Emphatically)* Cars are a constant headache and the cause of trouble.

Mother   *(entering from kitchen stage right with apron on and holding a large dish which she wipes slowly with a dish towel as she addresses Aunt Doris).* Oh, I thought I heard you come in, Doris. Something kept you working overtime?

Aunt Doris   *(sitting down in a chair stage right, with part of the newspaper snatched up from the couch where Grandmother sits reading. Kicks off her shoes).* No—just that blasted car of ours acting up again. Mac says it will be ready around seven.

Mother.   Well, I hope so, because I have a club meeting tonight, you know.

Aunt Doris   *(frowning slightly).* Oh, you do. Gee, I'm sorry Mary—I'd forgotten all about that. In fact, before the boss left, early this afternoon, I promised I'd stop by his house with some reports on my way home. *(Shrugs)* Then, that car of ours died *(shaking her head disgustedly)* and I had to be pushed to the garage. So-o-o, since I couldn't get out to the boss's place, I figured I'd run out there when I got the car back after supper.

boys

trouble. You could take a cab, George, for what it costs you to keep that thing going. *(Looking pointedly at George's profile)* You could even walk occasionally and be better off for it. *(Emphatically)* Cars are a constant headache and the cause of trouble.

Uncle Ed   *(entering from kitchen stage right while filling his pipe from a tobacco pouch).* Finally got home, eh George? They have you working overtime again?

Father   *(sitting down on a chair stage right, with part of the newspaper snatched up from the couch where Grandfather sits reading).* No—just that car of ours acting up again. Mac says it will be ready by seven or so.

Uncle Ed.   That's good 'cause I plan on going down to the club tonight.

Father.   You do, huh. I'd forgotten about that. In fact, the boss left early this afternoon and I promised I'd stop by his house with some reports on my way home. Then that clunker of ours died and I had to be pushed to the garage. So, I didn't get to the boss's place and figured I'd run out there when I got the car back after supper.

Uncle Ed   *(pondering).* H-m-m, that complicates things. *(Pause)* I've missed the last couple of meetings and I wanted especially to get to this one, George. *(Pause)* Since I figured the car would be available, I told Joe Robinson not to bother stopping for

| *mixed* | *girls* | *boys* |

Father *(growing annoyed)*. Well, I can drive you over to the Johnson's, pick up Helen, and take both of you to the meeting, I guess. Although we'll have to make it fast, because the boss is going to a play tonight about eight. *(Musing)* H-m-m–his place is way over on the other side of town too–exactly the opposite direction from your meeting. Maybe you'll have to ask Bill Johnson to pick you up instead.

Mother gives Father an exasperated look but continues drying the dish.

Grandmother. Bill will love that . . . driving way out here and then back downtown again. Cars are nothing but trouble.

Bob *(entering excitedly from stage right, carrying a pair of ice skates)*. Hi, Pop! Boy, am I glad to see you!

Father *(looks up from the newspaper he has made-believe he was reading)*. Yeah, well, that's unusual. Why the enthusiastic welcome?

Bob. 'Cause I've been waiting for you to get home with the car. Don't you remember? You told me I could have it tonight to take our mob out skating?

Father *(vaguely)*. Yes. *(Mock deference)* But, as a matter of fact, I do not have the car. The fuel pump gave up this time and Mac is working on it right now.

Bob *(protesting)*. Aw gee, Pop . . . and I'm supposed to pick up Liz at her

Mother *(frowning)*. Uh-oh, that is bad. It's lucky I have those meetings only once a month, isn't it? But I will need the car, because I told Helen Johnson I'd pick her up.

Aunt Doris *(mildly irritated and sighing)*. Well, why don't I drive you over to Helen's and take you both to the meeting on my way to the boss's house? *(Pause)* We'll have to make it fast though. The boss is going to a play tonight, I think. *(Musing)* And I just happened to remember that his place is way over on the other side of town. I wonder if Bill Johnson could pick you up instead?

Mother frowns, shakes her head negatively, but continues drying the dish.

Grandmother. Bill will love that . . . driving way out here and then back downtown again. Cars are nothing but trouble.

Bobbie *(entering excitedly from stage right, carrying a pair of ice skates and shouting enthusiastically)*. Hi, Aunt Doris! Wow, am I glad to see you!

Aunt Doris *(looks up from the newspaper she has made-believe she was reading)*. Oh, you are, eh? Why the enthusiastic welcome? I'm suspicious!

Bobbie. 'Cause I've been waiting for you to get home with the car. You *do* remember you promised me I could have it tonight to take the kids out skating, don't you?

Aunt Doris *(vaguely)*. Yes-s-s. But, as a

me.

Father. Well, don't worry; I think I can get you down there all right . . . . Although we'll have to make it fast, because the boss is going to a play tonight about eight and his place is in exactly the opposite direction from your meeting . . . . Maybe you'll have to get Bill Johnson to pick you up instead.

Uncle Ed frowns, looks annoyed, shakes his head from side to side once or twice, and, putting the tobacco pouch into his pocket, tamps the tobacco down in the pipe carefully with his thumb.

Grandfather. Bill will love that . . . driving way out here and then back downtown again. Cars are nothing but trouble.

Bob *(entering excitedly from stage right, carrying a pair of ice skates)*. Hi, Pop! Boy, am I glad to see you!

Father *(looks up from the newspaper he has made-believe he was reading)*. Yeah, well, that's unusual. Why the enthusiastic welcome?

Bob. 'Cause I've been waiting for you to get home with the car. Don't you remember? You told me I could have it tonight to take our mob out skating?

Father *(vaguely)*. Yes *(Mock deference)* But, as a matter of fact, I do not have the car. The fuel pump gave up this time and Mac is working on it right now.

mixed	girls	boys

mixed

place at 6:30 sharp and then go get the rest over at Doc's place. I feel let down. Now we're going to be really late getting to the rink. *(Glumly)* They'll murder me . . .

Father   *(with mock sympathy)*. Well, it's even worse than that, Bob, because I have to drop out to MacKenzie's with some reports. *(Turns back to his paper)*

Bob   *(thoroughly disappointed)*. Oh, no! But Pop, that's way over on the other side of town and it'll take you hours to get back.

Mother   *(who has stopped drying in order to listen to the discussion, interrupts frostily)*. And before going out to MacKenzie's your father has agreed to take me to my meeting. *(Exits stage right)*

Bob   *(completely defeated)*. That does it—the whole night shot! How could you all let me down this way. *(Shaking his head sadly and unbelievingly)*

Grandmother.   A car is nothing but trouble. All of you depend on it completely and when something goes wrong everybody is stuck. It's bad enough when the thing is running right . . .

Bob   *(interrupting snappishly sarcastic)*. Which is rare!

Grandmother.   Arguments, arguments— everybody's schedule is *so* important. A car is nothing but trouble.

Nancy enters from stage right with her coat

girls

matther of fact, I don't have the car, Bobbie. I think Mac said it's the fuel pump—or something like that—that's gone bad this time—and he's working on it right now.

Bobbie   *(wailing)*. Oh-h-h . . . and I'm supposed to pick up Liz at her place at 6:30 sharp and then go get the rest over at Doc's place. Gee, the kids were depending on me and now they're going to think I let them down. Besides, now we're going to be really late getting to the rink.

Aunt Doris   *(with mock sympathy)*. Well, it's even worse than that, Bobbie, because I have to run out to MacKenzie's with some reports. *(Turns back to her paper)*

Bobbie   *(throughly disappointed)*. Oh, no! But Aunt Doris, that's way over on the other side of town and it'll take you hours to get back.

Mother   *(who has stopped drying the dish in order to listen to the discussion, interupts frostily)*. And before going out to MacKenzie's your Aunt Doris has agreed to take me out to my meeting. *(Exits stage right)*

Bobbie   *(wails completely defeated)*. Oh-h-h . . . that just does it—all my plans—and—everything. The kids are going to be *terribly* disappointed too. *(Shaking her head sadly and unbelievingly)*

Grandmother.   A car is nothing but trouble. All of you depend on it com-

boys

Bob   *(protesting)*. Aw gee, Pop . . . and I'm supposed to pick up Liz at her place at 6:30 sharp and then go get the rest over at Doc's place. I feel let down. Now we're going to be really late getting to the rink. *(Glumly)* They'll murder me . . .

Father   *(with mock sympathy)*. Well, it's even worse than that, Bob, because I have to drop out to MacKenzie's with some reports. *(Turns back to his paper)*

Bob   *(thoroughly disappointed)*. Oh, no! But Pop, that's way over on the other side of town and it'll take you hours to get back.

Uncle Ed   *(who has just placed his pipe in his mouth, ready to light it, removes it and, pointing the stem at Bob, uses it to emphasize his words)*. And your father has agreed to take me to my meeting before going out to MacKenzie's. *(Exits stage right)*

Bob   *(completely defeated)*. That does it—the whole night shot! How could you all let me down this way. *(Shaking his head sadly and unbelievingly)*

Grandfather.   A car is nothing but trouble. All of you depend on it completely and when something goes wrong everybody is stuck. It's bad enough when the thing is running right . . .

Bob   *(interrupting snappishly sarcastic)*. Which is rare!

Grandfather.   Arguments, arguments—

mixed	girls	boys
on and carrying a violin case.	pletely and when something goes wrong everybody is stuck. It's bad enough when the thing is running right . . .	everybody's schedule is *so* important. A car is nothing but trouble.
Nancy *(cheerfully)*. Oh, I don't know, I think a car's pretty convenient, Grandma. Think of how tough it would be for me to get to orchestra practice tonight without our old wreck.	Bobbie *(interrupting snappishly sarcastic)*. Which is rare!	*John enters from stage right with his coat on and carrying a violin case.*
Bob *(who has walked upstage to stand behind the couch stage right and leaning on the back of the couch turns toward Nancy)*. Wreck is right. I've got news for you: it's out of action.	Grandmother. Arguments, arguments— everybody's schedule is *so* important. A car is nothing but trouble.	John. I wouldn't say that, Grandpa. If it wasn't for our old wreck, just think how tough it would be for me to get to orchestra practice tonight.
Nancy *(approaching stage center and facing Bob, disappointed)*. What again! And I counted on it too. Gee, probably the rest have all left and nobody can pick me up now. *(Turning to Father)* Any chance it will be ready tonight later?	*Nancy enters from stage right with her coat on and carrying a violin case.*	Bob *(who has walked upstage to stand behind the couch stage right and leaning on the back of the couch turns toward John)*. Wreck is right. I've got news for you: it's out of action.
Father *(talking while reading)*. Yes. *(Pause)* Mac is putting on a *(pause)* fuel pump. *(Shaking the paper as if to straighten it, continues reading and talking at once)* But, you're at the bottom of the list, I'm afraid. *(Pause)* I have to go to MacKenzie's, Mother has a club meeting, Bob has a skating date lined up . . .	Nancy *(cheerfully)*. Oh, I don't know, I think a car's pretty convenient, Grandma. Think of how tough it would be for me to get to orchestra practice tonight without our old wreck.	John *(approaching stage center and facing Bob)*. What again! Boy, and I counted on it too! *(Groaning)* The rest have all left by now and I'll have a hard time trying to get somebody to pick me up. *(Turning to Father)* Any chance it will be ready later tonight, Dad?
Nancy *(interrupting excitedly)*. But gee—just at the time I need it most. The concert is the 15th—just three weeks away—and we've only worked on half of the pieces. *(Whiningly)* Gee, I assumed you all knew that and would realize . . . oh-h-h. *(Disgusted and forlorn, places her violin case on*	Bobbie *(who has walked across to stand behind the couch, stage left, turns toward Nancy)*. Yes—but I have news for you: it is not running—*again*.	Father *(talking while reading)*. Yes. *(Pause)* Mac is putting on a *(pause)* fuel pump. *(Shaking the paper as if to straighten it, continues reading and talking at once)* But, you're at the bottom of the list, I'm afraid. *(Pause)* I have to go to MacKenzie's, Uncle Ed has a club meeting, Bob has a skating date lined up . . .
	Nancy *(approaching stage center and facing Bobbie, disappointed)*. What again! And I counted on it too. Gee, probably the rest have all left and nobody can pick me up now. *(Turning to Aunt Doris)* Any chance it will be ready tonight later?	John *(interrupting disgustedly)*. That's great! The concert is the 15th—just three weeks off—and we've only worked on half of the selections. And now, just when I need that heap most, it quits on us. *(Shaking his head,*
	Aunt Doris *(talking vaguely while reading)*. Oh, I don't know. Mac is doing something to the . . . fuel pump. But, anyway, when the thing's ready I have to go out to Mr. MacKenzie's, your mother has a club meeting, Bobbie has a skating date and . . . it looks like you're on the bottom of the list, dear.	

mixed

the table and turns her back toward the audience, facing upstage, stage center)

Bob   (hurt and glancing toward Nancy). Yeah—well what about the guys and girls who were depending on me. You can at least take a bus downtown. (Disgustedly) I feel let down. (Dropping his skates behind the couch, slumps into a chair)

Mother   (entering from kitchen, stage right and, removing her apron, speaks with frosty sarcasm). Well, that's just too bad, isn't it! You know very well that my meeting is held on the third Thursday of every month. And I should think that you'd have planned accordingly. (Goes to the cabinet near front door stage left, opens a cabinet drawer/door and begins rummaging around inside of the cabinet)

Bob.   But what will I tell the gang?

Nancy   (whirling around to face Bob angrily). The gang, the gang—and I've got this important concert coming up. (Turning to Father) Can't I take a cab, Daddy?

Father   (throwing down his paper and rising angrily). All right, cut it out! I'm fed up with the pack of you! Robert, go call up your friends and tell them to make other ride arrangements. Nancy, take your fiddle case in hand and get out to the bus stop. Mary, get dressed so that when I get back from Mac's with the car, you'll be ready to

girls

Nancy   (interrupting excitedly). But gee—just at the time I need it most. The concert is the 15th—just three weeks away—and we've only worked on half of the pieces. (Whiningly) Gee, I assumed you all knew that and would realize . . . oh-h-h. (Disgusted and forlorn, places her violin case on the table and turns her back toward the audience, facing upstage, stage center)

Bobbie.   Yeah, well what about all of the kids who were depending on me for rides. You can at least take a bus downtown. (Groaning) Gee, of all the times for this to happen! (Dropping skates in back of the couch, she slumps into a chair)

Mother   (entering from kitchen, stage right and, removing her apron, speaks with frosty sarcasm). Well, that's just too bad, isn't it! You know very well, that my meeting is held on the third Thursday of every month. And I should think that you'd have planned accordingly. (Goes to the cabinet near front door stage left, opens a cabinet drawer/door, and begins rummaging around inside of the cabinet)

Bobbie.   But what will I tell the gang?

Nancy   (whirling around to face Bobbie angrily). The gang, the gang—and I've got this important concert coming up. (Turning to Aunt Doris) Can't I take a cab, Aunt Doris?

Aunt Doris   (looking up from her paper

boys

places the violin case on the table and, thrusting his hands into his pockets, turns his back on the audience, facing upstage, stage center)

Bob   (hurt and glancing toward John). Yeah—well what about the guys and girls who were depending on me. You can at least take a bus downtown. (Disgustedly) I feel let down. (Dropping his skates behind the couch, slumps into a chair)

Uncle Ed   (entering from stage right, rolling down and buttoning his shirt cuffs and says, with mock commiseration). Well, that's tough, my boy! But my meetings don't come often and I plan to get to this one—as you all knew and could have allowed for. (Lays his pipe in an ashtray on the table, goes to the cabinet near the front door stage left, opens the door and begins rummaging around inside of the cabinet)

Bob.   But what will I tell the gang?

John   (whirling around to face Bob angrily). The gang, the gang—and I've got this important concert coming up. (Turning to Father) Can't I take a cab, Pop?

Father   (throwing down his paper and rising angrily). All right, cut it out! I'm fed up with the pack of you! Robert, go call up your friends and tell them to make other ride arrangements. John, take your fiddle case in hand and get out to the bus stop. Ed, get

mixed

go.

An ominous silence briefly follows Father's stormy commands. Nancy goes to the table and picks up her violin case. Bob starts slowly to get out of the chair and look for his skates behind the couch. Mother pulls a woman's hat from the cabinet, toys with it, turning it around and adjusting it several different ways, while standing before a mirror on the wall above the closet.

Grandmother   *(shaking her head).* A car is nothing but trouble . . . a constant headache.

Father   *(out of patience and turning with an annoyed frown toward Grandmother)* And, Mother, kindly stop emphasizing what is already obvious. Anyway, the car isn't a headache. It's a convenience. It's so convenient, in fact, that it is worn out with overuse . . . unnecessary use too, it seems to me.

Bob   *(emerging from behind the couch with skates in hand and joining in, as if to win his father's favor).* Yeah, there's nothing wrong with our car, Grandma. It's the people around here who cause the trouble. *(Glances at Nancy disgustedly)* . . . Violin players and such.

Nancy   *(turning and leaning toward Bob).* Oh, shut up! *(Haughtily and snippily)* I'm certainly tired of trying to sustain the cultural side of our family life against such constant opposition. There wouldn't be anything wrong with our car if it weren't

girls

annoyed). All right, let's cut it out. I'm getting pretty tired of all this nonsense. After all, I work in a noisy office all day, and it's no joy to come back at night to all this petty squabbling over the car. It's not my fault the thing has failed us again, is it? Bobbie, why don't you go call up your friends and tell them to make other ride arrangements. Nancy, just this once you can surely take the bus, so why don't you get out to the bus stop. Mary, if you'll get dressed and be ready I'll be able to pick you up here without wasting more time when I get back from the garage.

An ominous silence briefly follows Aunt Doris's stormy commands. Nancy goes to the table and picks up her violin case. Bobbie starts slowly to get out of the chair and look for her skates behind the couch. Mother pulls a woman's hat from the cabinet, toys with it, turning it around and adjusting it several different ways, while standing before a mirror on the wall above the closet.

Grandmother   *(shaking her head).* A car is nothing but trouble . . . a constant headache.

Aunt Doris   *(out of patience and turning with an annoyed frown toward Grandmother).* And, Mother, kindly stop emphasizing what is already obvious. Anyway, the car isn't a headache. It's a convenience. It's so convenient, in fact, that it is worn out

boys

dressed so that when I get back from Mac's with the car, you'll be ready to go.

An ominous silence briefly follows Father's stormy commands. John goes to the table and picks up his violin case. Bob starts slowly to get out of the chair and look for his skates behind the couch. Uncle Ed pulls a necktie out of the cabinet drawer, places it around his neck and ties it, carefully adjusting the knot while standing before a mirror on the wall next to the cabinet.

Grandfather   *(shaking his head).* A car is nothing but trouble . . . a constant headache.

Father   *(out of patience and turning with an annoyed frown toward Grandfather).* And, Father, kindly stop emphasizing what is already obvious. Anyway, the car isn't a headache. It's a convenience. It's so convenient, in fact, that it is worn out with overuse . . . unnecessary use too, it seems to me.

Bob   *(emerging from behind the couch with skates in hand and joining in, as if to win his father's favor).* Yeah, there's nothing wrong with our car, Grandpa. It's the people around here who cause the trouble. *(Glances at John disgustedly)* . . . Violin players and such.

John   *(now angered).* Oh, shut up! Nothing would be wrong with our poor car if it wasn't used all the time to haul a bunch of would-be athletes

mixed

used for all kinds of nonsensical errors—like hauling a pack of noisy kids all over. *(Sticks tongue out at Bob)*

Mother *(turning to the bickering children and speaking with assumed solemnity).* Yes, we've certainly spoiled both of you by letting you become so dependent on our poor car. *(Pause)* Although I do wonder sometimes if your selfish lack of consideration hasn't been inherited. *(Glances significantly at Father)*

Grandmother *(sarcastically).* Oh fine ... keep it up, all of you. Car, car, car. *(Mockingly)* "Our car," "my car," "*my* car." It's nothing but trouble, a constant headache.

Father *(now almost threateningly).* Yes, I do have a headache, thank you. But ... you all heard the orders. Bob, you'll just have time to phone one of the other fellows to pick you up. Nancy, I shall pick you up at the auditorium tonight right after your mother's meeting is over; there's a bus *(looks at wristwatch)* in three minutes. Get going. Mary, I'm going to Mac's and will be back in a half hour ... be ready. *(Pauses and then, with restrained cordiality, turns to Grandmother)* Mother ... I'll see you later.

Bob crosses to stage right as if to leave, followed by Mother. Nancy and Father start for the front door stage left. They almost reach it when the doorbell rings.

girls

with overuse ... unnecessary use too, it seems to me.

Bobbie *(emerging from behind the couch with skates in hand and joining in, as if to win her aunt's favor).* Gee, there isn't anything wrong with the car, Grandma. It's some of the people around here who're the real problem. *(Glances at Nancy disgustedly)* ... Violin players and such people ...

Nancy *(turning and leaning toward Bobbie).* Oh, shut up! *(Haughtily and snippily).* I'm certainly tired of trying to sustain the cultural side of our family life against such constant opposition. There wouldn't be anything wrong with our car if it weren't used for all kinds of nonsensical errands—like hauling a pack of noisy kids all over. *(Sticks tongue out at Bobbie)*

Mother *(turning toward the bickering children).* Well, I think the real trouble is that I've spoiled both of you by letting you become so dependent on our car. Certainly it hasn't been pleasant for me *(self-sympathizingly)* —a poor widow—trying to bring up two selfish girls. *(Seems about to weep)*

Grandmother *(sarcastically).* Oh fine ... keep it up, all of you. Car, car, car. *(Mockingly)* "Our car," "my car," "*my* car." it's nothing but trouble, a constant headache.

Aunt Doris *(annoyed and talking*

boys

and their silly-headed girlfriends all over town. *(Scowls ominously at Bob)*

Uncle Ed *(turning to the bickering children and interrupting).* Anyway, both you guys have gotten pretty spoiled 'cause we've let you depend on that poor car. *(Pauses and picks up his pipe from the ashtray on the table and, using it to emphasize his words)* If we hadn't let you use it, by now you'd both know how to get around without it *(scornfully)* instead of acting as if you were helpless.

Grandfather *(sarcastically).* Oh fine ... keep it up, all of you. Car, car, car. *(Mockingly)* "Our car," "my car," "*my* car." It's nothing but trouble, a constant headache.

Father *(now almost threateningly).* Yes, I do have a headache, thank you. But ... you all heard the orders. Bob, you'll just have time to phone one of the other fellows to pick you up. John, I shall pick you up at the auditorium tonight right after your Uncle Ed's meeting is over; there's a bus *(looks at wristwatch)* in three minutes. Get going. Ed, I'm going to Mac's and will be back in a half hour ... be ready. *(Pauses and then, with restrained cordiality, turns to Grandfather)* Father ... I'll see you later.

Bob crosses to stage right as if to leave, followed by Uncle Ed. John and Father start for the front door stage left. They almost reach it when the doorbell rings.

mixed	girls	boys

mixed

Father *(yanking open the door and snapping angrily)*. Well, what can I do for you?

Mr. Slocum *(smiling mechanically, hat in hand and poised on the threshold)*. Mr. Walters? My name is Slocum. I'm with Atlas Auto Insurance . . . your insurance company.

Grandmother *(looking toward the ceiling)*. Oh . . . now more trouble over that car!

Father *(exasperated)*. Yes, well look, I pay that premium yearly by check and I just paid it last month.

Mr. Slocum *(holding up his hand, palm toward Father, as if to reassure him)*. Oh, we received your check and your coverage has been extended. You are fully covered, Mr. Walters. Yes, indeed.

Mother *(who has paused and turned at the sound of the doorbell)*. Well, then, what do you want? I'm sorry, but we're all very busy and in a hurry just now.

Mr. Slocum *(apologetically)*. I know it will be bad news, Mr. Walters, but your car has been totally wrecked at Mac's garage. It seems it was rammed by a big tank truck just a little while ago.

Father *(as if stunned)*. Oh . . . well . . . why didn't Mac phone me?

Mr. Slocum. Couldn't very well. Slightly hurt himself and was taken to the hospital. I just happened to stop

girls

loudly*)*. Yes, of course I have a headache . . coming home to this lion's den! *(Very obviously restraining her annoyance and anger)* But I've told you all what you can do, haven't I? Bobbie, you'll just have time to phone one of the other girls to pick you up. Nancy, I shall pick you up at the auditorium after your mother's meeting is over; there's a bus *(looks at her wristwatch)* in three minutes, get going. Mary, I'm going to Mac's and will be back in a half hour . . . be ready. *(Pauses and then, with restrained cordiality, turns to Grandmother)* Mother . . . I'll see you later.

Bobbie crosses to stage right as if to leave, followed by Mother. Nancy and Aunt Doris start for the front door stage left. They almost reach it when the doorbell rings.

Aunt Doris *(yanking open the door and snapping angrily)*. Well, what can I do for you?

Mrs. Slocum *(smiling)*. Miss Walters? I'm Mrs. Slocum, representing Atlas Auto Insurance . . .

Grandmother *(looking toward the ceiling)*. Oh . . . now more trouble over that car!

Aunt Doris *(exasperated)*. Yes, well look, I pay that premium yearly by check and I just paid it last month.

Mrs. Slocum *(holding up her hand, palm toward Aunt Doris, as if to reassure her)*. Oh, we received your check and your coverage has been

boys

Father *(yanking open the door and snapping angrily)*. Well, what can I do for you?

Mr. Slocum *(smiling mechanically, hat in hand and poised on the threshold)*. Mr. Walters? My name is Slocum. I'm with Atlas Auto Insurance . . . . your insurance company.

Grandfather *(looking toward the ceiling)*. Oh . . . now more trouble over that car!

Father *(exasperated)*. Yes, well look, I pay that premium yearly by check and I just paid it last month.

Mr. Slocum *(holding up his hand, palm toward Father, as if to reassure him)*. Oh, we received your check and your coverage has been extended. You are fully covered, Mr. Walters. Yes, indeed.

Uncle Ed *(who has paused and turned at the sound of the doorbell)*. Well, then, what do you want? I'm sorry, but we're all very busy and in a hurry just now.

Mr. Slocum *(apologetically)*. I know it will be bad news, Mr. Walters, but your car has been totally wrecked at Mac's garage. It seems it was rammed by a big tank truck just a little while ago.

Father *(as if stunned)*. Oh . . . well . . . why didn't Mac phone me?

Mr. Slocum. Couldn't very well. Slightly hurt himself and was taken to the hospital. I just happened to stop

mixed	*girls*	*boys*
by there for gas and Mac told me it was your car. Thought I'd stop in to kind of reassure you on my way home.	extended. You are fully covered, Miss Walters. Yes, indeed.	by there for gas and Mac told me it was your car. Thought I'd stop in to kind of reassure you on my way home.

mixed

by there for gas and Mac told me it was your car. Thought I'd stop in to kind of reassure you on my way home.

Bob　*(who has stopped just at the exit stage right)*. Reassure us? That our car is a total wreck! *(This is said with biting sarcasm)*

Mr. Slocum　*(smiling mechanically and patronizingly)*. Yes, you see you've got complete coverage and our company will see to it that you have another car. In fact, I've already made out the report and if you'll just look it over *(extends paper to Father)* and sign it, I'll pick it up tomorrow and we'll take care of it right away. *(Still stunned, Father accepts the paper)* I'll stop by at about ten tomorrow morning then. Good evening. *(Exits stage left)*

Father　*(flatly)*. Good evening! *(Turning toward the family still standing stunned)* Well, I guess I'd better phone Mr. MacKenzie and tell him I won't be able to get there tonight. I'll get a cab for you, Mary. You kids will have to make your own arrangements. *(Exits quickly stage right)*

Bob　*(disgustedly)*. Gee . . . what a mess! *(Pause and then smiling vaguely)* But, now we can get something that will run regularly. *(Brightening)* Hey, how about one of those Alpines . . . man, have they got the power! *(Enthusiastically)*

Nancy　*(exasperated)*. Ridiculous! Can't you ever be sensible? We'll get one of

girls

extended. You are fully covered, Miss Walters. Yes, indeed.

Mother　*(who has paused and turned at the sound of the doorbell)*. Well, then, what do you want? I'm sorry, but we're all very busy and in a hurry just now.

Mrs. Slocum　*(apologetically)*. I know it will be bad news, Miss Walters, but your car has been totally wrecked at Mac's garage. It seems it was rammed by a big tank truck just a little while ago.

Aunt Doris　*(as if stunned)*. Oh . . . well . . . why didn't Mac phone me?

Mrs. Slocum.　He couldn't very well. He was slightly hurt himself and was taken to the hospital. I just happened to stop by there for gas and Mac told me it was your car. I thought I'd stop in to kind of reassure you on my way home.

Bobbie　*(who has stopped just at the exit stage right)*. Reassure us? That our car is a total wreck! *(This is said with biting sarcasm)*

Mrs. Slocum　*(smiling mechanically and patronizingly)*. Yes, you see you've got complete coverage and our company will see to it that you have another car. In fact, I've already made out the report and if you'll just look it over *(extends paper to Aunt Doris)* and sign it, I'll pick it up tomorrow and we'll take care of it right away. *(Still stunned, Aunt Doris accepts the*

boys

by there for gas and Mac told me it was your car. Thought I'd stop in to kind of reassure you on my way home.

Bob　*(who has stopped just at the exit stage right)*. Reassure us? That our car is a total wreck! *(This is said with biting sarcasm)*

Mr. Slocum　*(smiling mechanically and patronizingly)*. Yes, you see you've got complete coverage and our company will see to it that you have another car. In fact, I've already made out the report and if you'll just look it over *(extends paper to Father)* and sign it, I'll pick it up tomorrow and we'll take care of it right away. *(Still stunned, Father accepts the paper)* I'll stop by at about ten tomorrow morning then. Good evening. *(Exits stage left)*

Father　*(flatly)*. Good evening! *(Turning toward the family)*. Well, I guess I'd better phone Mr. MacKenzie and tell him I won't be able to get there tonight. You'd better call for a cab, Ed. And you kids will have to make your own arrangements. *(Exits quickly stage right)*

Bob　*(disgustedly)*. Gee . . . what a mess! *(Pause and then smiling vaguely)* But, now we can get something that will run regularly. *(Brightening)* Hey, how about one of those Alpines . . . man, have they got the power! *(Enthusiastically)*

John　*(exasperated)*. Ridiculous! Can't you ever be sensible! We ought to get

mixed

those cute little foreign sedans, just like Margie's, only blue instead of red.

Mother   *(decisively)*. I think we will do neither. We should get a nice medium-priced station wagon that we can use for shopping and vacationing.

Bob and Nancy   *(groaning in disgust)*. Oh, Mother, do we have to get one of those big, clumsy things?

Mother   *(with finality)*. Yes, and with power steering too.

Father   *(reentering from stage right as the bickering starts)*. We'll wait and see. I think, in fact, that we'll get another Ford two door sedan.

Mother   *(turning toward Father, annoyed at his resistance)*. Now, George . . . haven't we always needed a wagon?

Bob   *(in a voice filled with salesmanship)*. No, Pop, this is our chance to go sportscar!

Nancy   *(pleadingly)*. Dad . . . surely you won't listen to such talk . . . and you'll realize that a foreign sedan is our best choice.

Father   *(persistently)*. No, a Ford two door sedan will . . .

Mother   *(insistently)*. A large station wagon is . . .

Bob   *(still acting the part of the enthusiastic salesman)*. Power is what we need, power like . . .

Nancy   *(refusing to give up)*. Margie says she gets thirty miles to a gallon with her foreign car, and we will . . .

girls

paper) I'll stop by at about ten tomorrow morning then. Good evening. *(Exits stage left)*

Aunt Doris   *(flatly)*. Good evening! *(Turning toward the family still standing stunned)* Well, I guess I'd better phone Mr. MacKenzie and tell him I won't be able to get there tonight. Then you'd better call for a cab, Mary. And you kids will just have to make your own arrangements, I guess. *(Exits quickly stage right)*

Bobbie   *(disgustedly)*. Gee . . .what a mess! *(Pause and then smiling vaguely)* But now maybe we can get a car that will run regularly. *(Brightening)* Say, we could even get a convertible this time, couldn't we? *(Enthusiastically)*

Nancy   *(exasperated)*. Ridiculous! Can't you ever be sensible? We'll get one of those cute little foreign sedans, just like Margie's, only blue instead of red.

Mother   *(decisively)*. I think we will do neither. We should get a nice medium-priced station wagon that we can use for shopping and vacationing.

Bobbie and Nancy   *(groaning in disgust)*. Oh, Mother, do we have to get one of those big, clumsy things?

Mother   *(with finality)*. Yes, and with power steering too.

Aunt Doris   *(reentering from stage right as the bickering starts)*. I think we'd better think it over carefully. Maybe we ought to just get another Ford two door sedan.

boys

something durable and yet that can be fixed easily . . . like a Chevie.

Uncle Ed.   Yeah, well all that is fine—power and durability . . . but I say we ought to get something that we can carry stuff in during the hunting season . . . . nice station wagon maybe.

Bob and John   *(groaning in disgust)*. Oh, Uncle Ed, we don't need one of those big, clumsy things?

Uncle Ed   *(ignoring their comment)* . . . . And with a couple of sleeping bags and a tent we'd be all set for camping out.

Father   *(reentering from stage right as the bickering starts)*. We'll wait and see. I think, in fact, that we'll get another Ford two door sedan.

Uncle Ed   *(turning toward Father and adopting a persuasive tone)*. George, with a wagon we could take Tom and Joe along with the rifles and all their gear—and without crowding any of us.

Bob   *(in a voice filled with salesmanship)*. No, Pop, this is our chance to go sportscar!

John   *(pleadingly)*. Pop, don't let them give you that stuff. Let's get something standard sized that we can depend on . . . like a Chevie.

Father   *(persistently)*. No, a Ford two door sedan will . . .

Uncle Ed   *(insistently)*. A large station wagon is . . .

Bob   *(still acting the part of the enthusiastic salesman)*. Power is what we

mixed

They all begin to bicker, offering conflicting opinions.

Grandmother *(shaking her head and laughing amusedly).* Well, here we go again, arguing over a car, once more. A constant headache. Cars are nothing but trouble.

CURTAIN

Glossary

acting up—not working satisfactorily. This expression can also be used in referring to the bad behavior of a child.

any chance—is it possible

boy!—an exclamation with no specific meaning but conveying and perhaps emphasizing his feeling of excitement

cab—taxi

check—a paper form used instead of money

clumsy—awkward and without gracefulness

clunker—slang term for an automobile in poor condition

coming up—due, scheduled

cordiality—friendliness, pleasantness

count on—depend on

coverage—protection by insurance

cute—pretty, attractive

cut it out—stop it

damned—an expression of annoyance, here meaning *miserable* or *unreliable* (profanity)

died—slang meaning the engine stopped running

don't let them give you that stuff—don't

girls

Mother *(turning toward Aunt Doris, annoyed at her resistance).* Now, Doris, you know very well we should have had a wagon a long time, ago, don't you?

Bobbie *(pleadingly).* Oh, come on, Aunt Doris—this is our chance to get a really nice convertible.

Nancy *(pleadingly).* Aunt Doris . . . surely you won't listen to such talk . . . and you'll realize that a small foreign car is our best choice.

Aunt Doris *(persistently).* No, a Ford two door sedan will . . .

Mother *(insistently).* A large station wagon is . . .

Bobbie *(dreamily).* Just think of how nice it would be to ride along in a convertible with the breeze blowing your hair back and . . .

Nancy *(refusing to give up). Margie says she gets thirty miles to a gallon with her little car, and we will . . .*

They all begin to bicker, offering conflicting opinions.

Grandmother *(shaking her head and laughing amusedly).* Well, here we go again, arguing over a car, once more. A constant headache. Cars are nothing but trouble.

CURTAIN

Glossary

blasted—a term expressing annoyance or

boys

need, power like . . .

John. The essential things are economy and simplicity . . . like . . .

They all begin to bicker, offering conflicting opinions.

Grandfather *(shaking his head and laughing amusedly).* Well, here we go again, arguing over a car, once more. A constant headache. Cars are nothing but trouble.

CURTAIN

Glossary

all set—well equipped, able

Chevie—common abbreviation for Chevrolet, a low-priced American car

durable—strong

gang—group

gear—things, equipment

give you that stuff—tell you such nonsense

guys—boys or men

heap—a semi-affectionate slang reference to an old car

h-m-m/hū/—a question expression

not to bother stopping—not to come

pouch—an envelope-like container usually made of leather or plastic

silly-headed—foolish (here used derogatorily or sarcastically)

stuff—various things

tamps—presses down, as in filling a pipe with tobacco

would-be athlete—a disparaging reference to people pretending to be athletes

believe what they say

drop out to MacKenzie's—go out to MacKenzie's house

fed up—tired and annoyed by

fiddle case—violin case; *fiddle* is a colloquial term for violin

figured—thought, assumed, decided

fuel pump—device which draws the gasoline from the tank to the engine

gave up—stopped working

gee—an exclamation of strong feeling, with no specific meaning; a kind of emphasis

get going—colloquial form of a mildly threatening command meaning *go*

gets thirty miles per gallon—uses only one gallon (approx. four liters) of gasoline in going thirty miles (approx. fifty kilometers)

glumly—sadly

grandma/grandpa—informal reference to grandparents; *grandmother* and *grandfather* are not used very often by children in direct address

haughtily—disdainfully—assuming an attitude of superiority

hauling—carrying, usually used for objects rather than for people and therefore sarcastic here

here we go again (²here ²we ³go ²a ⁴gain)—we are again involved in a discussion of the same topic (i.e. the use the car)

hey/hey/—an exclamation of enthusiasm indicating a sudden thought or awareness

hi/hay/—familiar form of *hello*

huh/hə̄/— a kind of questioning expression,

dissatisfaction and meaning *miserable, disappointing, unreliable*. Used in place of profanity.

Bobbie—diminutive form of the boy's name Robert or the girl's name Roberta

convertible—a kind of car having a canvas top which may be lowered

cut it out—colloquial expression meaning *stop it*

died—stopped running

kids—usually this means *children*

lion's den—a noisy, unrestful place which may also be dangerous

no joy—not a pleasure, very unpleasant

petty squabbling—arguing over unimportant matters

pick her up—go by car to get her

say—an opening expression, indicating enthusiasm

uh-oh /³ə/²ow/—an expression, of sudden awareness of error or threat

widow—a woman whose husband has died

wow! /w⁴ æuw/—an expression of enthusism

mixed

equal to *is that so?*

I counted on it—I expected to use it; I relied on its being available

I'm with Atlas Auto Insurance—I work for the Atlas Auto Insurance Company

keep it up—continue what you are doing or saying, here used ironically

let down—disappointed; implies a feeling that he has been the victim of a kind of minor treachery

Liz—formerly an abbreviated form of Elizabeth, but now often used as a girl's full name

look it over—read it, examine it.

made out the report—wrote a report of the accident

make it fast—go there as quickly as possible

man—slang term of enthusiastic emphasis, which has no specific meaning

mob—group

mock—imitation, make believe, feigned

old wreck—one of many colloquial and semi-affectionate terms for an automobile

our chance to go sportscar—slang meaning to buy or own a sportscar

out of action—will not run, not available for use

overtime—more than the usual number of hours (usually more than eight hours)

pack—entire group, usually used for wolves or dogs—thus, sarcastically referring to the noise the characters are making in growling angrily at each other

pick you up—come to take you someplace by car

Pop—familiar term in addressing one's father

mixed

premium—a periodic payment made for insurance

profile—view from the side rather than from the front

rest—his other friends

rink—area used for ice-skating

rummaging—searching, looking for

run out there—drive to that place (stress is on *out*, not on *there*)

seven or so—about seven o'clock; in this case, 7 P.M.

shut up—be quiet

slumps—sprawls in a chair instead of sitting erect

snapping—speaking in a clipped, annoyed way

snippily—in a clipped, disagreeable manner

spoiled both of you—treated them too well, so that the children became selfish and inconsiderate

sticks tongue out—an expression of disrespect, used by children

stop in/drop by—a casual visit without a definite appointment

stuck—disappointed or frustrated

tank truck—a truck used for carrying liquids; here it was probably a gasoline truck

that *does* it—that is the final blow, the final disappointment (stress on *does*, not on *it*)

thing—a sarcastic reference to a car or any other object

threshold—right at the door and not beyond

tough—difficult

well look—pay attention (here indicating suppressed annoyance)

what a mess!—this is a miserable situation

mixed

what can I do for you—what do you want; this may sound harsh or discourteous, since it is a term used most frequently by clerks with customers rather than between friends or acquaintances (stress is on *you* here)

whole night shot—his plan for the evening has been destroyed

working on it—trying to fix or repair it

yanking—pulling very suddenly

yeah / ye ə /—an exclamation of doubt or skepticism

yup / yəp /—a colloquial form of *yes*

Structure

1. Colloquial usage typically contains a great many truncated expressions of various types:
   a. In this staging both Grandmother's "a little late" and George's reply "A little" as well as his "Had to stop . . ." and "Second time . . . ," or Mr. Slocum's "Couldn't very well" are all examples of common abbreviated structures from which the subject has been omitted.
   b. On the other hand, George's cautious "Why the enthusiastic welcome?" is a verbless construction, a kind of abbreviated form of *Why are you giving me an enthusiastic welcome?* The introductory "why" seems to signal the question, for the formula for the question form would be QVNVN?
   c. Nancy's "Any chance . . . later," meaning *Is there any chance . . . later,* is another example of a common verbless construction, but in this case the question is usually signaled by the rising intonation.
   d. Mother's "Something kept you working overtime" is interesting, for although it seems—from the rising intonation contour—to mean *Did something keep you working overtime?* the past verb form seems to indicate that *Something kept you working overtime, didn't it?* might be the full statement which has been abbreviated. We may speculate that perhaps attempts to determine the original full form of a statement are frustrated by the fact that the second possibility may convey a typically feminine softening, by way of the trailer question structure, which is carried over into the truncated version.

   Although these are fairly common constructions, mention of them is surprisingly rare in grammar texts, and foreign students should be given a great deal of practice in using them.

2. It may be necessary to call student attention to the fact that stress is rarely placed on pronouns in English. That is, many foreign students would distort the meaning of Mother's "I thought I heard you come in, George" by stressing *you* rather than *thought*, just as they would distort by stressing the pronoun rather than the following noun in Mother's statement, "My meeting is held . . . ," or by stressing *you* or *it* instead of *all* or *know* in her " . . . and you all know it." "Later, when the exasperated father tells the grandmother "will you kindly stop emphasizing what is already obvious," the word *you* might be stressed, but it is more likely that *stop* will receive the stress along with the first syllable of *obvious*. However, stressing is largely dependent on recognition of what elements are considered important in a context which is frequently much broader than the mere sentence. Throughout all of the various stagings in this text a great deal of meaning depends on effective, suitable stressing; it should be clear that not only would adequate notation and explanation require too many pages, but that ultimately the most effective way to teach the context is by student mimicking in the role as modeled by the teacher.

3. The expression *after all,* in Mother's "It's only once a month, after all," should be treated as one word, just as the transitions *however* or *nevertheless* are, although all syllables have almost equal stress in *after all,* and students should be discouraged from stressing the first syllable in *after*. The teacher might mention that if the *after all* occurs at the beginning of a statement, the stress, accompanied by a pitch rise, falls on the third syllable (i.e., *all*).

4. Pitch change not only tends to parallel stress change, but both may also be seen as devices to signal emotional attitude. As this staging is based on the frustration growing out of the thwarted demand for the use of the car, we can expect the rather open display of emotion. Quite typically, Nancy's projection is strongest and we find that her "What again!" is pronounced with a rising tone (i.e., from level 3 to level 4), indicating her disappointed surprise. Later, in her "just three weeks away," each word must be pronounced slowly and separately, as she tries to impress the family with the urgency, and the stress is on *away,* the second vowel sound, which is drawn out with a rising

pitch to produce a distraught wail. And finally, we get the signal of her complete frustration in her "oh-h-h" /²ow⁴/, which rises in pitch to level 4 as it is drawn out to reflect her disappointment.

Students can be shown a similar pattern in Bob's "Oh, no—but Pop . . . hours to get back," in which one finds a pitch rise to level 4 on the first two words to show Bob's excitement, there is also a sharp pitch rise on the words *Pop, town,* and *hours,* the vowel sounds which are drawn out so as to produce a kind of whine.

5. Much of the emotional reaction comes in the form of sarcasm or sarcastic mockery, however, and we find that in Bob's "Which is rare!" the drawing out of *rare* is accompanied by a pitch rise, just as *so* in Grandmother's "everybody's schedule is so important." The mocking note is made apparent in Nancy's scornful "the gang, the gang," and again in Grandmother's mechanical echoing in "Arguments, arguments" and "car, car, car," with the drawing out of each word to maximize the echoing effect. It comes to a focus in her "Oh fine, keep it up all of you," as the pitch rises to level 4 on *fine* and *up.*

However, the sarcasm in Mother's "Oh you do . . . bad" is obtained by employing pitch change in just the opposite way: there is a sharp drop in pitch on *do,* while the pitch drops—321—as each word in *just too bad* is pronounced separately. Sarcasm is related to irony, of course, and foreign students will need to be made aware that John's "That's great!" means exactly the opposite (i.e. John means that the situation is bad).

6. The teacher should point out that the use of contracted forms is so normal in colloquial usage that the use of the full verb and negative—as in Father's "I do not have the car"—rather than the contraction *don't,* produces a somewhat formal tone, reflecting annoyance, as does Father's use of the more formal less intimate *Robert* instead of Bob, but which also may seem rather comical in effect because of the incongruity of reversed deference positions.

7. Note that Grandfather's "a little late, h-m-m" /²hm³/ is not only an example of truncation but is an abbreviated form of a tag question: *you are a little late, aren't you?* in which the *h-m-m* takes the place of the tag part of the question. We often may find *eh?* /²ey³/ or *huh?* /²hə̃³/ used as the second part of a tag question.

Cultural Values

1. In order for many foreign students to understand the relationship of family members in this staging, it might be wise to try to make clear to them that in this country marriage is a matter of personal choice rather than an arrangement between families. This means that each couple does not merely join the family of the husband or of the wife, but, instead, forms a separate unit of its own; usually the couple and their children live in their own home apart from the parents of either the husband or wife. Occasionally, however, as in this staging, the grandparents may be invited to live in the home of one of their married children. When this occurs, usually everybody understands that the grandparents have no authority in the household. Usually, the wife is in charge of the house and the grandmother is expected to offer her opinion about housekeeping matters only when she is asked for it. Any attempt by the grandparents to dominate is usually resisted; if conflict should develop between the wife and her mother-in-law or mother, the husband is supposed to support his wife's side of the argument rather than his mother's.

Unlike the situation in many other countries, in America the relation between son-in-law and wife's mother is likely to be more difficult than the relation between daughter-in-law and husband's mother. That is, the husband is likely to be somewhat suspicious of his mother-in-law who, he may believe, can influence her daughter to make greater demands of him.

But the wife usually does not feel dominated by the husband's mother and, in fact, is about as likely to quarrel with her own mother as with her mother-in-law. Quite commonly the husband's mother will, in fact, support the wife in an argument against the husband, since an alliance of members of one sex against the other often may be somewhat stronger than family relations.

It might also be pointed out that since men are expected to be independent, the widowed grandfather will not like to be dependent on his married children. Thus, it is somewhat less common for the grandfather to live with his children than for the widowed grandmother to do so; large numbers of old men prefer to live alone. However, often when the husband's father does live in his son's house, his daughter-in-law will defend him against her husband, who may feel annoyed if his father seems to attempt to dominate the household.

2. Note that the son-in-law may address his mother-in-law as Mother, or more colloquially, as "Mom." It is not yet common for the son-in-law to use his mother-in-law's first name and to call her Mrs. would sound too formal and hostile. The mother-in-law, on the other hand, will probably call her son-in-law by his first name and, unless she is angry, will not call him Mr.

3. Cars are considered essential by most middle class Americans and even by a great many members of lower classes. And since many children learn automobile driving in high school, one of the main sources of conflict between parents and children, therefore, is the use of the family car. Very often several members of the family may wish to use the car at the same time and, in order to avoid arguments, it is sometimes necessary to make a kind of schedule so that each person will know when he can have the car. One of the most common and effective punishments with which parents may threaten a disobedient teenager, then, is to deny him (or her) the use of the family car for a specific period of time. Nowadays, family members who can afford to often buy their own cars in order to avoid such conflict. Since many people have their own cars, the use of taxis outside of large cities is much less common than it is in many other countries.

General Comment

1. This staging can be divided into four scenes: 1) the realization, by all members of the family, that the car is not available and their consequent annoyance as well as mutual hostility; 2) the ultimate outburst of the father and his subsequent directions to all other family members; 3) the arrival of and discussion with the Insurance Man; and 4) the renewed bickering of the family members. The climax, in a dramatic sense, comes in the third scene, as Mr. Slocum reveals that the compromise they have talked out will be impossible, since the car has been totally wrecked. The pace of the action speeds up to this point, is suddenly slowed down with the arrival of the Insurance Man, and then starts to speed up again after he leaves and the family again becomes embroiled in contention.

2. All family members quite openly state their annoyance and disagreement but the father remains the head of the family, despite the fact he does not dominate the members. This fact must be made clear by the loudness of his speech as he throws down his newspaper and begins to give orders to everyone. Everybody starts to obey those orders except Grandmother, and even her comments are silenced, with rather blunt courtesy, by the father.

3. The role of the Grandmother is very important because she states, and emphasizes by repetition, the fact that the car is the source of all trouble between the family members—and that is the main point of the staging. As she repeats this fact, the mutual hostility of the family members increases.

4. There is little movement involved in this situation and it is important, therefore, that the student actors resist the tendency to turn to face the one who is talking. In real-life conversation, comments are often made to no specific person and in an intimate group a remark can be directed toward someone even when the speaker does not face the person he is addressing.

5. The most difficult aspect of the performance of this staging will be that it requires each actor/actress to be occupied when not speaking. Grandmother and Father can pretend to read the

newspaper. Mother can pretend to dry the dish occasionally and later can adjust her hat. Bob and Nancy can best register their disgust and disappointment by merely looking forlorn or sulking; Nancy will be facing away from the audience, Bob might gloomily inspect his fingernails. These are all typical patterns of behavior common for characters in such a situation. But it is most important that each student should remember to exercise physical and oral patterns simultaneously rather than alternately.

Notes on Adaptation

1. Upon returning home, tired Aunt Doris "kicks off her shoes." Although many Americans—both men and women—do this to cool and rest their feet, it is more common among women. As women's shoes are made for style rather than comfort, women's feet may tire more quickly, particularly if women walk or stand longer than men.
2. As a middle class woman Aunt Doris is likely to substitute some other terms, such as "blasted," for the profanity men might use. This would be particularly true of a middle-aged woman even in the presence of women relatives, although it might not be true of younger women and teenaged girls.
3. In her statements "the fuel pump or something like that" and "Mac is doing something to the fuel pump," Aunt Doris displays a typical feminine vagueness about the source of trouble with her car. Although large numbers of American women drive automobiles, and some women may understand quite a bit about the mechanics of the automobile, they are not encouraged to learn anything about such matters, which are thought to be men's interests in their society; therefore, few girls will admit that they understand such matters. Actually few American men understand the mechanics of an automobile.
4. Note the use of typically feminine softening devices in the dialogue of this staging:
   a. The conversion of a statement to a question form, as in Aunt Doris's "Why don't I drive you" and in Bobbie's "You do remember . . . ,don't you?"
   b. Aunt Doris's use of the "I wonder if" construction to avoid the more direct *Maybe Bill Johnson could pick you up* or *Bill Johnson can probably pick you up.*
   c. The use of *really* in Bobbie's "really late" and "really disappointed," as an emotional intensifier, is not only more widely used among women but may be thought of as a linguistic manifestation of adolescent exuberance, for the effect of the use of the form is similar to that of other means of projecting the excitement of exaggeration.
   d. The affectionate "dear" is sometimes added as a kind of consolation device, as in Aunt Doris's "it looks like you're at the bottom of the list, dear," in speaking to the greatly disappointed Nancy.
   e. A softening effect is also achieved by Aunt Doris's use of the modifying phrase "just this once" and her use of *if* in "if you'll get dressed." It might be pointed out that in trying very hard to control her annoyance and anger Aunt Doris is being particularly polite; she is also showing the restraint which is expected more of women than of men.
5. Annoyance and even disappointment sometimes can be registered by the use of a truncated form, as in Bobbie's "Of all the times for this to happen," meaning *of all the times that this might have happened this is the worst time* or *now is the worst time for this to happen.*
6. Note the typically colloquial truncation in Uncle Ed's "Finally got home, eh George," meaning *you have finally arrived home* and John's "Any chance it will be ready later tonight, Dad?" meaning *is there any chance it will be ready tonight, Dad?* Uncle Ed has been able to omit the subject (i.e., you) because he is addressing Father directly, as is particularly clear from the fact he uses the father's first name (i.e., George). On the other hand, it is likely that there will be a rising pitch contour to indicate that John is asking a question, although such a rise would be less likely if the full statement with its significant shift in verb position were used.

7. Some of the differences in viewpoint separating older from younger teenagers can be seen in the impatience and annoyance expressed by John in his comments to the younger Bob. In complaining about the use of the car to carry "would-be athletes and their silly-headed girlfriends all over town," John is suggesting that Bob and his friends are not really athletes but merely pretend to be and, moreover, that the girls are frivolous rather than serious. Yet foreign students should be made aware that, unlike the situation in some societies, younger children in America rarely feel any sense of deference or respect for older brothers or sisters merely because of age difference. As the older boy, John feels somewhat superior to Bob's values, although at an earlier age John probably also pretended to be an athlete and began to be interested in girls. In fact, John's use of exaggerated expressions, such as "all the time" and "all over town" clearly indicates that he is still an adolescent.

8. Note the difference in attitude and greeting of the Mother in the version for girls and of Uncle Ed in the version for boys. Mother has probably been waiting and listening for Father's arrival, but although Uncle Ed realizes Father is late, he really hasn't been waiting for Father. Note also that the bantering tone of Uncle Ed's questions reveals that he sympathizes with the fact that employees are sometimes obliged to work overtime and he does not really want to hear an explanation of Father's lateness. On the other hand, Mother, who may be less acquainted with the business world, might like to know why Father is late. It should be pointed out, in support of this distinction, that Mother uses the vague and non-accusatory "something," in "Something kept you working overtime," while Uncle Ed uses the more direct "they" and even "somebody," showing that he tends to recognize that a worker is much more likely to work overtime because he is asked or ordered to by somebody. Although Mother may know this, she may tend to avoid admitting it.

    In general, the relationship between the two men is that of mutual understanding and sympathy, whereas that between Mother and Father is somewhat guarded and vaguely hostile, as if the relationship depended on a compromising of quite different values. The foreign student might be made aware that this attitude may characterize many relationships between men and women in America; the relative equality between the sexes may force this compromise.

9. Teachers might attempt to alert foreign students that irony is very common in colloquial usage and particularly in that of teenagers who may use it as a weapon in the generation conflict. We note, for instance, that when John says "That's great!" he really is expressing his disapproval of and annoyance with the situation, and he may also be expressing his resentment that everybody else will be able to use the car before he can use it. In any event, foreign students will have to become accustomed to the fact that a comment intended ironically must be interpreted in exactly the opposite sense than it ordinarily would have. Since such ironic usage depends largely on the situation, the foreign student must understand that situation in order to recognize the need for ironic interpretation. As ironic usage is inadequately dealt with by textbook writers, foreign students quite typically interpret ironic statements literally and thereby completely miss the meaning.

10. Two gestures which should be explained:

    a. Looking toward the ceiling by the grandparents is a conventional expression of the feeling that matters have gone beyond the limits of understanding or reason; probably this gesture is a kind of appeal for divine help when human reason has been exhausted or in some way failed.

    b. When a hand is held up by the Slocums, with the palm outward as a gesture of reassurance, it is an attempt to stop further explanation since there is no need to explain what the person otherwise would feel obliged to explain. Such a gesture can also mean *stop*.

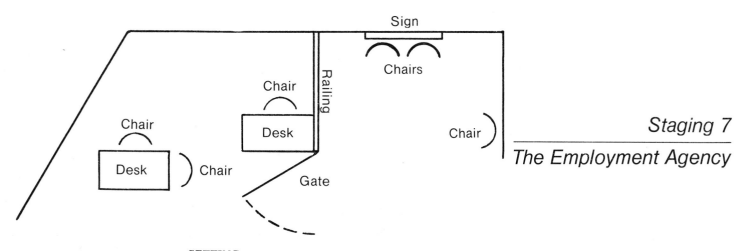

SETTING

A small business office. Midstage, a desk facing the audience. A railing attached to the left side of the desk and extending upstage to downstage forms a kind of barrier. Stage left of this barrier is a waiting room furnished with three chairs, two facing the audience and one far stage left facing stage right. A large sign hanging above the two chairs says Omega Employment Agency. Located stage right, halfway between the desk at midstage and the wings stage right, is another desk facing the audience. One chair is behind the desk and another chair is to the left of the desk, facing stage right. As the curtain rises, the Receptionist is writing at the desk stage left and an interviewer is talking with a man seated next to his desk stage right.

Mixed cast

Interviewer #1 (Charlie Melville)
Mr. Edwards
Receptionist (Julie)
Kim Thomas
Man #1 (Don Hoffman)
Man #2 (George Faber)
Mailman
Interviewer #2 (Joe)
Old Lady (Miss Abbie Wingate)

Girls' cast

Interviewer #1 (Martha Melville)
Mrs. Edwards
Receptionist (Julie)
Kim Thomas
Woman #1 (Donna Hoffman)
Woman #2 (Agnes Faber)
Woman Clerk
Interviewer #2 (Jenny)
Old Lady (Miss Abbie Wingate)

Boys' cast

Interviewer #1 (Charlie Melville)
Mr. Edwards
Interviewer #3 (Jim)
Thomas Harvey
Man #1 (Don Hoffman)
Man #2 (George Faber)
Mailman
Interviewer #2 (Joe)
Old Man (Albert Wingate)

mixed	*girls*	*boys*

mixed

Interviewer #1.   Now, Mr. Edwards, you have stated in your application that you can do light maintenance work. Could you be a bit more specific?

Mr. Edwards   *(drawing out his answer thoughtfully).* W-e-l-l . . . I've spent a number of years at it—and with fairly large companies too. *(Glancing at Interviewer)* Probably before your time, young feller.

Interviewer #1   *(smiling mechanically and mildly annoyed).* Yes, yes—that's very interesting. But we must have a clearer picture of exactly what kind of light maintenance you have done and can do.

Mr. Edwards   *(questioningly).* Light maintenance? Why, going around replacing electric bulbs and flourescent tubes, putting in new pull strings, checking fuse boxes . . . and even fixing wall switches and sockets now and then.

Interviewer #1   *(stunned).* Oh—I see— you mean light maintenance. *(Laughing nervously)* Usually we think of light maintenance as a kind of janitorial work, you know, Mr. Edwards.

Mr. Edwards   *(somewhat indignant).* Well, son, I always swept up when I finished a job—and I mopped too if I spilled anything over—yes, sir.

Girl enters stage left and goes to Receptionist's desk.

Receptionist   *(mechanically).* If you haven't been here before, please fill

girls

Interviewer #1.   Now Mrs. Edwards, you have stated in your application that you've had a great deal of experience in handling people. I wonder if you'd mind being a little more specific.

Mrs. Edwards   *(somewhat tartly).* Young lady, there's an art to not rubbing people the wrong way, and it takes a long time to acquire.

Interviewer #1   *(smiling mechanically and in an obviously ingratiating way).* Yes, I think I understand you, but I wonder if you'd tell me exactly in what capacity you've dealt with people.

Mrs. Edwards.   Oh, I see what you want—I thought I'd put down that I've made my living doing massaging in various health clubs and reducing salons. I've worked for quite a few and have the best references.

Interviewer #1   *(stunned).* Oh—now isn't that peculiar, I had somehow interpreted your note about handling people to mean you'd been in selling, personnel, or perhaps in public relations work.

Mrs. Edwards   *(smiling).* No-no-no . . . I've never done anything like that. I've always worked at massaging.

Girl enters stage left and goes to Receptionist's desk.

Receptionist   *(mechanically).* If you haven't been here before, please fill out an application. *(Points to a pile at*

boys

Interviewer #1.   Now, Mr. Edwards, you have stated in your application that you can do light maintenance work. Could you be a bit more specific?

Mr. Edwards   *(drawing out his answer thoughtfully).* W-e-l-l . . . I've spent a number of years at it—and with fairly large companies too. *(Glancing at Interviewer)* Probably before your time, young feller.

Interviewer #1   *(smiling mechanically and mildly annoyed).* Yes, yes—that's very interesting. But we must have a clearer picture of exactly what kind of light maintenance you have done and can do.

Mr. Edwards   *(questioningly).* Light maintenance? Why, going around replacing electric bulbs and fluorescent tubes, putting in new pull strings, checking fuse boxes . . . and even fixing wall switches and sockets now and then.

Interviewer #1   *(stunned).* Oh—I see— you mean light maintenance. *(Laughing nervously)* Usually we think of light maintenance as a kind of janitorial work, you know, Mr. Edwards.

Mr. Edwards   *(somewhat indignant).* Well, son, I always swept up when I finished a job—and I mopped too if I spilled anything over—yes, sir.

Man enters stage left and goes to Receptionist's desk.

Interviewer #3   *(mechanically).* Please fill out one of those application forms

mixed

out an application. *(Points to a pile at the corner of the desk)*

Miss Thomas.   Oh—I've been here before. My name's Kim Thomas and I filled out an application about three weeks ago, but I never heard from you.

Receptionist   *(surprised).* Three weeks! That *is* funny. *(Leafs swiftly through the cards in a file box on her desk. Looks puzzled)* There's something wrong—I don't have any card for you. Did you have an interview?

Miss Thomas.   Yes, that gentleman inside *(nodding toward Interviewer #1 conversing inaudibly with Mr. Edwards at a desk beyond Receptionist)* talked to me.

Two men enter stage left and sit down on the two chairs facing the audience. Receptionist quickly leafs through the file cards again and pulls out one.

Receptionist.   Here it is. *(Pause)* I see what happened. You wrote your first name first—where it states LAST NAME—and so your card was filed under Kim, Thomas Kim.

Miss Thomas.   No wonder I didn't get any call! *(Discouraged)* Gee, I guess I've been waiting for nothing all this time. *(Receptionist examines the card)*

Man #1   *(sitting in the waiting room).* So, I said to him, "Look, you people need me more than I need you"—and I left.

Man #2   *(sitting next to Man #1*

girls

the corner of the desk)

Miss Thomas.   Oh—I've been here before. My name's Kim Thomas and I filled out an application about three weeks ago, but I never heard from you.

Receptionist   *(surprised).* Three weeks! That *is* funny. *(Leafs swiftly through the cards in a file box on her desk. Looks puzzled)* There's something wrong—I don't have any card for you. Did you have an interview?

Miss Thomas.   Yes, that lady inside *(nodding toward Interviewer #1 conversing inaudibly with Mrs. Edwards at a desk beyond the Receptionist)* talked to me.

Two women enter stage left and sit down on the two chairs facing the audience. Receptionist quickly leafs through the file cards again and pulls out one.

Receptionist.   Here it is. *(Pause)* I see what happened. You wrote your first name first—where it states LAST NAME—and so your card was filed under Kim, Thomas Kim.

Miss Thomas.   No wonder I didn't get any call! *(Discouraged)* Gee, I guess I've been waiting for nothing all this time. *(Receptionist examines the card)*

Woman #1   *(sitting in the waiting room).* So, I said to him, "My dear, you need me more than I need you"—and I walked out.

Woman #2   *(sitting next to Woman #1 chuckles).* You really told him off,

boys

(points to a pile at the corner of the desk) and I'll try to take care of you right away.

Mr. Harvey   *(hesitating).* Er—my name's Thomas Harvey and I've been here before. Some woman had me fill out one of those applications when I was here three weeks ago. I haven't heard anything since.

Interviewer #3   *(frowning).* You haven't heard anything, eh? *That's* funny. *(Leafs swiftly through the cards in a file box on his desk)* I don't find any card for you and the Receptionist isn't here today so I don't know what she did with it. Were you interviewed?

Mr. Harvey   *(nodding).* Yeah—I think it was that feller over there, in fact. *(Nodding toward Interviewer #1 conversing inaudibly with Mr. Edwards at a desk beyond the Receptionist)*

Two men enter stage left and sit down on the two chairs facing the audience.

Interviewer #3   *(quickly leafs through the card file again).* Nope. *(Pause)* Wait a minute; here's your card, filed under Thomas *(shows Mr. Harvey the card)* because you wrote your first name where it says LAST NAME. So your card was out of place.

Mr. Harvey.   I really pulled a boner! No wonder I've been waiting for nothing all this time.

Man #1   *(sitting in the waiting room).* So, I said to him, "Look, you people need me more than I need you"—and I

mixed

chuckles). Boy, you really told him off. *(Pause)* How long is it since you worked?

Man #1.   Well, let's see . . . it must be about six months now. There's nothing in my line.

Man #2.   What do you do?

Man #1.   Me? I'm a veterinarian's assistant. I hold the dog while the vet gives him a shot. Kind of like a nurse. *(Man #2 nods understandingly)*

Man #2   *(half jokingly)*. Could be dangerous work—especially if the dog doesn't know he's supposed to be "man's best friend," eh? Then again, I used to have a big police dog that was gentle as a lamb, although a little speck of a fox terrier I had once was mean as they come.

Interviewer #1   *(smiling mechanically)*. Well, Mr. Edwards, we don't have many clients your age, and, of course, you realize that at seventy-three you may have some trouble getting even parttime work—but *(reaching out to shake hands with Mr. Edwards)* we'll do our best.

Mr. Edwards.   Anything at all will do—y'know, just a couple of hours a day. *(As Interviewer urges him toward the gate leading to the waiting room)* It's not the money, y'know. Just something to keep me busy.

Interviewer #1 nods still smiling mechanically as he turns to Receptionist.

Mr. Edwards.   Well, goodbye . . . and

girls

didn't you? But has it been a long time since you last worked?

Woman #1.   Well, let's see . . . it must be about six months now. There's nothing in my line.

Woman #2.   What do you do?

Woman #1.   Me? I'm a veterinarian's assistant. I hold the dog while the vet gives him a shot. Kind of like a nurse. *(Woman #2 nods understandingly)*

Woman #2   *(half jokingly)*. Could be dangerous work—especially if the dog doesn't know he's supposed to be "man's best friend," eh? Then again, I used to have a big police dog that was gentle as a lamb, although a little speck of a fox terrier I had once was mean as they come.

Interviewer #1   *(smiling mechanically)*. Well, Mrs. Edwards, jobs for . . . er . . . older women are a little tight, you know . . . even for parttime work. But *(patting Mrs. Edward's arm reassuringly)* we'll do our best to find something for you.

Mrs. Edwards.   Anything at all will do—y'know, just a couple of hours a day. *(As Interviewer urges her toward the gate leading to the waiting room)* It's not the money, y'know. Just something to keep me busy.

Interviewer #1 nods still smiling mechanically as she turns to Receptionist

Mrs. Edwards.   Well, goodbye . . . and thanks. *(Interviewer #1 waves goodbye to her as Mrs. Edwards exits stage*

boys

left.

Man #2   *(sitting next to Man #1 chuckles)*. Boy, you really told him off. *(Pause)* How long is it since you worked?

Man #1.   Well, let's see . . . it must be about six months now. There's nothing in my line.

Man #2.   What do you do?

Man #1.   Me? I'm a veterinarian's assistant. I hold the dog while the vet gives him a shot. Kind of like a nurse. *(Man #2 nods understandingly)*

Man #2   *(half jokingly)*. Could be dangerous work—especially if the dog doesn't know he's supposed to be "man's best friend," eh? Then again, I used to have a big police dog that was gentle as a lamb, although a little speck of a fox terrier I had once was mean as they come.

Interviewer #1   *(smiling mechanically)*. Well, Mr. Edwards, we don't have many clients your age, and, of course, you realize that at seventy-three you may have some trouble getting even parttime work—but *(reaching out to shake hands with Mr. Edwards)* we'll do our best.

Mr. Edwards.   Anything at all will do—y'know, just a couple of hours a day. *(As Interviewer urges him toward the gate leading to the waiting room)* It's not the money, y'know. Just something to keep me busy.

Interviewer #1 nods still smiling mechani-

mixed

thanks. *(Interviewer #1 waves goodbye to him as Mr. Edwards exits stage left)*

Interviewer #1   *(stage whispers to Receptionist while nods toward the departing Mr. Edwards).* A real bargain! *(Shakes his head wonderingly)*

Receptionist   *(to Interviewer #1).* Miss Thomas's card has been misfiled and so she hasn't been notified of vacancies, although she registered and was interviewed three weeks ago. I wonder if it's possible you may have something for her?

Interviewer #1.   Let me have the card. *(To Miss Thomas)* Please come in. *(Holds the gate for her to pass through, then goes to his desk, with Miss Thomas following; they both sit down and Interviewer, head resting in both hands, elbows on the desk, studies the card)*

Man #2   *(solemnly).* That's right—after you're forty-five it's pretty tough. Nobody needs you. They figure you're a bad risk and companies don't want to pay the high insurance rates.

Receptionist   *(glancing at the two men).* May I help either of you?

Man #1   *(scrambling to his feet, standing before her desk).* I'm Don Hoffman and I just wanted Mr. Hill to know I'm ready for work again. The doctor's got a lot of my money and I'm getting pretty low, so I'll need a job soon.

girls

left)

Interviewer #1   *(stage whispers to Receptionist and nods toward the departing Mrs. Edwards, while rolling her eyes toward the ceiling and shaking her head sadly).* A very tough case. Imagine, seventy-three!

Receptionist   *(to Interviewer #1).* Miss Thomas's card has been misfiled and so she hasn't been notified of vacancies, although she registered and was interviewed three weeks ago. I wonder if it's possible you may have something for her?

Interviewer #1.   May I have the card, please, Julie. *(Smiles mechanically at Miss Thomas and beckons)* Won't you please come in? *(Walks to her desk, followed by Miss Thomas, and they both sit down. Holding the card with thumb and forefinger of both hands, Interviewer studies it)*

Woman #2.   Oh, of course—you know as well as I do that at our age we can't compete with those slim young things. They want youthful decoration in most offices and it doesn't make much difference how much more efficient we might be.

Receptionist   *(glancing at the two women).* May I help either of you?

Woman #1   *(getting hastily to her feet and standing before the Receptionist's desk).* I'm Donna Hoffman and I wanted Mrs. Hill to know I'm out of the hospital now and available for

boys

cally as he turns to Interviewer #3.

Mr. Edwards.   Well, goodbye . . . and thanks. *(Interviewer #1 waves goodbye to him as Mr. Edwards exits stage left)*

Interviewer #1   *(stage whispers to Interviewer #3 while he nods toward the departing Mr. Edwards).* A real bargain! *(Shakes his head wonderingly)*

Interviewer #3   *(to Interviewer #1).* Say, Charlie, this guy's card was filed under his first name when he came around three weeks ago. What should I do with him? Have we got anything for him?

Interviewer #1.   Let me have the card. *(To Mr. Harvey)* Please come in. *(Holds the gate for him to pass through, then goes to his desk, with Mr. Harvey following; they both sit down and Interviewer, head resting in both hands, elbows on the desk, studies the card)*

Man #2   *(solemnly).* That's right—after you're forty-five it's pretty tough. Nobody needs you. They figure you're a bad risk and companies don't want to pay the high insurance rates.

Interviewer #3   *(glancing at the two men).* Can I help either of you two fellows? The Receptionist isn't in today.

Man #1   *(scrambling to his feet, standing before his desk).* I'm Don Hoffman and I just wanted Mr. Hill to know I'm ready for work again. The doctor's got

mixed	*girls*	*boys*

mixed

Receptionist.   Mr. Hoffman *(leafing through the card file and pulling out a card)*, we just have no calls in your line ... but we'll keep after it, of course. And be sure to let us know if you find something on your own, won't you?

Man #1   *(somewhat discouraged)*. Oh—well—thanks. *(Turning to Man #2)* Best of luck to you. *(Exits stage left, as Mailman enters and walks to Receptionist's desk holding a large mailing envelope)*

Man #2   *(to Man #1)*. Same to you. Hope you'll find something soon. See you around.

Miss Thomas   *(somewhat desperately)*. I've just got to get a job soon. I haven't had a paycheck for a month. I've been looking all over since I was here last time, but the restaurant business is off and they're not hiring any more waitresses. If I could type, I'd probably be able to pick up a job right away.

Mailman.   Say, I've got an envelope here, addressed to *(squints trying to read the writing on the envelope)* a George Faber, care of Omega Employment Agency.

Man #2   *(jumping up excitedly)*. That's me. Now there's luck for you! I just happened to be here at the right time. *(Explaining to Receptionist)* Since I've been moving around a lot I gave this place as my mailing address.

girls

work. *(Embarrassed, stares down at her pocketbook, held in both hands at about waist level)* The hospital bills added up pretty fast and I really do need the money.

Receptionist.   I'm awfully sorry, Mrs. Hoffman *(leafing through the card file and pulling out a card)*, but it is very slow right now ... although we're hoping we'll soon have something to offer you. *(Pause)* You will be sure to let us know if you find something yourself, won't you?

Woman #1   *(somewhat discouraged)*. Oh—well—thanks anyway. *(Turning and smiling to Woman #2)* Best of luck to you. *(Exits stage left as woman enters and walks to Receptionist's desk holding a large mailing envelope)*

Woman #2   *(to Woman #1)*. Same to you. Hope you'll find something soon. See you around.

Miss Thomas   *(somewhat desperately)*. I've just got to get a job soon. I haven't had a paycheck for a month. I've been looking all over since I was here last time, but the restaurant business is off and they're not hiring any more waitresses. If I could type, I'd probably be able to pick up a job right away.

Woman Clerk.   Excuse me, but this envelope *(holding it up and squinting as she tries to read the writing on the envelope)* addressed to an Agnes F-A ... looks like F-A-B-E-R ...

boys

a lot of my money and I'm getting pretty low, so I'll need a job soon.

Interviewer #3   *(nodding understandingly)*. Uh-huh. *(Leafing through the card file and pulling out a card)* I tell you, Mr. Hoffman, I don't find any calls listed in your line, right now. But I'll make a note here *(writes on the card)* for the Receptionist and she'll contact you when she gets back. Let her know if meanwhile you happen to get something on your own.

Man #1   *(somewhat discouraged)*. Oh—well—thanks. *(Turning to Man #2)* Best of luck to you. *(Exits stage left, as Mailman enters and walks to Receptionist's desk holding a large mailing envelope)*

Man #2   *(to Man #1)*. Same to you. Hope you'll find something soon. See you around.

Mr. Harvey   *(somewhat desperately to Interviewer #1)*. Look, I've got to get a job soon. I've been looking all over and haven't found anything. Construction is shut down all over town. It's getting tough with nothing coming in for the last month.

Mailman.   Say, I've got an envelope here, addressed to *(squints trying to read the writing on the envelope)* a George Faber, care of Omega Employment Agency.

Man #2   *(jumping up excitedly)*. That's me. Now there's luck for you! I just happened to be here at the right time.

mixed	*girls*	*boys*

mixed

Mailman hands him the package. He tears it open and pulls out several small booklets or pamphlets.

Man #2   *(to Receptionist and Mailman).* Excuse me, while I look over these free books I sent for. You never know—they might have some good ideas I can use. *(Reads the booklet titles aloud as he returns to his chair and sits down)* How to Improve Yourself; Ways to Make Money; 2500 Good Paying Jobs . . .

Mailman   *(to Receptionist).* Is this guy *(nodding at Man #2 who is engrossed in looking through the booklets)* here to find a job or does he use this place as a lounge?

Receptionist shrugs and shakes her head.

Mailman   *(nodding toward Man #2).* I'll bet he'd take off like a rabbit if you offered him a job. *(Turning toward Man #2 who sits contentedly reading the booklets)* But I don't envy him, being out of work at his age. *(Shaking his head sadly)* Probably has no training or skill to fall back on either. *(Sighing)* That's one thing about Civil Service—it's steady, even if the pay is low. *(Handing Receptionist a large bundle of mail)* Well, so long. *(Exits stage right)*

Interviewer #1   *(smiling mechanically at Miss Thomas).* There's nothing at the moment, but we'll see what we can do for you, Miss Thomas. I think we'll have something fairly soon. *(Gets up)*

girls

Faber, was delivered to our office, two doors down the hall, by mistake, and I thought it might possibly belong here.

Woman #2   *(jumping up excitedly).* That's me. Now there's luck for you! I just happened to be here at the right time. *(Explaining to Receptionist)* Since I've been moving around a lot, I gave this place as my mailing address.

Woman Clerk hands her the package. She tears it open and pulls out several small booklets or pamphlets.

Woman #2   *(to Receptionist and Woman Clerk).* Excuse me, while I look over these free books I sent for. You never know—they might have some good ideas I can use. *(Reads the booklet titles aloud as she returns to her chair and sits down)* How to Improve Yourself; Ways to Make Money; 2500 Good Paying Jobs . . .

Woman Clerk   *(puzzled stage whispers to Receptionist).* Do you think she *(nodding at Woman #2 who is engrossed in looking at the booklets)* has any real business here or does she just use this place as a lounge?

Receptionist shrugs and shakes her head.

Woman Clerk   *(snorting in mild disdain).* H-m-m! I imagine she wouldn't linger around here long if you threatened to give her a job. *(Turning toward Woman #2, who sits contentedly reading the pamphlets)* But, I don't envy her being out of work at her age. *(Shaking her head sadly)* I suppose she

boys

(Explaining to Interviewer #3) Since I've been moving around a lot I gave this place as my mailing address.

Mailman hands him the package. He tears it open and pulls out several small booklets or pamphlets.

Man #2   *(to Interviewer #3 and Mailman).* Excuse me, while I look over these free books I sent for. You never know—they might have some good ideas I can use. *(Reads the booklet titles aloud as he returns to his chair and sits down)* How to Improve Yourself; Ways to Make Money; 2500 Good Paying Jobs . . .

Mailman   *(to Interviewer #3).* Is this guy *(nodding at Man #2 who is engrossed in looking through the booklets)* here to find a job or does he use this place as a lounge?

Interviewer #3 shrugs and shakes his head.

Mailman   *(nodding toward Man #2).* I'll bet he'd take off like a rabbit if you offered him a job. *(Turning toward Man #2 who sits contentedly reading the booklets)* But I don't envy him, being out of work at his age. *(Shaking his head sadly)* Probably has no training or skill to fall back on either. *(Sighing)* That's one thing about Civil Service—it's steady, even if the pay is low. *(Handing Interviewer #3 a large bundle of mail)* Well, so long. *(Exits stage right)*

Interviewer #1   *(smiling mechanically at Mr. Harvey).* There's nothing at the

mixed

Goodbye!

Miss Thomas   (*disappointed*). I'm sure sorry I filled out that card wrong. (*She crosses to stage left to exit*) I hope something will turn up before my rent is due though, because I've stalled off the landlady long enough now. Well (*sadly*), g'bye. (*Exits*)

Interviewer #2   (*in shirtsleeves enters from stage right and crosses to Interviewer #1*). Say, Charlie, this will kill you! (*Holds out a card*) This guy I just interviewed told me he used to be a sword swallower (*chuckling*) and when I asked him why he quit he told me . . . he discovered it was a cut-throat business! (*Chuckles*) Can you imagine that!

Interviewer #1 laughs loudly and vigorously and is joined by Interviewer #2. While they are laughing a shabbily dressed old woman enters the waiting room, stage left, and goes to Receptionist's desk.

Old Lady   (*sternly*). I'm Abbie Wingate and I'd like to see the manager, young lady.

Receptionist   (*hesitating, embarrassed*). Er . . . have you made out an application?

Old Lady   (*snorting*). Application! No, you silly girl . . . at my age I'm not looking for a job. I own this agency. Now go and tell the manager I'm here and want to talk with him.

Receptionist   (*surprised and mildly frightened*). Yes, ma'am. (*Scurries over

girls

has no real training or skill to bargain with either. (*Sighing*) It's tough on a woman to get old—but (*shaking her head sadly*) it's happening to all of us. Well, glad I guessed right about that envelope belonging here anyway. (*Exits stage right*) Goodbye!

Interviewer #1   (*smiling mechanically at Miss Thomas*). There's nothing at the moment, but we'll see what we can do for you, Miss Thomas. I think we'll have something fairly soon. (*Gets up*) Goodbye!

Miss Thomas   (*disappointed*). I'm sure sorry I filled out that card wrong. (*She crosses to stage left to exit*) I hope something will turn up before my rent is due though, because I've stalled off the landlady long enough now. Well (*sadly*), g'bye. (*Exits*)

Interviewer #2   (*enters from stage right and crosses to Interviewer #1*). Say, Martha, this will just kill you! (*Holds out a card*) This woman I just interviewed told me she used to be a sword swallower (*giggling*) and when I asked her why she quit, she told me she discovered it was a cutthroat business! Isn't that just priceless! (*Giggles*)

Interviewer #1 laughs loudly and vigorously and is joined by Interviewer #2. While they are laughing a shabbily dressed old woman enters the waiting room, stage left, and goes to Receptionist's desk.

Old Lady   (*sternly*). I'm Abbie Wingate and I'd like to see the manager, young

boys

I'm not looking for a job, young man. (*Loudly*) I am the owner of this agency. (*Gesturing toward the inner moment, but we'll see what we can do for you, Mr. Harvey. I think we'll have something fairly soon. (*Gets up*) Goodbye!

Mr. Harvey.   I realize it's partly my fault, pulling that boner in filling out the card. But I'm behind in my rent and I don't know how long I can stall off the landlady. Well (*sighing sadly*), g'bye.

Interviewer #2   (*in shirtsleeves enters from stage right and crosses to Interviewer #1*). Say, Charlie, this will kill you! (*Holds out a card*) This guy I just interviewed told me he used to be a sword swallower (*chuckling*) and when I asked him why he quit he told me . . . he discovered it was a cut-throat business! (*Chuckles*) Can you imagine that!

Interviewer #1 laughs loudly and vigorously and is joined by Interviewer #2. While they are laughing a shabbily dressed old man enters the waiting room, stage left, and goes to Receptionist's desk.

Old Man   (*sternly*). I'm Albert Wingate and I'd like to see the manager, young man.

Interviewer #3   (*hesitating*). Our Receptionist is out today . . . er . . . have you made an application, sir?

Old Man   (*snorting*). Application! Of course not. What nonsense! At my age

mixed	girls	boys

mixed

to Interviewer #1's desk where the two interviewers are chatting and chuckling. Speaks nervously to Interviewer #1). Mr. Melville . . . *(They ignore her and continue chatting and chuckling)*

Interviewer #2 *(smiling).* And then, when I asked him what else he'd done, he told me he'd also trained fleas for a flea circus . . . only he was dissatisfied with the work . . . because he was barely scratching the surface of his talents. *(Again both roar with laughter while the Old Lady stares, annoyed and impatient)*

Interviewer #1 *(chuckling).* And he said it all with a straight face too. Isn't that something! *(Giggling)*

Interviewer #2. Maybe we should try to get him a job on TV. He's a lot more clever than most of the clowns they've got on. *(They both chuckle very audibly)*

Receptionist *(excitedly hissing to Interviewer #1).* Mr. Melville . . . there's a woman to see you . . .

Interviewer #2 *(still chuckling).* Does she have an appointment?

Receptionist *(shaking her head negatively and looking back over her shoulder toward the Old Lady who stands next to the gate, looking out over the audience frowning).* She says she owns the agency.

Both Interviewers gasp and abruptly stop laughing)

girls

lady.

Receptionist *(hesitating embarrassed).* Er . . . have you made out an application?

Old Lady *(snorting).* Application! No, you silly girl . . . at my age I'm not looking for a job. I own this agency. Now go and tell the manager I'm here and want to talk with her.

Receptionist *(surprised and mildly frightened).* Yes, ma'am. *(Scurries over to Interviewer #1's desk where the two interviewers are chatting and chuckling. Speaks nervously to Interviewer #1).* Mrs. Melville . . . *(They ignore her and continue chatting and chuckling)*

Interviewer #2 *(smiling).* And then, when I asked her what else she'd done, she told me she'd also trained fleas for a flea circus . . . only she was dissatisfied with the work . . . because she was barely scratching the surface of her talents. *(Again both roar with laughter while the Old Lady stares, annoyed and impatient)*

Interviewer #1 *(chuckling).* And she said it all with a straight face too? Isn't that perfectly priceless! *(Giggling)*

Interviewer #2. Maybe we should try to get her a job on TV. She's a lot more clever than most of the clowns they've got on. *(They both chuckle very audibly)*

Receptionist *(hissing to Interviewer #1).* Mrs. Melville . . . there's a woman

boys

office) Now go in and tell the manager I'm here. Want to talk with him. *(Gestures with both hands to urge Interviewer #3 on)*

Interviewer #3 *(surprised and mildly frightened).* Yes, sir. *(Scurries over to Interviewer #1's desk where the two interviewers are chatting and chuckling. Speaks nervously to Interviewer #1).* Mr. Melville . . . *(They ignore him and continue chatting and chuckling)*

Interviewer #1. And *(chuckling)* he said it all with a straight face too!

Interviewer #2. Maybe we should try to get him a job on TV. He's a lot more clever than most of the clowns they've got on. *(They both chuckle very audibly)*

Interviewer #3 *(to Interviewer #1).* Charlie . . . there's an old codger named Wingate out here to see you.

Interviewer #2 *(still chuckling).* Does he have an appointment?

Interviewer #3 *(nervously).* Look . . . cut it out, you guys. The old fellow says he owns the agency!

Both Interviewers gasp and abruptly stop laughing.

Interviewer #2 *(shocked).* Mr. Wingate! . . . the old boy himself, eh! Good luck, Charlie . . . see you later. *(He exits quickly stage right as Interviewer #1 rushes to his desk and motions to Interviewer #3 to bring in the Old Man)*

|| *mixed* | *girls* | *boys* |

mixed

Interviewer #2 *(shocked)*. Miss Wingate! Good luck, Charlie ... see you later. *(He exits quickly stage right as Interviewer #1 rushes to his desk and motions to Receptionist to bring in the Old Lady)*

Receptionist *(rushes back to her desk, opens the gate and with obviously exaggerated courtesy)*. Won't you come in, please, Miss Wingate? Mr. Melville will be happy to see you. *(Leads the way to Interviewer #1's desk. The Old Lady marches across the stage, following Receptionist. Interviewer #1 rises and comes around the desk enthusiastically to meet her, with a too beaming smile on his face. Receptionist scurries back to her desk)*

Interviewer #1 *(profusely)*. Miss Wingate! What a pleasant surprise!

Old Lady *(bluntly)*. Have you ever done any other kind of work, Mr. Melville? Can you get a job readily, do you suppose?

Interviewer #1 *(startled)*. Well ... *(giggling in nervous puzzlement)* as a matter of fact, I ...

Old Lady *(interrupting impatiently)*. This agency is a losing proposition, Mr. Melville, and if it doesn't begin to show a profit, I'm afraid I'm going to have to cut down on operating expenses. I thought I'd tell you personally of my decision—*(ominously)* so that you'd be prepared. Please inform the rest of your staff. Good day!

girls

to see you ...

Interviewer #2 *(still chuckling)*. Does she have an appointment?

Receptionist *(shaking her head negatively and looking back over her shoulder toward the Old Lady who stands next to the gate, looking out over the audience frowning)* She says she owns the agency.

Both Interviewers gasp and abruptly stop laughing.

Interviewer #2 *(shocked)*. Miss Wingate! Good luck, Martha ... see you later. *(She exits quickly stage right as Interviewer #1 rushes to her desk and motions to Receptionist to bring in the Old Lady)*

Receptionist *(rushes back to her desk, opens the gate and with obviously exaggerated courtesy)* Won't you come in, please, Miss Wingate? Mrs. Melville will be happy to see you. *(Leads the way to Interviewer #1's desk. The Old Lady marches across the stage following Receptionist. Interviewer #1 rises and comes around the desk enthusiastically to meet her, with a too beaming smile on her face. Receptionist scurries back to her desk)*

Interviewer #1 *(profusely)*. Miss Wingate! My, what a pleasant surprise!

Old Lady *(bluntly)*. Have you ever done any other kind of work, Mrs. Melville? Can you get a job readily, do you suppose?

Interviewer #1 *(startled)*. Well ...

boys

Interviewer #3 *(rushes back to Receptionist's desk, opens the gate with a flourish and with exaggerated courtesy)*. Please excuse the delay, Mr. Wingate. Come *(indicating the direction of Interviewer #1's office)* this way. *(Leads the Old Man stomping across the stage to Interviewer #1's desk. Interviewer #1, appearing to be studying some papers, glances up, quickly springs to his feet, as if surprised, and with a beaming but artificial smile on his face comes around the desk holding out his hand in greeting. Interviewer #3 quickly leaves, rushing back to Receptionist's desk where he sits, straining to hear the conversation)*

Interviewer #1 *(profusely)*. Mr. Wingate. *(Reaching to shake hands with Mr. Wingate, who unenthusiastically offers a very limp hand which Interviewer #1 shakes vigorously)* Why, what a rare pleasure this is, indeed!

Old Man *(flatly and slightly sarcastic)*. Yes, I'm sure. *(Bluntly)* Melville, have you ever done any other kind of work; could you get a job readily, do you think?

Interviewer #1 *(startled)*. Well ... *(giggling in nervous puzzlement)* as a matter of fact, I ...

Old Man *(interrupting)*. Melville, I'm going to have to cut down operating expenses here. It's been a losing prop-

mixed

(Turns and stamping across the stage, nods toward Receptionist's desk, and exits stage left)

Interviewer #1   *(dazed, stares after his departing guest, shrugs his shoulders, shakes his head, then calls to Receptionist).* Julie! . . . tell Joe to come here. I want to talk to you both.

Interviewer #2   *(gloomily emerging stage right and walking slowly toward Interviewer #1's desk).* Never mind . . . I heard the whole thing, Charlie . . . (Shakes his head sadly) And I've been expecting it, the way things have been going.

Receptionist   *(crossing the stage to Interviewer #1's desk and sighing sadly)* Yeah . . . me too. In the last couple of months this place hasn't made a dime.

They all stand in silent gloom gazing at the floor before Interviewer #1's desk for a few seconds.

Interviewer #1   *(sadly).* Well *(sighing)* I guess that's it. *(Reaching for a card file on his desk)* Maybe we'd better see if there are any jobs in here . . . for *ourselves* . . . just in case.

CURTAIN

girls

(giggling in nervous puzzlement) as a matter of fact, I . . .

Old Lady   *(interrupting impatiently).* This agency is a losing proposition, Mrs. Melville, and if it doesn't begin to show a profit, I'm afraid I'm going to have to cut down on operating expenses. I thought I'd tell you personally of my decision— *(ominously)* so that you'd be prepared. Please inform the rest of your staff. Good day! *(Turns and, stamping across the stage, nods toward Receptionist's desk, and exits stage left)*

Interviewer #1   *(dazed, stares after her departing guest, shrugs her shoulders, shakes her head, then calls to Receptionist)* Julie! . . . tell Jenny to come here. I want to talk to you both.

Interviewer #2   *(gloomily emerging stage right and walking slowly toward Interviewer #1's desk).* Never mind . . . I heard the whole thing, Martha . . . (Shakes her head sadly) And I've been expecting it, the way things have been going.

Receptionist   *(crossing the stage to Interviewer #1's desk and sighing sadly).* Yeah . . . me too. In the last couple of months this place hasn't made a dime.

They all stand in silent gloom gazing at the floor before Interviewer #1's desk for a few seconds.

Interviewer #1   *(sadly).* Well *(sighing)* I guess that's it. *(Reaching for a card file*

boys

osition for too long. *(Ominously)* I want you and your staff to be prepared for the possibility I may have to close this office so I'm giving you fair warning now. Good day! *(Turns and, stamping across the stage, nods a curt goodbye to Interviewer #3, and exits stage left)*

Interviewer #1   *(dazed, stares after his departing guest, shrugs his shoulders, shakes his head, then calls to Interviewer #3).* Jim! . . . get Joe in here. I've got to talk to both of you right away.

Interviewer #2   *(gloomily emerging stage right and walking slowly toward Interviewer #1's desk).* Never mind . . . I heard the whole thing, Charlie . . . (Shakes his head sadly) And I've been expecting it, the way things have been going.

Interviewer #3   *(crossing the stage to Interviewer #1's desk and sighing sadly).* Yeah . . . me too. In the last couple of months this place hasn't made a dime.

They all stand in silent gloom gazing at the floor before Interviewer #1's desk for a few seconds.

Interviewer #1   *(sadly).* Well *(sighing)* I guess that's it. *(Reaching for a card file on his desk)* Maybe we'd better see if there are any jobs in here . . . for *ourselves* . . . just in case.

CURTAIN

mixed

fail

beaming—very broad

before your time—before you were born

boy—an exclamation of enthusiasm, having no specific meaning

business is off—no business, no customers

can you imagine that!—exclamation of surprise (this does not mean *isn't that surprising*)

care of—the mail will be kept for the person it is addressed to

cut down—reduce

cutthroat business—very competitive, and therefore, risky

eh/²ey³/—expresses a question

er /ər/—expression of hesitation

feller—a sound spelling of *fellow*, also occasionally spelled *fella*

figure—to assume, calculate, imagine, think

fill out—answer all of the questions on a form

find something—find a job

fall back on—depend on

flea circus—a kind of entertainment in which trained fleas pull tiny carts, fight with each other, etc.

funny—peculiar, unusual, odd

gee—exclamation of enthusiasm

gentle as a lamb—very gentle

getting pretty low—needs money badly

gloom—sadness, dejection

good day—a somewhat old-fashioned and formal sounding *goodbye*

guy /gay/—fellow, man, person

g'bye—common colloquial form of *goodbye*

hasn't made a dime—there has been little or

girls

on her desk) Maybe we'd better see if there are any jobs in here . . . for *ourselves* . . . just in case.

CURTAIN

Glossary

a little tight—not available, a very few or little

forefinger—finger next to the thumb

handling people—getting along with people, working with people

health club—a kind of gymnasium having equipment for exercising

h-m-m-/h²ã/—this explosive sound expresses doubt

in what capacity—what relationship

ingratiatingly—an obvious attempt to seem friendly

just priceless—very interesting, amazing

massaging—rubbing the body to soothe aching muscles

my dear—a rather old-fashioned and stilted form of address, here used as ironic sarcasm

personnel—in charge of employees, usually in a large company

public relations—in contact with customers, including advertising

reducing salons—special gymnasiums equipped to help fat people lose extra weight

rubbing people the wrong way—annoying or angering people

slim young things—young girls

boys

Glossary

behind in my rent—owes rent to his landlady, rent is overdue

codger—old man; *old fellow* and *old boy* are terms of a similar meaning

cut it out—stop it

fair warning—warning with time enough so that other plans may be made

get Joe in here—ask Joe to come here

getting tough—becoming difficult to live

limp—without life or strength

look—sentence opener reflecting a kind of impatience or exasperation

losing proposition—unprofitable

nope—colloquial form of *no*

nothing coming in—receiving no salary

pulled a boner—made a silly mistake

scurries—rushes in an uncoordinated, clumsy way

shut down—stopped, not operating

uh-huh /ə̃ + hə̃/—expression meaning *yes*

mixed

no profit from the business

hollowly—without emotion (here, the manager is suffering from a kind of shock and therefore speaking in a dazed way)

I'll bet—I think, I'm sure

it's steady—the work is regular, there are no periods of unemployment

just in case—if some possibility becomes actual; here, just in case they lose their jobs

keep after it—will try hard to find

last name—family name

leaf—look at, search, examine

let's see—an expression of calculation or reflection

line—specialty

look—a sentence opener, frequently reflecting a kind of impatience or annoyance

losing proposition—unprofitable

mailing envelope—envelope, usually made of strong brown paper, for mailing books or other small items

mean as they come—very vicious

my line—the special kind of work I can do

no wonder—the reason is very obvious

on your own—by yourself, without assistance

pick up a job—find a job

pull string—the string used to switch on an electric light

same to you—a courtesy expression used in replying to someone who has wished for your good fortune or happiness

say—sentence opener to call attention

see you around—a slang form of *goodbye*

girls

tough on a woman—difficult for a woman

very slow right now—not much business, few customers at this time

youthful decoration—attractive girls

mixed (continued)

shot—injection of medicine by a hypodermic needle

so long—form of *goodbye*

something will turn up—some job will develop or appear

something wrong—some mistake, unusual situation

speck—very small unit

stall off the landlady—ask the landlady to postpone the collection of the rent

steady—continues with no interruption of work

straight face—without smiling, quite seriously

sword swallower—a kind of entertainer who can put a sword down his throat or appear to

take off—run away

that's it—it's the way matters stand, unfortunately; it's final or the end

the way things have been going—recent

mixed (continued)

events indicate

the whole thing—the entire conversation

this will kill you—a colloquial exaggeration meaning this will make you laugh very heartily because it is very funny

told him off—made your opinion very clear and forcefully, denounced him

tough—difficult

veterinarian—doctor for animals, abbreviated colloquially as vet

waiting for nothing—waiting unnecessarily

well—a sentence opener having no specific meaning

what do you do?—what kinds of work can you do?

why—sentence opener with no specific meaning

yeah /yeə/—colloquial form of *yes*

you never know—it is impossible to predict

y'know—you understand, you realize

Structure

1. Since it would be impossible to provide students with examples of all the regional dialects they might encounter, only one is represented in the dialogue of the various stagings. Indeed most textbook authors will readily admit to using their own dialect. Yet, it should be recognized that distinctions between dialects often are not sharply drawn in the sense that most people—including authors—probably speak mixed dialects. Moreover, in America where urbanization has been a particularly strong tendency, the distinctions between regional dialects are not only reduced but may tend also to correlate with age level. Thus, we often find dialect characteristic of rural areas in the speech of older urban people. In this staging, we find the old man, Mr. Edwards, using the word *feller*, of rather low frequency in many parts of the country, and pronouncing it with a final *r* sound, as is shown in the adjusted spelling, rather than with the /ow/ that the spelling seems to suggest or the /ə/ common in several other parts of the country. We also find him using an attenuated sentence opener We-l-l, which is also a feature of speech in several regions.

    Additionally, the stress seems to vary from first to second syllable of the word *maintenance* as spoken by people from various parts of the country, and that fact may account for the possible confusion of *líght maintenance* with *light máintenance*. Obviously the stress we usually depend upon to distinguish these two is that of word stress on *light* rather than the syllable stress within *maintenance*. Yet, the two kinds of stress often seem in conflict. Not only does the pun on *light maintenance* depend on stress difference but also in the expressions "that is funny" and its contracted form "that's funny," the student must not be permitted to stress the word *funny*, for with such stressing the word tends to mean *comical* or *humorous* rather than *peculiar* or *unusual*.

2. Another matter of intonation deserving mention is the one characterizing exclamations. In this staging we find characters saying "no wonder I didn't get any call!" which would probably be said with a stress and a strong pitch rise on *wonder*, and "Now there's luck for you!" which would probably be said with stress on either *there's*, with a considerable pitch rise, or *luck*, mainly set off by stress.

3. In the expression "Here it is" we find a peculiar kind of demonstrative emphasis achieved by displacing the normally final position of *here*, as in the usual order, or the stress can move to *is* accompanied by a pitch rise. Such demonstratives are quite common, as in *There you are* or *Up she goes*. The teacher should be aware that there will be a tendency on the part of many foreigners to stress the pronoun incorrectly in such sentences.

4. Although the *let's* or *let us* form is often presented as a device useful to soften a command, giving it the tone of a request, the similar use of *let me,* as in "let me have the card" frequently goes unmentioned. The use of this device, in conjunction with the question form, as in *Let me have an apple, will you* is quite common as a softening device in women's speech.

5. Again, some truncated structures should be pointed out:

    a. The most common is that used where there is mutual recognition or understanding—usually as a consequence of prior mention in discourse—as in "Light maintenance" or "Could be dangerous work" or "A real bargain!" In all instances the subject is omitted and there is an unstated reference back to something mentioned earlier. This is evidence of the pertinence—as well as complexity—of the concept of context sensitivity which is thus far little explored.

    b. Certain kinds of truncation are rather illusory in the sense that the written form may falsely indicate separate sentences although a speaker may merely pause or slow down the sound stream and what follows is something like a continuation, afterthought, or aside, as in "Just something to keep me busy" or "Probably has no training or skill to fall back on."

c. The expressions of amenities are frequently truncated, since they are cliche' forms well known to all, as in "See you around" or "Same to you" or even "Hope you'll find something soon." Note that such truncation reflects a kind of informality and, therefore, understanding or sympathy.

My experience indicates that such truncations occur more commonly in some regions than in others, and that there seems to be a slight tendency for men to use this device more often than women—perhaps reflecting a characteristically greater taciturnity and narrower scope of emotional expression among men. Or, on the other hand, male familiarity may be reflected in this usage rather than in the intonational shifts and elaborate use of intonation characteristic of women's speech.

6. Note the repetition as Interviewer #1 says "Yes, yes—that's very interesting," which indicates mild impatience and actually gives an ironic quality to *interesting*—he means he is *not* interested. A similar impatience is apparent as Mrs. Edwards says "No, no, no . . . I've never done anything like that," but here instead of impatience the echoing of *no* seems to reflect a kind of amusement at the absurdity of the Interviewer's assumption. The old woman's amusement is apparent from her laugh, a common softening device employed by women particularly.

Cultural Values

1. Although English is not characterized by elaborate honorific devices, common in many other languages, we have seen that generational conflict may be reflected in various references to age. Again, in this staging, we find old Mr. Edwards attempting to retain control of the conversation by using such expressions as "young feller" or "before your time" or "son." The need he feels to exert control can be seen as stemming from the recognition by all concerned that his bargaining position is poor, since at seventy-three he is far beyond ordinary working age. The waiting-room conversation between the two clients also underlines the sad tendency to correlate age and usefulness, as one man points out that after forty-five nobody needs you, since you're considered a bad risk. On the other hand, we find Miss Wingate's "at my age" expressing her indignation at the suggestion she seeks employment. Here it seems more reasonable to suppose that she is reluctantly—and somewhat bitterly even—accepting and expressing society's value rather than expressing her own opinion of age.

Although people seventy-three years old usually do not look for employment, many foreign students are surprised that everybody in America does not receive a retirement pension and, therefore, some are obliged to work even when old. However, in many cases old people who do have some income still prefer to work at least part-time and the foreign student should be made aware that the reason for this—although complex—is largely because in our society individual worth tends to be measured by one's productivity. Many people who have no work at all feel lazy, or somehow guilty, about their leisure. Yet, there is rarely work available for older people, partly because—as Man #2 states—most companies are unwilling to pay the high insurance rates. The emphasis on youth is also apparent in Woman #2's statement that young girls—even those less efficient than older women—are in demand. The unsolved problem of what to do with old people is peculiar to most industrialized societies and foreign students should be made aware of that fact, since it is both a cause and effect of various attitudes prevailing among English-speaking people and is reflected in many aspects of daily life.

Attention of the foreign student should be called to the fact that Interviewer #1 hesitates about referring directly to Mrs. Edwards' age. This hesitation indicates the tendency in our society to value youth, and the consequent implied insult in alluding to one's age. Although many foreign students may readily understand that society is more likely to avoid referring to the age of women than of men, some foreigners will have to be warned about this peculiar social value. Note, also, the old people's underlying resentment of the young interviewers that is likely to be heightened by their realization that they are unemployed merely because of their advanced age. This resentment is reflected in Mr. Edward's indignation at what he feels is an implication he has been an untidy worker.

2. The relation of client and employee in the employment agency may require further discussion for some students will be completely unfamiliar with the process of independent, individual job seeking. The relation between client and employee is that of mutual dependence and mutual benefit, although employees may at times tend to forget that their jobs depend on the satisfaction of customers. Moreover, the general employer-employee relationship is also made clear in this staging as we are shown the behavior of the agency employees toward Abbie Wingate, the agency owner. Although rather exaggerated deference and courtesy is shown, it is very clear to all concerned that the employees will remain with a company only as long as they find it personally advantageous and, on the other hand, they will be retained by the employer only as long as it is to his personal advantage. This idea of personal advantage is expressed by one man in the waiting room telling another of his attitude toward his employer—"You people need me more than I need you"—just before he quit his job. This kind of typical independence may seem fantastic to many foreign students who are familiar only with a paternalistic business relationship in which they are obliged to feel unswerving personal gratitude, and even life-long loyalty, to an employer.

   It might even be pointed out that the exaggerated, old-fashioned deference displayed toward Abbie Wingate seems to emphasize the gap between the generations; the young people behave toward her as they believe she wants them to, although little or no sincerity underlies their behavior—and Miss Wingate is, unfortunately, well aware of that fact.

3. The typically indirect, extremely qualified language of women can be seen in the courteous expression "I wonder if it's possible you may," in which we find indecisive tentativeness in the *wonder,* the *possible,* and the *may.* Such compounding is not

only characteristic of women's speech but is typical academic hedging designed to project an attitude of proper scholarly caution. Foreign students will certainly become acquainted very quickly with this form of qualification.

4. The foreign student should be made aware that varying degrees of familiarity and respect can be conveyed through the choice of forms of address as when Mr. Wingate says "Melville" instead of *Mr. Melville.* In general, foreigners will find that Americans quite readily assume a kind of familiarity by quickly using a person's first name, avoiding the use of *Mr., Miss,* or *Mrs.* with the family name usually used for more formal relationships. On the other hand, the use of the family name without the *Mr.* seems to reflect an attempt to be neither familiar nor distant; it is a kind of middle position which we often find men using, and almost never find women using when addressing men. Although girls and women may use this form of address with each other (i.e., the family name without *Miss* or *Mrs.*), men do not address or refer to them in this way. That is, whenever the first name of a girl or woman is not used, men should use *Miss* or *Mrs.* before her family name.

   Students may be surprised to learn that English first names and family names are not always distinguishable. There are a number of names, such as Thomas, George, Scott, Townsend, Lee, Forest, Lynne, Ruth, Marion, Russell, Henry, Lewis, Hamilton, Nelson, Francis, Dean, Craig, Raymond, Arthur, Harvey, Franklin, Wallace, James, Arnold, which are used both for a first name and a family name, although such interchange-ability would be impossible in many other cultures.

5. Note what may seem a somewhat offhand, impersonal attitude on the part of the Receptionist toward the people who enter the waiting room. Students may have to learn that such an attitude reflects no personal dislike but is thought to express a kind of objectivity indicating that all people will be treated equally and without favoritism, although it may actually be evidence of the worker's boredom with a dull, routine job.

6. Many students will have to learn that although we usually write

our family name last—and therefore it is called the "last name"—for convenience in a filing system the family name is often written first. Since Americans are unfamiliar with foreign names, the foreign student should read instructions carefully so as to avoid the kind of confusion of first and last names apparent in this staging in which we are shown that even some American names may occasionally be confused.

General Comment

1. As in the case of the two stagings, "Quiet Please" and "Flight 641," we have a set in the form of an entry gate through which various characters enter; in this staging the entry gate is presided over by the Receptionist. However, most of the action does not focus on this entrance, but instead, consists of a series of conversational exchanges held loosely together by the role of Interviewer #1, who appears in at least half of the dozen exchanges into which this staging might be divided. This series of conversational exchanges is made up of a fairly regular alternation of sad and comic references, in an attempt to introduce students to the simultaneity of these elements in the same situation. Even the character of Abbie Wingate, who resolves the alternation by casting a pall over the situation, can be seen as a somewhat comical figure with her rather formal, old-fashioned reserve. Students should be urged not to imagine that a situation will be entirely of one emotional tone; they will have the opportunity to experience the contrasting values producing these opposing impressions and learn the behavior patterns so they may project them appropriately.

2. The comic parts consist of a kind of pun on *light maintenance,* based on a shift of stress and juncture, and the play of words on the phrase "handling people" with reference to the work of the woman who has always done massaging: the double meaning in her comment about there being an art to not rubbing people the wrong way—since this expression literally refers to massaging whereas figuratively it means not annoying people, and may

therefore be seen as a veiled reference to her annoyance with the interviewer's questioning. Also comical are the overinflated reference to the veterinarian assistant's duties and the two set jokes having to do with the sword swallower and the flea circus. The set jokes are based on bizarre possibilities but also depend upon puns which may induce vocabulary building. That is, "cutthroat business" can refer to the literal fact that a sword swallower could easily cut his throat, as well as to the figurative fact that if too many people become sword swallowers the business will become highly competitive; on the other hand, the person training fleas is likely to be scratching his flea bites and, since there is not much opportunity for advancement in the work of training fleas, a person involved in such work may feel his talents are scarcely used.

However, the main hope is not only that students will learn to understand the humor but also that they will learn when and when not to laugh. As students they may find the humor of the puns amusing but when staging communication they will learn how to laugh suitably within the situation; there are many kinds of laughs, depending on the social evaluation of a situation. The way of telling a joke is culturally determined and must be rehearsed, as all toastmasters know. Since the foreign student is not likely to become a professional comedian, he practices for logical ordering, for pronunciation, and for pacing, so that he can effectively deliver the punchline; his involvement with the joke is only a means to the end of refining his control of English communication.

3. The atmosphere of an employment agency is likely to be rather gloomy. If jobs are readily available, there is no need for the agency's services, except for inadequate people unable to find jobs for themselves. If jobs are not readily available, then most clients of the agency are doomed to disappointment. And yet the basic inadequacy of the clients in this staging may itself provide a kind of gallows humor. Perhaps more importantly, however, the situation furnishes insight into the mutuality of a relationship which is essentially that of business.

Notes on Adaptation

1. Many types of employment have been sex linked in America, that is usually only women are employed as receptionists and telephone operators in American companies. Recently, perhaps in conformity with certain civil right legislation, Post Office authorities have begun to employ women as mail carriers, but it is still not a job held by many women. Roles in this staging have been adjusted accordingly.

2. Attention has been called to the use of puns in the original staging. We find additional use made of this device in the adaptation for women in which we find the surprised Interviewer discovering that in using the expressions "handling people" and "rubbing them the wrong way," Mrs. Edwards was speaking quite literally of her experience in massaging rather than in the figurative sense in which these expressions are usually intended. This switch from figurative to literal interpretation is a standard humor device which may serve to acquaint the student with the elasticity of the language. He should be made aware, moreover, that not only does all language consist of metaphor, in a certain sense, but that the relationship between literal and figurative usage—exactly what is seen as similar to what and how they are similar—reflects the cultural values underlying the language.

3. The adaptation for women shows the various softening devices employed by the Receptionist in addressing the older Mrs. Edwards as contrasted with her way of speaking to young Miss Thomas who is her contemporary. The student's attention should be called to the fact that since women more than men compete in job hunting on the basis of physical appearance and beauty, they are more likely to be concerned with age. The Woman Clerk realistically if ruefully states, "It's tough on a woman to get old—but it's happening to all of us". Women's language particularly tends to reveal their concern with age in its preference for ambiguous, euphemistic, and relative expressions, such as "older women" rather than *old women*.

4. Scrutinizing the adaptations for softening devices more likely to be found in women's speech than in men's, we find the Interviewer in addressing Miss Thomas, using the question form "Won't you please come in?" although even in being deferential to age and social status Interviewer # 3 can say very directly "Please excuse the delay, Mr. Wingate. Come in. This way to Mr. Melville's desk." Of course, individual variation, reflecting both idiolect and social dialect can be expected, but the incisive attitude in men's speech is so normal that indirection or circumlocution may seem like sarcasm or disingenuousness.

A tendency toward attenuation has been seen as peculiar to women's speech and in the adaptation of this staging we find a woman, Interviewer #1, telling another woman, Mrs. Edwards, that jobs are a "little tight," using modification to soften the actual impossibility of employment for a seventy-three year old woman. The reductive modifier *little* is used to relieve somewhat the impact, just as the woman speaker is likely to employ the older verb form "really *do* need" instead of *really need* to intensify without seeming curt or assertive. Examples of such softening modification devices have been found in dialogue of earlier stagings. In the adaptation of this staging for women we find, additionally, that a woman, Interviewer #2, uses the expressions "just priceless" and "perfectly priceless," although it is very unlikely that a man would attempt this kind of modification. In general, men are expected to be less communicative and more taciturn than women. In fact, articulateness and fluency are thought rather suspect feminine traits mirroring the greater emotional spectrum permitted in women's discourse.

5. However, we do find a tendency, noted earlier, for some degree of deference toward age to soften the speech of a young man toward an older man, just as we find some possibility of paternalism underlying Mr. Wingate's blunt urging of Interviewer #3 to report the owner's arrival to the manager of the agency. Students should be made aware that it is very unlikely that a younger man could employ such a authoritarian, bullying tone successfully in addressing an older man. Women do not use such address at all, except in very special communal situations, such as in women's military organizations or in girls' dormitories.

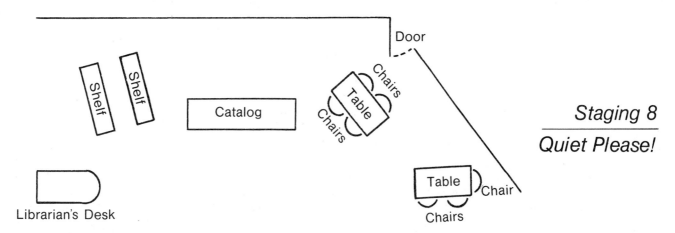

SETTING

A small public library. Stage right downstage is Librarian's desk. To the rear of it and slightly upstage are a couple of book shelves facing stage left. Upstage center is a card catalogue. Stage left downstage is a table (long side facing the audience) at one end of which Scholar sits facing stage right. About halfway between the card catalogue and Scholar's table is another table (long side facing Librarian's desk) occupied by Young Man and Young Girl, seated on the upstage, long side of the table. As the curtain rises, several people, one by one, come to check out books. This is done almost silently for a few seconds, to establish the scene. The sound of a radiator banging can be heard occasionally throughout the play.

Mixed cast	*Girls' cast*	*Boys' cast*
Librarian (Dorothy Johnson)	Librarian (Miss Dorothy Johnson)	Librarian (Mr. Fred Johnson)
Librarian's Assistant	Librarian's Assistant	Librarian's Assistant (Bob)
Young Man (Steve)	Young Girl	Student
Young Girl (Alice)	Student	Scholar
Scholar	Scholar	Page (Robert)
Page (Robert)	Page (Roberta)	Guide
Guide (Mrs. Townsend)	Guide	Boy A (Stanley)
Boy A (Stanley)	Girl A (Debbie)	Boy B (Roger)
Boy B (Roger)	Girl B (Joan)	Boy #1
Girl #1	Girl #1	Boy #2
Girl #2	Girl #2	Janitor
Janitor	Janitress	

mixed

Librarian's Assistant.   May I see your card, please? *(Pause while person produces a card from his pocket)* Thank you. *(Person exits and Librarian says to the next person)* Do you have your library card?

Person spoken to   *(may be played by Janitor wearing a hat)*. Uh-huh . . . it's right here. *(Pause while digging in his pocket and producing the card)* There you are. *(Extending the card which is stamped; Librarian shuffles several cards together as person waits)*

Librarian.   Not many people in today. We're usually a lot busier.

Librarian's Assistant   *(to person waiting)*. Thank you. *(Handing book)* There you are. That book is due in two weeks. Oh, by the way, notice the date stamp . . . that other one *(pointing to a book the person is holding)* is a three-day book.

Person checking out the book.   Thanks for reminding me . . . I'll get it back in time. *(Exits stage right)*

Young couple sitting at table holding hands have been gazing at each other contentedly. Old scholarly looking fellow sitting opposite them at the table studies on without paying attention to the conversation.

Young Man   *(seated at the table, to the young girl whose hand he continues to hold)*. What kind of books do you like

girls

Librarian.   May I see your card, please? *(Pause while person produces a card from her pocket)* Thank you. *(Person exits and Librarian says to next person)* Do you have your library card?

Person spoken to   *(may be played by Janitress wearing a hat)*. Uh-huh . . . it's right here. *(Pause while digging in her pocket and producing the card)* There you are. *(Extending the card which is stamped; Librarian shuffles several cards together as person waits)*

Librarian's Assistant.   Golly, I expected it would be much busier here. It isn't always this way, I suppose, though, is it?

Librarian   *(preoccupied with checking out the books)*. Oh, it picks up later . . . in the evening. *(Pause)* You'd better always make sure to stamp the three-day books, by the way.

Person checking out the book.   Thanks for reminding me . . . I'll get it back in time. *(Exits stage right)*

Librarian's Assistant   *(nodding)*. Uh-huh and Mr. Daly told me we're supposed to collect a five-cent fine for every day a three-day book's overdue.

Student with a pad and pencil walks from the card catalogue to Librarian's desk.

Student   *(to Librarian)*. Excuse me, Miss, but do you happen to know

boys

Librarian.   May I see your card, please? *(Pause while person produces a card from his pocket)* Thank you. *(person exits and Librarian says to next person)* Do you have your library card?

Person spoken to   *(may be played by Janitor wearing a hat)*. Uh-huh . . . it's right here. *(Pause while digging in his pocket and producing the card)* There you are. *(Extending the card which is stamped; Librarian shuffles several cards together as person waits)*

Librarian's Assistant   *(to Librarian)*. Is it always this quiet here? I figured there'd be much more business.

Librarian   *(preoccupied with checking out books)*. It will pick up . . . later. It's always busy in the evening. *(Pause)* Always be sure to stamp the three-day books, do you hear, Bob?

Person checking out the book.   Thanks for reminding me . . . I'll get it back in time. *(Exits stage right)*

Librarian's Assistant.   O.K. . . . and Mr. Daly told me to be sure to get the five-cent fine for each day a three-day book's overdue.

Student with a pad and pencil walks from the card catalogue to the Librarian's desk.

Student   *(to Librarian)*. Say, where could I get some figures on how many books are published annually? *(Explaining)* I'm writing a term paper on

mixed	*girls*	*boys*

mixed

to read, Alice?

Young Girl.   Well, I don't read much ... but I like to read stories of people ... you know ... *(pauses and looks away from him)* stories about girls and fellas, mostly.

Young Man.   You do? *(Pause)* I guess they're all right, but I like adventure stories ... Westerns. They're more realistic, I think.

Young Girl   *(overenthusiastically)*. You do? ...

Scholar   *(quietly interrupting the conversation between the couple, in a polite attempt to veil his annoyance at their disturbing chatter)*. No ... *you don't. (Wagging a finger from side to side and vigorously shaking his head negatively and then emphatically)* You don't talk in the library. You must not disturb others who have come here to study.

Librarian looks up from her work, points toward the scholar and the couple, and seems about to speak. But she does not.

Young Man   *(talking to young girl, tapping his temple significantly and rolling his eyes toward the ceiling)*. Funny how you always find such strange people in the library.

Young Girl   *(giggling)*. Don't make me laugh, Steve.

Scholar peers sternly over the top of his glasses at the talkers until they become embarrassed, then sighing, he continues reading. Page walks by noisily, staggering

girls

where I could find some figures ... er ... statistics ... on how many books are published annually? *(Explaining)* I have a paper to write for school ... on the publishing business.

Librarian's Assistant   *(to Student)*. Probably *Publishers' Weekly (turning to Librarian who is busily sorting cards)*, don't you think?

Librarian   *(preoccupied and not looking up from her work)*. Figures on publication? H-m-m ... yes, that would be a good place to start. But you'd better go help her look up some studies that have been done on the publishing business.

Librarian's Assistant   *(while walking noisily to the card catalogue, followed by Student)*. Now, let me see, are you interested in commercial publication only, or do you want to include university presses, government publications, and all that?

Student   *(laughing nervously)*. We-l-l ... I really don't know. What do you think?

Librarian's Assistant   *(looking rather disgusted and speaking somewhat scoldingly)*. Oh my—you should have found out before starting on this—but I think you'd better start with commercial publishing anyway.

Scholar   *(quietly interrupting the conversation between Librarian's Assistant and Student, in a polite attempt to veil her annoyance at their disturbing chat-*

boys

the publishing business.

Librarian's Assistant   *(to Librarian). Publishers' Weekly?*

Librarian   *(preoccupied with paper work before him)*. Publication figures? Yeah, that would be a good start. But take him over to the card catalogue and help him look up several studies under Publishing.

Librarian's Assistant   *(while walking noisily to the card catalogue, followed by Student)*. Now, let me see, are you interested in commerical publication only, or do you want to include university presses, government publications, and all that?

Student.   Gee, I don't know. The teacher who gave us the topic didn't say.

Librarian's Assistant   *(sighing and frowning at Student in distaste)*. Well, you'd better start with commercial publishing and see how much you can find on that.

Scholar   *(quietly interrupting the conversation between Librarian's Assistant and Student, in a polite attempt to veil his annoyance at their disturbing chatter)*. No ... you don't. *(Wagging a finger from side to side and vigorously shaking his head negatively and then, emphatically)* You don't talk in the library. You must not disturb others who have come here to study.

Librarian looks up from her work, points toward Scholar and seems about to speak.

mixed

beneath a large pile of books he's carrying, lurches, and—after a desperate struggle to hold on to the books—finally drops them and they crash noisily to the floor.

Page.   Damn!

Scholar   *(turning startled and indignant)*. Is this a library or a bowling alley? How can we concentrate with all that noise?

Page   *(apologetically)*. I'm sorry, sir. *(Bends to pick up the books)*

Young Girl and Young Man remain completely self-absorbed and seemingly unaware of the racket.

Scholar   *(shaking his head and grumbling)*. H-m-m . . . with all this noise, I've been reading the same page for ten minutes. Just like a foundry in here today! (*Returns, still grumbling, to his reading)*

Young Man   *(to Young Girl)*. What's your favorite TV show, Alice?

Young Girl.   Oh, I like them all . . . especially the stories. *(Pondering)* There's one on Channel 7 on Tuesday evenings— around 9 o'clock—that has the cutest fellow. You know who I mean, don't you? I can't think of his name.

Young Man   *(pondering)*. H-m-m. I think I've caught that one . . . but I can't think of his name either. *(To Page, who has almost finished picking up the fallen books and is stacking them on the table)* Hey, who's in that show on Channel 7 on Tuesday nights

girls

ter). *(Wagging a finger and shaking her head negatively)* You mustn't talk in the library, you know. Others have come to study and we must be considerate of them, mustn't we?

Librarian looks up from her work, points toward Scholar, and seems about to speak. But she does not. Student and Librarian's Assistant both stare at Scholar, who returns to her reading.

Student   *(giggling)*. Wasn't she funny though—there are always such strange people in a library.

Scholar peers sternly over the top of her glasses at the talkers until they become embrassed, then, sighing, she continues reading. Page walks by noisily, staggering beneath a large pile of books she's carrying, lurches, and—after a desperate struggle to hold on to the books—finally drops them and they crash noisily to the floor.

Page   *(giving a little gasp and quickly putting her hand over her mouth as she realizes she's created a disturbance)*. Oh, my . . .

Scholar   *(turns startled and annoyed)*. Oh, now come on! Is this a library or a bowling alley? How can we concentrate with all this noise?

Page   *(embarrassed and apologetic)*. I'm terrible sorry, Ma'am, I didn't mean . . . .*(Bends quickly to pick up the books)*

Librarian's Assistant and Student remain completely self-absorbed and seemingly unaware of the racket.

boys

But he does not. Student and Libarian's Assistant both stare at Scholar, who returns to his reading.

Librarian's Assistant   *(in a slightly quieter voice)*. I guess we were too noisy and disturbed him. *(Stage whispering)* We'll have to be more careful.

Student   *(shaking his head)*. You always find odd ones like that *(nodding toward Scholar)* in a library, it seems.

Scholar peers sternly over the top of his glasses at the talkers until they become embarrassed, then, sighing, he continues reading. Page walks by noisily, staggering beneath a large pile of books he's carrying, lurches, and—after a desperate struggle to hold on to the books—finally drops them and they crash noisily to the floor.

Page.   Damn!

Scholar   *(turning startled and indignant)*. Is this a library or a bowling alley? How can we concentrate with all that noise?

Page   *(apologetically)*. I'm sorry, sir. *(Bends to pick up the books)*

Librarian's Assistant and Student remain completely self-absorbed and seemingly unaware of the racket.

Scholar   *(shaking his head and grumbling)*. H-m-m . . . with all this noise, I've been reading the same page for ten minutes. Just like a foundry in here today. (*Returns, still grumbling, to his reading)*

Librarian's Assistant   *(looking up reflec-*

mixed

around 9 o'clock?

Page *(pondering)*. That's funny . . . I can't remember his name either. I don't watch it much. *(Smiles at Young Girl)*

Scholar squirms in annoyance and looks sternly at them over his eyeglasses.

Young Girl *(noticing the scholar)*. Say, Mister, do you happen to know the name of the cute boy who's on Channel 7 on Tuesday nights around 9?

Scholar *(loudly and indignantly)*. I certainly do not, and, furthermore *(revealing his annoyance)* I wish you would continue that discussion outside. *(Points toward the door, stage right)*

Librarian *(officiously looking in the direction of Scholar)*. Quiet please! We don't allow talking in the library. If you insist on making noise, I'll have to ask you to leave.

Couple can hardly suppress their laughter, hiding their faces in their hands, while Scholar registers dismay at being reprimanded.

Scholar *(grumbling as he returns to his studying)*. Of all the nonsense . . !

Middle-aged person, serving as a tour guide, appears stage right, followed by Boys A and B.

Guide *(smiling at Librarian)*. Hello, Dorothy—well, it seems I have only two students for orientation today. *(Officiously, to the two boys)* All

girls

Scholar *(shaking her head)*. Oh my, what a day! So much distraction! I've read the same page for ten minutes. *(Sighing heavily)* It seems more like a foundry than a library. *(Returns, still grumbling, to her reading)*

Librarian's Assistant *(looking up reflectively)*. Wait a minute . . . I think the Sunday *Times* had an article on the publishing business not long ago. I think I'll go look. *(Walks briskly stage right and disappears behind shelf near Librarian's desk)*

Student *(continuing to look through a drawer of cards as Librarian's Assistant leaves)*. Thanks . . . I'll just copy down some of these titles. *(Tries to write, copying from a card, picks up pen, looks at the point, taps it on the paper, draws circles. Frowns at the realization the pen is empty. Sees Page, who has almost finished picking up the fallen books and is stacking them on the table. Walks over to Page)* Say, you don't happen to have a pen I can borrow, do you?

Page *(shaking her head negatively)*. No, I don't even have a pencil. I usually carry one, but I lost mine somewhere yesterday. It was a good one . . . and I only had it a week too.

Scholar squirms in annoyance and looks sternly at them over her eyeglasses.

Student *(noticing the dignified woman scholar)*. Say, Miss—er—lady—do you have a pen you could lend me . . . just

boys

tively)*. Wait a minute . . . I think the Sunday *Times* had an article on the publishing business not long ago. I think I'll go look. *(Walks briskly stage right and disappears behind shelf near Librarian's desk)*

Student *(continuing to look through a drawer of cards as Librarian's Assistant leaves)*. Thanks . . . I'll just copy down some of these titles. *(Tries to write, copying from a card, picks up pen, looks at the point, taps it on the paper, draws circles. Frowns at the realization the pen is empty. Sees Page who has almost finished picking up the fallen books and is stacking them on the table. Walks over to Page)* Say, you don't happen to have a pen I can borrow, do you?

Page *(pondering)*. No, I lost mine yesterday. A good one too. I only had it a week . . . and left it somewhere, I guess.

Scholar squirms in annoyance and looks sternly at them over his eyeglasses.

Student *(noticing Scholar)*. Say . . . er . . . sir, could I borrow your pen for awhile?

Scholar *(loudly and indigantly)*. You certainly could not! *(Grumbling aloud and revealing his extreme annoyance)*. Indeed! What a nerve! *(Student, chastened, quickly returns to the card catalogue)*

Librarian *(officiously looking in the direction of Scholar)*. Quiet please! We

mixed

students should learn to use the library properly. After all, a library is a scholar's main tool. *(Nodding toward Librarian)* This is Miss Johnson, the librarian.

Scholar looks up annoyed at this noisy interruption and then, head resting on one hand, looks disgustedly and resignedly out over the audience, drumming his fingers on the table as the chatter continues.

Librarian's Assistant   *(giving the boys each a booklet and taking one step to stage right behind the desk).* There's an explanation of our cataloguing system. *(Smiling mechanically)* I'll be happy to answer any question or help you find any book you may want.

One boy immediately stuffs the booklet into his pocket without looking at it; the other boy leans on the librarian's desk, thumbing idly through one book after the other that he finds there.

Guide   *(stepping to the card catalogue at midstage and mechanically starting a monotonously rehearsed speech).* Now this is the card catalogue. It contains cards for each book in the library. *(Opens a file drawer and points to one of the file cards. Boys A and B follow but are obviously bored and not listening.)*

Young Man who has been gazing at Young Girl—who, shyly, gazes down at the table while occasionally darting a glance at Page—is attracted by the sound of Guide's high voice. He listens.

Guide.   Yes, there are cards filed both

girls

for a minute or so?

Scholar   *(loudly and indignantly).* Why! I most certainly do not, young lady. *(Smiling icily)* And if you're going to keep chatting I wonder if you'd mind doing it outside. *(Nods toward the door, stage right)*

Librarian   *(officiously looking at Scholar).* Quiet please! We don't permit loud talking in the library. People who insist on talking will be asked to leave the library.

Student, giggling as Scholar registers dismay and consternation at being reprimanded, quickly turns toward the card catalogue, as if to avoid being seen laughing, but her shoulders continue to shake with laughter as her back is turned to the audience.

Scholar   *(indignantly aghast).* Why—I never was so . . . It's unbelievable!

Middle-aged person, serving as a tour guide, appears stage right, followed by Girls A and B.

Guide   *(smiling at Librarian).* Hello, Dorothy—well, it seems I have only two students for the orientation today. *(Officiously, to the girls)* All students should learn to use the library properly. After all, a library is a scholar's main tool. *(Nodding toward Librarian)* This is Miss Johnson, the librarian.

Scholar looks up annoyed at the noisy interruption and then, head resting on one hand, looks disgustedly and resignedly out over the audience, drumming her fingers on the table

boys

don't allow talking in the library. If you insist on making noise, I'll have to ask you to leave.

Student, bursting into laughter at the dismayed look on the face of the reprimanded Scholar, who stands with mouth open and eyes widened in consternation and disbelief, quickly turns toward the card catalogue as if to avoid being seen laughing, but his shoulders shake as he continues to laugh with his back turned to the audience.

Scholar   *(grumbling as he returns to his studying).* Of all the nonsense . . . !

Middle-aged person, serving as a tour guide, appears stage right, followed by Boys A and B.

Guide   *(smiling at Librarian).* Hello, Fred—only two for the orientation today. *(Officiously, to the two boys)* All students should learn to use the library properly. After all, a library is a scholar's main tool. *(Nodding toward Librarian).* This is Mr. Johnson, our librarian.

Scholar looks up annoyed at this noisy interruption and then, head resting on one hand, looks disgustedly and resignedly out over the audience, drumming his fingers on the table as the chatter continues.

Librarian   *(giving the boys each a booklet and taking one step to stage right behind the desk).* There's an explanation of our cataloguing system. *(Smiling mechanically)* I'll be happy to answer any question or help you find any book you may want.

mixed

for author and book title, so there are two cards filed for each book. The number shows the order of the books on the shelves.

Young Man   (interested). Huh! (Surprised and incredulous) What do you know about that! Each book has two cards! (Stares at Guide)

Guide.   The card catalogue is the heart of the library, and you must learn how it works. (Noisily pulls out a file drawer)

Young Girl   (not listening but now completely absorbed with Page).Oh, yes. (Continuing to stare smilingly at Page) So interesting!

Young Man   (rising). Be right back, Alice. I gotta see this. (Gets up and goes over to the card catalogue. Guide shows him a card)

Scholar, signaling to Librarian for quiet, points toward the source of noise and holds his index finger to his lips significantly.

Librarian smiles mechanically toward Scholar and goes back to her work. Scholar looks away from her toward the audience, makes a sour face, shakes his head, and goes back to his reading, one hand over each ear.

Boy A   (to Boy B). Ever been here before?

Boy B   (to Boy A). Uh-uh.

Boy A.   I don't get the point—how come she brought us over here?

Boy B   (shrugging). I don't know. I guess she just likes to show people around.

girls

as the chatter continues.

Librarian   (giving the girls each a booklet and taking one step to stage right behind the desk). There's an explanation of our cataloguing system. (Smiling mechanically) I'll be happy to answer any question or help you find any book you may want.

One girl immediately rolls the booklet into a tube which she taps against the desk several times and finally squints through as a telescope; the other girl leans on the librarian's desk, thumbing idly through one book after another which she finds there.

Guide   (stepping to the card catalogue at midstage and mechanically starting a monotonously rehearsed speech). Now this is the card catalogue. It contains cards for each book in the library. (Opens a file drawer and points to one of the file cards. Girls A and B follow but are obviously bored and not listening)

Student, almost pushed aside by Guide, scrambles to pick up her papers from where they've been scattered on a pulled out file drawer and on top of the card catalogue. She stands aside listening to Guide.

Guide.   Yes, there are cards filed both for author and book title, so there are two cards filed for each book. The number shows the order of the book on the shelves.

Student looks slightly bored, taps her toe impatiently, and shrugs as Librarian's Assistant, who has entered stage right carrying a

boys

One boy immediately stuffs the booklet into his pocket, without looking at it; the other boy leans on Librarian's desk, thumbing idly through one book after the other that he finds there.

Guide   (stepping to the card catalogue at midstage and mechanically starting a monotonously rehearsed speech). Now this is the card catalogue. It contains cards for each book in the library. (Opens a file drawer and points to one of the file cards. Boys A and B follow but are obviously bored and not listening)

Student, almost pushed aside by Guide, scrambles to pick up his papers from where they've been scattered on a pulled out file drawer and on top of the card catalogue. He stands aside listening to the Guide.

Guide.   Yes, there are cards filed both for author and book title, so there are two cards filed for each book. The number shows the order of the books on the shelves.

Student, looks slightly bored and, shaking his head sadly, shrugs as Librarian's Assistant, who has entered stage right carrying a newspaper, passes around upstage of the card catalogue and holds out the newspaper before the student.

Guide.   The card catalogue is the heart of the library, and you must learn how it works. (Noisily pulls out a file drawer while peering distastefully at Student and Librarian's Assistant who merely stand aside waiting)

mixed	girls	boys

mixed

Boy A.   How much longer do you think this will last?

Boy B   *(shaking his head)*. It beats me . . . but I sure wish I could get out of here.

Boy A.   Yeah—it's kind of dead in here. So quiet, it makes you feel sort of sleepy. *(Yawns)*

Boy B.   It sure does. *(For the first time noticing Young Girl sitting at the table)* But she's kind of cute, huh? *(He nods toward the girl)*

Young Man remains in conversation with Guide. Both have backs to the audience and they seem engaged in enthusiastic conversation. Scholar sits with cheek resting on his hand, disgusted look of long suffering on his face, and shakes his head as he stares out over the audience.

Boy A.   U-m-m *(spoken appraisingly)* . . . not bad at all. The dopey guy she was with *(thumbing toward Young Man who is eagerly listening to Guide)* left her *(sourly)* . . . for scholarship. *(This last word is spoken with strong sarcastic emphasis)*

Boy B.   He's out of his mind . . . but at least it keeps Mrs. Townsend *(nodding toward Guide)* off our backs.

Guide   *(interrupting the two boys snappishly as they wander along the bookshelves stage right upstage)*. Stanley . . . Roger *(threateningly)* . . . we're over here.

Both boys quickly join Guide who then moves from the card catalogue to the book

girls

newspaper, passes around upstage of the card catalogue and holds the newspaper before the student.

Guide.   The card catalogue is the heart of the library, and you must learn how it works. *(Noisily pulls out a file drawer while peering distastefully at Student and Librarian's Assistant who merely stands aside waiting)*

Librarian's Assistant   *(to Student)*. Here's the issue I was referring to. It's a pretty thorough article and I think you'd better read it as a starter. There is a lot of information you can use, I'm sure.

Student.   Oh, thanks loads! I guess I'd better do that—particularly since *(nodding toward Guide and speaking sarcastically and slightly louder)* the card catalogue seems to be in use and *(with pointed emphasis)* unavailable right now.

Holding the newspaper, Student goes to the table near Scholar, stage left, sits down and starts to read the newspaper.

Scholar   *(signaling to Librarian for quiet, points toward the source of noise)*. If you please. *(Holds her index finger to her lips significantly)*

Librarian smiles mechanically toward Scholar and goes back to her work. Scholar looks away from her toward the audience, makes a sour face, shakes her head, and goes back to her reading, one hand over each ear.

Girl A   *(to Girl B)*. Ever been here before?

boys

Librarian's Assistant   *(to Student)*. Here's the issue I was referring to. It's a pretty thorough article and I think you'd better read it as a starter. There is a lot of information you can use, I'm sure.

Student.   Gee, thanks. I'll do that right away—since *(nodding toward Guide and speaking sarcastically and slightly louder)* I can't get at the card catalogue right now anyway.

Holding the newspaper, Student goes to the table near Scholar, stage left, sits down and starts to read the newspaper. Scholar, signaling to Librarian for quiet, points toward the source of noise and holds his index finger to his lips significantly. Librarian smiles mechanically toward Scholar and goes back to his work. Scholar looks away from him toward audience, makes a sour face, shakes his head, and goes back to his reading, one hand over each ear.

Boy A   *(to Boy B)*. Ever been here before?

Boy B   *(to Boy A)*. Uh-uh.

Boy A.   I don't get the point—how come he brought us over here?

Boy B   *(shrugging)*. I don't know. I guess he just likes to show people around.

Boy A.   How much longer do you think this will last?

Boy B   *(shaking his head)*. It beats me . . . but I sure wish I could get out of here.

Boy A.   Yeah—it's kind of dead in here.

mixed

shelves. *Young Man, obviously dazzled, also follows Guide. Scholar who throughout the conversational noise has been crouched with outstretched hands pressing against the table as if ready to spring, bends his head determinedly over his book.*

Guide   *(as she walks to shelves).* And over here we have the reference volumes. *(She points to the shelves)* The *Cumulative Book Index*—or *C.B.I.* as we call it—and the *Readers' Guide to Periodical Literature* are particularly important.

Young Man   *(bends over to look at the books on a lower shelf).* They're sure big and heavy looking, but why are they so important?

Guide   *(mechanically).* Because all books published are listed in the *C.B.I.*—and in the *Readers' Guide to Periodical Literature* you can find an index of all articles from most leading magazines and journals.

Young Man   *(wonderingly).* Yeah? So you don't have to waste a lot of time looking through all the magazines just hoping to find something you're interested in.

Guide smiles mechanically and nods reassuringly. All three boys stand facing the row of books as Guide pulls out first one and then another, seemingly talking about them—she has her back to the audience and faces the boys, nodding occasionally toward first one boy, then another, as if in conversation. They nod in response.

girls

Girl B   *(to Girl A).* Uh-uh.

Girl A.   I don't get the point—how come she brought us over here?

Girl B   *(shrugging).* I don't know. I guess she just likes to show people around.

Girl A.   How much longer do you think this will last?

Girl B   *(shaking her head).* It beats me . . . but I sure wish I could get out of here.

Girl A.   Yeah—it's kind of dead in here. So quiet, it makes you feel sort of sleepy. *(Yawns)*

Girl B.   It sure does. What a day for this! How I'd like to be down at the beach.

Girl A.   U-m-m. *(Sighing)* Wouldn't that be great . . . but . . . we'd better get going. *(Nods towards Guide)*

Guide   *(interrupting the two girls snappishly as they wander along the bookshelves stage right upstage).* Debbie . . . Joan *(threateningly)* . . . we're over here.

Both girls quickly join Guide who then moves from the card catalogue to the book shelves. Scholar who throughout the conversational noise has been crouched with outstretched hands pressing against the table as if ready to spring, bends her head determinedly over her book.

Guide   *(as she walks to shelves).* And over here we have the reference volumes. *(She points to the shelves).* The *Cumulative Book Index*—or *C.B.I.* as

boys

So quiet, it makes you feel sort of sleepy. *(Yawns)*

Boy B.   It sure does. *(Sighing)* Boy, how I'd like to be at the beach now.

Boy A.   U-m-m. *(Sighing)* Wouldn't that be great! *(Sarcastically)* In fact, wouldn't any place else be great! But let's get going. *(Nods toward Guide)*

Guide   *(interrupting the two boys snappishly as they wander along the bookshelves stage right upstage).* Stanley . . . Roger *(threateningly)* . . . we're over here.

Both boys quickly join Guide who then moves from the card catalogue to the book shelves. Scholar who throughout the conversational noise has been crouched with outstretched hands pressing against the table as if ready to spring, bends his head determinedly over his book.

Guide   *(as he walks to shelves).* And over here we have the reference volumes. *(He points to the shelves)* The *Cumulative Book Index*—or *C.B.I.* as we call it—and the *Readers' Guide to Periodical Literature* are particularly important.

Boy A   *(bends over to look at the books on a lower shelf, then, frowning, says boredly).* They're big, heavy looking, and dusty.

Boy B   *(smiling mechanically at Guide).* I don't see how they could be so important if they're not used more than that.

Guide   *(pointedly ignoring Boy B con-*

mixed

Two girls enter stage left and stand just behind Scholar chatting.

Girl #1   *(using her hands to describe a dress as she talks)*. It had a little round collar and came out here *(gestures)*, you know, and the skirt was just darling. Gee, I wish I could remember which magazine it was in.

Girl #2   *(shaking her head negatively)*. It might look good on you, but I need something more tailored...like *(enthusiastically beaming)*—did you see that simply gorgeous suit in Mimi's window?

Scholar raises his head, glances over his shoulder, removes his glasses, rubs his eyes, and shakes his head sadly as he sits with bowed head, pinching the bridge of his nose, wearied and disgusted, as they continue to chatter.

Girl #1.   Yeah...but it's the wrong color for me. I just couldn't wear it—with my hair. *(Negatively shaking off the idea)* Uh-uh.

Girl #2.   I saw just what you need at the Mode Shop. You'd look great in it. It was...

Scholar whirls and lashing out with his arm savagely, silently motions them away.

Looking back over their shoulders at him the two girls exit hurriedly stage left, puzzled at the reaction of Scholar who continues to glare at them as they exit.

Young Girl   *(to Page)*. How do you like working here?

Page   *(not very enthusiastically as he*

girls

we call it—and the *Readers' Guide to Periodical Literature* are particularly important.

Girl A   *(bends over to look at the books on a lower shelf, then frowning, says in a bored way)*. They're big, heavy looking and *(running her finger over the standing book edge)*...very dusty. *(Rubs fingers together with a look of distaste)*

Girl B   *(smiling mechanically at Guide and with mock innocence)*. But they certainly can't be so important if they're not used more than that, can they, Mrs. Townsend?

Guide   *(pointedly ignoring Girl B continues her mechanical speech)*. All books published are listed in the *C.B.I.*, and the *Readers' Guide to Periodical Literature* is an index of all articles from most leading magazines and journals.

Girl A   *(clapping her hands together in mock wonder)*. And so, you don't have to waste a lot of time looking through all the magazines! *(Exaggeratedly)* How perfectly marvelous!

Guide grimaces disgustedly in recognition of the girls' sarcastic impudence and then roughly grabbing an arm of each girl, so that Guide is in the middle with one girl on each side, she faces them toward the book shelves. Then, with her back toward the audience, Guide pulls first one book and then another from the bookshelves, seemingly talking about them. She nods occasionally

boys

tinues his mechanical speech)*. All books published are listed in the *C.B.I.*, and the *Readers' Guide to Periodical Literature* is an index of all articles from most leading magazines and journals.

Boy A   *(dully and bored)*. So you don't have to waste a lot of time looking through all the magazines for stuff you might want. *(Sarcastically)* Great!

Guide grimaces disgustedly in recognition of the boys' sarcastic impudence and then roughly grabbing an arm of each boy, so that Guide is in the middle with one boy on each side, he faces them toward the bookshelves. Then, with his back toward the audience, Guide pulls first one book and then another from the bookshelves, seemingly talking about them. He nods occasionally toward first one and then the other boy as if in conversation. Resignedly and obviously bored, the two boys nod dully in response. Two boys enter stage left and stand just behind Scholar chatting.

Boy #1.   Yeah, she's pretty smart but she's not much for looks.

Boy #2.   I wouldn't even mind that, but that kid sister of hers is a pain in the neck. Elaine has to take care of her all the time, because her mother is working...and that kid is just spoiled.

Scholar raises his head, glances over his shoulder, removes his glasses, rubs his eyes, and shakes his head sadly as he sits with bowed head, pinching the bridge of his nose, wearied and disgusted, as they continue to

mixed

continues stacking books carefully on the table). It's O.K. *(shrugs)* . . . just a job . . . and it doesn't pay much.

Young Girl. But it's kind of interesting, I guess—I mean, all the books and . . . everything. *(Smiles encouragingly)*

Page. Well *(smiling)* some of the people here are . . . very nice . . .

Scholar *(hissing in annoyance).* Quiet please! *(Wagging a finger at them reprovingly)* I have already asked you several times to be quiet.

Page, startled at the sudden reprimand, knocks all the books he has been carefully stacking on the edge of the table, and they all fall noisily to the floor again. A loud crash results. Scholar winces painfully at the noise and, shaking his head disgustedly, pulls off his glasses, groaning as he covers his eyes with his hands.

Librarian. Quiet, please! *(Exasperated)* Robert *(stressing with obviously forced politeness)* kindly pick up all of those books and bring them here *(again with threatening emphasis)* right away.

Page hurriedly and nervously begins to pick up the books again.

Young Girl *(rising from her chair and going over to help).* Here . . . let me help you *(She helps pick up the books) books)*

It is quiet for a few seconds with only the muffled conversation of Guide and the boys and the sound of books being stacked on the table. The radiator bangs more often, how-

girls

toward first one and then the other girl as if in conversation. Resignedly and obviously bored, the two girls nod dully in response.

Two girls enter stage left and stand just behind Scholar chatting.

Girl #1 *(using her hands to describe a dress as she talks).* It had a little round collar and came out here *(gestures),* you know, and the skirt was just darling. Gee, I wish I could remember which magazine it was in.

Girl #2 *(shaking her head negatively).* It might look good on you, but I need something more tailored . . . like *(enthusiastically beaming)*—did you see that simply gorgeous suit in Mimi's window?

Scholar raises her head, glances over her shoulder, removes her glasses, rubs her eyes, and shakes her head sadly as she sits with bowed head, pinching the bridge of her nose, wearied and disgusted, as they continue to chatter.

Girl #1. Yeah . . . but it's the wrong color for me. I just couldn't wear it—with my hair. *(Negatively shaking off the idea)* Uh-uh.

Girl #2. I saw just what you need at the Mode Shop. You'd look great in it. It was . . .

Scholar *(coughing artificially to gain their attention).* Ahem! *(But the two chatting girls continue to ignore her)*

Girl #1. It was blue, wasn't it? . . . and they had it in the window last week.

Girl #2 *(shaking her head negatively).*

boys

chatter.

Boy #1. She sure is . . . and she's always hanging around too. *(Pause)* What are we going to do here?

Boy #2. I figured we could kill an hour looking at the magazines maybe. We should've come earlier and worked on that term paper *(sarcastically)* like the great scholar. *(Nods toward Student)*

Boy #1 *(scornfully).* Him? I bet he just got here too.

Scholar whirls and lashing out with his arm savagely, silently motions them away.

Boy #1 *(looking at Boy #2 and tapping his head significantly as they step back).* Funny how you find such strange people in the library.

Boy #2 *(nodding).* It sure is. Let's get away from this guy.

Looking back over their shoulders the two boys exit hurriedly stage left, puzzled at the reaction of Scholar who continues to glare at them as they exit.

Student *(looking up).* How do you like working here?

Page *(not very enthusiastically as he continues stacking books carefully on the table).* It's O.K. *(shrugs)* . . . just a job . . . and it doesn't pay much.

Student *(smiling).* But it could be interesting . . . the books . . . and the chance to meet girls that drop in now and then . . .

Page. Yeah . . . there are fringe benefits, all right. *(Smiling)* I've met some good-looking girls here . . .

mixed

ever, and more loudly. Yet Scholar studies on, a contented smile on his face. Page and Girl carry the books to the Librarian's desk and set them down.

Page   (to Young Girl). Gee, thanks a lot. (Looks at his wristwatch) It's time for my break. Want a coke?

Young Girl   (glancing quickly at Young Man who still listens to Guide). Sure! They quickly exit stage right as Janitor carrying a large wrench enters.

Librarian   (looking up at Janitor and smiling). Well, you're finally here, eh? That radiator's been banging like that all day.

Janitor   (laying the wrench on Librarian's desk and leaning on the desk as he talks). Pretty loud, ain't it? (Pause as the radiator bangs) Probably a little air in the line. Gets that way now and then. They ought to install a new furnace in this place. (Pause) But that's not likely. (Chuckles) No budget. (Pause) I guess we'll just have to put up with that old one for awhile. (Chuckling) Maybe another ten years. Scholar, who has been disturbed at the sound of the conversation, looks up from his book and clears his throat pointedly.

Janitor   (ignoring Scholar's hint and gazing around the room). Say, business is kind of quiet in here today ... not much of a crowd. (Smiling at Librarian) What're you doing, Miss Johnson, scaring 'em away? (Laughs noisily at his own joke, although

girls

No, not that one. I mean the brown knit they ...

Scholar   (whirling and, shaking her finger violently as if to reprimand them, hisses). Now, see here—I've had just about enough of your silly chatter ... (With a quick, waving movement motions with her hand for them to leave)

Startled, the two girls jump back. Then, they exit hurriedly stage left, looking back over their shoulders at her, frightened yet mildly puzzled and even amused by the violence of Scholar's behavior.

Young Girl   (to Page). How do you like working here?

Page   (not very enthusiastically as she continues stacking books carefully on the table). It's O.K. (shrugs) just a job ... and it doesn't pay much.

Young Girl   (chattily). But it must be kind of interesting ... I mean all the books ... and the boys ...

Page.   Well, there are fringe benefits. (Pauses smiling) Some of the fellas are pretty nice.

Scholar   (hissing in annoyance). Quiet, please! (Wagging a finger at them reprovingly) I have already asked you several times to be quiet.

Page, startled at the sudden reprimand, knocks all the books she has been carefully stacking on the edge of the table, and they all fall noisily to the floor again. A loud crash results. Scholar winces painfully at the noise and, shaking her head disgustedly,

boys

Scholar   (hissing in annoyance). Quiet please! (Wagging a finger at them reprovingly) I have already asked you several times to be quiet.

Page, startled at the sudden reprimand, knocks all the books he has been carefully stacking on the edge of the table, and they all fall noisily to the floor again. A loud crash results. Scholar winces painfully at the noise and, shaking his head disgustedly, pulls off his glasses groaning as he covers his eyes with his hands.

Librarian.   Quiet, please! (Exasperated, Robert (with obviously forced politeness), kindly pick up all of those books and bring them here (with threatening emphasis) right away.

Page hurriedly and nervously begins to pick up the books again.

Student.   Boy, you did it again! Put them on the table ... I'll give you a hand. (Stoops to help gather up the books)

It is quiet for a few seconds with only the muffled conversation of Guide and the boys and the sound of books being stacked on the table. The radiator bangs more often, however, and more loudly. Yet Scholar studies on, a contented smile on his face. Page and Student carry the books to Librarian's desk and set them down.

Page   (to Student). Thanks. (Looks at his wristwatch) It's time for my break and I think I'd better get out of here for awhile. (Nods significantly toward the frowning Librarian) Let's get a

mixed

Librarian looks mildly displeased)

Scholar *(jumping up and, facing Librarian, implores).* Quiet please—that's all I ask. I came here to do some important work and there have been constant noisy interruptions.

Librarian's Assistant *(leaning over her desk toward Scholar, finger to lips, speaking in a tense stage whisper).* Quiet, please! I'm sorry, sir, but I must ask you again not to speak so loudly in the library.

Guide *(can be heard saying to the boys).* Yes, that's right . . . always try to find what you want by yourself—quietly of course. *(Raising her voice for emphasis)* We must always be quiet in the library.

Stunned, Scholar slowly sits down, drums his fingers on the table irritably, and desperately tries to control his anger.

Janitor *(embarrassed at the exchange).* Well, I guess I'd better get to work. *(Exits stage left)*

There is a moment or two of silence during which Scholar takes up his book and begins to read again. Librarian busies herself at her desk. Then, suddenly, a very loud sound of a hammer beating on a pipe can be heard off stage left.

Scholar *(angrily throwing down his book).* That's the last straw! That does it! *(Grabbing up his papers from the table and flinging them into his briefcase, he snatches up his hat and his briefcase and stamps noisily across the*

girls

pulls off her glasses groaning as she covers her eyes with her hands.

Librarian. Quiet, please! *(Exasperated)* Roberta *(with obviously forced politeness)* Kindly pick up all of those books and bring them here *(with threatening emphasis)* right away . . . *(with obviously fake affection)* de-ar.

Page hurriedly and nervously begins to pick up the books again.

Young Girl *(rising from her chair and going over to help).* Here . . .let me help you. *(She helps pick up the books)*

It is quiet for a few seconds with only the muffled conversation of Guide and the girls and the sound of books being stacked on the table. The radiator bangs more often, however, and more loudly. Yet Scholar studies on, a contented smile on her face. Page and Young Girl carry the books to Librarian's desk and set them down.

Page *(to Young Girl).* Gee, thanks a lot. *(Looks at her wristwatch)* It's time for my break. Let's get a coke.

Young Girl *(hesitating as she glances at Librarian's Assistant who stares back at her solemnly).* O.K.

Young Girl dashes to the table, picks up a small change purse and rushes after Page, who is exiting stage right as Janitress carrying a large bucket and mop enters.

Librarian *(looking up at Janitress and smiling).* So, you're finally going to mop the place, eh. Well, it certainly needs it.

boys

coke.

Student. I've got a lot to do. *(Glances at Librarian's Assistant who gazes back at him solemnly)* But . . . let's go . . .

They quickly exit stage right as Janitor carrying a large wrench enters.

Librarian *(looking up àt Janitor and smiling).* Well, you're finally here, eh? That radiator's been banging like that all day.

Janitor *(laying the wrench on Librarian's desk and leaning on the desk as he talks).* Pretty loud, ain't it? *(Pause as the radiator bangs)* Probably a little air in the line. Gets that way now and then. They ought to install a new furnace in this place. *(Pause)* But that's not likely. *(Chuckles)* No budget. *(Pause)* I guess we'll just have to put up with that old one for awhile. *(Chuckling)* Maybe another ten years.

Scholar, who has been disturbed at the sound of the conversation, looks up from his book and clears his throat pointedly.

Janitor *(ignoring Scholar's hint and gazing around the room).* Say, business is kind of quiet in here today . . . not much of a crowd. *(Smiling at Librarian)* What're you doing, Mr. Johnson, scaring 'em away? *(Laughs noisily at his own joke, although Librarian looks mildly displeased)*

Scholar *(jumping up and, facing Librarian, implores).* Quiet please—that's all I ask. I came here to do some important work and there have been constant

mixed

room toward the door stage right)

Librarian   (not looking up from her work and speaking very mechanically as Scholar tramps noisily past Librarian's desk). Quiet, please! I'll have to ask you to be quiet in the library!

Scholar   (turning on his way out and laughing wildly). Quiet, quiet! Ha, ha! (And then, sarcastically) Please! Bah! (Stamps angrily out as the startled Librarian rises from her desk and leans over the ledge gazing after Scholar, amazed as he exits noisily into the right wing.)

CURTAIN

Glossary

after all—it is a fact, indeed

ain't it—uneducated colloquial form of *isn't it*

air in the line—air in the pipe

a starter—a way to begin the job, an approach

awfully sorry—very sorry

bah! /bæə/—expression of disgust

bangs—making a loud noise

book is due—book should be returned

break—a rest period

cataloguing system—system for filing book cards representing the subject and order of books on the shelves

caught—seen

channel 7—the station number for a TV

girls

Janitress   (setting the bucket down in front of Librarian's desk and leaning on the desk as she talks). Pretty dirty, all right. (Chuckling) I don't see how you people get this place so dirty. (Frowning) I think that old furnace just keeps the dust blowing around in here. (Sighing) But . . . I doubt if they'll install a new one . . . unless they get a fatter budget. (Smiling) So . . . I guess we'll just have to put up with it . . . like everything else around here!

Scholar, who has been disturbed at the sound of the conversation, looks up from her book and clears her throat pointedly.

Janitress   (oblivious to Scholar's annoyance, gazes around the room). Say, you haven't got much of a crowd in here today, have you? (smiling), or have you chased some of the noisy ones out already? (Laughs noisily at her own joke)

Scholar   (half rising and leaning on the table, facing Librarian, implores). All I've asked for . . . (frostily) repeatedly today . . . is quiet. I have some very important work to do here, young lady, but I certainly cannot do it with all these noisy interruptions.

Librarian   (leaning over her desk toward Scholar, fingers to lips, speaking in a tense stage whisper). Quiet, please! I'm sorry, madam, but I must ask you again not to speak so loudly in the library.

boys

noisy interruptions.

Librarian   (leaning over his desk toward Scholar, finger to lips, speaking in a tense stage whisper). Quiet, please! I'm sorry, sir, but I must ask you again not to speak so loudly in the library.

Guide   (can be heard saying to the boys). Yes, that's right . . . always try to find what you want by yourself— quietly, of course. (Raising his voice slightly for emphasis) We must always be quiet in the library.

Stunned, Scholar slowly sits down, drums his fingers on the table irritably, and desperately tries to control his anger.

Janitor   (embarrassed at the exchange). Well, I guess I'd better get to work. (Exits stage left)

There is a moment or two of silence during which Scholar takes up his book and begins to read again. Librarian busies himself at his desk. Then, suddenly, a very loud sound of a hammer beating on a pipe can be heard off stage left.

Scholar   (angrily throwing down his book). That's the last straw! That does it! (Grabbing up his papers from the table and flinging them into his briefcase, he snatches up his hat and his briefcase and stamps noisily across the room toward the door stage right.)

Librarian   (not looking up from his work and speaking very mechanically as Scholar tramps noisily past Librarian's desk). Quiet, please! I'll have to ask you to be quiet in the library!

mixed

broadcast

'coke—usually Coca Cola, but sometimes used for any kind of soft drink

cutest—attractive, good-looking

damn—expression of annoyance (profanity)

date stamp—rubber ink stamp used to show the date on which a book must be returned

dazzled—astonished, fascinated

doesn't pay much—provides small wages

dopey guy—slang meaning silly or foolish fellow

eh? /ey/—a questioning expression coming at the end of a statement sentence

'em—contracted form of *them*

flinging—throwing

foundry—a factory where metal is cast; usually a very noisy place just as a bowling alley is

funny—strange, peculiar

gee—a sentence opener expressing enthusiasm, emphasizing what follows

golly /galiy/—mild expression of surprise

gotta—careless pronunciation of *got to* (meaning *have to* or *must*)

here, let me help you—please let me help you

hey—somewhat rude expression to attract someone's attention

hm-m-m /hm/—expression of thought or speculation

how come?—why?

huh! /hə̃/—an expression of surprise, spoken very abruptly almost as a grunt

huh? /²hə³/ — question expression spoken with a rising pitch

girls

Guide   *(can be heard saying to the girls).* Yes, that's right . . . always try to find what you want by yourself—quietly, of course. *(Raising her voice slightly for emphasis)* We must always be quiet in the library.

Stunned, Scholar slowly sits down, drums her fingers on the table irritably and desperately tries to control her anger).

Janitress   *(embarrassed at the exchange).* Well, I guess I'd better get to work. *(Stamps noisily across the stage and exits stage right, slamming the door loudly)*

Scholar   *(angrily yanking off her eyeglasses).* That's the last straw! I just cannot stand it another second. *(Folding her glasses and slamming them into her purse, she tosses her papers into a folder, snatches up the folder, and stamps noisily toward the door stage right)*

Librarian   *(not looking up from her work and speaking very mechanically as Scholar tramps noisily past Librarian's desk).* Quiet please! I'll have to ask you to be quiet in the library!

Scholar   *(turning on her way out and laughing wildly).* Quiet, quiet! Ha, ha! *(And then, sarcastically)* Please! Incredible! (Stamps angrily out as the startled Librarian rises from desk and leans over the ledge gazing after Scholar, amazed as she exits noisily into the right wing.)*

CURTAIN

boys

Scholar   *(turning on his way out and laughing wildly).* Quiet, quiet! Ha! ha! *(And then, sarcastically)* Please! Bah! *(Stamps angrily out as the startled Librarian rises from his desk and leans over the ledge gazing after Scholar, amazed as he exits noisily into the right wing)*

CURTAIN

Glossary

boy, you did it again!—sarcastic reference to a repeated error or failure

business—rather sarcastic reference to library students as if they were a business

can't get it—can't use, because it is being used by somebody else

chastened—subdued because scolded

do you hear—do you understand

figured—thought, imagined

fringe benefit—something in addition to a salary or wage

give you a hand—help you

good start—good place to begin looking

get going—move

great scholar—a sarcastic reference

hanging around—remaining, idling

I bet—I think, I imagine

kid—child

kid sister—younger sister

kill an hour—waste some time

not much for looks—not very pretty, unattractive

O.K.—yes

CURTAIN

mixed

I don't get the point—I don't understand

it beats me—it puzzles me, I don't understand it

it's kind of dead in here—very quiet and uninteresting

just a job—merely a means to earn money, uninteresting and temporary rather than a career

just darling—very good or nice

kind of cute—rather pretty, attractive

let me see—expression of thought or reflection

look great—appear very beautiful

not bad at all—very good

officiously—in a too impersonally efficient way

off our backs—keep from annoying or bothering us

O.K.—fair, not excellent but passable

orientation—lecture to accustom, acquaint, or make familiar with something

out of his mind—impractical, foolish, crazy

put up with—to endure or tolerate

racket—noise

radiator—device made of iron pipe to convey heat from a furnace to a room

reprimanded—scolded

say—an expression used to call attention in opening a conversation

show people around—guide people

simply gorgeous—very beautiful

stamps—walks very loudly, pressing one's feet hard against the floor

sure wish—wish very much

tailored—having very sharply defined contours, like a uniform

girls

Glossary

ahem /ə + hem/—sound of throat clearing, sometimes to draw attention

copy down—copy (i.e., *down* has no specific meaning, as in *write down*)

fatter budget—bigger budget

get going—move

had just about enough—cannot tolerate more

implores—begs, beseeches, appeals for sympathy

incredible—so obviously absurd as to be unbelievable

it sure is—it definitely is true

look up—search for

now let me see—expression of thought or reflection

oh my—mild and nervous expression of concern

Oh, now come on—an expression of annoyed disbelief

O.K.—yes

perfectly marvelous—wonderful, fine

picks up—increases

see here—an expression to focus attention, usually expresses annoyance

tailored—plainly cut, without feminine elaboration

thanks loads—thank you very much

wait a minute—an expression of sudden memory or realization

wouldn't that be great?—that would be very good or pleasant

boys

pain in the neck—an annoyance

pretty—rather, very

quiet—not busy

say—a signal to open a sentence or to attract attention

smart—clever, intelligent

spoiled—ill-mannered, selfish

sure is—certainly is

what a nerve!—expression of indignation, annoyance

yeah/ yeə/—yes

mixed

temple—side of the head between eye and ear (the gesture of tapping the temple indicates the opinion that another person is crazy)

that does it!—an expression of annoyance (meaning *that is all I can endure*)

the last straw—the final and decisive annoyance, the limit to what can be tolerated or endured

there you are—here it is, an expression used when offering or completing some service

three-day book—book which can be taken from the library for only three days

uh-huh /ə̃+hə̃/—yes

uh-uh /ə̃+ə̃/—a negative expression

u-m-m /um/—expression of pleasure, appreciation

veil—to mask or keep from being seen

Westerns—cowboy movies (often shown on TV)

what do you know about that!—expression of surprised insight, discovery, amazement

wrench—a tool for turning nuts or bolts

wrong color—unsuitable color

yeah? /yeə/—Yes? but expressing a kind of surprise or doubt

Structure

1. As we have seen in examining the dialogue of other stagings, there is a marked tendency to use abbreviated structures in spoken expression. Partly this is a consequence of the pressure of time in speaking as well as of the mutual awareness of the subject of conversation and the possibility for immediate correction or clarification in face to face exchange. In this staging we find further evidence of this in such expressions as: "Ever been here before?" "So you don't have to waste a lot of time looking through all the magazines just hoping to find something you're interested in?" "No budget." But we also find that intensity of emotional reaction also tends to truncate structures, as in: "Just like a foundry."—expression of irritation/annoyance; "Of all the nonsense!"—expression of annoyance; "Not bad at all!"—expression of approval; "Pretty

loud, isn't it"—expression of mild disapproval. These expressions reflect an attitude or focus of attention rather than denotative contents.

2. There is another type of shortened form which expresses a kind of judgment or evaluation yet is somewhat more than a mere emotional signal; we find it exemplified in such expressions as: "Funny how you always find such strange people in a library," i.e., *It is strange how.* . . . We note that frequently this type of expression can appear in the form of a rhetorical question: *Isn't it funny how you always find such strange people in a library?* and in this case the intonation contour is that of a statement rather than that of the usual BE + N question structure. Certain phrases from the dialogue of this staging are, of course, untruncated yet are essentially rhetorical in nature and mainly project an emotional attitude: "Is this a library or a bowling alley?" "Wouldn't that be great?" "How can we concentrate with all that noise?" And we also note that still another type of rhetorical question utilizes a peculiar kind of question and answer combination structure: "What are you doing . . . scaring 'em away?" i.e.—Are you scaring them away?

3. The student will have to be shown that to convey the frustration in the scholar's "Is this a library or a bowling alley," he must not only have a juncture after *library* but he must have a pitch rise on *library* and a pitch rise on *alley.* Although it may be too subtle a point for most students, some, in fact, may be able to see that the *or* of exclusion must not become the *or* of alternation. Incidentally, but not insignificantly, the teacher must insist that the stress on *bowling alley* must fall on the first syllable of *bowling* rather than on the first syllable of *alley.*

4. Women, children, and adolescents are permitted a greater range of emotional expression and, as we have seen earlier, we find this fact reflected particularly in the woman's extensive use of intensifiers, such as "just darling" or "simply gorgeous." These, then, are typical women's language and are not likely to be used by males of any age. Two expressions used in the dialogue of this staging and characteristic of woman's language, although largely confined to the speech of adolescent girls, are the fairly simple "thanks loads" and the more complicated "the cutest fellow." The latter expression is complicated because girls use it in discussing boys and both boys and girls would use "cute" in referring to girls, but boys would not do so discussing other boys.

5. Lexical items to be found in the staging and deserving special recognition, as peculiar to spoken expression, are:
   a. *With* meaning *because of,* as in the expression "with all this noise I've been reading the same page for ten minutes" or "I just couldn't wear it—with my hair." Note that in the second expression *with my hair* means *because it does not harmonize with the color of my hair.*
   b. *So* meaning *therefore,* as in the expression "So you don't have to waste a lot of time looking through all the magazines just hoping to find something you're interested in." Note that *so* is also a kind of conversation connective device, similar to *well,* imparting a kind of native quality to speech, and, therefore, useful for foreign students to acquire.
   c. "Hey" and "say" are used as sentence openers, usually to attract or focus the attention of the person to whom a statement is addressed. However, it should also be noted that unlike *well,* another common sentence opener, such expressions are very often used to preface a request to make it seem somewhat less blunt. And the student should be warned that, improperly used, *hey* may seem somewhat rude.
   d. "Why!" may also be a sentence opener but, again, students must be warned that when strongly aspirated this word usually expresses indignation, somewhat like the use of *indeed!*

6. There are certain words which seem mainly to serve as emphasizers, although they may have other functions as well:
   a. *How* used as a sentence opener as when one of the bored boys declares, "How I'd like to be down at the beach," means *I would like very much to be at the beach,* although

the sentence may seem almost like a rhetorical question. It might be noted in passing, that the *down* of "down at the beach" is actually without meaning; the *over* in "over here" is another example of a word without meaning.

b. *Do you hear* tied to the end of a sentence seems to serve a similar emphasizing function, although it also means *do you understand.*

c. *Certainly* is not only a strong intensifier but, when used before a negative expression, may convey indignation or annoyance, as in the Scholar's "I certainly do not."

d. Although it may be largely a regional usage, *sure* is widely used as an intensifier meaning *certainly* or *very much*, as in "it sure is" or "I sure wish . . . "

7. Adolescents in particular tend, perhaps defensively, to mask their emotional attitudes by a kind of feigned inarticulateness, reflected in the use of *kind of*, meaning *quite* or even *very*, as in "kind of cute" or in "kind of dead." *Sort of* is a frequent alternate for *kind of*. An extension of this masking device is to be found in a use of *you know*, of such high frequency in adolescent speech as to seem almost an oral punctuation device or a juncture signal. Moreover, this expression is not confined to adolescent usage but seems to be an expression of a kind of feigned coyness.

8. Note the remoteness obtained by the avoidance of personal pronoun reference, as the woman Librarian warns the woman Scholar, "We don't permit loud talking in the library. People who insist on talking will be asked to leave the library." The foreign student will have to learn that the *we*, as plural, is impersonal; by omission of the agent, in the passive voice construction used in the second sentence, an impersonal or anonymous quality can be gained.

9. Note the use of *that* instead of *who* in the Boy Student's "girls that drop in now and then." This usage is very common colloquially, perhaps signifying the erosion of distinction between reference to objects and to persons, although that distinction is still widely taught. Similarly, the distinction between object and subject personal pronouns shows some deterioration in the fact that, although *whom* is taught, it has probably vanished from the speech of most people.

10. Two examples of the use of stress to convey emotional coloring should be pointed out to the students:

a. When Scholar says: *"You don't talk in the library,"* each word is spoken slowly, separately, and with equal stress. This extreme form of emphasis is used in scolding or in warning.

b. When Guide says: "Roger [or Joan] (threateningly) . . . . we're over here," the word *here* is given primary stress to contrast emphatically with *there* where Roger [or Joan] has remained standing instead of following the Guide. There is an implied threat because Guide indicates that the boy or girl is expected to follow and may be punished for not following.

Cultural Values

1. It should be recognized that the average man in America lives in what has been called an adolescent centered society. This emphasis on youth may be an extension of the high valuation placed on time, but is most certainly an extension of the fact that education has traditionally been seen as the way to rise in a very fluid social structure. That is, the adolescent years are essentially those spent after acquiring basic training in reading and writing, during which the adolescent is directly prepared for making his own way in the world. Moreover, since independence and self-reliance are extensions of the national ideal of individualism, the adolescent spends a great deal of time in social activity and particularly in dating, which is supposed to supply the experience with people on which he will have to base his individual choice of a marriage partner.

In America this period of adolescence is considered a time of rebellion although generational conflict certainly seems almost a universal in human society. The foreign student will need to understand something of the particular tensions of these years of adolescence seen as complex ramifications of certain national values already noted. In addition to our experience with roles in this staging, we have observed the behavior of adolescents in a number of stagings. Whether these attitudes and patterns of behavior are somehow imposed on teenagers or have been derived, by observation of teenagers by adults, is probably impossible to ascertain. Of course this must be largely generalization, then, and not every adolescent will fit the pattern exactly. But there are attitudes and behavior patterns widely thought to be representative and accepted even by adolescents or teenagers.

2. The attention of foreign students should be called to the fact that:

   a. Television has pretty much supplanted radio as well as reading for many teenagers and they have a pantheon of TV performers. But since they are likely to be distracted by interest in social activities, they are likely to be inattentive even in watching TV.

   b. The library is often considered as merely a social meeting place although adolescents may also make dates to study together there. A kind of experimental romance is the main purpose, little genuine studying is really accomplished, and the library is likely to be rather noisy as a consequence.

   c. Typically, adolescents have little interest in scholarly matters or, in fact, in serious problems of national and international social importance, as the focus of their attention tends to be on their immediately personal and largely physical gratification. The library is merely a convenient meeting place with an aura of respectability. It is a place where parents cannot observe them.

   d. Girls manifest this focus of attention in their interest in clothes—buying them rather than making them—in cosmetics, and in hair styling. In these interests is reflected the widely accepted idea that women are largely decorative and there is a great pressure on girls to occupy themselves with self-decoration and ornamentation.

   e. Boys manifest their concern with physical gratification largely through an interest in sports—frequently vicariously as audience for professional athletes—and, even more typically, by a preoccupation with automobiles which, by extension, are seen as a means to personal power over space and time. Since driving is taught in most high schools, many teenagers can drive and many boys either own their own cars or have access to their family cars. This, of course, facilitates dating—which compounds the distraction.

   f. However, perhaps the main focus of adolescent interest is overwhelmingly on each other. That is, both boys and girls are likely to spend a great deal of time and effort attracting each other and in each other's company. Even in the adaptations for a cast of one sex we find evidence of this concern for the opposite sex.

3. Perhaps the most obvious manifestation of adolescence, and frequently related to the rebelliousness characteristic of these years, is the very casual social behavior. Actively fostered by commercial interests, teenage clothing styles are widely adopted. We also note, in this staging, the disregard for social amenities, and the seeming discourtesy in conversation among adolescents. Very direct, they tend to become acquainted quickly, easily—and rather shallowly. Although foreigners may find their behavior a kind of disrespectful mockery of love, adolescents quite openly display their mutual affection while engaged in the socially approved experimentation called dating.

4. The masking and reversal in emotional reference are very commonly reflected in colloquial usage. The boy appraising the young girl decides she is "not bad," but mildly enthusiastic as this expression may seem, it might indicate considerable interest. Similarly, the comment that another girl, is "pretty smart," is another example of probable understatement meaning *very smart, very clever, very intelligent*. Since such understating modifiers are usually omitted from texts, the foreigner may easily underestimate a comment or evaluation—just as he may tend to take such an ironic expression such as Boy A's "Great!" quite literally, rather than ironically as it is intended—and then

be puzzled about the characterization, such usage deserves some attention.

5. Note the fact that the girl addresses the woman Scholar first as "Miss" and then as "lady." This points up the rather delicate problem of determining age—since *Miss* is usually used to address young women whose marital status is unknown whereas *Madam* is likely to be used for older women whose marital status is unknown. However, there is a clash of cultural values here too, for not only is youth very highly valued, and therefore every attempt is made to appear young, but since single people beyond the age of thirty-five or so are still thought somewhat comical— for their failure to marry—the implied reference to marital status in either *Miss* or *Madam* may seem insulting. *(Mrs.* is not used in direct address unless it is accompanied by the woman's last name.) The perplexed girl, therefore, avoids the problem of address by choosing the neutral term "lady."

6. In notes to earlier stagings in this text under the heading of Structure, extensive comment has been made on certain manifestations of what we might think of as woman's language. However, it should be apparent that many such manifestations might as justifiably be considered under the heading of Cultural Values, since they reflect the peculiar role patterns allocated to women. That is, we might point out that the contraction of modal auxiliary and the negative, in the word *mustn't* of the lady scholar's dialogue—but also to be found in other combinations, such as *oughtn't* or even *shouldn't*—indirectly convey that mild admonishment, reprimand, or even a kind of softened command, more typical of women's speech. Moreover, women further soften this construction by using *we* rather than *you* as the subject of *mustn't*, and often by placing the combination in the second clause of the trailer or tag question. Similarly, the woman's use of "Oh, now come on" makes a kind of plea for cooperation, in which the exasperation is softened, in typical feminine fashion, of what might otherwise seem the quite blunt and aggressive demand more common in male speech.

On the other hand, another device more commonly ex-ploited by women than by men is the stretching of the vowel or diphthong for purposes of strengthening emphasis. Most texts show emphasis as the consequence of stress intensification or the use of modifiers and intensifiers. But, it is apparent that although "de-ar" /^{2}diy-^{3}ər/, which the lady librarian uses, is characterized by stress intensification, the ironical, mock expression of attention reflecting her annoyance is conveyed by sound stretching. In fact, it might be seen that in slowing down the speech pace, by such sound stretching, attention is drawn to that word just as it would be by the greater loudness provided by ordinary stress intensification.

Thus, it seems likely that since what may appear characteristic softening devices—in the sense of devices providing indirection—are actually employed by women to intensify and focus effect, the term *softening* as we have used it is clearly a not completely satisfactory improvisation. As in all areas of experience, difference—such as that distinguishing the behavior of men from that of women—need not imply valuational contrast.

General Comment

1. There are certain similarities between this staging and "Flight 641":
   a. The set in both stagings consists of a room having one entrance—past the Airline Agent's/Librarian's desk.
   b. The dialogue consists of patterns of alternation between pairs of conversants, although there is somewhat less interaction between pairs in this play than in "Flight 641." In both stagings the pairs are distributed around the set so that exchanges take place in various parts of the stage, but in "Flight 641" all action tends toward the desk of the Agent and Assistant, whereas in "Quiet Please!" most characters have little if any close contact with the Librarian; indeed, most of them ignore the Librarian.
   c. Although the setting for both stagings is a public place and focuses on the relations of characters with a bureaucracy, we

note that the situation of "Flight 641" is complicated because the passengers as customers are dealing with representatives of a large private company while the characters in "Quiet Please!" are citizens and taxpayers dealing with a kind of minor government official.

    d. About half of the characters in this staging are adolescents who feel neither direct responsibility to nor interest in the library; they are mere casual visitors. These adolescents may be seen to be largely rebelling against a parental figure of authority rather than offering conscious opposition to a bureaucracy.

All of these similarities and differences can explain the peculiarities of behavior characterizing the characters in this staging.

2. This staging is constructed as a rather complex and somewhat involuted collection of conversational exchanges, but basically it consists of exchanges in six scenes following a kind of introductory opening:

    a) the young couple interrupted by the Page and the Scholar
    b) the guide and the boys
    c) the two girls
    d) the girl and the Page
    e) the Librarian and the Janitor
    f) the Scholar and the Librarian

Although the Scholar is the focus of attention, and it is his reaction which ties the events together, he does not really interact but, instead, interrupts until the final scene. Thus, the function of the Scholar may be seen as serving to emphasize the ironic fact that those whose duty it is to enforce silence frequently are noisiest. The staging builds up to a kind of climax which has undergone slow development throughout, when the scholar finally explodes in exasperation over the continuous series of disturbances and total lack of concern for his rights. All of those annoyances are apparently routine rather than unusual and it is the scholar who in such an atmosphere must seem odd or deviant.

3. We note that about half the exchanges in the original staging are changed in the adaptations offered. And these necessary changes for the most part provide the student with useful evidence of important distinctions between the values and attitudes of men in contrast to women, as reflected in behavior in our society. The different interests and attitudes distinguishing girls from boys has received comment earlier. It might be a good idea, however, to point out that although the Scholar is finally defeated and driven out, whether the role is played by a man or by a woman, the woman Scholar, even in dealing with girls and other women, speaks and acts in ways subtly different from those which characterize the man Scholar. Because her growing annoyance is not as bluntly and aggressively displayed, her ultimate outburst may seem more surprising to students who cannot adequately interpret the evidence of her attitude which she has provided along the way.

4. Although a secondary and peripheral benefit, this staging may help to acquaint students with expected library behavior—behavior *not* displayed by the characters. It also may give them some acquaintance with typical library facilities. Many students will be quite unfamiliar with an open shelf system, giving equal access to all books. In fact, many foreign students may have difficulty with this concept as part of their difficulty in understanding that equal access on a much broader basis which characterizes our society. They may be ill-prepared to understand the general lack of age and class distinctions which they will encounter. On the other hand, since many will also be aware of our failure to reach perfection in extending the idea of equal access throughout our society, they will be keenly aware of the shortcomings, many of which cannot be justified.

    Odd as it may seem, those coming from places having very rigid social class, and even caste stratification patterns, may feel most dissatisfied with what may seem to them the waste of such freedom on those of our people who, from their standpoint, are not ready, willing, or able to make any use of the extensive opportunities which exist here. Some foreigners may become quite incensed that so much should be wasted here on those they find undeserving because they imagine natives of their own countries and elsewhere could better utilize it. Students coming from scarcity societies will have to be helped to understand attitudes prevailing in societies characterized by plenty, surplus —and even waste.

5. Although it is not dealt with directly in this staging, the adolescent attitude toward work is important to an understanding of the adolescent and the relation of the adolescent and adult. Since the play activity of teenagers is largely social, it will appear to many foreigners that they are lazy and irresponsible, frivolous rather than serious. Yet the foreigner will have to recognize that another part of the cultural value scheme encourages large numbers of teenagers to work at least part-time. In fact, many businesses and industries depend on such part-time labor of teenagers. Yet, since they are essentially unskilled and frequently have no focused interest, most teenagers work at jobs they are not interested in merely to gain the money necessary for the culturally valued displays of independence and individualism. For many of them, therefore, the work is "just a job," only a means of making money and by no means a career.

Notes on Adaptation

1. Since the romantic interest peculiar to American adolescents underlies much of the staging, there are serious complications to be met in adaptation for performance by a cast comprising a single sex. That is, the romance between the Young Man and Young Girl, that between the Young Girl and Page, and the conversation between the two boys had to be considerably changed. Of course, part of the problem could be solved by dropping out the young couple and modifying dialogue of other characters accordingly. However, I have chosen to provide adaptations which retain the same number of roles as in the original staging whenever possible. The role of the Guide is readily changed, due to its inherent officiousness and the insistence on being impersonal, and so is the role of the Janitor. Similarly, since the role of the Librarian is one of bureaucratic impersonality, it can readily be converted to a man's role.

2. Clearly this staging provides the best opportunity since "The Meeting" to examine the world of the adolescent and his relation with adults. We have witnessed attempts of the elderly to gain respect from the young, by calling them "young man"/"young lady." This is, of course, a manifestation of the continuing struggle between the generations, as the elders attempt to stem the challenge of youth. That challenge takes many forms, and often the mutual hostility is rather subtly expressed. Often there is a mock respect, a sarcastic element in the adolescent use of seemingly deferential expressions since in a society valuing youth, no reference—no matter how indirect or seemingly polite—can actually be complimentary. We also find a kind of feigned courtesy or affection, commonly used between women members of two generations, as when the woman, who obviously disapproves of the girl's behavior, manages to stretch her pronunciation of "dear" in an exaggerated way, to make a kind of veiled threat of it, already noted. It is important for foreign students to learn that compounding of courtesy seems incongruous and a kind of sarcastic mockery in English, for, in contrast, many cultures intensify politeness by such compounding or use of stilted expression and there is no sarcastic mockery or insult implied.

3. The foreigner will have to learn that there is a great deal of sarcasm and irony in spoken expression and that "kidding" or making sly attempts to deceive or to tease is very common, particularly among young people. Three common ways of attaining a sarcastic effect are:

   a) Stilted diction which contributes a kind of comical incongruity in the use of such uncommon words or combinations as *"perfectly splendid"* or even in the more ordinary word *"wonderful"* when applied to something obviously undeserving of such exaltation.

   b) Intonation, particularly an exaggerated or excessive pitch change reflecting an enthusiasm which, again, is incongruous in the situation, in this staging when a girl says "just imagine" or when a boy says "Great—just great."

    c) Exclamation—particularly when the facts show the situation quite obviously warrants no exclamation: when the girl says "What a day for this!" meaning that the weather is too fine to be wasted on such dull indoor activity.

4. Note the older woman Scholar's annoyed and even bitter use of "indeed" which alerts us because it seems rather quaint and even part of the literary rather than of the spoken expression. A similar usage for the expression of disapproval or annoyance is that of full form structure rather than abbreviated or contracted. In the adaptation for women, the woman Scholar says, "I *cannot* do so with all these noisy interruptions" instead of using *can't*; by this device she can intensify the negative which is somewhat depressed in the contraction forms. Note also that earlier this woman has used the excessively formal, and therefore sarcastic, "if you please."

5. Attention must again be called to the quality of hesitancy and indirectness characteristic of the speech of many women. We have seen in examining earlier stagings that there are several devices which are particularly common in producing this effect:

    a) The attenuation of syllables, as in "we-l-l";

    b) Addition of such expressions as "I guess," "I suppose," or the use of the prefatory "I wonder if . . . .";

    c) The utilization of a question form instead of either statement or command, particularly common is the use of "What do you think?";

    d) The use of the even less direct negative question structure, as in "You don't happen to have a pen I can borrow, do you?"

It should be recognized that a discussion of the usages peculiar to women's language can provide the means to consideration of the directness of expression typical in exchange between men. And this can be particularly valuable since foreigners from many cultures readily interpret such direct, sparse, and incisive statement as discourteous, although no such interpretation is warranted.

6. A certain slangy quality, which is partly the result of truncation as well as of unusual use of words, is quite common in the speech of adolescents, perhaps as another aspect of rebellion against standard behavior patterns. Since slang is likely to become quickly dated and drop out of the usage, many teachers may feel it is not worthwhile teaching it to foreign students. Some may, on that basis, question the use of dialogue of these stagings. It should be pointed out, therefore, that although every attempt has been made to limit the use of slang, all usage changes and the goal of teaching usage in the living language presupposes some risk, since all living language is, in a sense, dying language. I have chosen to risk the datedness of colloquial usage rather than the blandness of a dateless textbookese. The process of language learning is a continuing one involving growth as well as total involvement.

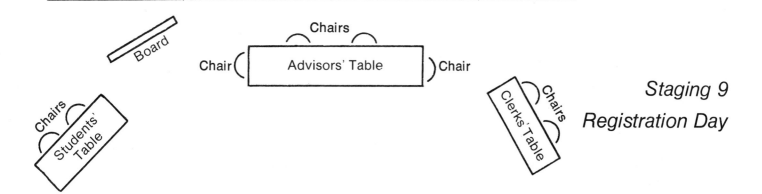

SETTING

A large room used for college registration, almost symmetrically furnished: clerk's table, stage left downstage, one end turned slightly upstage; students' table, stage right downstage, one end turned slightly upstage; advisors' table, stage center. A large board containing course titles and numbers is hanging or standing to the rear of the students' table stage right. As the curtain rises, two clerks sit talking at their table stage left.

Mixed cast	*Girls' cast*	*Boys' cast*
Clerk #1 (Connie)	Clerk #1 (Connie)	Clerk #1 (Don)
Clerk #2	Clerk #2	Clerk #2
Prof. Jones (Bob)	Prof. Jones (Louise)	Prof. Jones (Bob)
Prof. Smith	Prof. Smith	Prof. Smith
John	Joan	John
Frank Thompson	Fran Thompson	Frank Thompson
Ruth	Ruth	Ray
Linda	Linda	Lenny
Shirley	Shirley	Charlie
Joseph Blake	Janet	Joseph Blake

Clerk #1. Let's hope it isn't another day like yesterday. Wow—I thought I'd die with the mob we had . . . must	Clerk #1. Let's hope it isn't another day like yesterday. Wow—I thought I'd die with the mob we had . . . must	Clerk #1. Boy, I hope it's not like yesterday. We must have had five thousand kids here. Really murder!

183

mixed

have been five thousand kids here.

Clerk #2.   Glad I missed it. But maybe it won't be so tough today. (Pεη˘ξ) I think we've got the S's through the Z's, haven't we?

Clerk #1   *(nodding).* Yeah. *(Looking into the wings stage left, and stage whispering)* Here comes Prof. Jones—right on time, for a change.

Prof. Jones enters briskly stage left.

Prof. Jones   *(briefcase tucked under his arm and rubbing his hands together with exaggerated mock enthusiasm).* Good morning, ladies! Another exciting day ahead of us, eh? *(Shaking his head and chuckling as he marches to the advisors' table midstage)* Nothing like good old registration. *(Tossing his briefcase on the table, pulling out the chair, removing his suit coat and sitting down)* No sir . . . nothing like it!

Prof. Smith   *(entering from stage left).* Nothing like what, Bob?

Two clerks busy themselves setting up boxes of cards before them while Prof. Smith walks to the advisors' table, tosses down his briefcase, removes his coat, and sits down.

Prof. Jones   *(smiling broadly).* Welcome to registration, Prof. Smith! *(Pulling a small box from his pocket)* Have an aspirin? *(Holds out the box)*

Prof. Smith   *(frowning and looking stage right distastefully).* Not yet . . . save them for later . . . I'm sure we'll need them. *(Glancing toward the wings stage left and exclaiming melo-*

girls

have been five thousand kids here.

Clerk #2.   Glad I missed it. But maybe it won't be so tough today. *(Pause)* I think we've got the S's through the Z's, haven't we?

Clerk #1.   Uh-huh *(looking into wings stage left and stage whispering)* and here she comes . . . Prof. Jones . . . right on time as usual.

Prof. Jones enters briskly stage left.

Prof. Jones   *(leather folder under her arm, removes her gloves with exaggerated flourish).* Good morning, girls! Another exciting day ahead of us. *(Walks slowly to the advisors' table midstage, rubs her hand over the surface, frowns distastefully as she rubs dust together between thumb and forefinger)* Good old registration! *(Leans down and, after blowing across the tabletop, places her leather folder on the table. Opens the folder, pulls out a handkerchief, flicks it across the chair seat, and sits down)* Absolutely nothing like it! *(This last sentence should be spoken very musically with a rising pitch)*

Prof. Smith   *(entering from stage left).* Fortunately, Louise, fortunately!

Two clerks busy themselves setting up boxes of cards before them while Prof. Smith walks to the advisors' table, repeats Prof. Jones's inspection for dust, and sits down.

Prof. Jones   *(smiling broadly and with very dramatic enthusiasm).* Welcome, my dear, to registration! *(Pulling a box*

boys

Clerk #2.   Glad I missed it. But maybe it won't be so tough today. (Pεη˘ξ) I think we've got the S's through the Z's, haven't we?

Clerk #1   *(nodding).* Yeah. *(Looking into the wings, stage left, and stage whispering)* Here comes Prof. Jones—right on time, for a change.

Prof. Jones enters briskly stage left.

Prof. Jones   *(brief case tucked under his arm and rubbing his hands together with exaggerated mock enthusiasm).* Good morning, Gentlemen! Another exciting day ahead of us, eh? *(Shaking his head and chuckling as he marches to the advisors' table midstage)* Nothing like good old registration. *(Tossing his brief case on the table, pulling out the chair, removing his suit coat and sitting down)* No, sir . . . nothing like it!

Prof. Smith   *(entering from stage left).* Nothing like what, Bob?

Two clerks busy themselves setting up boxes of cards before them while Prof. Smith walks to the advisors' table, tosses down his briefcase, removes his coat and sits down.

Prof. Jones   *(smiling broadly).* Welcome to registration, Prof. Smith! *(Pulling a small box from his pocket)* Have an aspirin? *(Holds out the box)*

Prof. Smith   *(frowning and looking stage right distastefully).* Not yet . . . save them for later . . . I'm sure we'll need them. *(Glancing toward the wings stage left and exclaiming melo-*

mixed	*girls*	*boys*

mixed

dramatically) Lo, our first customer approaches!

John enters stage right, sits down at the students' table, picks a form from the pile stacked there, pulls a paper from his pocket, and turns to face the large board upstage right. While he glances from the paper before him to the board, the two professors consult together over a paper on the advisors' table.

John   *(flatly, as if talking aloud to himself).* Just as I figured . . . Econ. 274 . . . Soc. 511 . . . Poli. Sci. 436 . . . and the French . . . all closed! Damnit! *(Sighing, turns the paper over and starts flipping desperately through the course bulletin he finds on the table)*

Frank enters stage right, carrying a notebook, and going directly to the advisors' table, sits down at the end next to Prof. Jones.

Frank.   My name is Frank Thompson and I was scheduled to register yesterday. But I had to work late and by the time I got here the building was closed. I think this is O.K., Prof. Jones. *(Pulls a form from the notebook he is carrying and offers it to Prof. Jones who takes it and looks it over)*

John, scribbling on his papers, consulting the course catalog on the desk, and glancing at the board, grunts in satisfaction, shuffles the papers together, gets up, crosses to the advisors' table,and slumps down, placing the papers on the table before Prof. Smith.

girls

from a purse she has removed from her leather folder) Would you like your aspirin now or later?

Prof. Smith   *(frowning and looking distastefully stage right toward the board).* I believe I'll have mine later . . . when I'll certainly need it more. *(Glances toward the wings stage left)* Oh, the avalanche has started!

Joan enters stage right, sits down at the students' table, picks a form from the pile stacked there, pulls a paper from her pocket, and turns to face the larger board upstage right. While she glances from the paper before her to the board, the two professors consult together over a paper on the advisors' table.

Fran enters stage right, carrying a notebook, and going directly to the advisors' table, sits down at the end next to Prof. Jones.

Fran.   My name is Fran Thompson and I was scheduled to register yesterday. But I had to work late and by the time I got here the building was closed. I think this is O.K., Prof. Jones. *(Pulls a form from the notebook she is carrying and offers it to Prof. Jones who takes it and looks it over)*

Joan, scribbling on her papers, consulting the course catalog on the desk, and glancing at the board, grunts in satisfaction, shuffles the papers together, gets up, crosses to the advisors' table, and slumps down, placing the papers on the table before Prof. Smith.

Clerk #2   *(to Clerk #1).* Is anything else closed, beside what's on the board?

boys

dramatically) Lo, our first customer approaches!

John enters stage right, sits down at the students' table, picks a form from the pile stacked there, pulls a paper from his pocket, and turns to face the large board upstage right. While he glances from the paper before him to the board, the two professors consult together over a paper on the advisors' table.

John   *(flatly, as if talking aloud to himself).* Just as I figured . . . Econ. 274 . . . Soc. 511 . . . Poli. Sci. 436 . . . and the French . . . all closed! Damnit! *(Sighing, turns the paper over and starts flipping desperately through the course bulletin he finds on the table)*

Frank enters stage right, carrying a notebook, and going directly to the advisors' table, sits down at the end next to Prof. Jones.

Frank.   My name is Frank Thompson and I was scheduled to register yesterday. But I had to work late and by the time I got here the building was closed. I think this is O.K., Prof. Jones. *(Pulls a form from the notebook he is carrying and offers it to Prof. Jones who takes it and looks it over)*

John, scribbling on his papers, consulting the course catalog on the desk, and glancing at the board, grunts in satisfaction, shuffles the papers together, gets up, crosses to the advisors' table, and slumps down, placing the papers on the table before Prof. Smith.

mixed

Clerk #2 *(to Clerk #1)*. Is anything else closed, beside what's on the board?

Clerk #1 *(consulting some papers)*. No-o-o . . . oh, wait a minute; here's one I forgot to post last night. I'd better post it. *(Takes a card containing course title and number printed in large black letters and numerals and, crossing to the board, posts it and then returns to her spot behind the clerks' table)*

John *(gloomily to Prof. Smith)*. I wanted to take the History Survey, but there's only one section and that's at four o'clock. I start work at three o'clock on Wednesdays—so that's out. *(Shrugs and shakes his head resignedly)*

Prof. Smith *(nodding)*. Are you working everyday?

John. No, only Wednesday—and then over the weekends too, of course.

Prof. Smith *(glancing at the board)*. Anyway, that Psych. course you've listed . . . 269 . . . is closed.

John *(shocked)*. What! *(Glances at the board)* How did I miss it! *(Gloomily)* oh boy . . . now I've got to juggle the whole works around again. *(Sighs and picks up the paper before Prof. Smith and trudges wearily back to the students' table. He sits down and again begins desperately flipping through the course bulletin and checking the board listings)*

Prof. Jones. Now let's see . . . you've

girls

Clerk #1 *(consulting some papers)*. No-o-o . . . oh, wait a minute; here's one I forgot to post last night. I'd better post it. *(Takes a card containing course title and number printed in large black letters and numerals and, crossing to the board, posts it and then returns to her spot behind the clerks' table)*

Joan *(to Prof. Smith)*. I wanted so much to take the History Survey—you know, the Modern European—but it's at four o'clock and I have to be at my job at three o'clock on Wednesdays. *(Sighing)* So-o-o . . . I guess I've got to find something else.

Prof. Smith *(nodding)*. Are you working everyday?

Joan. No, only Wednesdays—and then over the weekends too, of course.

Prof. Smith *(glancing at the board)*. Anyway, that Psych. course you've listed . . . 269 . . . is closed.

Joan *(shocked)*. Oh-h-h! *(Wailing as she stares at the board)* And I thought I had everything worked out so beautifully too. *(Frowning)* Oh, that makes me so mad! *(Snatches up her papers and marches stiffly to the student table. She sits down and again begins desperately flipping through the course bulletin and checking the board listings)*

Prof. Jones. Now let's see . . . you've met the science requirement, I suppose . . . H-m-m . . . what about the

boys

Clerk #2 *(to Clerk #1)*. Is anything else closed, beside what's on the board?

Clerk #1 *(consulting some papers)*. No-o-o . . . oh, wait a minute; here's one I forgot to post last night. I'd better post it. *(Takes a card containing course title and number printed in large black letters and numerals and, crossing to the board, posts it and then returns to his spot behind the clerks' table)*

John *(gloomily to Prof. Smith)*. I wanted to take the History Survey, but there's only one section and that's at four o'clock. I start work at three o'clock on Wednesdays—so that's out. *(Shrugs and shakes his head resignedly)*

Prof. Smith *(nodding)*. Are you working everyday?

John. No, only Wednesdays—and then over the weekends too, of course.

Prof. Smith *(glancing at the board)*. Anyway, that Psych. course you've listed . . . 269 . . . is closed.

John *(shocked)*. What! *(Glances at the board)* How did I miss it! *(Gloomily)* Oh boy . . . now I've got to juggle the whole works around again. *(Sighs and picks up the paper before Prof. Smith and trudges wearily back to the students' table. He sits down and again begins desperately flipping through the course bulletin and checking the board listings)*

Prof. Jones. Now let's see . . . you've

mixed

met the science requirement, I suppose ... H-m-m ... what about the English sequence? *(Glancing up at Frank)*

Frank.   I had the basic course sequence and the Shakespeare 219 ... so I figure I've got three more courses to go. *(Prof. Jones nods and continues to examine the forms)*

Ruth   *(entering from stage left, stops before the clerks' table smiling)*. Hi, Connie ... it's times like these I wish I was Baker or Conners instead of Walters.

Clerk #1.   Oh, they may open a few sections if you stick around *(smiling)* ... until next term!

Ruth nods and, crossing to the advisors' table, sits down before Prof. Smith.

Ruth   *(enthusiastically)*. Hi, Prof. Smith! Gee, it seems as if I haven't seen you in such a long time! *(Innocently)* I hope your American Lit. Survey isn't closed, is it?

Prof. Smith   *(smiling and glancing to the right at the large board)*. Yes, it seems that way ... but do you need it? When do you finish?

Ruth.   Well, it's my last year and I've got to practice teach this quarter, so I'm going to be tied up, I guess ...

Prof. Smith   *(nodding)*. How about the Criticism ... There's an evening section you could get into. *(Glances at the board)* Yeah, that would fit in O.K.

girls

English sequence? *(Glancing up at Fran)*

Fran.   I had the basic course sequence and the Shakespeare 219 ... so I think I need three more courses, don't I?

Ruth   *(entering from stage left, stops before the clerks' table smiling)*. Hi, Connie ... it's times like these I wish I was Baker or Conners instead of Walters.

Clerk #1.   Oh, they may open a few sections if you stick around *(smiling)* ... until next term!

Ruth nods and, crossing to the advisors' table, sits down before Prof. Smith.

Ruth   *(enthusiastically)*. Hi, Prof. Smith! Gee, it seems as if I haven't seen you in such a long time! *(Innocently)* I hope your American Lit. Survey isn't closed, is it?

Prof. Smith   *(smiling and glancing to the right at the large board)*. Yes, it seems that way ... but do you need it? When do you finish?

Ruth.   Well, it's my last year and I've got to practice teach this quarter, so I'm going to be tied up, I guess ...

Prof. Smith   *(nodding)*. How about the Criticism ... I think there's an evening section you could get into, isn't there? *(Glances at the board)* Yes, that would work out very well, wouldn't it?

Ruth   *(somewhat coyly feigning embarrassment)*. Oh ... but I've heard it's such a good course and I've been so anxious to take your survey ... if I

boys

met the science requirement, I suppose ... H-m-m ... what about the English sequence? *(Glancing up at Frank)*

Frank.   I had the basic course sequence and the Shakespeare 219 ... so I figure I've got three more courses to go. *(Prof. Jones nods and continues to examine the forms)*

Ray   *(entering from stage left, stops before the clerks' table smiling)*. Hi, Don ... it's times like these I wish I was Baker or Conners instead of Walters.

Clerk #1.   Oh, they may open a few sections if you stick around *(smiling)* ... until next term!

Ray nods and, crossing to the advisors' table, sits down before Prof. Smith.

Ray.   Hi, Prof. Smith ... I haven't seen you in a long time. Is your American Lit. Survey closed yet?

Prof. Smith   *(smiling and glancing to the right at the large board)*. Yes, it seems that way ... but do you need it? When do you finish?

Ray.   This is my last year and, with practice teaching, they've got me tied up.

Prof. Smith   *(nodding)*. How about the Criticism ... There's an evening section you could get into. *(Glances at the board)* Yeah, that would fit in O.K.

Ray   *(smiling)*. Yeah, I know, but I'd sort of counted on that survey, if

mixed

Ruth   *(somewhat coyly feigning embarrassment).* Oh . . . but I've heard it's such a good course and I've been so anxious to take your survey . . . if I possibly could.

Frank.   As a history major I ought to have at least one history course each term—although *(gloomily)* they conflict with almost everything else. And, of course, I've still got to meet the language requirement . . . somehow.

Prof. Jones   *(nodding in agreement).* Um-m-m *(studying Frank's papers),* I see you have Spanish here. *(Pointing to the form)* Didn't you tell me you were taking German? *(Looks up at Frank)*

Frank   *(nodding grimly and somewhat embarrassed).* I flunked it—so I figured I'd better switch to Spanish . . . and maybe have a better chance of passing.

Prof. Jones   *(nodding).* Maybe so . . . maybe so. *(Writes on the paper and hands it to Frank)* O.K. . . . there you are, Frank.

Frank, mumbling "thanks," gets up and goes to the clerks' table, offering the form to Clerk #2 who takes it and begins pulling several cards from the box before him.

Prof. Smith muses over Ruth's papers.

Ruth.   I just couldn't find anything else to fit in, the way the Ed. courses are scheduled . . .

Prof. Smith   *(nodding).* Yes, it *does* seem that way, doesn't it? Well, I guess I can squeeze one more into that class.

girls

possibly could.

Fran.   As a history major I ought to have at least one history course each term—although *(gloomily)* they conflict with almost everything else. And, of course, I've still got to meet the language requirement . . . somehow.

Prof. Jones   *(nodding).* I see you have Spanish here *(pointing to Fran's papers),* although I thought you told me you were taking German, didn't you? *(Looks at Fran)*

Fran   *(nodding grimly and somewhat embarrassed).* I flunked it and so I decided to try Spanish instead . . . and I really hope I can do better with that.

Prof. Jones   *(nodding, but noncommittally).* Uh-huh . . . I imagine so. *(Writes on the paper and hands it to Fran)* All right, there you are, Fran.

Fran, mumbling "thanks," gets up and goes to the clerks' table, offering the form to Clerk #2 who takes it and begins pulling several cards from the box before her.

Prof. Smith muses over Ruth's papers.

Ruth.   I just couldn't find anything else to fit in, the way the Ed. courses are scheduled . . .

Prof. Smith   *(nodding).* Yes, it does seem that way, doesn't it. Well, I guess I can squeeze one more into that class. *(Signs the form and hands it to Ruth)*

Fran   *(stage whispering to Clerk #2).* Oh, I feel so lucky . . . that's the last card, isn't it? I just knew that section would fill fast! *(Pauses)* By the way,

boys

possible.

Frank.   As a history major I ought to have at least one history course each term—although *(gloomily)* they conflict with almost everything else. And, of course, I've still got to meet the language requirement . . . somehow.

Prof. Jones   *(nodding in agreement).* Um-m-m *(studying Frank's papers),* I see you have Spanish here. *(Pointing to the form)* Didn't you tell me you were taking German? *(Looks up at Frank)*

Frank   *(nodding grimly and somewhat embarrassed).* I flunked it—so I figured I'd better switch to Spanish . . . and maybe have a better chance of passing.

Prof. Jones   *(nodding).* Maybe so . . . maybe so. *(Writes on the paper and hands it to Frank)* O.K. . . . there you are, Frank.

Frank, mumbling "thanks," gets up and goes to the clerks' table, offering the form to Clerk #2 who takes it and begins pulling several cards from the box before him.

Prof. Smith muses over Ray's papers.

Ray.   The Ed. courses have me blocked.

Prof. Smith   *(nodding).* Um-hm. *(Pause)* Well, I guess I can squeeze one more into that class. *(Signs the form and hands it to Ray)*

Frank   *(to Clerk #2).* Boy, am I lucky! That's the last card. I figured that section would fill up fast. By the way, how many cards are left for that Introductory German?

mixed

(Signs the form and hands it to Ruth)

Frank *(to Clerk #2).* Boy, am I lucky! That's the last card. I figured that section would fill up fast. By the way, how many cards are left for that Introductory German?

Clerk #2 *(counting the cards).* Lots of them . . . twenty.

Frank *(nodding and smiling).* So far he's got five, then. *(Shaking his head)* If they only knew . . . he's terrible! *(Gathers up the cards)* Thanks. *(Exits stage left almost bumping Linda as she enters)* Oh—s'cuse me. *(Glances over his shoulder at Linda, smiling and whistling softly in appreciation as he exits)*

Ruth (beaming). Gee, thanks so much, Prof. Smith. See you in class. *(Crosses to clerks' table and hands forms to Clerk #1)*

Linda pauses midstage, gazing at the board on her way to the students' table, shakes her head disgustedly, and continues on to the students' table where she sits down, glances at the board again, and consults the course bulletin on the table.

Prof. Jones *(stretching and then banteringly to Prof. Smith).* I can't understand why you get all the good-looking ones while the clods all come to me.

Prof. Smith *(smiling and nodding toward Ruth).* She's a pretty bright kid too. I think I gave her a B in the 120 a couple of years ago.

girls

are there many cards left for that Introductory German?

Clerk #2 *(counting the cards).* Lots of them . . . twenty.

Fran *(nodding and smiling).* So far only five kids have signed up, then. *(Shaking her head)* Gee, if they only knew that she's *(pause)* such an awful teacher. *(Gathers up the cards)* Thanks. *(Exits stage left, passing Linda as she enters)*

Ruth *(beaming).* Gee, thanks. It's awfully sweet of you to let me in, Prof. Smith. See you in class. *(Crosses to clerks' table and hands her form to Clerk #1)*

Linda pauses midstage, gazing at the board on her way to the students' table, shakes her head disgustedly, and continues on to the students' table where she sits down, glances at the board again, and consults the course bulletin on the table.

Prof. Jones *(banteringly to Prof. Smith).* Soft-hearted Nellie *(and then mocking solemnly)* . . . although I'm sure I can't think of anything she'd find more profitable, of course. *(Smiling)*

Prof. Smith *(smiling and nodding toward Ruth).* She's a pretty bright kid too. I think I gave her a B in the 120 a couple of years ago.

Prof. Jones *(nodding with a sly smile).* She looks like such a nice girl—and I'm sure she knows precisely how few B's you give out too.

boys

Clerk #2 *(counting the cards).* Lots of them . . . twenty.

Frank *(nodding and smiling).* So far he's got five then. *(Shaking his head)* If they only knew . . . he's terrible. *(Gathers up the cards)* Thanks. *(Exits stage left, passing Lenny entering)*

Ray *(beaming).* Gee, thanks, doc. *(Crosses to clerks' table and hands forms to Clerk #1)*

Lenny pauses midstage, gazing at the board on his way to the students' table, shakes his head disgustedly, and continues on to the students' table where he sits down, glances at the board again, and consults the course bulletin on the table.

Prof. Jones *(stretching and banteringly to Prof. Smith).* Fairly elastic class rolls, you have, eh, Prof. Smith?

Prof. Smith *(in mock seriousness and sly pomposity).* Even they recognize quality *(sighing with mock sadness),* although I often wish there was someone whom I might entrust to share the burden of cultivating their eager young minds. *(Chuckles)*

Prof. Jones *(nodding in mock piety).* Modesty will do it every time!

Ray *(in stage whisper to Clerk #1).* Well, the old faker let me in, thank God. *(Clerk nods, chuckling, and hands him some cards)* See you later; I've got to get downtown to work. *(Exits briskly stage left)*

Charlie enters stage right and, seeing Lenny, immediately rushes up to him.

mixed

Prof. Jones   *(nodding with a sly smile).* Understandable . . . quite understandable.

Ruth   *(in stage whisper to Clerk #1).* Well, the old faker let me in, thank God. *(Clerk nods, chuckling, and hands her some cards)* See you later; I've got to get downtown to work. *(Exits briskly stage left)*

Shirley enters stage right and, seeing Linda, immediately rushes up to her.

Shirley   *(enthusiastically).* Gee, Linda, where have you been? I've been looking everywhere for you. Can't you do all this later . . . you've got all day. I've got such a lot to tell you. *(They talk together inaudibly, half turned away from the audience)*

Prof. Jones   *(sarcastically to Prof. Smith).* Two prizes! *(Nodding toward the two girls chatting. The two professors watch the pair disgustedly)*

Shirley   *(turning toward the audience and talking to Linda whose face is also visible).* And was he cute!

Linda   *(somewhat annoyed).* Well, look, Shirley, that's all great, but I've got to get registered today and get to work by three *(looking at her wristwatch)* and it's two o'clock now. *(They again turn slightly away from the audience and chat inaudibly)*

Clerk #2 meanwhile exits stage left and, returning with several large cards containing course titles and numbers, hangs them on the board stage right.

girls

Ruth   *(in stage whisper to Clerk #1).* Well, the old faker let me in, thank God. *(Clerk nods, chuckling, and hands her some cards)* See you later; I've got to get downtown to work. *(Exits briskly stage left)*

Shirley enters stage right and, seeing Linda, immediately rushes up to her.

Shirley   *(enthusiastically).* Gee, Linda, where have you been? I've been looking everywhere for you. Can't you do all this later . . . you've got all day. I've got such a lot to tell you. *(They talk together inaudibly, half turned away from the audience)*

Prof. Jones   *(sarcastically to Prof. Smith).* Two prizes! *(Nodding toward the two girls chatting. The two professors watch the pair disgustedly)*

Shirley   *(turning toward the audience and talking to Linda whose face is also visible).* And was he cute!

Linda   *(somewhat annoyed).* Well, look, Shirley, that's all great, but I've got to get registered today and get to work by three *(looking at her wristwatch)* and it's two o'clock now. *(They again turn slightly away from the audience and chat inaudibly)*

Clerk #2 meanwhile exits stage left and, returning with several large cards containing course titles and numbers, hangs them on the board stage right.

Shirley   *(turning back toward the audience and talking to Linda whose face is again visible).* I know, but I wanted

boys

Charlie   *(frowning and annoyed).* Lenny, where have you been? I've been looking all over. *(Glancing at the papers Lenny is carrying)* Gee, you can fool around with this stuff later. I want to talk to you. *(They talk together inaudibly, half turned away from the audience)*

Prof. Jones   *(sarcastically to Prof. Smith).* Two prizes! *(Nodding toward the two boys chatting. The two professors watch the pair disgustedly)*

Charlie   *(turning toward the audience and talking to Lenny whose face is also visible).* And she was real good-looking, too!

Lenny   *(somewhat annoyed).* Well, look, Charlie, that's all great, but I've got to get registered today and get to work by three *(looking at his wristwatch)* and it's two o'clock now. *(They again turn slightly away from the audience and chat inaudibly)*

Clerk #2 meanwhile exits stage left and, returning with several large cards containing course titles and numbers, hangs them on the board stage right.

Charlie   *(turning back toward the audience and talking to Lenny whose face is again visible).* Yeah, I know all that, but I figured if you could pick up a date the four of us could go out to the Cave together tonight.

Lenny.   How're we going to get out there?

Charlie   *(smiling).* In her brand new

mixed

Shirley   *(turning back toward the audience and talking to Linda whose face is again visible).* I know, but I wanted to tell you he's going to call me tonight and I figured maybe you could get a date and we all could go out to the Cave together.

Linda.   Has he got a car?

Shirley.   A car! Only a brand new Buick convertible! *(Excitedly)* His name is Blake and he's a really bright guy. I think he's in some kind of research or something.

Linda   *(impatiently).* Shirley, it sounds terrific . . . except I've got to be at work at three and I've got to register right now. *(Obviously trying to end the conversation)*

Shirley   *(dreamily).* I met Joe at a dance last night . . . *(Sighs)*

Joseph Blake enters briskly, goes immediately to the chair opposite Prof. Smith and sits down.

Linda   *(gazes at Shirley and shakes her head).* Yeah . . . *(sarcastically)* fate, but I've got to register, right now. *(Gets up and, going over to Prof. Jones's table, places her forms on the table and sits down)*

Prof. Smith   *(cheerily).* Back again, Mr. Blake? I'd heard that you are financially embarrassed and you might not be with us this term . . .

Linda listens attentively to the conversation between Prof. Smith and Joseph, having glanced quickly at the latter.

girls

to tell you he's going to call me tonight and I figured maybe you could get a date and we all could go out to the Cave together.

Linda.   Has he got a car?

Shirley.   A car! Only a brand new Buick convertible! *(Excitedly)* His name is Blake and he's a really bright guy. I think he's in some kind of research or something.

Linda   *(impatiently).* Shirley, it sounds terrific . . . except I've got to be at work at three and I've got to register right now. *(Obviously trying to end the conversation)*

Janet enters briskly, goes immediately to Prof. Smith's desk and sits down.

Shirley   *(dreamily).* I met Joe at a dance last night . . . *(Sighs)*

Linda   *(gazes at Shirley and shakes her head).* Yeah . . . *(sarcastically)* fate, but I've got to register, right now. *(Gets up and, going over to Prof. Jones's table, places her forms on the table and sits down)*

Prof. Smith   *(surprised).* Back again, Janet? Didn't I hear that you had a wedding planned for this month?

Janet   *(cautiously).* Yes . . . Joe and I were planning to get married . . . you may remember we were in your class together . . . but we . . . er . . . ran into some financial troubles. Now we've postponed it while we both work and save some money.

Linda listens attentively to the conversation

boys

Buick convertible . . . she got as a Christmas present from her father who's a banker in Chicago! Her name is Sandra. *(Repeats the name slowly as if relishing the sound)* Sandra! . . . And she's really class. I think she does modeling or something.

Lenny   *(impatiently).* Charlie, it sounds terrific . . . except I've got to be at work at three and I've got to register right now. *(Obviously trying to end the conversation)*

Joseph enters briskly, goes immediately to Prof. Smith's desk and sits down.

Charlie   *(smiling broadly).* And to think I just happened to drop in at the dance in Newton where I met this doll . . . sheer chance! *(Shakes his head in disbelief)*

Lenny   *(gazes at Charlie and shakes his head).* Yeah . . . *(sarcastically)* fate, but I've got to register, right now. *(Gets up and, going over to Prof. Jone's table, places his forms on the table and sits down)*

Prof. Smith   *(cheerily).* Back again, Mr. Blake? I'd heard that you are financially embarrassed and you might not be with us this term . . .

Lenny listens attentively to the conversation between Prof. Smith and Joseph, having glanced quickly at the latter.

Joseph.   Frankly, I almost dropped out of school to get a job—I planned on getting married this month. *(Pauses, noticing Prof. Smith's quizzical look)*

mixed	*girls*	*boys*

mixed

Joseph.   Frankly, I didn't think I was going to be able to raise the tuition.

Prof. Smith   *(reflectively).* That's odd, ... I recall seeing you driving a new Buick convertible downtown as recently as last night, Joe. Did you sell it?

Joseph   *(shaking his head solemnly).* That isn't mine. It belongs to my uncle who's a traveling salesman. He's heading east and, since he had a stop to make here in town, let me drive it last night.

Prof. Jones turns and looks at the board, frowns, and then pointing to Linda's papers, gestures toward the board.

Linda   *(startled because she has been straining to hear the conversation between Joseph and Prof. Smith).* Oh . . . (Then wailing) O-h-h . . . no—they've closed the Math, too. (Angrily grabs up her papers, glances nervously at her watch, and rushes back to the students' table)

John   *(to Linda).* Rough, isn't it! I had the same problem. You just get a good schedule worked out and then they close a section. Ph-t-t—it's gone!

Linda   *(wailing gloomily).* I don't know what I'm going to do *(glancing nervously at her wristwatch)* and I've got to get to work.

John   *(glancing at Linda's schedule).* Try Poli. Sci. 234 . . . they've got three sections left and you've got to take it sooner or later 'cause it's required.

girls

between Prof. Smith and Janet, having glanced quickly at the latter.*

Prof. Smith   *(reflectively).* Oh, I had assumed Joe was from a rather wealthy background. In fact, it seems to me I saw him driving a new convertible downtown just last night . . .

Janet   *(surprised and looking down, slightly embarrassed).* Oh, that isn't his—unfortunately. His uncle's a traveling salesman and lent it to Joe when he stopped on the way through town last night.

Prof. Jones turns and looks at the board, frowns, and then pointing to Linda's papers, gestures toward the board.

Linda   *(startled because she has been straining to hear the conversation between Janet and Prof. Smith).* Oh . . . (Then wailing) O-h-h . . . no—they've closed the Math, too. (Angrily grabs up her papers, glances nervously at her watch, and rushes back to the students' table)

Joan   *(smiling and shaking her head in sympathy as Linda drops into the chair gloomily).* Isn't it just terrible? I had the same problem . . . they close a section just as you get a good schedule worked out and *(shrug)* you're dead . . . just like that . . . and have to start all over.

Linda   *(wailing gloomily).* I don't know what I'm going to do *(glancing nervously at her wristwatch)* and I've got to get to work.

boys

her name's Williams . . . she was in your class too . . .

Prof. Smith.   I gather that you've . . . er . . . changed your plans, then?

Joseph   *(nodding).* She's an orphan and the people who adopted her can't help us at all, so we agreed I should finish school first. *(Pause)* I guess I'll sell my Buick convertible . . . since I really can't keep up the payments and I need the money.

Prof. Jones turns and looks at the board, frowns, and then pointing to Lenny's papers, gestures toward the board.

Lenny   *(startled because he has been straining to hear the conversation between Joseph and Prof. Smith).* Huh! (Annoyed) What! They closed the Math? (Signing resignedly) Well, I'll have to give it another try. (Grabs up his papers, glances nervously at his wristwatch, and rushes back to the students' table)

John   *(to Lenny).* Rough, isn't it! I had the same problem. You just get a good schedule worked out and then they close a section. Ph-t-t—it's gone!

Lenny.   Always the same story . . . but *(glances nervously at his wristwatch)* I've got to get to work today.

John   *(glancing at Lenny's schedule).* Try Poli. Sci. 234 . . . they've got three sections left and you've got to take it sooner or later 'cause it's required. *(Shows him the course bulletin)*

Lenny   *(looks at the schedule and then*

mixed

(Shows her the course bulletin)

Linda (looks at the bulletin and then at her papers). Say, that does work, doesn't it! (Scribbles on the paper and, rushing to Prof. Jones's desk, throws her papers down and leans on the back of the chair before him instead of sitting down)

Prof. Jones Well, that was quick! (Examines her paper, glances at the board)

Prof. Smith But in any event, you have rejoined us . . . doubtless to make up the six incompletes still on your—er—unusual record, eh Mr. Blake? . . . and thereby raise that grade point to a towering two point two five?

Joseph (trying to look very serious). Prof. Smith, I'm not kidding you, I've turned serious. (Trying desperately to sound convincing) I haven't had a single date all summer and I won't have until I get those term papers in (noting Prof. Smith's skeptical look) . . . within a week, I promise.

Prof. Jones (looking up and smiling). Looks like you've done it. (Scribbles on the papers and hands them to Linda, who glances at Joseph, still engaged in conversation with Prof. Smith, and then rushes to the clerks' table)

Clerk #1 (nudges Clerk #2 and nods toward Joseph as she stamps Linda's papers). Listen to that liar! (Chuckling) I doubt if he even knows how to

girls

Joan (glancing at Linda's schedule). Why don't you try Poli. Sci. 234 in there. I think there are about three sections left and it's required, so you've got to take it sooner or later it seems. It might fit.

Linda (looks at the bulletin and then at her papers). Say, that does work, doesn't it! (Scribbles on the paper and, rushing to Prof. Jones's desk, throws her papers down and leans on the back of the chair before her instead of sitting down)

Prof. Jones. Now, that wasn't so hard evidently . . . was it? (Examines her paper, glances at the board)

Prof. Smith. I see. But, as I recall, Mr. Blake has a rather weak academic record, hasn't he? (Acidly) Perhaps it will be better if he drops out of school to work for awhile.

Janet (feigning shock). Oh, he isn't going to leave school! In fact, he has become very serious about getting his degree. (Piously, noting Prof. Smith's skeptical look) We haven't had a single date for a couple of months, because he's been studying so hard.

Prof. Jones (looking up and smiling). Looks like you've done it. (Scribbles on the papers and hands them to Linda, who glances at Janet, still engaged in conversation with Prof. Smith, and then rushes to the clerks' table)

Clerk #1 (nudging Clerk #2 and chuck-

boys

at his papers). H-m-m! That might work! (Makes a few notes on the paper, looks up beaming happily) Yeah, it sure does! (Shaking his head disbelievingly) I should have thought of that earlier. (Grabs up the papers and, rushing to Prof. Jones, places his papers down carefully on the table, glancing at his watch again as he drops into the chair)

Prof. Jones. Well, that was quick! (Examines his paper, glances at the board)

Prof. Smith. H-m-m. I assumed you might have sold it, since I hadn't seen you driving it around town. (Ominously) In fact, I haven't seen you at all lately, Mr. Blake.

Joseph (seriously). I've been cracking the books pretty hard, trying to get off probation and I haven't even had time to date my fiancée. She's been using my car to drive out to see her sick sister over in Newton. (Pause) I guess her sister is pretty sick too, because she drove out last night and is driving out again tonight. In fact, she says she drives out there about every night.

Prof. Jones (looking up and smiling). Looks like you've done it. (Scribbles on the papers and hands them to Lenny, who glances at Joseph, still engaged in conversation with Prof. Smith, and then rushes to the clerks' table)

mixed

read.

Linda *(nodding toward Joseph).* Do you know him?

Clerk #2 *(wry-faced).* Know him! Why, Joe Blake is the one truly professional con man on our beloved campus.

Linda *(attentively, accepting her papers).* Did you say Joe Blake?

Clerk #2 nods, Linda, shocked, rushes over to the students' table and is surprised to find Shirley gone.

John *(looking up as she approaches).* Hi ... say, your friend just left. She seemed to be in a kind of daze and wandered away muttering something about a "dream man" she met last night. Some guy named Blake, I think.

Linda *(excited).* Gee, I'll have to find some way to get in touch with her somehow later, I guess. I've got something very important to tell her. Oh—er—thanks a lot for that advice. *(Quickly rushing away)* G'bye. *(Crosses stage and exits stage left)*

John. G'bye. *(Pauses and then bending seriously over his papers talks aloud to himself)* Now let's see ... if I shift the French to two o'clock and the Poli. Sci. to three o'clock, then ...

CURTAIN

Glossary

am I lucky—exclamation meaning *I am lucky*
beloved campus—sarcastic reference to the

girls

ling). I wonder if Joe's kidding her too—or whether she's trying to kid Prof. Smith. *(Chuckling)* Frankly, I doubt if Joe even knows how to read, don't you?

Linda *(nodding toward Joan).* Do you happen to know the fellow she is talking about?

Clerk #2 *(wry-faced).* Know him! Why, Joe Blake is the one truly professional con man on our beloved campus.

Linda *(attentively, accepting her papers).* Did you say Joe Blake?

Clerk #2 nods, Linda, shocked, rushes over to the students' table and is surprised to find Shirley gone.

Joan *(looking up and smiling).* Back again? Your friend just wandered off, still muttering about a "dream man" she met at a dance last night ... some fellow named Blake.

Linda *(excited).* Gee, I'll have to find some way to get in touch with her somehow later, I guess. I've got something very important to tell her. Oh—er—thanks a lot for that advice. *(Quickly rushing away)* G'bye. *(Crosses stage and exits stage left)*

Joan. I'm glad for you that it worked. I wish I could find such an easy solution to my own problem here. *(Calling after Linda who exits quickly stage left)* G'bye. *(Pauses and then bending seriously over her papers, talks to herself)* Now, let's see—if I shift the French to two o'clock and the Poli.

boys

Clerk #1 *(nudges Clerk #2 and nods toward Joseph as he stamps Lenny's papers).* Listen to that! She's even got his new convertible ... so she can visit her "sick sister"! *(Sarcastically)* The "sister" she was dancing with out at Newton last night looked pretty healthy to me! *(Chuckles)*

Lenny *(nodding toward Joe).* Do you know the girl he's engaged to?

Clerk #2 *(wry-faced).* Who doesn't know Sandra Williams—the biggest female con artist and all around gold digger on campus.

Lenny *(attentively accepting his papers).* Did you say her name's Sandra Williams?

Clerk #2 nods. Lenny, scowling, walks back to the students' table, looking around for Charlie.

Lenny *(to John who is still working on his papers).* Thanks for that advice—it worked out fine. Say, ya seen the guy I was talking with before?

John *(looking up).* Yeah, he wandered off muttering something about some wonderful girl named Sandra. *(Looks down at his papers again)*

Lenny *(nodding).* Um-hm. *(Frowning)* Guess I'll have to phone him the bad news. Thanks. See you around! *(Crosses stage and exits stage left)*

John *(preoccupied).* G'bye. *(Pauses and talking aloud to himself)* Now, let's see ... if I shift the French to two o'clock, and the Poli. Sci. to three

mixed

school

brand new—recently new, just purchased

bright guy—clever, intelligent fellow

clods—dull, uninteresting people

closed—filled and not available to more students

con man—one who makes a living by lying to people to induce them to give him money

convertible—an automobile with a canvas roof that can be lowered in good weather

customer—sarcastic reference to a student

cute—handsome, attractive

damnit!—profane expression of annoyance, anger

does work—is possible

dream man—a slang expression referring to a man so ideal as to seem a dream figure rather than real

eh /^{3}ey^4/—isn't that true?

figure—calculate, think, expect

financially embarrassed—without money

finish—graduate

flunked—failed

fool around—become involved with, waste time on

for a change—usually he is late; it is unusual for him to be on time

get a date—arrange for an acquaintance of the opposite sex to accompany

get in touch with—contact, talk to personally or by telephone

gloomily—sadly

good-looking ones—pretty girls

grade point—a kind of system for averaging grades and course credits

great—very good

girls

Sci. to three o'clock, then . . .

CURTAIN

Glossary

avalanche—a landslide; used figuratively it means a mob or large crowd

awfully sweet—very nice, kind

had a wedding planned—going to marry

just like that—happening as quickly as the words themselves are pronounced

piously—with exaggerated seriousness

ran into some financial trouble—needed money

skeptical—doubtful, unbelieving

soft-hearted—too kind, overly sympathetic, lacking determination

uh-huh /$\widetilde{ə}$ + h$\widetilde{ə}$/—yes

work out—be possible

you're dead—blocked, finished, you've failed

boys

o'clock, then . . .

CURTAIN

Glossary

boy—exclamation of excitement (for emphasis)

con artist—one who makes a living by lying, a notorious liar

cracking the books—student slang meaning *studying*

doc—familiar abbreviation for *doctor*

doll—a kind of slang term meaning an attractive or pretty girl

drop in—stop by, go to

elastic class rolls—no real limit to class size, willingly lets students enter

give it another try—try again

gold digger—a woman who pretends sincere affection in order to get a man's money

good-looking—pretty, attractive

h-m-m /hm/—sound made while considering or speculating

huh /h$\widetilde{ə}$/—expression of surprise

it sure does—it certainly does, it does (with emphasis)

keep up the payments—continue to pay for it in monthly installments

modesty—tendency to avoid reporting own achievements, here used ironically

orphan—a child whose parents are dead

pick up a date—get a date

probation—status of students having unsatisfactory grades

mixed	*girls*	*boys*

mixed	*boys*
hi/hay/—colloquial, familiar form of greeting, *hello* h-m-m/hm/—expression of reflection or speculation in a daze—preoccupied, inattentive, out of contact with reality incompletes—unfilled requirements for a course I thought I'd die—it was a great strain, very difficult juggle the whole works—rearrange everything kidding—fooling, trying to persuade by lying, making jokes, not serious lo—archaic poetic exclamation to attract attention, display emotion look—expression of emphasis (as a sentence opener usually) mob—large group mock—imitation muttering—speaking unclearly in a very low voice nothing like it—ironic comment: could mean uniquely bad as well as uniquely good now, let's see—expression indicating intention to examine something oh boy—expression of weariness and depression O.K.—satisfactory, all right old faker—derogatory expression implying that somebody is not sincere, not honest, not competent ph-t-t /fit/—sound of something going past very quickly or disappearing post—to put up a sign indicating or notifying practice teach—several months of actual classroom teaching for training while	really class—wealthy, cultured, sophisticated really murder—very difficult (slang) see you around—somewhat slangy colloquial form of *goodbye* stepparents—people who adopt or raise an orphan terrific—very good the bad news—the information that Sandra has lied to Charlie tied up—no time available um-hm /m + hm/—expression indicating understanding or confirmation of a suspicion

mixed (continued)	*mixed (continued)*
supervised by an experienced teacher pretty bright kid—fairly intelligent child prizes—sarcastic reference to their stupidity, lack of ability raise the tuition—obtain the money to pay his tuition rough—very difficult scribble—write very hurriedly and carelessly section—one version of a course squeeze one more—allow a student to enter the course although the maximum has been reached stick around—remain, stay, wait switch—change take—register for, as a student terrific—very good, typical exaggerated expression of a teen-ager that's out—that's impossible there you are—expression used when	handing something to someone or completing some service three courses to go—three courses yet to be taken tied up—no time available, very busy tough—difficult trudge—walk wearily tucked—held um-hm / m + hm/—yes um-m-m /əm/—expression of reflection or speculation unusual record—ironic comment (since *unusual* can mean unusually bad as well as unusually good) wow /wæuw/—exclamation of excitement (for emphasis) yea /yeə/—common colloquial form of *yes* you've done it—you've succeeded you've got all day—you have plenty of time

Structure

1. Again, we find examples of various truncated structures characteristic of colloquial usage.
   a. Lenny: "Say, ya seen the guy I was talking with before?" meaning *Have you seen . . . ?* Auxiliary and subject have been omitted, but the intonation rise makes the auxiliary unnecessary, since the irregular *seen* is clearly part of a perfect tense form. The subject *ya* is a colloquial distortion of *you.*
   b. Another truncated structure is that of John's "Rough, isn't it!" which might be seen as an abbreviated form of the standard tag/trailer question pattern *It is rough, isn't it?* or as a simple rhetorical question with the *rough* displaced to the position of sentence opener for greater emphasis to be gained from the onomatopoeic harsh /r/
   c. It should be noted that eh /e^{3}y/ serves as substitute for the second clause in tag/trailer questions
   d. " 'cause it's required" displays a common dropping of unstressed first syllable in *because.* Another common example of this usage is found in "g'bye" in which the ending of *good* is dropped, particularly in rapid speech.
   e. Clerk #2's "know him!" another truncated structure, syntactically may seem to be an abbreviated form of the question *Do I know him?* Yet, actually the intensification of stress coupled with the pitch rise on *know* reveals it as an exclamation rather than a question.
2. There is a considerable amount of sarcastic humor in the staging, much of it attained by unusual shifts in the intonation contour. For instance, Prof. Jones's exaggerated enthusiasm, projected by exploitation of a broader than usual spectrum of pitch change: "Go^{4}od ·mór^{2}ning, ^{3}ladies.^{2} ^{2}Another . . . ^{3}eh? Nothing like good old re^{2}gistra^{4}tion.
   The irony in this enthusiasm is heightened by the mock formality, particularly apparent in the male version as Prof. Jones says: "Good morning, *ladies and gentlemen.*" Note that Prof. Smith's querying reply: "^{2}Nothing like ^{3}what, ^{2}Bo^{3}b?" another example of displacement of usual order, is identifiable as a question largely by the pitch rise on the last word. Later, we find Prof. Smith announcing, "^{3}Lo, ^{2}our first customer appr^{3}oaches" which derives its sarcastic comedy as much from his mock exclamatory tone as from his use of the archaic word *Lo* and his quaint use of simple present tense instead of progressive. Humorous incongruity stems from exploitation of such obvious intonation ranges as in an otherwise flat line like "Understandable, ^{3}quite understandable." We again see the exaggerated intensity of pitch-stress combinations in Ruth's conversation with Prof. Smith—particularly as emphases for her intensifiers *such* and *so*—as contrasted with the flatness of her later comment about him to the two clerks. Note that Ruth's exaggerated intonation patterns exceed even those usually permitted women as contrasted with men. Similarly, Dr. Smith's amused skepticism about Joe's motives and intentions can be communicated by exaggerated intonation, as in "^{3}That's ^{2}odd^3, be^{2}cause it seems to ^{3}me I ^{2}dis^{3}tinctly ^{2}recall seeing ^{3}you driving a new Buick convertible downtown—as ^{3}recently, ^{2}in fact, as ^{2}last night, ^{3}Joe."
   Although the exaggerated range of intonation contour far exceeds the limits of the usual notation, indicating the gross sentence contour rather than the subtle pitch shifts within a word, such exaggeration does not represent mere theatricality, nor can it be seen as the mere phonetic eccentricity of an idiolect. Only a few of the most obvious of these intonation patterns have been suggested here; moreover, since few linguists have interested themselves in such aspects of communication, we have no really adequate notation for such features. Yet, this exaggeration is an intonational cliché as important for foreigners to learn as logical and idiomatic clichés are. The teacher will have to provide oral models for the intonation patterns to be mimicked.

3. Notice should be taken of the sarcasm in Prof. Smith's comment to Joe Blake: "doubtless to make up the six incompletes still on

your—er— unusual record." That Prof. Smith is pretending to believe Joe intends to do some studying, and that he realizes Joe wants him to believe this, is clear from the use of the word *doubtless*. A *two point two five,* only slightly above a passing level, represents a very mediocre performance.

The sarcasm in Linda/Lenny's "Yeah . . . fate!" is based on an attempt to deflate the romantic cliché of chance meeting, a typical feature of melodrama. When the clerk uses "beloved campus," she is similarly using an obvious cliché to get an effect of comic irony.

4. The teacher should point out that in the statement "only a brand new Buick convertible," the *only* signals an obvious understatement which becomes even more obvious when we come to *brand new Buick,* since possession of a new automobile of a moderately expensive kind is very desirable and not at all to be disparaged. Thus, Shirley/Charlie is making a kind of ironic reply, reflecting something similar to false modesty, which emphasizes the desirability of the situation.

5. Although the order of subject and verb are reversed in Frank's exclamation, "Boy, am I lucky" in what seems the usual cue for a question, actually the statement is somewhat like the rhetorical question because it requires no reply. It is merely an exclamation, the form of which may indicate that the speaker is half questioning the actuality of whatever has excited him.

The student will have to be shown that the exclamation is to be distinguished from John's use of "Oh boy," which is not enthusiastic but expresses a sudden realization of failure, defeat, or frustration. Unlike Frank's exclamation, which is probably characterized by increased pitch/stress intensities on *Boy,* John's expression has a falling intonation contour possibly reaching level one.

6. Note that in the expression "you just get a good schedule worked out and then they close a section," the present tense is used as in the statement of natural laws or consistent happenings. Here, in exaggeration, John comments on the consistency of the pattern of misfortune or disaster he and others have experienced.

7. When the clerk states "if you stick around . . . until next term!" the apparent hope which seems to be offered is destroyed by the last three words functioning as a kind of anticlimax.

8. "By the way" is a common colloquial expression which foreign students should learn. It precedes a question which is secondary and indicates a kind of afterthought.

9. In the expression "right on time," meaning *exactly on time,* we have an instance of redundancy very common, particularly in colloquial usage. The *right* may provide emphasis. *Go over to his house* and *come on along* similarly display redundancy in the inclusion of the essentially meaningless *over* and *on.*

10. Clerk #1's "No-o-o" is drawn out to indicate a kind of tentative or provisional negation, probably spoken in a preoccupied way while still thinking about the problem, rather than at the conclusion of thought. On the other hand, when Joan says "So-o-o . . . I guess" she draws out or stretches the vowel to express a kind of reluctance to change.

Cultural Values

1. The rehearsal of this staging can provide a fine opportunity for discussion of the characteristics of American university life. University students or young people generally may find this quite interesting, particularly if it is presented as a series of contrasts with the university life they may be familiar with. But even older students may find this interesting if some attempt is made to point out that the structure and operation of the university reflects certain broader social values which must be understood by those learning to communicate in the language. Most foreign students, for instance, will be immediately impressed by the fact that in the United States generally it is relatively easy to gain acceptance as a student at a university but relatively difficult to remain a student. That is, although equality of opportunity is fairly unlimited, in contrast to the situation in many other countries, the necessity of proving one's ability is a

continuing one. Students may be surprised to find that here regular attendance is necessary, as is daily study rather than semi-annual cramming. There may be many sections offered for a course. Class size or enrollment for each section is limited and when the limit is reached the section is closed. But quite often student demand for a course will result in creation of new sections of that course, just as the number of students desiring to enter the university will lead to expanding the enrollment. In other words, unlike the situation in many other countries, in American schools there is not a fixed number of places for which students compete; instead, the number of places varies according to student need and demand. In general, the student must recognize that his understanding of American education as a part of American life will require a major reorientation of values.

Some students will find even the alphabetical registration according to family name quite surprising and will, therefore, be puzzled by Ruth's/Ray's wish her/his name began with a *B* or *C* (as in *B*aker or *C*onners), instead of a *W* as in *W*alters, since they may not understand that students registering earlier will have a better choice of courses. In fact, the presentation of the same course in different sections given at different times will be totally unfamiliar, particularly to those who, having no experience with student employment, have no idea how important differences in time can be for working students.

Similarly, many students will not understand the several functions of the faculty advisor to see that students meet basic course requirements for graduation, that they are not taking more courses than they can successfully manage, and that they are aware of course offerings which may be both of individual interest and significant in terms of individual student goals and future plans. The mechanics of the registration process will dazzle some foreign students used to a less mechanical, bureaucratic procedure while it will baffle others. And even standard abbreviations for subject areas (i.e., Econ/iˈykan/; Soc. /sows/; Poli Sci /paliy + saiy/; Psych /sayk/) will puzzle most foreign students.

2. Students will have to learn something about social relations between teacher and student as well as between students. They will probably find that the role and status of the teacher, as reflected by the two professors in our staging, are quite unfamiliar. The lack of austerity and the casual behavior of teachers may seem "undignified" to many foreign students who will find it peculiar that teachers do not form a separate, distinguishable class in society but are quite accessible, demanding little or no deference. Perhaps they may recognize that the prevalent sarcasm, found even in the banter between the two professors, functions as a kind of social leveler, as they discover that the teacher is a kind of advisor/guide rather than a master or leader. The teacher here is easily approached in that he is approached only when a student has a problem within the teacher's professional competence; yet teachers are fairly objective and reluctant to become involved in a student's personal affairs. Many foreign students may find even the concept of "personal affairs" quite incomprehensible, since in their society a teacher may be looked upon as a kind of wise man who may either be consulted on all sorts of matters or whose opinions have the force of commands.

Nevertheless, the foreigner will also need to recognize that there are definite limits to informality in the relationship between faculty and students. Ray's use of "doc," for instance, in addressing Dr. Smith may be considered in bad taste, if not disrespectful, because it is too familiar, particularly if used by a student not very well acquainted with the professor.

Incidentally, it might be noted that most American professors prefer to be addressed as Mister—rather than Professor—or Doctor, although most foreign students who come from strongly status-conscious societies may find this odd.

3. The status and self-image of the American teacher as a kind of specialist or technician reflect social values to be found underlying the American notion of education itself, many aspects of which are revealed in attitudes of characters in the staging. That generally teachers in America are not content with mere time-serving is clear from the professor's wry comment, "Nothing like

good old registration," which is an ironic expression of his sense of boredom at the prospect of a dull routine day. The dullness of this prospect is emphasized, incidentally, by the irony in the use of an obvious cliché pose of enthusiasm, "No sir . . . nothing like it." There is also, of course, a kind of bravado in this prevalence of joking banter and the foreign student should be given some idea of the basis of the need for it as well as the meaning of the expressions used to express it.

4. Active student participation in class will be quite unfamiliar to some foreign students who have experienced only the large lecture system; they will be quite startled to learn that not only must they attend classes regularly but that lecture courses usually have discussion and quiz sections. Parenthetically, it might be noted that the lack of fluency of some of those foreign students who have studied English many years may be traceable to this lack of active participation in their native school system.

   For many, the necessity of earning a grade by persistent and sustained effort and display of ability will seem fantastic, and they will be quite surprised to find that there is no special social status separating students from the general population, since virtually anyone who can demonstrate his ability can be a student, while those demonstrating a lack of ability can expect to "flunk out." The possibility of failure and the consequent exclusion from the university of a student will be beyond the wildest imagination of many foreign students familiar only with the ideas of university entrance tightly limited by a single examination, and the inevitable graduation for the elite who gain admission. They will be unprepared, therefore, for the American student's constant concern with grades, credits and his Grade Point Average. Some may find the underlying equalitarianism objectionable, resenting even the alphabetical designation, as earlier noted. Others will see a contradiction in the need to meet specific course requirements while enjoying the privilege of free election; they will have to learn that the system is contrived to prevent the excessive skewing, which would obviate breadth of education, while fostering the exploration and development of individual ability.

5. For many, the provision for manifestation of individualism will seem ridiculous, since the special student social status to be found in many societies is, in a sense, recognition of a kind of sub-adult standing. The individual responsibility accorded students here will not be readily understood by many foreign students as linked to what will seem great freedom of choice. The fact that large numbers of students work at least part-time, demonstrated by the students in this staging, and that many students support themselves and even their families by working at full time jobs is understandably difficult to grasp for foreigners who think in terms of a special student status. They will also find the strong desire for independent self-reliance which drives many students to reject parental financial aid very hard to understand and they may be amazed that students readily engage in hard manual labor without stigma. Similarly they will find it peculiar that students should be involved with dating and with concern for boy/girl relations in this staging, since for many foreign students university life is set sharply apart, almost an isolated stage, of one's life rather than merely a part of the life of anyone motivated enough to want it and capable of profiting from the experience.

   This is not to say that there is no distinct student culture in America, but it is to say that the student culture is likely to find its manifestation in social activities—dances, football games, the existence of distinctly student "hang outs," such as the Cave in this staging, rather than in intellectual activities. It is also likely to find expression in student language—as part of the cult of youth—featuring exaggerated dictional choice, such as "terrific," "beautiful," and "great." Although student evaluation of teachers is probably universal, the openness of statement may surprise foreign students who would not think of speaking other than respectfully of a teacher and who might, therefore, be surprised by Frank's "he's terrible" or Fran's "she's such an awful teacher."

   But these are only a few points which the alert teacher may

extract from this staging to enlighten foreign students about important underlying cultural values. More important than the presentation of long explanatory lectures, which challenge only the student's powers of aural comprehension, is the possibility that staging communication offers the student an opportunity to be an active participant immersed in the situation and, through total mimicry of his teacher, to acquire those behavior patterns necessary for appropriate communication. Most important, that process of meticulous observation necessary for total mimicry may become a learning habit, thereby providing the means to expand the power of communication.

General Comment

1. This staging consists of a series of exchanges but without an explicit active ending which "Flight 641" or "Quiet Please!" or "The Employment Agency" provides. This play does not build up to an obvious climax, but students should recognize that often—as in real life situations—we are instead confronted by bits of contradictory evidence which accumulate to arouse doubt and may raise questions about what has seemed clear. We may begin to suspect that the real importance of situation does not lie in surface event and action but underneath the surface. The situation at the opening of this staging seems quite routine, even as we discover the complications which frustrate registration, the ways students meet that frustration and, more specifically, the various demands on their time. Against this background, we gradually realize that not only are students and faculty mutually masked but students are masked from each other. Thus, the pacing is fairly slow until Joesph arrives and Linda overhears his conversation; from that point the pace speeds up and the staging ends.

2. There is much frustration in the situation shown and there is also much which is comic. Some of the humor is a product of the incongruity existing in the inevitable opposition between the seeming freedoms of choice when it is not clear that real choices exist: the students are free to choose courses—within the limits of certain sequence requirements—but the available sections of courses are not convenient in terms of other obligations. For many foreign students, since the entire university atmosphere may seem fraught with ominousness and solemnity, any hint of levity may seem bizarre. Thus, only by mimicking can they hope eventually to acquire suitable behavior patterns.

3. Some of the humor, moreover, has its source in the fact that what is a new if frustrating experience for students is a repetition of situations year after year as students come and go. The teachers are rarely convinced of their own seeming importance, and are quite well aware that few students can understand the teachers' goals or purposes, let alone approve or enjoy them—despite the occasional student pretense to the contrary. Despite the relative lack of formality in student-teacher relationships in America, students are virtually unaware of the prevalance of humor in relations between teachers.

4. Although the required coordination of simultaneous physical movement and speech—in the sense of having characters speak while moving across the stage—is not excessive, dialogue must be reinforced by suitable postures and facies. The professors' distraction or preoccupation, signaled by their "Um-m-m" and "Maybe so" and "Um-hm," must be conveyed by adequate combinations of physical appearance and speech. Similarly, the sarcastic quality of Prof. Jones's mock gaiety upon entering the room is communicated as much by his brisk walk and casual tossing of his briefcase as by the exaggerated intonational structure of his dialogue.

5. However, the main source of humor lies in our realization that a great deal of pretense separates faculty and students. Although both are caught up in a bureasucratic system, they have quite different goals and values. We find from their comments—and particularly from their comments about each other—that they live in two quite distinct and separate worlds which, in effect, mirror the generational conflict that we have seen characterizes relations between adults and children generally, such as when the

student refers to a professor from whom the student imagines he/she has just charmed or flattered a favor, as "the old faker." Another similar instance lies in Joseph's comic attempt to convince Prof. Smith of his change of heart, of his newly acquired sincerity of purpose, when the professor obviously is skeptical if not completely unbelieving. Of course, Joseph's attempt is rendered more humorous since the audience is aware that although Joseph imagines he is wise enough to fool others, he has been fooled himself by his fiancée who pretends to visit a sick sister, but is actually going dancing with other men. But to catch this the foreign student will need to acquire some knowledge of the comic possibilities of equality between the sexes, the dating experimentation process, the nature of other aspects of the battle of the sexes in this country; otherwise, he is very likely to conclude with great solemnity that the girl is unworthy of his observation.

Comically, each side in the generational conflict imagines it can truly evaluate the behavior of the other. Although the students do not really know the faculty members, they tend to consider the faculty as a part of the oppressive world of adult power. On the other hand, although the faculty members have, of course, once been young and led the life of students, they do not really know the values and attitudes of the young people as well as they imagine—for time and age have mercifully allowed them to forget what once seemed so desperately important.

Notes on Adaptation

1. Since most foreign students are probably more familiar with schools attended by students of one sex rather than with coeducational systems, adapting this play for a cast of one sex should pose no problem. And even the possibility of women professors, as in the adaptation for a cast of girls, should not seem peculiar except perhaps to a few students coming from cultures in which this would be virtually impossible. Thus, the most difficult problem in adaptation has been that posed by

teenage romantic relations. And a solution has been found in shifting active relationships between characters on stage to allusions to figures never seen. That is, in the girls' version Linda overhears Janet talking about Joseph, whom we never see; and in the boys' version Lenny overhears Joseph talking about Sandra who never appears on stage.

2. Yet, the changing of roles is not accomplished by merely changing the names of characters, for relative status is revealed through the dialogue and other behavior patterns. The adaptation for a female cast, therefore, opens with a typically feminine concern for dust which may soil her clothes. We would much more rarely find such a concern displayed in man's behavior. We also find, once again, the extensive use of intensifiers—particularly the use of *such* and *so*—characterizing the woman's expression of a broader emotional spectrum than society allows the man. Joan says, "That makes me *so* mad; Ruth says, "it's *such* a good course"; and Shirley says, "I've got *such* a lot to tell you." Other typically feminine structures would be Fran's "I think I need three more courses, don't I ?" and Prof. Jones's "I thought you told me you were taking German, didn't you?" or Linda's "That does work, doesn't it?"—all expressing feminine indirection by the tag/trailer question.

In comparing the adaptations of the play we discover that the dialogue used by a girl student in addressing a woman professor is likely to be quite different from that she might use in addressing a man professor: Ruth is not nearly so flip and seemingly offhand with Mrs. Smith as she is with Mr. Smith. We find similarly that the tone of banter between the two women professors is quite different from that between the men professors: the "kidding" is not so free and they seem to feel the need to make clear to each other that no criticism is really intended. Prof. Jones kids Mrs. Smith about being too softhearted in yielding to the student's wishes, and then half facetiously moderates her statements by suggesting that actually Prof. Smith has given the student something the student needed. We note too, that although the male Prof. Jones sustained and augmented his cliché pose of enthusiasm for registration by the mock formal "ladies and gentlemen," Mrs. Jones greets those present with the homelier term, "girls."

In general, then, although the adaptation for an all girl cast is relatively simple, the dialogue must reflect the less open, somewhat guarded strong concern for psychological subtlety and nuance that we have seen as more characteristic of woman's less aggressive, unassertive, and even indecisive behavior pattern.

3. We have suggested that men tend to be somewhat freer in their expression although they may express a more limited range of emotional attitudes than women. Turning to the version for a cast of men, we find these tendencies reflected in the somewhat more extensive use of slang and other less regular, more idiomatic structures. We also find a teasing and sarcastic note in the dialogue exchanges between the two male professors. Perhaps the freedom of expression reflects a greater group comraderie among men—evidenced particularly by Ray's somewhat impudent use of "doc" in addressing Prof. Smith—as well as a lack of that personal competitiveness which many Americans see as springing from a kind of sense of mutual threat felt toward each other by girls and women.

It might be noted that the social values encourage women to develop greater sensitivity to slight changes within a social situation. In the adaptation for a cast of men, Charlie and Lenny discuss Sandra in comparatively unemotional terms. That is, Charlie is seemingly less caught up in romantic fantasy than is Shirley, in the version for women, and more impressed with his good fortune as well as with Sandra's wealth and beauty. Although the contrast between a woman's view of romance as a possible means to developing a new identity and, the man's view of romance as merely a phase in the enhancement of an identity, will be readily familiar to most students as a characteristic that distinguishs women from men, some students may have difficulty recognizing that in American society women are often expected to be romantic dreamers, more emotional, and less practical. For some students, such are the very characteristics attributed to men in their society. Students may find this mythology particularly difficult to accept as they encounter insistence on equality between the sexes; in fact, for some the roles of men and women as they have known them may seem reversed in America.

4. Another instance of the exaggeration or emphasis attained by shifting from question to a kind of rhetorical question form: Shirley states "and was he cute." Since the rhetorical question is characterized by the fact that its answer is obvious, this usage seems to imply the ultimate or maximum emphasis. Again, it might be pointed out that the word *cute* is applied by both boys and girls to girls, and by girls to boys, but it is never applied by boys to boys.

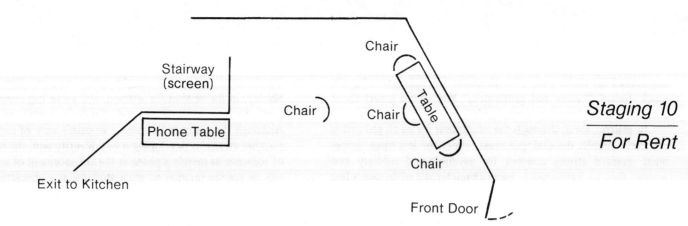

SETTING

The living room of a middle class home, late afternoon or early evening in fall. A telephone table with a phone on it stands stage right just in front of a large screen, which is supposed to be the stairwell for stairs leading to the second floor. A large lounge chair stands at midstage. Doorway to kitchen is at stage right downstage. The front door leading outside is far stage left downstage. As the curtain rises Mr. Martin sits in the large chair midstage reading a newspaper. Aunt Martha is speaking on the telephone, stage right. Grandpa is slowly and thoughtfully setting the table, stage left.

Mixed cast

Aunt Martha (Mrs. Martin's sister)
Mrs. Martin
Mr. Martin (George)
Miss Townsend ⎱ (potential tenants)
Miss Randall ⎰
Grandpa
Georgie (Mr. Martin's son, about 15)
Detective
Uncle Stan (Aunt Martha's husband)
Mrs. Ferguson ⎱ (next door neighbors)
Mr. Ferguson ⎰

Girls' cast

Aunt Martha (Mrs. Martin's sister)
Mrs. Martin
Mabel (older daughter)
Miss Townsend ⎱ (potential tenants)
Miss Randall ⎰
Grandma
Jeanie (younger daughter)
Mrs. Robinson (neighborhood association representative)
Aunt Sarah (Mrs. Martin's sister)
Mrs. Ferguson ⎱ (neighbors)
Mrs. Clark ⎰

Boys' cast

Ray, an older son
Mr. Martin (George)
Uncle Bob
Mr. Townsend ⎱ potential tenants
Mr. Randall ⎰
Grandpa
Georgie
Detective
Uncle Stan
Mr. Clark ⎱ neighbors
Mr. Ferguson ⎰

mixed	*girls*	*boys*

mixed

Aunt Martha.   Yes, it's on the second floor and it's *so* nicely decorated. In fact, we just . . .

Doorbell rings interrupting her and she glances at Mr. Martin who remains oblivious as he continues reading.

Aunt Martha   *(continuing her conversation).* . . . It's just been painted . . . a gorgeous blue. *(Disappointed)* Oh— you don't like blue . . .

Doorbell rings again. Aunt Martha motions impatiently to rouse Mr. Martin but, still oblivious, he reads on. Doorbell continues ringing as Aunt Martha snaps her fingers and tries in every way to attract Mr. Martin's attention as she continues the telephone conversation with, "uh-huh" . . . "yes" . . . "of course" . . . "that's right." Mrs. Martin, dressed in an apron, enters from the kitchen stage right, stirring something in a saucepan.

Aunt Martha   *(shouting).* George!

Mr. Martin   *(looking at her over the top of his lowered newspaper).* Did you call me, dear?

Mrs. Martin motions towards the door just as the bell rings again. She watches as he gets up, goes stage left to open the door. As he beckons the two girls to enter, Mrs. Martin exits hurriedly stage right. Miss Townsend and Miss Randall enter, looking around apprehensively and appraisingly.

Aunt Martha   *(back on the phone and suddenly embarrassed as she realizes she hasn't covered the phone receiver).* No, no—everything's all right here. *(Laughing nervously)* . . . Oh no—it

girls

Aunt Martha.   Yes, it's on the second floor and it's *so* nicely decorated. In fact, we just . . .

Doorbell rings interrupting her and she glances at Mabel who remains oblivious as she continues reading.

Aunt Martha   *(continuing her conversation).* . . . It's just been painted . . . a gorgeous blue. *(Disappointed)* Oh — you don't like blue . . .

Doorbell rings again. Aunt Martha motions impatiently to rouse Mabel but, still oblivious, she reads on. Doorbell continues ringing as Aunt Martha snaps her fingers and tries in every way to attract Mabel's attention as she continues the telephone conversation with, "uh-huh" . . . "yes" . . . "of course" . . . "that's right." Mrs. Martin, dressed in an apron, enters from the kitchen stage right, stirring something in a saucepan.

Mrs. Martin   *(shouting).* Mabel!

Mabel.   Yes, Mom . . . did you want something?

Mrs. Martin motions toward the door just as the bell rings again. She watches as Mabel gets up, goes stage left to open the door. As she beckons the two girls to enter, Mrs. Martin exits hurriedly stage right. Miss Townsend and Miss Randall enter, looking around apprehensively and appraisingly.

Aunt Martha   *(back on the phone and suddenly embarrassed as she realizes she hasn't covered the phone receiver).* No, no — everything's all right here . . . Oh no—it really is a very quiet place.

boys

Ray.   Yeah, it's on the second floor and was just painted . . . *(Louder)* I say we just painted it . . .

Doorbell rings interrupting him and Ray glances at Mr. Martin who remains oblivious as he continues reading.

Ray.   Kind of a bright blue . . . sea blue, they call it . . . *(Disappointed)* You don't like blue . . .

Doorbell rings again. Ray motions impatiently to rouse Mr. Martin who, still oblivious, reads on. Doorbell continues ringing as Ray snaps his fingers and tries in every way to attract Mr. Martin's attention as he continues the telephone conversation with, "uh-huh" . . . "yes" . . . "of course" . . . "that's right" Uncle Bob, dressed in an apron, enters from the kitchen stage right, stirring something in a saucepan.

Uncle Bob   *(shouting).* George, can't you get that?

Mr. Martin.   What's that, Bob . . . you call me?

Uncle Bob motions toward the door just as the bell rings again. He watches as Mr. Martin gets up, goes stage left to open the door. As he beckons the two men to enter, Uncle Bob exits hurriedly stage right. Mr. Townsend and Mr. Randall enter, looking around apprehensively and appraisingly.

Ray   *(chuckling).* Naw—everything's O.K. here . . . a nice quiet place.

Mr. Townsend.   Say, we saw your ad and would like to find out about that basement apartment.

Mr. Martin.   Uh-huh . . . well *(smiling)*

mixed

really is a very quiet place.

Miss Townsend   *(to Mr. Martin, holding her purse with both hands before her).* We saw your ad and would like to know about the room.

Mr. Martin   *(obviously fascinated by the chance to chat with two attractive young women, stands up very straight to hide his paunch, and smiles in an artificially friendly way).* Yes, yes, of course!

Aunt Martha   *(continuing her phone conversation with exaggerated sweetness while glaring at Mr. Martin).* Oh yes . . . there's lots of space.

Mr. Martin   *(to the girls).* Well, it's not very big . . . kind of cosy, y'know. And it's just been painted. Did it myself. Has a double bed. *(Chuckling)* I've always liked a double bed myself . . .

Miss Randall   *(nervously).* The rent . . . how much is the rent?

Grandpa   *(interrupting).* And it's pretty close to the john too . . . I mean the bathroom. We all share the bath . . . not at the same time, of course. *(Laughs heartily as he continues to set the table)*

Aunt Martha   *(into the phone).* Yes, it's practically a private bath . . . well . . . you'd have it to yourself . . . almost.

Miss Townsend   *(somewhat icily).* But we'd like to know the rent.

Mr. Martin   *(again ignoring the question).* It's a nice quiet place too.

girls

Miss Townsend   *(to Mabel, holding her purse with both hands before her).* We saw your ad and would like to know about the room.

Mabel   *(smiling at the two girls).* Oh yes . . . won't you come in. *(Stepping behind them to close the door and glancing appraisingly at their clothing as she does so)* I'll be glad to talk to you about it.

Aunt Martha   *(continuing her phone conversation with exaggerated sweetness while glaring at Mabel).* Oh yes . . . there's lots of space.

Mabel   *(to the girls).* Well, it's kind of small . . . and has a double bed . . . *(quickly)* but it really would be big enough for two, I guess—if you don't mind that. And it's very clean . . . my father just finished painting it, in fact.

Miss Randall   *(nervously).* The rent . . . how much is the rent?

Grandma   *(interrupting).* And it's pretty close to the john too . . . I mean the bathroom. We all share the bath . . . not at the same time, of course. *(Laughs heartily as she continues to set the table)*

Aunt Martha   *(into the phone).* Yes, it's practically a private bath . . . well . . . you'd have it to yourself . . . almost.

Miss Townsend   *(somewhat icily).* But we'd like to know the rent.

Mabel.   It's such a quiet place too.

A terrific blast of sound comes from behind

boys

we'll be glad to tell you fellows about it . . . and even give you a l at the place.

Ray   *(continuing the phone con sation).* Yeah, it's pretty big. Runs whole length of the basement, in f

Mr. Martin   *(to the two boys).* T fellows from the college lived in it year—although there's really only big rooms. I finished painting it week . . . so you can move right in.

Mr. Randall   *(nervously).* The rent how much is the rent?

Grandpa   *(interrupting).* Got its john even . . . though the tub's upst and we all share it. Heavy traffic tight schedules sometimes *(chuckl* but we managed pretty well last y

Ray   *(into the phone).* Well, the bat on the second floor—but you'd hav to yourself . . . almost.

Mr. Townsend   *(somewhat icily).* we'd like to know the rent.

Mr. Martin   *(again ignoring the que tion).* It's a nice quiet place too.

A terrific blast of sound comes from beh the screen stage right, startling everybody very noisy jazz recording is being played full volume. The two potential tenants are startled they both step back and, turn toward the stairwell, stare toward the cei since the sound is supposed to be com from upstairs. Ray winces and placing hand over the phone turns toward the st well.

Uncle Bob   *(carrying a saucepan, ent*

mixed

A terrific blast of sound comes from behind the screen stage right, startling everybody. A very noisy jazz recording is being played at full volume. The two potential tenants are so startled they both step back and, turning toward the stairwell, stare toward the ceiling since the sound is supposed to be coming from upstairs. Aunt Martha winces and placing her hand over the phone turns toward the stairwell.

Mrs. Martin   *(carrying a saucepan, enters hurriedly from the kitchen stage right and shouts but is hardly audible against the noise coming from up- stairs).* Georgie!

Mr. Martin, raising one hand apologetically, gives an embarrassed smile and, turning, runs across the stage, disappearing behind the screen stage right up stage. Sound of foot- steps running upstairs, a loud shout, and the loud music stops very abruptly. A moment of silence.

Aunt Martha   *(lifting the phone receiver to her ear).* Hello! . . . hello! *(Shrugs, looks at the receiver, and places the receiver on the hook. With a tense and artificial smile, turns to the two girls who, having moved toward the door stage left, stand looking at each other as if undecided whether to leave)*

Mrs. Martin   *(putting the saucepan down on the telephone table, wipes her hands on her apron and crosses to the two girls).* Oh, please don't rush off. *(Grabbing one arm of each girl and, walking between them, leads*

girls

the screen stage right, startling everybody. A very noisy jazz recording is being played at full volume. The two potential tenants are so startled they both step back and, turning toward the stairwell, stare toward the ceiling since the sound is supposed to be coming from upstairs. Aunt Martha winces and plac- ing her hand over the phone turns toward the stairwell.

Mrs. Martin   *(carrying a saucepan, enters hurriedly from the kitchen stage right and shouts but is hardly audible against the noise coming from upstairs).* Jeanie!

Mabel, winces painfully holding her hands over her ears, then with an embarrassed smile shakes her head and runs across the stage, disappearing behind the screen stage right up stage. Sound of footsteps running upstairs, a loud cry, and the blasting music stops very abruptly. A moment of silence.

Aunt Martha   *(lifting the phone receiver to her ear).* Hello! . . . hello! *(Shrugs, looks at the receiver, and places the receiver on the hook. With a tense and artificial smile, turns to the two girls who, having moved toward the door stage left, stand looking at each other as if undecided whether to leave)*

Mrs. Martin   *(putting the saucepan down on the telephone table, wipes her hands on her apron and crosses to the two girls).* Oh, please don't rush off. *(Grabbing one arm of each girl and, walking between them, leads them across the stage toward the stair-*

boys

hurriedly from the kitchen stage right and shouts but is hardly audible against the noise coming from up- stairs). Georgie!

Mr. Martin, raising one hand apologetically, gives an embarrassed smile and, turning, runs across the stage, disappearing behind the screen stage right up stage. Sound of foot- steps running upstairs, a loud shout, and the loud music stops very abruptly. A moment of silence.

Ray   *(lifting the phone receiver to his ear).* Hello! . . . hello! *(Shrugs, looks at the receiver, and places the receiver on the hook. With a tense and artificial smile, turns to the two boys who, having moved toward the door stage left, stand looking at each other as if undecided whether to leave)*

Uncle Bob   *(putting the saucepan down on the telephone table, wipes his hands on his apron and crosses to the two prospective tenants).* Well, fellas, you don't want to rush off until you get a look at that apartment, huh? *(Walks in back of them to get between them, slapping both on the back, then motioning them to follow him, he crosses the stage toward the stairwell. Ray picks up the saucepan and exits to the kitch- en stage right. Sound of footsteps coming downstairs. Georgie enters ap- parently propelled by a shove from Mr. Martin who, frowning, enters be- hind him)*

mixed

them across the stage toward the stairwell. Aunt Martha picks up the saucepan and exits to the kitchen stage right. Sound of footsteps coming downstairs. Georgie enters apparently propelled by a shove from Mr. Martin who, frowning, enters behind Georgie)

Georgie   *(confronting the two girls, whistles appreciatively).* Say, I just got here in time! *(Running his hand through his hair and adjusting his tie)* I didn't realize we had company. *(Pause)* It's a swell room—I know you'll like it. And it sure will be great to have you around here to liven up this place. My name is Georgie, by the way, and . . .

Mrs. Martin   *(pushing the beaming Georgie aside, leads the two girls behind the stairwell screen).* Just wait 'til you see it; it's such a lovely room! I'm sure it's just what you girls want. *(Sound of footsteps going upstairs)*

Mr. Martin   *(angrily hissing at Georgie).* Just when we finally have a couple of prospective tenants you start that damned racket up there. *(Raises a hand as if to strike Georgie who ducks away)*

Grandpa   *(who has been standing before the table, stage left, listening to the discussion).* Don't be too hard on the boy, George—you were the same at his age . . . *(chuckling)* and maybe even worse.

Georgie   *(crosses the stage and slumps in*

girls

well. Aunt Martha picks up the saucepan and exits to the kitchen stage right. Sound of footsteps coming downstairs. Jeanie enters apparently propelled by a shove from Mabel who, frowning, enters behind Jeanie)

Jeanie   *(confronting the two girls).* Oh hi! I'm Jeanie. I suppose you came to look at the room, huh? Well, it's not bad really, since my dad painted it. *(To Miss Townsend)* Gee, that's a nice dress; it's just right for you . . . not too loud.

Mrs. Martin   *(pushing the beaming Jeanie aside, leads the two girls behind the stairwell screen).* Just wait till you see it; it's such a lovely room! I'm sure it's just what you girls want. *(Sound of footsteps going upstairs)*

Mabel   *(angrily hissing at Jeanie).* Oh, I could just murder you! We finally have a couple of prospective roomers and you make such a racket up there that we can't even talk to them. You really are a pain, isn't she, Grandma?

Grandma   *(drily).* Um-hm . . . but I remember it wasn't too long ago that somebody else was just as silly—maybe worse even. *(Looks pointedly at Mabel and Jeanie. Jeanie crosses the stage toward Grandma, who has been standing near the table, turns and sticks her tongue out at Mabel*

Jeanie   *(slumping into the big chair at midstage).* Gee, this place is so dull and some of the people here are just

boys

Georgie   *(confronting the two prospective tenants).* You guys are here to look at the apartment, I'll bet—and I guess that puts an end to the ping pong games down there for awhile—unless *(hopefully)* either of you like ping pong. My name is Georgie, by the way, and . . .

Uncle Bob   *(pushing Georgie aside, leads the two prospective tenants behind the stairwell screen).* It's just what you fellas have been looking for. Come along and look it over. *(Sound of footsteps going downstairs)*

Mr. Martin   *(angrily hissing at Georgie).* Just when we finally have a couple of prospective tenants you start that damned racket up there. *(Raises a hand as if to strike Georgie who ducks away)*

Grandpa   *(who has been standing before the table, stage left, listening to the discussion).* Don't be too hard on the boy, George—you were the same at his age . . . *(chuckling)* and maybe even worse.

Georgie   *(crosses the stage and slumps in the large chair midstage, speaking sullenly).* Aw gee, Pop, this place is like a morgue and I just wanted to liven things up a little. Besides, Uncle Stan told me I could play his records whenever I wanted to.

Doorbell rings and Grandpa goes to open the door stage left.

Detective   *(entering but standing just in-*

mixed

the large chair midstage, *speaking sullenly). Aw gee, Pop, this place is like a morgue and I just wanted to liven things up a little. Besides, Uncle Stan told me I could play his records whenever I wanted to.*

Doorbell rings and Grandpa goes to open the door stage left.

Detective   *(entering but standing just inside the door).* Detective Arnold, 24th Precinct. *(Holds out his opened wallet to Grandpa, then slips it back into his coat pocket as Grandpa beckons him in and closes the door)* We've had several complaints from your neighbors about the noise here.

Mr. Martin   *(embarrassed and frowning slightly).* Oh . . . well . . . I'm awfully sorry. Once in awhile the kid *(motioning toward Georgie)* acts up a little. *(Smiling)* We keep after him to be quiet . . . but *(smiling)* you know how kids are.

Georgie   *(grumbling).* Aw gee, how can a little noise now and then bother anybody . . . what a bunch of old crabs.

Detective   *(frowning).* It seems to happen pretty often. A violation of the public nuisance ordinance, y'know *(reaches into the inside breast pocket of his jacket)* and so I guess I've got to give you a ticket. *(Pulls out a pad and begins writing on it)*

Georgie.   Gee and I always thought cops were supposed to hunt for crooks and

girls

dead. And *(sarcastically)* just for your information *(turning toward Mabel)* Aunt Sarah told me I can play her records whenever I want to. So there! *(Makes a face at Mabel)*

Doorbell rings and Grandma goes to open the door stage left.

Mrs. Robinson   *(entering but standing just inside the door).* I'm Mrs. Robinson *(smiling automatically and nervously)* Er--at the last meeting of the neighborhood association there were several complaints about noise and I was asked to talk with you about . . .

Mabel   *(embarrassed).* Oh, well, it does get a little noisy here sometimes, I guess *(glancing at Jeanie)*, particularly on weekends and during school vacations . . .

Jeanie   *(sarcastically).* So some of the neighborhood fuddy duddies really don't sleep 24 hours a day then, it seems . . . *(shaking her head)* such cranks.

Mrs. Robinson   *(mildly surprised and annoyed).* Well, apparently it's pretty noisy here most of the time and this *is* a residential area, you know. *(Begins writing on a sheet of paper attached to a clipboard)*

Jeanie.   The last meeting of the neighborhood association was so noisy that we couldn't get to sleep until one. *(Snorting with indignation)* And they have the nerve to complain about a

boys

side the door).* Detective Arnold, 24th Precinct. *(Holds out his opened wallet to Grandpa, then slips it back into his coat pocket as Grandpa beckons him in and closes the door)* We've had several complaints from your neighbors about the noise here.

Mr. Martin   *(embarrassed and frowning slightly).* Oh . . . well . . . I'm awfully sorry. Once in awhile the kid *(motioning toward Georgie)* acts up a little. *(Smiling)* We keep after him to be quiet . . . but *(smiling)* you know how kids are.

Georgie   *(grumbling).* Aw gee, how can a little noise now and then bother anybody . . . what a bunch of old crabs.

Detective   *(frowning).* It seems to happen pretty often. A violation of the public nuisance ordinance, y'know *(reaches into the inside breast pocket of his jacket)* and so I guess I've got to give you a ticket. *(Pulls out a pad and begins writing on it)*

Georgie.   Gee and I always thought cops were supposed to hunt for crooks and try to stop crime, like on TV, I sure didn't think they had time to look after every old crank's complaint about a little noise.

Detective looks up, annoyed, and, glancing at Mr. Martin, scowls.

Grandpa   *(attempting to sound stern).* Georgie, we've heard enough from you. I think you'd better go over to

mixed

try to stop crime, like on TV. I sure didn't think they had time to look after every old crank's complaint about a little noise.

Detective looks up, annoyed, and, glancing at Mr. Martin, scowls.

Grandpa   *(attempting to sound stern).* Georgie, we've heard enough from you. I think you'd better go over to Tommy's house until around supper time.

Georgie   *(lurches to his feet, sighing audibly, and, hands jammed into pants pockets, marches past the detective, Mr. Martin, and Grandpa).* O.K., Grandpa. See you later. *(Exits out front door stage left)*

Sound of footsteps coming downstairs and the two girls emerge smiling from behind the stairwell screen, followed by Mrs. Martin. The three men watch as the girls seem entirely unaware of their presence.

Miss Randall   *(to Mrs. Martin).* It's such an awfully nice room.

Miss Townsend   *(nodding in agreement).* Yes, it's really so nice . . . much nicer than I expected . . . and I think we should take it, don't you?

Miss Randall   *(turning to Miss Townsend).* Yes, we've looked at so many places . . . and I don't think we can find anything better . . . or as conveniently located.

Miss Townsend   *(enthusiastically).* It *is* close to the school. *(To Mrs. Martin)* This is our first year of teaching.

girls

little noise here!

Mrs. Robinson looks up, annoyed, and, glancing at Mabel, scowls.

Grandma   *(attempting to sound stern).* Jeanie, we've heard enough from you. I think you'd better go over to Mary's house until around supper time.

Jeanie   *(lurches to her feet, sighing audibly).* O.K., Grandma. *(Almost running past Mrs. Robinson, Mabel, and Grandma)* See you later. *(Exits out front door stage left)*

Sound of footsteps coming downstairs and the two girls emerge smiling from behind the stairwell screen followed by Mrs. Martin. The three women watch as the girls seem entirely unaware of their presence.

Miss Randall   *(to Mrs. Martin).* It's such an awfully nice room.

Miss Townsend   *(nodding in agreement).* Yes, it's really so nice . . . much nicer that I expected . . . and I think we should take it, don't you?

Miss Randall   *(turning to Miss Townsend).* Yes, we've looked at so many places . . . and I don't think we can find anything better . . . or as conveniently located.

Miss Townsend   *(enthusiastically).* It *is* close to the school. *(To Mrs. Martin)* This is our first year of teaching.

Miss Randall.   We wouldn't have to waste a lot of time commuting every day.

Miss Townsend   *(still speaking to Mrs. Martin).* And, since you say we can

boys

Tommy's house until around supper time.

Georgie   *(lurches to his feet, sighing audibly, and, hands jammed into pants pockets, marches past the detective, Mr. Martin, and Grandpa).* O.K., Grandpa. See you later. *(Exits out from door stage left)*

Sound of footsteps coming upstairs and the two prospective tenants emerge, smiling, from behind the stairwell screen followed by Uncle Bob. The three other men watch from stage right.

Mr. Randall   *(positively).* I like it . . . it's a pretty nice apartment.

Mr. Townsend   *(nodding in agreement).* I think so too . . . it's better than I expected and it's conveniently located.

Mr. Randall   *(turning to Mr. Townsend).* It's the best we've seen, certainly, and I don't think we can find anything better.

Mr. Townsend.   It's close to school anyway. *(To Uncle Bob)* This is our first year at college and it's probably going to be rough.

Mr. Randall.   Yeah, we won't waste any time commuting.

Mr. Townsend   *(still speaking to Uncle Bob).* We can save a little too, eating a couple of meals here everyday.

Uncle Bob nods smiling.

Mr. Randall   *(turning to Uncle Bob).* O.K. then . . . what's the rent?

Mr. Townsend.   Yeah, and *(chuckling)* remember, we're just poor university

mixed

Miss Randall. We wouldn't have to waste a lot of time commuting every day.

Miss Townsend *(still speaking to Mrs. Martin)*. And, since you say we can have a hot plate, we could even eat breakfast here.

Mrs. Martin nods smiling.

Miss Randall *(turning to Mrs. Martin)*. It sounds so good, But what's the rent?

Miss Townsend. Yes, that's very important . . . because the salary for beginning teachers isn't much, you know.

Detective *(who has been standing listening with pencil poised over his pad, clears his throat)*. Ahem! *(Says with sarcastic emphasis to Mr. Martin)* You couldn't be thinking of renting out rooms in a neighborhood zoned for family residence only, could you?

The women all turn as if noticing the men for the first time.

Mr. Martin *(piously, feigning surprise)*. Family residence only, eh? First time I've heard about that. *Pauses and then as if convinced)* But, if you say so . . . *(Turns toward the tenants and speaks sternly)* Well, that's the law and we certainly don't want to break it, of course. *(And as he urges them toward the door, walking close behind them)* Sorry.

Miss Townsend *(puzzled and faintly resisting)*. But, couldn't we . . . well,

girls

have a hot plate, we could even eat breakfast here.

Mrs. Martin nods smiling.

Miss Randall *(turning to Mrs. Martin)*. It sounds so good. But what's the rent?

Miss Townsend. Yes, that's very important . . . because the salary for beginning teachers isn't much, you know.

Mrs. Robinson *(who has been standing listening with pencil poised over her clipboard, clears her throat)*. Ahem! That reminds me, some of the members of the neighborhood association have seen your ads, and I've been asked to remind you that, since this area is zoned for family residence only, renting of rooms is, of course, prohibited.

The two prospective tenants and Mrs. Martin turn as if noticing the others for the first time.

Mabel *(feigning surprise)*. Is that so? Well, I'm sure none of us realized that. *(Piously)* We certainly had no intention of breaking the law, you understand.

Grandma *(nervously, reinforcing Mabel's position)*. Why, of course we didn't. *(Laughs with nervous overloudness)* I'm sure it's all just a little misunderstanding. *(She urges the prospective tenants toward the door)*

Miss Townsend *(puzzled and faintly resisting)*. But, couldn't we . . . well, you

boys

students.

Detective *(who has been standing listening with pencil poised over his pad, clears his throat)*. Ahem! *(Says with sarcastic emphasis to Mr. Martin)* You couldn't be thinking of renting out rooms in a neighborhood zoned for family residence only, could you?

The men all turn as if noticing the other men for the first time.

Mr. Martin *(piously, feigning surprise)*. Family residence only, eh? First time I've heard about that. *(Pauses and then as if convinced)* But, if you say so . . . *(Turns toward the tenants and speaks sternly)* Well, that's the law and we certainly don't want to break it, of course. *(And as he urges them toward the door, walking close behind them)* Sorry.

Mr. Townsend *(puzzled and faintly resisting)*. Gee, but there ought to be some way around it . . . Couldn't we just . . . We would sure like to take it.

Mr. Randall *(interrupting)*. Yeah, we can give you a deposit right now if . . .

Grandpa *(interrupting and anxiously urging them out the door and, in fact, pressing the door against them as they stand on the threshold)*. No, no, we can't do it; that's all there is to it . . . Sorry about it. *(Hurriedly closes the door, shouting "G'bye." As Detective stares, frowning suspiciously, Grandpa then turns from the door and, going over to the table, picks up the news-*

mixed

you advertised and we really like the place so much . . .

Miss Randall   (interrupting). Yes, we're ready to take it, if the rent . . .

Grandpa   (interrupting and anxiously urging them out the door and, in fact, pressing the door against them as they stand on the threshold). No, no, we can't do it; that's all there is to it . . . Sorry about it. (Hurriedly closes the door, shouting "G'bye." As Detective stares, frowning suspiciously, Grandpa then turns from the door and, going over to the table, picks up the newspaper. He sits down at the table and seems to be completely absorbed in reading the newspaper)

Mrs. Martin   (nervously explaining to the detective). Some friends . . . just wanted them to see how nicely we decorated the upstairs. (Gives a false smile and nervous giggle)

Detective   (suspicious). Um-hm. (Pause) Now about that noise . . .

Mr. Martin   (soothingly). Well . . . Georgie is a little noisy at times, Officer . . . but . . . we were all boys once, you know. (Chuckling hollowly)

Detective   (nods reflectively). Well, I hate to ticket you . . . but you've got to keep him quiet 'cause the people around here are really making it hot for us at the precinct. (Tears the ticket in half, walks toward the door and opens it)

Uncle Stan   (bumping the detective,

girls

advertised and we really like the place so much . . .

Miss Randall   (interrupting). Yes, we're ready to take it, if the rent . . .

Grandma   (urging the girls out the door and pressing it against them as they hesitate on the threshold). We're really awfully sorry for putting you to such trouble, girls. (Stammering with embarrassment, she seems to plead for their cooperation) I know you'll . . . understand . . . we didn't realize . . . well . . . er . . . g'bye. (She closes the door while Mrs. Robinson stares frowning suspiciously)

Mable has meanwhile crossed the stage and seating herself at the table, stage left, pretends to read the newspaper.

Mrs. Martin   (nervously explaining to Mrs. Robinson). Some friends . . . just wanted them to see how nicely we decorated the upstairs. (Gives a false smile and nervous giggle)

Mrs. Robinson   (to Grandma). Yes . . . but now about the noise here . . .

Grandma   (soothingly). Well . . . Jeanie is a little noisy at times, I must admit . . . but . . . we were all young once, you know . . . and that's how kids are. (Chuckling hollowly)

Mrs. Robinson   (nods mildly embarrassed). Yes . . . and of course the association really doesn't want to cause you any trouble. We just want to keep up neighborhood standards. (Moves toward the door and holds the

boys

paper. He sits down at the table and seems to be completely absorbed in reading the newspaper)

Uncle Bob   (nervously explaining to the detective). A couple of friends . . . of my son. Er . . . I just wanted them to see what a nice job we did downstairs. (Forced smile)

Detective   (suspicious). Um-hm. (Pause) Now about that noise . . .

Mr. Martin   (soothingly). Well . . . Georgie is a little noisy at times, Officer . . . but . . . we were all boys once, you know. (Chuckling hollowly)

Detective   (nods reflectively). Well, I hate to ticket you . . . but you've got to keep him quiet 'cause the people around here are really making it hot for us at the precinct. (Tears the ticket in half, walks toward the door and opens it)

Uncle Stan   (bumping the detective, staggers in carrying a huge round canvas covered bundle). Boy! That door just opened in time, 'cause this thing is really heavy. (Carefully places the bundle on the floor)

Detective   (annoyed to Mr. Martin). Now wait a minute . . . who is this . . . (Sarcastically) Another friend?

Mr. Martin   (chuckling nervously.) Well, no, as a matter of fact, he's my brother-in-law, Stan . . . he and his wife live with us.

Detective   (suspiciously). Yeah? Well, that's very interesting. (Leans over and

mixed

staggers in carrying a huge round canvas covered bundle). Boy! That door just opened in time, 'cause this thing is really heavy. *(Carefully places the bundle on the floor).*

Detective   *(annoyed, to Mr. Martin).* Now wait a minute . . . who is this . . . *(Sarcastically)* Another friend?

Mr. Martin   *(chuckling nervously).* Well, no, as a matter of fact, he's my brother-in-law, Stan . . . he and my wife's sister live with us.

Detective   *(suspiciously).* Yeah? Well, that's very interesting. *(Leans over and starts to open the cover on the bundle which Uncle Stan has set down)* Mind if I just look this over . . .

Uncle Stan   *(pushing the detective away and adjusting the wrapping on his bundle).* Now look, who're you?

Detective   *(annoyed).* Detective Arnold, 24th Precinct. What's that? *(Points toward Uncle Stan's package resting on the floor}*

Uncle Stan.   My Drum. *(Peevishly)* I bring it home to practice on almost every night. *(Pointedly)* And I don't like anybody to mess around with it . . . *(flashing a look of annoyance at Mrs. Martin),* even that damned nephew of mine.

Detective   *(glancing at Mr. and Mrs. Martin, who stand looking very embarrassed).* So, he practices the drum here every night, eh? Well *(turning toward Uncle Stan and stabbing his forefinger*

girls

doorknob) Actually they merely asked me to mention the problem to you and see if I could get you to keep it a little quieter here. *(Smiles and opens the door)*

Aunt Sarah   *(bumping Mrs. Robinson, staggers in carrying a large French horn case, groans audibly).* Oh — my! That door just opened in time! I'm just about dead. *(Kicks off her shoes and places the French horn case on the floor)*

Mrs. Robinson   *(stoops to pick up her clipboard which Aunt Sarah has knocked to the floor and touches up her hair with the other hand as she rises).* Pardon me . . . you must be *(speaks rather sarcastically)* another friend, I guess.

Grandma   *(chuckling and shaking her head).* No, she's my other daughter . . . Sarah and her husband live with us. *(Reaches down and picks up the newspaper Mabel has left on the table)*

Mrs. Robinson   *(coolly).* Really! Well, that's very interesting . . . and *(looks down at the French horn case)* French horn, isn't it?

Aunt Sarah   *(wearily).* Yes, yes . . . and after blowing that thing in rehearsal all afternoon, I'm just done.

Mrs. Robinson   *(coolly).* Yes, I imagine so . . . and the noise must be tiring too, I suppose, isn't it?

Aunt Sarah   *(wearily).* Oh, I suppose so . . . although I hardly notice that. I

boys

starts to open the cover on the bundle which Uncle Stan has set down) Mind if I just look this over . . .

Uncle Stan   *(pushing the detective away and adjusting the wrapping on his bundle).* Now look, who're you?

Detective   *(annoyed).* Detective Arnold, 24th Precinct. What's that? *(Points toward Uncle Stan's package resting on the floor)*

Uncle Stan.   My drum. *(Pointedly)* I bring it home to practice on almost every night. *(Pointedly)* And I don't like *anybody* to mess around with it . . . *(flashing a look of annoyance at Mr. Martin)* even that damned nephew of mine.

Detective   *(glancing at Mr. Martin, who stands looking very embarrassed).* So, he practices the drum here every night, eh? Well *(turning toward Uncle Stan and stabbing his forefinger toward him to emphasize each word),* you better find some other place to practice *(turning to Mr. Martin)* 'cause if we get just *one* more complaint I'm going to have to ticket you. *(Marches stiffly to the door)* Goodnight! *(Exits stage left)*

Mr. Martin   *(sighing in relief).* Phew! He almost had us on two counts: zoning violation and noise.

Uncle Stan   *(shaking his head disgustedly).* Neighbors complaining again, eh? Well, I make a lot less noise with this *(pats the drum)* than Georgie makes playing the record player. And,

mixed

toward him to emphasize each word), you better find some other place to practice *(turning to Mr. Martin)* 'cause if we get just *one* more complaint I'm going to have to ticket you. *(Marches stiffly to the door)* Goodnight! *(Exits stage left)*

Mr. Martin   *(sighing in relief).* Phew! He almost had us on two counts: zoning violation and noise.

Uncle Stan   *(shaking his head disgustedly).* Neighbors complaining again, eh? Well, I make a lot less noise with this *(pats the drum)* than Georgie makes playing that record player. And, by the way, when I came back from the store last night while you were out, I found him pounding on my drum while that record player was turned up as loud as it would play. No wonder the neighbors complain!

Mrs. Martin   *(sadly preoccupied as she sits down in the big chair midstage and ignores Uncle Stan).* Gee, and those two were all set to rent that place we've advertised for so long. *(Shaking her head disgustedly)*

There is a knock at the door and when Grandpa, still holding the newspaper, gets up to open it, Mr. & Mrs. Ferguson rush in.

Mrs. Ferguson   *(excitedly to Mrs. Martin).* Gracie, we've got such wonderful news . . . (Breathlessly) They bought our old place . . . *(as if dazzled)* for $10,000. Just imagine!

Mr. Ferguson   *(beaming toward Mr.*

girls

usually practice home a couple of hours every night and nobody seems to mind.

Mrs. Robinson.   But, as a matter of fact, it does contribute to the noise which the neighborhood association has asked me to call to your attention *(Pauses)* I'm sure, however, that since I've mentioned it, you'll all try to be a little quieter so as not to annoy your neighbors . . . *(threateningly)* who'd hate to have to take harsher action. *(Forcing a smile)* It's been so nice meeting you all. Goodnight! *(Exits stage left)*

Mabel   *(rising as the door closes and sighing audibly).* Phew! She certainly got an eyeful and an earful here. It sure didn't take her long to spot the zoning violation—and some of the noise sources, too. *(Crosses stage and sits down at the telephone table stage right)*

Aunt Sarah.   That was nasty . . . referring to my music as noise. But she ought to know what real noise is . . . since she must have heard Jeanie playing that record player. *(Turning to Grandma)* By the way, when I came home from the store last night about midnight—before the rest of you got back—that thing was turned up to full volume and that kid was sitting right next to it. No wonder the neighbors complain!

Mrs. Martin   *(sadly preoccupied as she*

boys

by the way, when I came back from the store last night while you were out, I found him pounding on my drum while that record player was turned up a loud as it would play. No wonder the neighbors complain!

Uncle Bob   *(sadly preoccupied as he sits down in the big chair midstage and ignores Uncle Stan).* Gee, and those two were all set to rent that place we've advertised for so long. *(Shaking his head disgustedly)*

There is a knock at the door and when Grandpa, still holding the newspaper, gets up to open it, Mr. Ferguson and Mr. Clark rush in.

Mr. Clark   *(enthusiastically).* Boy, Bob, what news we've got! They bought my old place *(pronouncing the figure very slowly)* for TEN THOUSAND DOLLARS. Can you imagine that!

Mr. Ferguson   *(beaming toward Mr. Martin).* That's right, George. A fellow who's putting up an all night drive-in came around and snapped up my place . . . *(snaps his fingers)* like that.

Ray enters from kitchen stage right and crosses to midstage where he stands listening just behind Uncle Bob's chair.

Mr. Clark.   He said they decided they wanted to make a parking lot out of the property.

Mr. Ferguson.   And we've got to get out in two weeks 'cause they're going to start tearing down the house. *(Chuckling happily)*

mixed

Martin). That's right, George. A fellow who's putting up an all night drive-in came around and snapped up my place like that. *(Snaps his fingers)*

Aunt Martha enters from kitchen stage right and crosses to midstage where she stands listening just behind Mrs. Martin's chair.

Mrs. Ferguson.   He said they decided they wanted to make a parking lot out of the property.

Mr. Ferguson.   And we've got to get out in two weeks 'cause they're going to start tearing down the house. *(Chuckling happily)*

Mrs. Ferguson.   And imagine, Gracie . . . $10,000 for our old place. *(Shaking her head unbelievingly and smiling)* I'll be so glad to get out of there.

Mr. Ferguson.   Yeah . . . me too. Everything in the place needed fixing. I couldn't keep up with it anymore.

Grandpa.   Well, well — that's certainly good news, Tom . . . glad to hear it.

Aunt Martha   *(laughing).* An all night drive-in! Now it will *really* be noisy around here, won't it?

Mrs. Martin.   I wish we could get out too.

Mr. Ferguson   *(eagerly).* But that's just what we came over to tell you. The guy said he'd be over here tomorrow morning to try to talk you into selling too!

Mrs. Martin   *(excitedly).* What! Why that's marvelous! It's too good to believe!

girls

sits down in the big chair midstage and ignores Aunt Sarah). Gee, and those two were all set to rent that place we've advertised for so long. *(Shaking her head disgustedly)*

There is a knock at the door and when Grandma, still holding the newspaper, gets up to open it, Mrs. Ferguson and Mrs. Clark rush in.

Mrs. Ferguson   *(excitedly to Mrs. Martin).* Gracie, we've got such wonderful news . . . *(Breathlessly)* They bought our old place . . . *(as if dazzled)* for $10,000. Just imagine!

Mrs. Clark.   That's right, Gracie. A guy who's putting up an all night drive-in came around and snapped up my place like that. *(Snaps her fingers)*

Aunt Martha enters from kitchen stage right and crosses to midstage where she stands listening just behind Mrs. Martin's chair.

Mrs. Ferguson.   He said they decided they wanted to make a parking lot out of the property.

Mrs. Clark.   And we've got to get out in two weeks 'cause they're going to start tearing down the house. *(Chuckling happily)*

Mrs. Ferguson.   And imagine, Gracie . . . $10,000 for our old place. *(Shaking her head unbelievingly and smiling)* I'll be so glad to get out of there.

Mrs. Clark   *(nodding).* Me too. Everything in our place needed fixing and my husband just couldn't keep up with it anymore.

boys

Mr. Clark   *(excitedly).* Boy, oh boy . . . $10,000 for that old place! *(Shaking his head unbelievingly and smiling)* Will I be glad to get out of there!

Mr. Ferguson.   Yeah . . . me too. Everything in the place needed fixing. I couldn't keep up with it anymore.

Grandpa.   Well, well—that's certainly good news, fellas . . . glad to hear it.

Ray   *(laughing).* An all night drive-in restaurant, huh? Wow . . . it will really be noisy around here now!

Uncle Bob   *(shaking his head sadly).* It sure will. I wish we could get out too.

Mr. Ferguson   *(eagerly).* But that's just what we came over to tell you. The guy said he'd be over here tomorrow morning to try to talk you into selling too!

Uncle Bob   *(excitedly).* What! Why, that's *really* swell! Maybe our troubles are over then!

Grandpa   *(slowly reflecting).* H-m-m . . . well, maybe . . . but where will we all live?

Mr. Clark.   Why, you can rent a place . . . like we're going to do.

Mr. Ferguson.   Sure, and you can stop trying to rent out rooms.

Uncle Bob   *(beaming).* No more struggling to rent rooms to people. *(Chuckling)* In fact, we can even become renters ourselves! *(Gets up and, grabbing the newspaper from Grandpa's hand, turns to the classified ads)*

Mr. Clark   *(holding one side of the*

mixed

Grandpa (slowly reflecting). H-m-m ... well, maybe ... but where will we all live?

Mrs. Ferguson. Why, you can rent a place ... like we're going to do.

Mr. Ferguson. Sure, and you can stop trying to rent out rooms.

Mrs. Martin (happily excited). Oh, I feel so good! Why, we can even become renters ourselves, can't we? (Gets up and, grabbing the newspaper from Grandpa's hand, turns to the classified ads)

Mrs. Ferguson (holding one side of the newspaper, peers at it with Mrs. Martin). Just listen to this (reads mechanically), "Beautiful 8 room house, 3 bedrooms, clean, newly decorated, utilities included, nice quiet neighborhood."

Aunt Martha stands behind Mrs. Ferguson and Mrs. Martin, peering over their shoulders as they eagerly examine the newspaper.

Mrs. Martin (excitedly). Hey ... here's another good one. (Reads) "For Rent ...

CURTAIN

Glossary

acts up—behaves badly as a child

ahem! /əhem/—sound made by clearing the throat

all night drive-in—a kind of restaurant open

---

girls

Grandma. Well, that *is* good news for both of you, isn't it? ... I'm so glad to hear it.

Aunt Martha (laughing). An all night drive-in! Now it will *really* be noisy around here, won't it?

Mrs. Martin. I wish we could get out too.

Mrs. Clark. But that's just what we came over to tell you. The man said he'd be over here tomorrow morning to try to talk you into selling too!

Mrs. Martin (xcitedly). What! Why that's marvelous! It's too good to believe!

Grandma (slowly reflecting). H-m-m ... well, maybe ... but where will we all live?

Mrs. Ferguson. Why, you can rent a place ... like we're going to do.

Mrs. Clark. Sure, and you can stop trying to rent out rooms.

Mrs. Martin (happily excited). Oh, I feel so good! Why, we can even become renters ourselves, can't we? (Get up and, grabbing the newspaper from Grandma's hand, turns to the classified ads)

Mrs. Ferguson (holding one side of the newspaper, peers at it with Mrs. Martin). Just listen to this (reads mechanically), "Beautiful 8 room house, 3 bedrooms, clean, newly decorated, utilities included, nice quiet neighborhood."

Aunt Martha stands behind Mrs. Ferguson

---

boys

newspaper, peers at it with Uncle Bob). Just listen to this (reads mechanically), "Beautiful 8 room house, 3 bedrooms, clean, newly decorated, utilities included, nice quiet neighborhood."

Ray stands behind Mr. Ferguson and Uncle Bob, peering over their shoulders as they examine the newspaper.

Uncle Bob (excitedly). Hey ... here's another good one. (Reads) "For Rent ...

CURTAIN

Glossary

basement apartment—an apartment located in the basement, below ground level; such apartments are usually less expensive

get out—move, change to another house

get that—answer it

going to be rough—will be difficult

huh /²hə̃³/—expression signifying a question

I'll bet—I suppose, imagine, think, guess

just what you've been looking for—exactly what you want

look it over—look at it

naw /nɔ/—colloquial form of *no*

No more struggling to rent apartments to people!—a truncated form of something like, "We won't have to struggle anymore to rent apartments to people" or "Since we are now free, we won't have to worry about renting apartments."

see what a nice job we did—see how well our work was done

mixed

all night and at which waitresses serve people who remain in their automobiles; this kind of place is very popular with teenagers particularly and, therefore, is noisy

all set—ready

a ticket—a printed form issued by the police to people who violate a law; usually the receiver must go to the police station or to a court

aw gee—expresses a kind of whining or grumbling

beckon—motion with the hand to call or attract

boy!—emphatic expression; a kind of intensifier of the meaning of the phrase which follows

classified ads—section of newspaper where jobs, houses, and things for sale are listed systematically

commuting—traveling daily over the same route

cops—policemen

cosy—attractive, comfortable, and giving a secure feeling although small

crooks—thieves or criminals in general

damned—expression of annoyance or dissatisfaction; profanity

damned racket—terrible noise

dear—mild term of affection

decorated—painted

don't be too hard on—don't be so severe with, don't make unreasonable demands

double bed—a bed made big enough for two people

eh/ey/—a questioning expression

girls

and Mrs. Martin, peering over their shoulders as they eagerly examine the newspaper.

Mrs. Martin   *(excitedly)*. Oh, and here's another good one. *(Reads)* "For Rent . . .

CURTAIN

Glossary

ads—advertisements in a newspaper, here referring to advertising a room for rent

an eyeful and an earful—saw and heard a lot

er/ər/—an expression of hesitation while trying to decide how to continue

fuddy duddies—dull, conservative, unimaginative, uninteresting people

have the nerve—don't hesitate (to be hypercritical)

I could just murder you!—an exaggerated expression of exasperation

just about dead—very tired, exhausted

just done—completely exhausted

just right—suitable

keep up neighborhood standards—keep the neighborhood clean and quiet

makes a face at Mabel—the distortion of facial features to express annoyance; sticking out the tongue is one common expression

Mom—colloquial form of *mother*, used in addressing your own mother

oh-my—a kind of feminine intensifier of the meaning of the phrase that follows

some of the people here are just dead—the people are not interesting; they are dull

boys

Will I be glad to get out of there!—although in the form of a question, this is not even a rhetorical question but is merely an exclamation, usually indicated by raised pitch and stress on *there*

wow! /w æ uw/—expression of excited emphasis

mixed

forefinger—finger next to the thumb

gee/²jiy/—a kind of intensifier of the meaning or implication of the phrase which follows

gorgeous—very beautiful

great—very good, pleasant

guy—colloquial term for man

have it to yourself—you would be the only person using it

hey/hey/—an expression used to call attention

h-m-m/hm/—expression of thought, speculation

hot plate—a small, electric stove

john—a common colloquial term for toilet; *bathroom* is more formal usage

keep after him—keep scolding him

keep up with—do as much as necessary

kid—child; here it refers to Georgie

liven things up—make more lively and interesting

look after—investigate, take care of

lurch—to walk clumsily, in an uncontrolled way

making it hot for us—complaining about it and scolding us constantly, making us uncomfortable

marvelous—expression of pleasant surprise, meaning *very good* or *wonderful;* usually used by women rather than by men

mess around with—disturb, play with

mind if I just look this over—may I look at this, examine this

morgue—a building used for storing dead bodies before a funeral, here an exaggerated reference to the quiet and dullness

girls

people

soothingly—attempting to calm

so there—expression of annoyance or antagonism

stop—to see, observe

too loud—having very bright, clashing colors

wince—to draw back the head suddenly as if in pain

you really are a pain—you are very troublesome, annoying, a pest; an expression of annoyance or anger

mixed (continued)

no wonder—quite understandably

now look, who're you?—who are you?
Neither *now* nor *look* have any specific
meaning but both indicate an attempt to
mask impatience or annoyance

old crabs—people who constantly complain

old crank—another term for somebody who
complains constantly

on two counts—for two violations

parking lot—an area where automobiles may
be parked or left temporarily

paunch—fat stomach sticking out

phew/fyu/—an expression of relief from
pressure

piously—very seriously

poised—held steady and unmoving

precinct—area of police administration

preoccupied—thinking of something else and
not aware of surrounding activity

propelled—driven or pushed

public nuisance ordinance—a law against
various kinds of annoying disturbance

putting up—constructing, building

really heavy—very heavy

saucepan—a small cooking pot

mixed (continued)

scowl—a facial expression of anger or
annoyance

snapped up—purchased very quickly

swell—very nice

talk you into—persuade, convince

tearing down—removing, razing

that's all there is to it—I refuse to discuss the
matter further

there ought to be some way around it—there
should be some way to solve or avoid the
problem

they—somebody, people unspecified; here
the people who expect to build the
drive-in

troubles are over—troubles have disappeared;
we have no more troubles

turned up—volume raised

um-hm/²əm+³hm/—expression of understanding or agreement, here used
ironically

utilities—gas and electricity

we've heard enough from you—be quiet; you
talk too much

we were all boys once—we must remember
that we were also noisy once and,

mixed (continued)

therefore, must not be too severe

yeah? /²ye³ə/—expresses some doubt or
disbelief

you know how kids are—you know that all
children are difficult to control

you were the same at his age—you behaved
as badly when you were as young as he is

zoned—given a certain classification showing
the kind of use which can be made of
buildings in that area

Structure

For the most part the syntactic structures used in the dialogue of
this staging are common, regular patterns. However, there are several
structures which deserve comment because they can be found so
widely in colloquial usage and because they diverge from standard
structures to be found in most textbooks.

1. We often find what seem to be mixtures of two question forms,
as if the speaker had abruptly changed his mind after starting
one pattern or as if he is answering his own question. In this
staging, for instance, the detective says, "Who is this—another
friend?" and we can understand that although he means "Is this
another friend?" he means more than that, for the apparent
change of mind is actually a cue for the communication of

sarcasm or disbelief. Thus, the detective is really saying something like, "Well, I suppose you are now going to pretend that this person is merely another friend and not someone renting rooms here," or "Surely, you don't expect me to believe that this person is only a friend." Yet, the cue is not entirely syntactic, for we note that the sarcasm is a product of the stress/pitch rise on *friend*; that is, the intonation shift tends to come on the last word. In this instance, there may also be a pitch/stress rise on—*other*.

2. We often find truncation in exclamations, and in this staging when Mr. Martin says "First time I've heard about that" he means *It is the first time I have heard about that.* Later Uncle Stan says, "No wonder the neighbors complain!" meaning "I think it is no wonder that the neighbors complain" or "I can understand why the neighbors complain." It might be noted that in this typical truncated exclamation structure, the pitch/stress rises occur on either *wonder* or *complain* with an accompanying sustained terminal (single bar) juncture. Note a similar exclamatory pitch/stress shift to *really* in Aunt Martha's line, "Now it will really be noisy around here," although the unexclaimed form would probably place the pitch/stress rise on *noisy*. It is also possible that the exclaimer might use a pitch/stress rise on *will*, if *really* is omitted or precedes *will*.

   Although structurally it is a full statement, when Mrs. Martin says "Gee, and those two were all set to rent that place we've advertised for so long," she has used *Gee* not with the usual meaning of happy excitement but to express her disappointment. She means *I am very disappointed that we have lost the opportunity to rent the room to those two people who were so anxious to rent it.* There is a similar kind of unstated, implicit emotional content in Aunt Sarah's statement "that kid was sitting right next to it," which means that she thinks the girl was sitting too close.

3. Often *eh* /³ey⁴/? is substituted for the question phrase in the trailer or tag question structure, as when the detective says, "So, he practices the drum here every night, eh?" or when Uncle Stan says, "Neighbors complaining again, eh?" or when Mr. Martin says, "Family residence only, eh?"

   We find that huh/²h ɔ̃³/ is sometimes substituted for eh /ey/ and either usage is usually accompanied by a pitch rise signaling that a question is intended. Yet, usually this is more like a comment/exclamation or a rhetorical question, since no reply is expected. The student should be advised that, as in the case of the question formed by using a rising intonation with a statement structure, this usage may communicate an attitude of sarcasm, impatience, or derision. He must be prepared to recognize this cue, then, and must realize the possible response to his own production of the structure.

4. Although I have not attempted to furnish all contractions and elisions which would actually be used in everyday speech, since much of that cannot readily be conveyed in writing but, as part of the dynamic integration of speech, must be modeled by the teacher orally and mimicked by the students, I have had Mr. Martin say "y'know" for *you know* and the Detective " 'Cause" for *because*. I may seem inconsistent here, unless I take this occasion to sensitize teachers to the need for extensive contraction throughout the various stagings, not only if colloquial usage is to be sustained but also if the differentials which distinguish the status of the various roles are to be recreated. That is, the spoken expression and the roles utilize contractions to varying degrees reflecting the status and social relationship of communicants.

5. The teacher will have to model, and the student will have to mimic, the various behavior patterns necessary to communicate the following general attitudes distinguishing roles:

   Aunt Martha—sweetly persuasive;

   Grandpa—playful and uninhibited;

   Two prospective tenants—inexperienced and rather timid, apprehensive;

   Mr. Martin—changing from flirtatious to stern and falsely pious;

   Detective—suspicious and sarcastic;

... ᵗʰᵃⁿ is available to men,
ᵐᵘⁿication by
... ᵗ a
... a
... ᵍ and is
... ᵗʰᵉ syntax

alisms, such as "um-hm," although this expression may defy written form. One reason for this difficulty in notation is that subtle changes in utterance communicate quite different meanings. For example, in this staging Aunt Martha, speaking on the telephone, uses this expression as a kind of signal of agreement, as a kind of continuator which does not disrupt the stream of speech of the one she is listening to. On the other hand, by shifting from a fairly level and equal pitch/stress on both parts of this two-part expression to a slight rise on the second part, the Detective communicates his doubt, his suspicion, which is complexly related to his sarcastic tone. Most native Americans are conscious neither of the frequency with which they employ such expressions, the range of communication possible in that utilization, nor the serious confusion for a foreigner, stemming from the fact that range embodies semantic opposites. The student will need to learn such expression by aural/oral means and learn to associate the sounds and the meanings by mimicry just as he would any other words; his problem is complicated, however, because there is no adequate notation for such expressions.

7. Reference has been made to examples of typical woman's language to be found in other stagings. In this staging we note Aunt Martha's use of "gorgeous" which is not usually part of the man's vocabulary. We also note many examples of that feminine use of intensifiers *so* and *such* in the expressions, "such a lovely room," "so nice," "so good," "such a nice room." Students will want to learn to use the language as it is used by most members of their own sex and it will be particularly important for girls or women to acquire control of both these intensifiers,

indicates that this *why* does not signal a ...

Cultural Values

1. For many foreigners and particularly for those who come from societies in which the home is not open to strangers and rarely—in a sharply limited way—to acquaintances, the custom of renting out rooms of one's house to strangers will seem quite odd. For many foreigners the family house may seem almost sacred and inviolable since it is very closely tied to the continuity of family tradition. For some, therefore, the joy of the Martin family upon receiving news they will be able to sell their home will be almost inconceivable, for they may tend to think of property ownership as a main source of social status. Thus, their first tendency may be to pity the Martin's, particularly since foreigners frequently are unaware of the relative high wages of such skilled craftsmen as carpenters and painters in this country. They will be quite surprised to learn that the cost of having one's property maintained by professional craftsmen accounts in large measure for the fact that many American homeowners themselves do most repairs on their own property. For many foreigners, who come from rigidly stratified societies, it is impossible to imagine a clerical worker or college professor, let us say, doing manual labor or any sort.

2. The student is exposed to some aspects of generational conflict which he found in the earlier staging "Our Car." In this play he finds that children taught to be aggressive and self-reliant may become rebellious against the older generation which has taught them. Georgie does not get along with most adults and he will seem quite disrespectful and rebellious to many foreign students.

Yet, grandparents are sometimes more successful in establishing contact with teenagers—largely, as in the case of Grandpa and Georgie, because grandparents can recall the parents own foolish behavior and cannot feel so concerned about the teenager's behavior. Unfortunately, we might also point out that since the child, in attacking the adult world, is challenging the society's power structure, his unwillingness to grant even grudging authority to the grandparents may be a subtle clue as to the social impotence of old people in this country.

3. Despite the generational conflict which makes teenagers a kind of nightmare for many parents, the children tend to acquire the general form of parental values and standards. In the flirtatious behavior toward the two prospective tenants, by both Mr. Martin and Georgie, the student will be able to see the wisdon of the popular saying "like father, like son"—which is, of course, understandable since the parents inevitably serve, to some considerable extent, as models for their children.

However, there is another aspect to this flirtatiousness which should be noted, for those students from strongly status-conscious societies will be quite amazed at the casualness of relations between people, particularly between members of the opposite sex. Mr. Martin's sly and slightly ribald reference to the double bed would be impossible in many societies although Grandpa's reference to "the john," which seems comical because of the incongruity of such uninhibited allusion to bodily functions which are taboo in our society, might seem quite normal. It is difficult, of course for foreigners to learn which areas are taboo; they will also find it hard, though essential, to recognize the circumstances and for whom the violation of taboo areas is possible. Grandpa displays the typical old person's disregard for one of society's taboos. In a certain sense, old people are permitted to behave with a somewhat childlike irreverence; yet the foreign student must not imagine that Grandpa is displaying the childlike symptoms of senility.

4. Many foreigners, unaware of America's glorification of youth, will be surprised that the all night drive-in mentioned in this staging is, perhaps, the most popular meeting-place for large numbers of suburban teenagers. This fact points up the commonality of teenagers' access to automobiles and that they have money to spend on their own entertainment. Often this is difficult for foreigners to understand and particularly when they learn many such teenagers are high school and college students who buy cars and pay for their entertainment with money they have themselves earned; in many societies student status demands at least a pretense of austere dignity while automatically obviating the possibility of engagement in manual labor by which students in America often earn money.

Moreover, even in fairly industrialized and urbanized societies, earlier farm traditions still prevail, decreeing early retirement to bed and early rising. For them the idea of extensive activity—restaurants, movies, traffic—throughout the night will seem very odd, indeed; many who have never stayed up beyond midnight, except possibly to cram for their semi-annual exams, will be astounded at the spectacle of teenagers dancing until 3. In fact, I have noted that the pace of teenage activity, the extent of teenagers' energy overwhelm many foreign students—at least until they observe the great quantities of high energy food teenagers consume; parenthetically, it may be stated that the volume of food consumption of *all* Americans is a revelation to many foreigners.

5. Since police are often feared and avoided in many parts of the world, some foreigners will have trouble imagining any kind of informal contact with them, such as is shown in this staging. The student may be quite surprised to find that here a policeman is generally considered a kind of public servant to be dealt with respectfully perhaps but not deferentially, that persuasion and even argument may be employed in dealing with police, and that police are expected to enforce laws objectively without regard for social status of the lawbreaker. Students from status-conscious societies will find it difficult to realize that policemen are usually fairly well paid and, as residents in middle class sections of the city, engage quite freely in ordinary social

1. Although the staging is complicated by a number of exits and entrances, it may be divided into four main scenes:
   a. Arrival of prospective tenants (Miss Randall and Miss Townsend);
   b. Arrival of Detective;
   c. Departure of prospective tenants and of Detective;
   d. Arrival of the Fergusons.

   The decision to rent one of their rooms determines the manner of communication of Aunt Martha, Mrs. Martin, and Mr. Martin, while it also determines the strength of their reaction against Georgie. It might also be noted that this decision to rent a room explains the gloom and consequent slackening of pace following the departure of the prospective tenants, even though the Martins have not been ticketed by the Detective. This gloom, in turn, contrasts with the excited happy discovery which brings the play to a close.

2. Many of the exits and entrances must be well planned and will require students to coordinate—and not merely alternate—movement and speech if the stage is not to be overcrowded. Note that Mrs. Martin re-enters as Mr. Martin exits, followed by Aunt Martha. After meeting briefly with the entering Georgie and re-entering Mr. Martin, Mrs. Martin exits with the prospective tenants. The Detective enters and, soon after, Georgie exits. Then, the prospective tenants exit just shortly before Uncle Stan's entrance, which precedes the Detective's exit. Uncle Stan's exit is followed by the entrance of the Fergusons and by Aunt Martha's re-entrance.

   Grandpa is the sole character who is on stage during the entire play, then, and it will be necessary for him to remain do some of the minor household chores so he will not feel he is a charity recipient, but he does not often interfere in serious family matters.

3. Staged telephone communication is, of course, different from ordinary dialogue, since we can only hear one side of the conversation on stage. The playwright must provide adequate clues, in the form of partially echoed words or phrases and even visual effects, such as gestures or facies of the person listening, so that the audience can guess the content of the unheard half. This is interesting from the standpoint of theatrical contrivance, but since our interest is primarily in teaching students everyday English, we will utilize the situation in other ways.

   As an exercise, giving students one half of a telephone conversation aurally and having them supply the other half can be useful to focus their attention so that they may learn to pick out the clues provided. In addition, they can be taught to recognize the need to supply substitute patterns for the visual ones—which cannot be communicated on the phone. Most students will recognize that in phone conversations between people who do not know each other well—who therefore cannot visualize each other's characteristic visual behavior patterns—communication is either sparse and starkly functional or else some substitution in oral communication patterns is necessary.

   Substitution usually takes the form of supplementation or exaggeration of intonational features, but absolute speed as well as relative pacing of speech is likely to be difficult in a phone conversation, since most people tend to focus their attention better and organize their phone speech much more carefully. They may be more direct, and may feel themselves under some pressure to complete the phone conversation more quickly; their phrasing and periods of silence may also be controlled and distributed differently from those speech features experienced in ordinary face-to-face conversation.

Notes on Adaptation

In general, some of the humor of the outrageously contrasting lines in the description of the place for rent and the humor of parallel father-son mildly flirtatious behavior of the original play have been somewhat sacrificed in the adaptations. The typically exaggerated reactions of the teenagers, Jeanie and Georgie, are comical, however, as are the uninhibited comments of Grandma and Grandpa. There is also comic shock—even for a native English speaker—in Uncle Bob's appearance in an apron although the foreign student will have to learn that such a spectacle is quite possible; it will teach him something further about the social values which make such a spectacle comical even for natives. That is, many foreign students often learn, rather painfully if they are men, that bachelors with limited funds may have to do their own cooking and other housework in this virtually servantless land.

Yet much of the comedy is grounded on incongruity stemming from the exploitation of intonation possibilities. The students must, through mimicry, be sensitized to such situational comic exaggeration, again not because they will become drama students but because they will want to recognize what the laugh is all about. Such focusing of student attention reinforces a habit important for later self teaching and acquaints the student with social values involved in the question of what is thought funny in a society whose language he is learning. Language teaching is inevitably repetitious, but if some attempt is made to utilize aspects of humor, it need not be the grim business it frequently is.

If we examine separately, the adaptations for girls and boys, we find that several specific comments can be made about each:

1. In the girls' adaptation the plot situation remains essentially unchanged although several roles have to be shifted. With role shifts the tenor of certain scenes is quite different. For instance, there is a major problem in the scene between the Detective and Uncle Stan, even when the role of the Detective is changed to that of Mrs. Robinson, the lady representative of the Neighborhood Association, and the role of Uncle Stan becomes that of Aunt Sarah; Mrs. Robinson, who has an entirely different status function, cannot behave as the Detective does and Aunt Sarah, a woman, would neither play nor carry a large bass drum. A French horn, often played by a woman, is substituted. In referring to the bundle, Mrs. Robinson uses the truncated structure "French horn, isn't it?" from which both the subject and the verb are omitted but indicated by the direction of her looking.

2. Moreover, Jeanie, also a typically troublesome, rebellious teenager, cannot behave as Georgie does, since she cannot flirt with the two women who come to inquire about the room, and as a girl she may not deal so bluntly, so sarcastically, with the detective. But we note that both Georgie and Jeanie share the typical teenager's awareness of the hypocritical attitudes of society, although Jeanie is more pointed in her observation of her neighbor's behavior whereas Georgie's comment about his neighbors is very general; instead he criticizes the police directly rather than the society which supports the police.

3. In further distinguishing between these two teenagers, we note Jeanie's typical teenage girl's interest in Miss Townsend's clothes, Mabel, a late teenager, also eyes the clothing of the prospective tenants as they enter, but we find that she is more reserved and less rebellious than Jeanie, although Grandma reminds the older girl that she was quite recently just as annoying as Jeanie is.

4. Earlier reference has been made to typically feminine expression and particularly to the use of intensifiers. For example, Miss Townsend says "We *really* like the place *so* much." Other typically feminine characteristics are shown in the emphasis on the cleanliness of the room; we note also that Aunt Sarah immediately kicks off her shoes as many women do when tired.

5. On the other hand, Mrs. Robinson becomes quite threatening

adding "It's been so nice meeting you all," using the typical feminine intensifier *so*.

However, as a neighbor representing other neighbors, Mrs. Robinson is likely to receive somewhat more polite and reserved treatment than would be given to the detective who is merely an official whose relationship with the Martins is objective rather than neighborly. The Martins may never see the detective again, but they will be in close contact with their neighbors during their residence in the community. Many foreign students will have difficulty understanding both the American attitude toward police and the peculiar attitude most Americans have toward neighbors, since attitudes toward either of these members of society vary considerably with the society.

6. In contrasting the two adaptations, however, we find that Ray's phone dialogue is quite a bit more blunt than Mabel's or Aunt Martha's; as a man, Ray tends to use shorter, more direct phrases lacking emotional toning. Similarly, Mr. Randall and Mr. Townsend speak in typically short, clipped phrases, expressing their opinions directly without softening or modification. Mr. Townsend does not hesitate about reminding the Martins that he and Mr. Randall can pay only a low rent because "we're just poor university students," whereas Miss Townsend is somewhat less direct in stating that "the salary for beginning teachers isn't very much." Again, this contrast should be considered less a matter of idiosyncrasy, distinguishing an individual character, than a reflection of the fact that our social values still require "ladylike" behavior of women in public or when dealing with strangers; the foreign student, whose observation is restricted mainly to the rather specialized liberality of behavior granted the

although it is probably used as often by young women.

8. The dialogue for Grandma is virtually interchangeable with that for Grandpa, since many of the behavior patterns of the sexes seem to blur and become less distinct with age. Younger people in somewhat formal conversation with strangers would be less likely to refer to the "john," although older people frequently lose such inhibitions and are typically less embarrassed by such allusions to elemental bodily functions.

Conclusion

This book, based on a commitment to communication quite different from the defective view of language on which most teaching is now grounded, may seem to have involved me in self-contradiction. Some readers may feel I have written a book on language teaching in which I insist that language teaching cannot be done from a book. It, therefore, seems that further clarification is necessary.

The main point I have tried to make is that there must be more general recognition that good language students have always, consciously or not, mimicked more than the teacher's oral expression. Intuitively and by chance these few good students have learned the behavior patterns that can be taught to all students openly and systematically. Indeed, my purpose in writing this book has been to present the idea that these features must be taught systematically if the student is efficiently to learn communication instead of the artificial and inadequate oral expression which many foreign students now acquire.

The communication situations that, for want of a better term, I have called stagings, then, are merely examples of vehicles I have found suitable for the conveyance of students into an unfamiliar and foreign world. I have tried to focus teacher attention on the use of such stagings to facilitate total mimicry of communication patterns. Yet, in fact, although more suitable—for reasons I have discussed in some detail earlier—for the job of staging communication, the stagings included in this book of themselves represent little that is startlingly new. Their newness lies mainly in their implementation of the concept of language as communication.

In commentaries, and in the more conventional stage notes, I have attempted to provide for that implementation. I have furnished information as to what behavior patterns were suitable, how they should be projected, and why they are necessary for communication. Yet, certainly the material provided for those stagings will not and cannot supply the student with exhaustive explanation about the necessary patterns. Admittedly, there is no notation at present to represent certain features of communication, although work might be done to supply much notation that linguists have not provided. We might, for instance, try to adapt some of the pause cueing and emotional toning devices used by such poets as E.E. Cummings. Some of us have also toyed with the idea of using modified and augmented ballet notation—Laban or otherwise—as a means to noting postures, movements, and perhaps even facies necessary for staging communication.

However, any visualization of sound features can at best produce only a static rendition of what in ordinary communication is a dynamic process. That there is no adequate way to set down in writing the specific detail of all audio-visual features and relations required in a specific communication situation does not deny the possibility that we may recognize and write about the fact that such integrated features exist. But it is precisely the dynamic integration of oral expression and complementary movement as well as other visible features that must be learned. And the only way we can teach such communications patterns is by demonstrating them.

Obviously, since this approach greatly increases the responsibilities of and demands on the capabilities of teachers, some resistance to its adoption may be expected. Many teachers will insist on imagining that they will need training in as well as an acquaintance with theater work, although, it has been pointed out that the approach is essentially not theatrical or dramatic. Others may feel disturbed because there really is no new authority to which they can surrender—but, indeed, as linguists have long quite rightly contended, the teacher as native speaker must always be the final authority.

It is likely, however, that any reluctance will be a measure of the degree to which we have allowed our understanding of language as communication to become distorted. Some teachers may find it hard to recognize that communication is total behavioral response and not merely fluency in that part of oral expresion which has been taught in conventional language courses In short, the teacher will have to develop a greater sensitivity to the true nature of communication. I have, moreover, pointed up the indispensability of

in a new way. He will have to know what behavior patterns, what features, characterize his language and he will have to know when each is employed. In enhancing the role of the teacher, this approach provides for overt recognition of the teacher as a person, a communicant. He will have to remain analytical while behaving naturally as a native speaking communicant.

Most foreign language teaching, however, is done by teachers whose native language is that of their students. Obviously, these teachers will not be able to "behave naturally" in the way my approach suggests. Theirs is, instead, a doubly difficult task, for they will have to become more conscious of themselves in yet another way, in contrast with the native speakers of the language they teach. Teachers whose native language is not English will have to attempt to approximate the native speaker's fluency with *all* the integrated patterns necessary for communicating attitudes in various social situations. The foreign teacher, therefore, will have to recognize that not only is the good mimic likely to be a good language student but also he will probably be a better language teacher. To that end, many foreign teachers will have to stop focusing exclusively on the mere speech of native speakers of the language they teach, while ignoring the visible, physical behavior. They will have to realize that they must drop their familiar patterns of behavior and that they must mimic the native speaker's total behavior; they will have to be able to model that behavior for their students to mimic. Many of these foreign teachers will be obliged to recognize the simple fact that the most effective teacher is the model.

of the language, and a truly vicarious communication experience requires exposure to visual features as well. We are all aware that much English is being taught in places where no native English speaking models are available. And teachers there who accept this approach lack opportunity for the kind of observation they need to master the necessary communications patterns. If we hope to create teacher models for students to mimic in learning to communicate in another language, we must provide them with the opportunity for observation. Where native speakers cannot be made available, sound movies and even television—although lacking the dynamics of immediacy of exchange attainable through vis-a-vis contact—can serve as partial substitutes. Therefore, no effort should be spared to furnish short sound films of stagings, such as have been provided in this text, to those foreign teachers who have no opportunity for direct observation of behavior patterns of native speakers whose communication they are mastering.

Thus, while hoping to generate a desire to teach communication rather than merely language, I must warn all teachers—native speakers and foreigners alike—that certainly the greater demands for development and implementation of awareness required for staging communication will tax the teacher more heavily. But, measured in terms of that peculiar sense of satisfaction and accomplishment which increased student learning gives—an experience available only to the dedicated teacher—I am confident the added burden will seem worthwhile, indeed.

Richard C. Bedford is professor of English at Doshisha Women's College, Kyoto, Japan. He received his B.A. degree from Olivet College in 1947; his M.A. (1951) and Ph. D. (1960) degrees from the University of Iowa. He has taught at Wayne State University, the University of Alaska, and has been guest professor of English at Osaka University of Foreign Studies, Osaka, Japan.

The manuscript was edited by Marguerite C. Wallace. The book was designed by Richard Kinney. The typesetting is set IBM Press Roman. The Display face is Alphatype's Helvetica.

The book is printed on Ann Arbor text paper and bound in Columbia Mills' Fictionette cloth. Manufactured in the United States of America.